A PEOPLE UNDER
SIEGE

Aaron Edwards is a Senior Lecturer in Defence and International Affairs at the Royal Military Academy Sandhurst and an Honorary Research Fellow in the School of History, Politics and International Relations at the University of Leicester. Born in Belfast in 1980, he obtained his PhD in Politics from Queen's University Belfast in 2006 and was elected a Fellow of the Royal Historical Society in 2012. He is the author of several acclaimed books, including *Mad Mitch's Tribal Law: Aden and the End of Empire* (Transworld Books, 2014), *UVF: Behind the Mask* (Merrion Press, 2017) and *Agents of Influence: Britain's Secret Intelligence War Against the IRA* (Merrion Press, 2021). His work has appeared in *Fortnight*, *The Irish Times*, *The Irish News*, *Belfast Telegraph*, *Belfast News Letter*, *Irish Independent* and the *Dublin Review of Books*.

Also by Aaron Edwards:

Agents of Influence: Britain's Secret Intelligence War Against the IRA

UVF: Behind the Mask

Strategy in War and Peace: A Critical Introduction

War: A Beginner's Guide

Mad Mitch's Tribal Law: Aden and the End of Empire

Defending the Realm? The Politics of Britain's Small Wars since 1945

The Northern Ireland Troubles: Operation Banner, 1969–2007

The Northern Ireland Conflict: A Beginner's Guide (with Cillian McGrattan)

A History of the Northern Ireland Labour Party: Democratic Socialism and Sectarianism

Transforming the Peace Process in Northern Ireland: From Terrorism to Democratic Politics (edited with Stephen Bloomer)

A PEOPLE UNDER SIEGE

The Unionists of Northern Ireland,
from Partition to Brexit and Beyond

Aaron Edwards

MERRION
PRESS

First published in 2023 by
Merrion Press
10 George's Street
Newbridge
Co. Kildare
Ireland
www.merrionpress.ie

© Aaron Edwards, 2023

978 1 78537 299 5 (Paper)
978 1 78537 302 2 (Ebook)

A CIP catalogue record for this book
is available from the British Library.

All rights reserved. No part of this publication may be reproduced, stored in a retrieval system, or transmitted, in any form or by any means (electronic, mechanical, photocopying, recording or otherwise), without the prior written permission of both the copyright owner and the publisher of this book.

Typeset in Minion Pro 11/15.5 pt

Cover design by riverdesignbooks.com

Front cover image courtesy of Abaca Press/Alamy Stock Photo
Back cover image courtesy of the Edwards collection

Merrion Press is a member of Publishing Ireland.

Printed and bound in Great Britain by TJ Books Limited, Padstow, Cornwall

'The sweetest thing in all my life has been the longing – to reach the Mountain, to find the place where all beauty came from – my country, the place where I ought to have been born. Do you think it all meant nothing, all the longing? The longing for home? For indeed it now feels not like going but going back. All my life the god of the Mountain has been wooing me. Oh, look up once at least before the end and wish me joy. I am going to my lover. Do you not see now – ?'

From C.S. Lewis, *Till We Have Faces: A Myth Retold*, pp. 75–6

CONTENTS

List of Abbreviations	ix
Prologue: A Sense of Belonging	xi
Introduction	1
1. A State Born in Violence	16
2. The People of Independent Thought	29
3. Masters of Our Own House	47
4. Whipping Up the New Recruits	58
5. Responsible Members of the Community	69
6. An Ulster Divided Against Itself	87
7. A Regime Under Fire	107
8. A Very Loyalist Coup	121
9. Prisoners of the IRA's Strategy	138
10. The Duisburg Formula	153
11. An Image Problem	164
12. Lifting the Siege	173
13. Ulster's Answer to Leaderless Resistance	192
14. The Changing of the Guard	206
15. A People Under Siege (Again)	215
16. Toppling the New Tower of Babel	225

17.	Circling the Wagons	235
18.	Political Unionism and the Greater Good	247
	Epilogue: Everyday Patriotism	256

Endnotes 262
Bibliography 309
Acknowledgements 321
Index 323

LIST OF ABBREVIATIONS

ACE	Action for Community Employment
CLMC	Combined Loyalist Military Command
CLR	Campaign for Labour Representation
DUP	Democratic Unionist Party
GOC	General Officer Commanding
HQNI	British Army Headquarters Northern Ireland (Thiepval Barracks)
INLA	Irish National Liberation Army
IRA	Irish Republican Army
JIC	Joint Intelligence Committee
LCC	Loyalist Communities Council
LOL	Loyalist Orange Lodge
LVF	Loyalist Volunteer Force
MI5	Military Intelligence, Section 5 (Security Service)
MLA	Member for the Legislative Assembly
NCO	Non-Commissioned Officer
NICRA	Northern Ireland Civil Rights Association
NIHE	Northern Ireland Housing Executive
NILP	Northern Ireland Labour Party
NIO	Northern Ireland Office
PBPA	People Before Profit Alliance
PIRA	Provisional Irish Republican Army
PONI	Police Ombudsman for Northern Ireland
PRONI	Public Record Office of Northern Ireland
PSNI	Police Service of Northern Ireland

PUP	Progressive Unionist Party
RAF	Royal Air Force
RDA	Rathcoole Defence Association
RSHG	Rathcoole Self-Help Group
RHC	Red Hand Commandos
RIC	Royal Irish Constabulary
RUC	Royal Ulster Constabulary
SAS	Special Air Service (British Army Special Forces)
SDLP	Social Democratic and Labour Party
TUV	Traditional Unionist Voice
UDA	Ulster Defence Association
UDI	Unilateral Declaration of Independence
UDP	Ulster Democratic Party
UDR	Ulster Defence Regiment
UESA	Ulster Ex-Servicemen's Association
UFF	Ulster Freedom Fighters
ULDP	Ulster Loyalist Democratic Party
UPA	Ulster Protestant Association
UPL	Ulster Protestant League
UPRG	Ulster Political Research Group
USC	Ulster Special Constabulary
UUC	Ulster Unionist Council
UULA	Ulster Unionist Labour Association
UUP	Ulster Unionist Party
UVF	Ulster Volunteer Force
UWC	Ulster Workers' Council
UWUC	Ulster Women's Unionist Council

PROLOGUE
A Sense of Belonging

> I did not learn the Protestant version of history from books, but by word of mouth passed on from generation to generation. The 'quality', who had education and leisure, knew the details and the dates, but ordinary folk like ourselves carried the facts – or alleged facts – of history in our very bones and in our hearts. We were the people who had never surrendered and would never surrender. As each Twelfth of July came round, Protestant fervour would rise again and be reaffirmed.
>
> Robert Greacen, *The Sash My Father Wore: An Autobiography*[1]

Whitewell Road, North Belfast, 12 July 2001

THE BRICKS AND BOTTLES RAINED down thick and fast. I ducked to avoid a golf ball hurtling in my direction. I wove to narrowly miss a bottle smashing on the ground beside me. Up ahead was a solid line of police Land Rovers blocking the bridge. Royal Ulster Constabulary (RUC) officers in full riot gear huddled closely together in front of their vehicles in a well-disciplined formation, holding their reinforced shields tightly to their chests.

Facing off against the police officers were about thirty Orangemen, who had also formed up in orderly ranks, their standard-bearer spearheading their advance towards police lines. The young man carrying the bright blue, gold and red bannerette depicting the local lodge's emblem – a crest emblazoned with the words 'For God and Ulster' – was a friend of mine. We grew up in the same housing estate and occasionally socialised together. As I stood observing the lodge at close quarters, I felt like I was amongst friends. Amongst people like me. The lodge regalia was completed with a huge banner depicting a painting of soldiers from the 36th Ulster Division going over the top in the trench warfare of the First World War. The soldiers on the banner were portrayed as stoic, defiant and determined. It flapped in the warm July breeze, a reminder of the slaughter of the Somme, held aloft by two Orangemen as bricks and other debris flew above our heads, thrown by angry nationalists behind police lines. Adrenaline coursed through my veins. A red mist descended over those around me. Fear, anger and frustration animated them, and I could see it was taking considerable willpower for the Orangemen to maintain their dignity in the face of such violent provocation.

The lodge had walked the short distance from the Master of the Lodge's home in White City to hand over a letter of protest to the police. No band accompanied them. 'Party Tunes', as they are known, were banned. They wanted to cross Arthur's Bridge and make their way down the Longlands Road, up Church Road and past a cluster of out-of-town shops before entering the Rathcoole estate, about a mile away, the home of most of the members of the lodge. For generations Orangemen like these had walked along what they called their 'traditional route'. What they did not know at the time was that the labelling of this parade as 'contentious' was not a by-product of the Troubles, nor of the recent Drumcree, Ormeau Road and Derry controversies. Many Orangemen perceived these protests to be a deliberate Sinn Féin strategy of forming residents' groups against parades as a means of stopping them from performing their age-old tribal rites,[2] though, in reality, such actions had a long history that predated the formation of Sinn Féin and even Northern Ireland itself.

The local Loyal Orange Lodge (LOL) 658 in Greencastle had been formed a few hundred yards from this spot in 1886, amidst frequent disputes between local Protestants and Catholics over parading. Indeed, there had been frequent rioting in the Greencastle and neighbouring Whitehouse areas in 1867, and then again in 1887 and in 1897, commonly involving clashes between Orangemen, bandsmen and the police.[3]

In July 1899 one local, who went by the *nom de plume* 'Unionist', wrote to the *Belfast News Letter* to complain about the treatment of the Orangemen of Greencastle and was at considerable pains to state that it was not a nationalist district and, out of the 225 families living there, 135 were

Protestant. The 'rowdier elements' amongst the remaining ninety Catholic families, he said, were 'like a lot of Smithfield corner-boys'.[4] Complaining about heavy-handed treatment by the police, he called on his local MP to 'find out the reason why a rebel procession can walk in Belfast when a procession of men sworn to uphold the empire is not allowed'.[5] The *News Letter* agreed and chastised nationalists who 'glorify rebellion; they express over and over again their unabated hostility to England; and their great aim is to fracture and weaken the Empire'. As far as the newspaper was concerned, nationalism was 'at its old game – trying to bring discredit on Orangeism'.[6]

Other letters flooded the *News Letter* columns, each one arguing that loyalists had not been responsible for disturbing the peace in the district.[7] One even went as far as to suggest it was 'time that something was done to prevent the Nationalists from taking possession of the village'. The Protestant people, the letter writer said, 'must be blind, or they have closed their eyes, to what has been going on for the past few years, otherwise they would have been up in arms long since'.[8] Another loyalist, signing his letter 'Anti-Rebel', stated 'that they won't have any more of this nonsense. All that the Protestants of Greencastle want is equality of rights, and this much they intend having.'[9]

Most of those who wrote letters blamed the trouble on the rise in the number of Roman Catholic police officers stationed in the area, although one letter writer refuted this allegation, arguing that the Greencastle nationalist band was 'prohibited by the Roman Catholic sergeants here from entering the neighbouring village of Whitehouse just as the Protestant bands are prevented from entering the Roman Catholic village of Greencastle'.[10] In the final correspondence published by the *News Letter*, 'Unionist' said the 'Nationalists have had too much of it their own way in this district, but the Protestant people do not intend to tolerate it any longer.'[11]

Violence never seemed far from the surface in Greencastle, though it was not until a generation later, during serious civil unrest in the 1920s, that gunmen opened fire at a funeral of a local Protestant, Herbert Hazard, killing one man, Hugh McNally, and wounding another, Thomas McBride. At the same time, it was claimed that a loyalist mob had wrecked the Emmett Hall, chasing a few Catholics out of the area.[12] Then came a long détente lasting half a century.

With the re-emergence of violence in the early 1970s, Greencastle's strong grassroots leadership was tested, with community activist Joe Camplisson lamenting how intercommunal rioting in July 1971 led to a serious deterioration in community relations in the area.[13] It would get worse. Much worse.

On 6 January 1973, eighteen-year-old William Rankin was shot dead as he inflated his car tyres at the corner of Mill Road and the Shore Road.[14] A few years later, a particularly grisly double murder of a Catholic couple, twenty-six-year-old Mervyn McDonald and his wife, twenty-four-year-old Rosaleen, was carried out in front of their two young children – one aged two-and-a-half, the other four months – at their home on the Longlands Road on 9 July 1976. One neighbour was watching television when they heard the shots. 'I looked through the curtains and saw two people coming down the path from the house. One of them was carrying a gun. They were so casual it was unbelievable.'[15] The Ulster Freedom Fighters (UFF) terror group subsequently claimed responsibility, which the nationalist Social Democratic and Labour Party (SDLP) claimed was part of 'a deliberate murderous campaign' to 'drive Catholics from Newtownabbey, Whitehouse and Greencastle'.[16] The Ulster Volunteer Force (UVF) subsequently murdered David Nocher, a member of the Workers' Party, as he cleaned a shop window on the Mill Road in Greencastle on 29 October 1983.[17] A few weeks later, the UVF shot and killed Irish National Liberation Army (INLA) member Joe Craven, a neighbour of Nocher's from Bawnmore Park, while he collected his dole money at the benefits office on the edge of the Rathcoole estate.[18]

Against this backdrop, tensions remained high between the two communities in the Greencastle area. Changing demographics also conspired to challenge claims to tribal rites the Orange Order may once have exercised in areas like this.[19] And so, in July 2001, as I watched the local lodge register its solitary act of protest, I couldn't help but wonder about the motivations of the youths from the nationalist community on the other side of the bridge. They had gathered at police lines to express their displeasure at what they saw as an act of loyalist defiance. Some of them had empty milk bottles, which they fashioned into Molotov cocktails, known locally as petrol bombs, as well as broken paving slabs, golf balls, and bottles filled with urine. Yet, ironically, the police were facing in my direction, where no one had resorted to violence, only peaceful protest. In any event, the battle lines had been firmly drawn in the minds of the authorities and the other community, no doubt shaped by generations of antagonism.

For much of my life until that point, we had called the persistent conflict between Catholics and Protestants the 'Troubles', which was a reflection of earlier sporadic violence in the early 1920s. But there was nothing sporadic about those three decades of sustained and organised slaughter. With the signing of the Belfast Agreement in 1998, we were led to believe such violence had finally abated, once and for all. It was hard to square this myth with the reality as another bottle of piss whizzed past me.

I began to question why I was even here. The truth was I liked to accompany this lodge every Twelfth of July. It was my grandfather's lodge. Like my grandmother, he had been born and reared a few hundred yards along the Whitewell Road in a tough, working-class row of terrace homes in Barbour Street. Those were hard times, when the shadow of the Great Depression touched their lives and the lives of their Catholic neighbours in what was known locally as 'Pope's Row'. Relations between the two communities were generally good except for times, such as in the mid-1930s, when loyalist and republican gunmen re-emerged to wreak havoc. After my grandparents married, they moved to Mill Road, a few hundred yards across what was now Arthur's Bridge, before finally settling in East Way, Rathcoole, in the mid-1960s. As the Troubles picked up pace in the 1970s, between 8,000 and 15,000 families were intimidated out of their homes, leaving places like Greencastle, Bawnmore, Longlands and the Whitewell Road predominantly Catholic and nationalist, while Protestant families moved in large numbers to the neighbouring White City and Rathcoole estates.[20] Against this backdrop of changing demographics, my grandfather and his Orange brethren were confronted by the harsh reality of social and political upheaval. Their traditional route, which had never fully been 'theirs' anyway, was impassable.

Unexpectedly there came a lull in the fracas as the angry shouts and sounds of broken glass and crashing masonry died down. Out of the corner of my eye I spotted some community activists from the local branch of the Progressive Unionist Party (PUP) emerge from a side street to seek a peaceful resolution, and within a few minutes the violent protest had ended.

The Orangemen returned to the White City side of the Whitewell Road, where they were bused out of the area and to Rathcoole to complete the remainder of their filter parade to join the much larger Twelfth celebrations. Many of the Orangemen on the bus that day felt their tribal rights had been infringed. It left them deflated and humiliated. There were plenty of people to blame: quite apart from the other side, the police – who they had come to see as *their* police – were singled out for especially harsh criticism. History repeated itself that day in North Belfast.

Later that evening, in a social club in Rathcoole, the Orangemen recalled how 'the Provies' had prevented them from walking 'their traditional route' and how they were lucky the police were there to prevent matters 'getting out of hand'. All they wanted was 'their rights' respected. Where was 'their parity of esteem' promised by the recent Belfast Agreement? The conversation soon turned to great danger lurking round every corner.

During a visit to Belfast in the late 1970s, writer Dervla Murphy spent time in the company of loyalists like these, pondering 'for how long more can the dying Orange tradition linger on? It is very much a wary, close-the-ranks tradition, always suspecting threats, plots betrayals, conspiracies, always on the look-out for danger ... As a social force it is as negative and destructive as the Republican hatred of England.'[21] I can't now remember the exact moment it dawned on me that I was amidst this 'close-the-ranks tradition', but I knew that as a young man I had begun to think to the contrary. I had got to know nationalists during three years as an undergraduate at the University of Ulster. Quite a few were committed republicans from Belfast, Derry and Armagh, who had their own version of history and understanding of politics. I was aware that their reading of the past was, like the unionist and loyalist interpretations of history, frequently manufactured from misperceptions and misremembrances. As historian Brian Walker has so eloquently observed, the 'Unionist sense of history ... with its great emphasis on 1641, 1689 and 1690, and with the accompanying idea of constant conflict between Protestant and Catholic, is highly selective.'[22]

In working-class communities, where oral tradition is the principal means of passing on history, customs and tradition, this lived experience was streetwise knowledge designed to keep us safe, while republican violence and political agitation posed an existential threat to our very existence.

While my undergraduate history degree had taught me to be sceptical of received wisdom, to question everything I was being told, I knew that being on the Whitewell Road that day, amongst loyalists who felt themselves to be under siege, meant I was part of something greater than myself. I was part of a community, both real and imagined. We were Protestants loyal to Her Majesty the Queen, her heirs and successors, and to the Union between Great Britain and Northern Ireland. Above all, though, we were loyal to each other. Some might even have called us 'loyalists'. It felt good to belong, even if we felt embattled by our physical encounter on the bridge that day or in the stories that sprang from our lived experience.[23]

I was born in 1980 and grew up at a time when the armed conflict on the streets was winding down, though the violence continued to shape and influence our lives in both direct and indirect ways. Family and friends seemed consumed by a state of heightened anxiety, occasionally punctuated by outright fear when, for instance, republican terrorists gunned down a member of the local community. Fifty-one-year-old John Gibson was shot dead as he arrived home from work on 21 October 1993 not far from my front door. The Provisional Irish Republican Army (PIRA) justified his murder on the basis that he worked for a construction company that rebuilt police and army barracks. Then there was my father's friend, forty-three-year-old Sergeant Robert Irvine, who was shot dead at his sister's home in Rasharkin a year earlier, on 20 October 1992, because the PIRA deemed him a 'legitimate target' for belonging to the local battalion of the Royal Irish Regiment. I had a schoolfriend whose father, thirty-eight-year-old John McConnell, a civilian contractor, was murdered on his way home from work, when the IRA detonated a 1,500lb bomb at the Teebane crossroads between Omagh and Cookstown on 17 January 1992. The Provos said he and his co-workers were legitimate targets because they helped to rebuild security force bases. Finally, there was forty-four-year-old Gerry Evans, who had just opened a fishing tackle shop in Glengormley. My father had been talking to him a few hours before he was gunned down by the PIRA on 27 April 1994. The mere fact that he was a loyalist was enough for them to sign his death warrant.[24]

One thing all these people had in common was their community identity. They were unionists. Although they were very different as individuals, the local insistence on ascribing political identities to everyone meant they were part of an imagined community that saw their murders as a common assault on all of us.[25] As far as we were concerned, these people were our kith and kin – part of a broader unionist family. An insidious feeling of fear gripped us in the wake of their deaths. It made us paranoid that we were on the verge of destruction – about to be eradicated like those communities in the Balkans and elsewhere we read about in newspapers and saw on television. We hunkered down. Our enemies were out to get us. They could be anywhere. We were a people under siege.

When I think back to those years, I can still feel the fear and anxiety I experienced, as death or serious injury skulked around every corner. You carry it in your bones and your blood forever. During times of great uncertainty, we all want to belong. It's what makes humankind the social species it has become.

A People Under Siege is a book about the sense of belonging felt by the unionist community in Northern Ireland, but it is much more than that – it is an attempt to articulate what is meant by unionism. In taking this approach it is necessary to confront both the narrow, sectional beliefs and prejudices of unionists and loyalists, as well as the more positive and forward-thinking aspects of this political creed. As a people, I believe unionists in Northern Ireland are capable of being great innovators, problem-solvers and thinkers. 'Northern Protestants have an eloquent artistic and intellectual tradition,' wrote journalist Susan McKay, 'though it is often obscured.'[26]

However, McKay is generally dismissive of unionists and even more so of loyalists, lampooning them for their flags, their Orangeism, their values, and going as far as to stereotype them as counting 'inflexibility' amongst 'traditional Unionist virtues'.[27] She is not alone. Unionists have frequently been misrepresented in Great Britain by journalists like Max Hastings, who once claimed his memory was 'far too unreliable to offer valid testimony' to the Saville Inquiry into Bloody Sunday,[28] yet has, nonetheless, been especially vivid in his recollections of 'several hundred thousand embittered "Proddies"'[29] who 'have been able to sustain a sorry pantomime, conscious that they are unloved beyond their own streets'.[30] There may be some truth to this, but it does not excuse attempts to misrepresent and denigrate an entire community.

I no longer live in Northern Ireland. I relocated to England when I was in my late twenties, though I return home regularly to the place of my birth to try to understand its people and what makes them tick and, importantly, why the community I grew up alongside continues to harbour the sort of deep-seated feelings of fear and anxiety I once felt. I believe unionism is a political fraternity that has the potential to be much more benevolent, positive and inclusive than its critics admit, and so it is important to spell out how and why it can realise this potential. *A People Under Siege*, therefore, seeks to explain key developments within unionism from the point of view of its prominent personalities and political parties, including the forms of unionism and loyalism that run like tributaries into a fast-flowing river of British national identity. It also attempts to examine how they are seen from the perspective of others beyond their community.

Political unionism in Northern Ireland is much more than a sense of belonging. It is also about how people organise themselves according to their relationship with one another, with those they elect to govern on their behalf, and how, as a people, they contribute to their country, the United Kingdom. At a time of considerable domestic political turmoil and global uncertainty, I have seen much more pragmatism than pessimism, and more self-reflection than the flagrant displays of primordial sectarian bigotry you read about in the columns of denigratory journalism. It is for this reason that a new book on Northern Irish unionists is badly needed. If we do not acknowledge, accept and respect our differing political outlooks, we may never move to a position of mutual acceptance, tolerance and understanding that will help us build a lasting peace in this troubled part of the world.

INTRODUCTION

[T]here can be no right to power except what is either founded upon, or speedily obtains, the hearty consent of the body of the people.

Francis Hutcheson, *A Short Introduction to Moral Philosophy*[1]

NATION STATES ARE IN CRISIS. Everywhere, from the United States to Europe and the Middle East to Central Asia and beyond, identity politics are on the rise, calling into question who we are and forcing us to rethink how we live our lives and how we organise ourselves politically.[2] Humankind appears to be in the grip of constant fear, anxiety and uncertainty about what the future holds.

The advent of identity politics did not create this crisis. Rather, this struggle for security has been going on since time immemorial. We can trace its intellectual origins to the birth of the modern state in the mid-seventeenth century, which sprang from the smouldering embers of the Thirty Years' War (1618–48).[3] Philosophers like Thomas Hobbes (1588–1679) were among the first to grapple with the idea of reconciling our individual liberties with the benefits offered by banding together with others for greater collective security. Hobbes had a deeply cynical view of life. As far as he was concerned, humankind was locked in a state of perpetual conflict where individuals had to resign themselves to the depressing certainty that 'every man is Enemy of every man', where he or she was locked in a persistent nightmare of 'continuall feare, and danger of violent death', and where people were destined to live out a life that was 'solitary, poore, nasty, brutish, and short'.[4] Hobbes' seminal book *Leviathan* (1651) reflected a world where this 'state of nature' reigned supreme and where humankind was destined to fight out a 'war against all'. People were 'continually in competition for Honour and Dignity ... and consequently amongst men there ariseth on that ground, Envy and Hatred, and finally Warre'.[5] As an antidote to such feelings of insecurity, Hobbes suggested that people required a 'Common Power, to keep them in awe, and to direct their actions to the Common Benefit'.[6] In practice, this meant ceding individual rights and liberties to a political authority or what he called a 'Common-Wealth'.

Hobbes was writing at a time when the evidence for his theory of perpetual conflict was all around. In the decade leading up to the publication of *Leviathan*, the English Civil War had seen the arrest, trial and execution of King Charles I (1600–49). The British Civil War, as it is more correctly termed by most historians nowadays, drew in other parts of the Stuart kingdom too, with significant battles taking place in Ireland.

Under Charles' father, James I (1566–1625), the plantation of Ireland had seen the influx of economic migrants from England and Scotland, who rapidly presided over the confiscation of land from the native Irish and 'Old English'.[7] The colonisation of the country from the early seventeenth century left the door open to the more intensive planation of Ulster after the flight of the local Gaelic earls.[8] However, this resolved little of the insecurity felt by Protestants there. A Catholic insurrection in Ulster in 1641, in which many planters were massacred, 'left a deep impression upon Ulster Protestants',[9] who promptly raised militias to defend themselves against further attack.[10]

Formed in the aftermath of the massacres, the Laggan Army was one such fighting force.[11] Raised by two wealthy landowning brothers, Sir William and Sir Robert Stewart, the Laggan Army initially operated in Donegal but would fight several key battles during the Civil War. Robert Stewart was the army's titular military chief, on account of his extensive military experience in the Thirty Years' War. He knew the value of Protestants banding together for collective security and in 1643 committed himself to the Solemn League and Covenant in Coleraine.[12] This was an agreement between the English Parliamentarians and the Scots, by which the latter gave an undertaking to support the former in their disputes with the Royalists who sided with King Charles I.[13] Although it was couched in explicitly religious language aimed at protecting the Presbyterian Church of Scotland, for Ulster Protestants the Covenant provided a 'public band against the danger, now all too apparent, from the natives'.[14] The idea of covenanting stretched back to biblical times, but in mid-seventeenth-century Ulster it meant an evolving contractual relationship between Ulster Protestants and the sovereign authority.[15] Covenanting was, therefore, seen as a spiritual means of binding people together in a contract or agreement as they embarked on a joint venture – in Ulster, this meant defending themselves against external threats.

By the end of the seventeenth century, Presbyterians had come to be seen as Dissenters in the eyes of the Established Episcopalian Church,[16] which was closely linked to the Church of England after the Restoration of King Charles II. With Presbyterianism marginalised, the Established Church formed the 'fountain of privilege in Ireland'.[17] Ulster Presbyterians, therefore, became leading advocates of the 'Protestant Succession', by which they hoped to preserve the Protestant royal lineage. One of the most influential Presbyterian radicals was a clergyman from Drumalig in County Down, John Hutcheson, who had assumed a key role in recruiting men to bear arms in anticipation of a 'Protestant Succession'.[18] His son, Francis, was born on 8 August 1694 and would rise to prominence, first as a leading academician in the principal Dissenter Academy in Dublin in the 1720s, and then as Professor of Moral Philosophy at Glasgow University from 1729 until his death in 1746.[19] While at Glasgow, Hutcheson taught and corresponded with David Hume (1711–76) and Adam Smith (1723–90) and was regarded by both as a major intellectual influence on their work.[20]

As a key architect of the Scottish Enlightenment, if not its leader,[21] Francis Hutcheson became renowned in his lifetime for his work on ethics, aesthetics and moral philosophy, but his greatest contribution was, perhaps, 'in the field of politics'.[22] This included the concept of political union, which saw him depart significantly from Hobbes' understanding of a 'state of war'. For Hutcheson, in what he characterised as a 'civil society', people did sometimes disobey the law by stealing or being violent towards one another, but that did not necessarily mean a 'political state is a state of war among men thus united'.[23] Although he acknowledged the imperfection of humankind, Hutcheson maintained that they must have observed 'dangers or miseries attending a state of anarchy' to know that they were much greater than 'any inconveniences to be feared from submitting their affairs along with others to the direction of certain governors or councils concerned in the safety of all'.[24] For it was in that realisation, Hutcheson believed, that people 'would begin to desire a political constitution for their own safety and advantage, as well as for the general good'.[25] In one of his most important observations on political unions, Hutcheson concluded that as men were 'naturally endued with reason, caution, and sagacity; and civil government, or some sort of political union must appear, in the present state of our nature, the necessary means of safety and prosperity to themselves and others, they must naturally desire it in this view; and nature has endued them with active powers and understanding for performing all political offices'.[26]

Hutcheson's radical ideas on the relationship between the people and their rulers made him a 'standard author in pre-Revolutionary America', in France and in Ireland.[27] His ideas percolated through those countries' revolutionary movements and, along with other Enlightenment thinkers like Kant, Locke and Paine, 'provided inspiration and political ideas to Irish Catholic (and Presbyterian) radicals in the 1790s', prompting an uprising by the United Irishmen in 1798.[28] In Ireland, the emergence of these revolutionary ideals also prompted the formation of a counter-revolutionary movement, the Orange Order, following a skirmish between an offshoot of the Protestant Peep o' Day Boys and the Catholic Defenders at the Diamond near Loughgall on 21 September 1795. The Order sought the preservation of the Protestant ascendancy[29] and the exclusion of Catholics from public life. This acted as a catalyst to the 1798 Rebellion of the United Irishmen. Their leader, Wolfe Tone, thought the British by 'birth, breeding and bigotry' feared the 'Irish infant of 82' and the 'natural development of its capacities and its powers', which brought a fear of 'political and religious schism' and of Defenderism, Presbyterianism, Catholicism, United Irishism that 'may, gradually, yet not slowly, change into PATRIOTISM'.[30]

The Act of Union, which came into effect on 1 January 1801, was 'intended to heal and manage these divisions'.[31] Under Article VI of the Act, it promised that 'his Majesty's subjects of Ireland shall have the same privileges, and be on the same footing as his Majesty's subjects of Great Britain'.[32] William Drennan, one of the founders of the United Irishmen, had parted ways with that organisation in 1794,[33] but he opposed the Union, and wrote of his 'fixed abhorrence, and my instinctive antipathy, against this legislative and incorporating Union, that takes away the BODY, as well as SOUL of the Irish people'.[34]

According to historian Richard English, 'The 1790s were a crucial decade in the emergence of modern Ireland,' giving birth to 'popular republicanism, separatism, loyalism and Orangeism ... [and] nationalist Ireland'.[35] Throughout the nineteenth century these ideologies gradually began to offer competing world views about how the state and its people should be organised. Orangeism, loyalism and unionism became entrenched in reaction to a 'resurgent Irish Catholicism and nationalism', with a 'pan-Protestant, ethno-national formation'[36] taking shape in the form of Ulster unionism towards the end of the century. Unionism in Ulster 'grew from a process whose origins preceded organised nationalism', which was largely attributable to the manipulation of Belfast conservatives in establishing their 'authority over both the urban working class and rural tenant farmers by outflanking the traditional landed elite'.[37] The growth of a new capitalist class undoubtedly intersected with the manufacture of a form of unionism that owed more to attempts to invent a form of territorial-based nationalism than to the global ideas of political unionism first articulated by Francis Hutcheson.[38] As Britain's colonial authority decayed in Ireland, two communities emerged as 'national peoples in conflict for the same land' in what came to be called an 'ethnic frontier'.[39]

In the late nineteenth century, Ulster unionists mobilised in vast numbers against British government plans to push through a policy of Home Rule for Ireland. Lord Randolph Churchill exploited the opportunism of the 'Orange Card', 'declaring that "Ulster will fight and Ulster will be right," in an address to Conservatives and Orangemen at the Ulster Hall in Belfast'.[40] It was the alliance between Conservatives and Liberal Unionists in 1886, however, that would lay the foundations of a political party organisation that would eventually emerge in 1905 under the auspices of the Ulster Unionist Council (UUC). At the time, the Irish Nationalist Party remained dismissive of the unionist situation, despite the latter's embattled position and the British government's attempts to remove them from the United Kingdom without their consent.[41]

Supporters of Home Rule found it difficult to understand the rationale for unionist attachment to the Union between Great Britain and Ireland. 'With all their hard-headedness and practicality, the men of Belfast and Ulster ... true to their Scottish origin, are a singularly emotional people,' opined the English Home Ruler Sydney Brooks in 1909.[42] 'Their political creed is really a political cult, a compound of fears, instincts, hatreds and suspicions in which facts are metamorphosed out of all semblance to reality,' he complained. Brooks regarded unionists as little more than an 'English garrison' in Ireland and dismissed them when writing about his adopted Sinn Féin cause, which, he claimed, aimed to 'make the Irish politically virile, united and constructive'.[43] Like other champions of Home Rule, Brooks underestimated the strongly held belief of unionists that they were better off both economically and in terms of their physical security within Britain's imperial orbit, incorporating two territories under one parliament, rather than carving out a future as part of an independent, small island nation.

The unionist mobilisation against Home Rule involved all members of the community, including women and young people. By 1911, thousands of women had come together to form the Ulster Women's Unionist Council (UWUC), effectively giving them a political voice despite them being unenfranchised until the passing of the Representation of the People Act (1928) seventeen years later.[44] Formed under the presidency of Mary Anne, 2nd Duchess of Abercorn, the UWUC saw 40,000–50,000 women enrol in its first twelve months. In a mass gathering at the Ulster Hall on 18 January 1912, the Duchess of Abercorn told the audience how they were assembled for one purpose – 'to protest with one voice against the action of the present government in trying to force Home Rule upon Ireland and the people of Ireland'. To rapturous applause, she continued: 'I cannot understand why anyone should want Home Rule, and by it to relegate Ireland to the wretched position of importance held by the Isle of Man. The only hope for a small island like ours is to be incorporated for all legislative purposes with a powerful country such as Great Britain.'[45] The Countess of Kilmorey reminded the same audience how:

> [The] women of Ireland had a great part to play in the political struggle, and complete confidence in their own leaders as well as in those comrades, the loyal men of Ireland, they would go forward, hand in hand, with a firm determination to fight to a finish for the unimpaired maintenance of the Union, until the battle was won and the victory theirs.[46]

The UWUC served as 'an effective illustration of the degree of political interest many women possessed in the early years of the twentieth century, even years before they possessed the right to vote'.[47]

On 26 September 1912, almost half a million men and women signed the Ulster Solemn League and Covenant, which reiterated the unionist belief that Home Rule 'would be disastrous to the material well-being of Ulster as well as the whole of Ireland, subversive of our civil and religious freedom, destructive of our citizenship and perilous to the unity of the Empire'. It expressed the loyalty of its signatories to King George V, pledging 'in solemn Covenant throughout this our time of threatened calamity to stand by one another in defending for ourselves and our children our cherished position of equal citizenship in the United Kingdom'. Crucially, the Covenant's signatories agreed to use 'all means which may be found necessary to defeat the present conspiracy to set up a Home Rule Parliament in Ireland', refusing to recognise the authority of such a parliament should it be forced upon them. With the Covenant pledge, some people signing in their own blood, Ulster unionism had now adopted all the trappings of a nationalist movement.

In one of the most famous books on the development of this Ulster movement, *Ulster's Stand for the Union*, Ronald McNeill MP observed how its leader, Sir Edward Carson, 'may not have succeeded in bringing the Ulster people into a Promised Land', but 'he had at least conducted an orderly retreat to a position of safety'.[48] McNeill continued:

> The almost miraculous skill with which he [Carson] had directed all the operations of a protracted and harassing campaign, avoiding traps and countless crises, frustrating with unfailing adroitness the manoeuvres both of implacable enemies and treacherous 'friends', was fully appreciated by his grateful followers, who had for years past regarded him with an intensity of personal devotion seldom given even to the greatest of political leaders.[49]

McNeill disputed the notion that unionism's mobilisation against Home Rule was really a rebellion in the proper sense, especially when the aim was to preserve what he believed to be the democratic will of the people. 'It was resistance to the transfer of a people's allegiance without their consent,' he stated, and 'to their forcible expulsion from the Constitution with which they were content and their forcible inclusion in a Constitution which they detested. This was the very antithesis of Revolution.'[50] McNeill, perhaps more than any other politician and author at the time, did more to legitimise the idea of unionism as a form of nationalism centred on the ancient province of Ulster (though Protestants only enjoyed a numerical majority in six of the nine counties), a province which was prepared to fight for its right to oppose political designs being hatched at Westminster on the future organisation of self-government for the entire island of Ireland.[51]

In opposing Home Rule for Ireland, unionists lobbied instead for the creation of a new state based on a Protestant head count in Ulster. They saw this as the best way to avoid being subsumed within a Catholic-dominated all-island political structure. However, the establishment of Northern Ireland between the passing of the Government of Act (1920), which partitioned Ireland, and the reporting of the Boundary Commission in 1925, which confirmed the course of the Irish border as outlined in the Act,[52] left Ulster unionists with a mammoth task ahead of them. They had won a veto on Home Rule for Ireland but were left to administer 'a form of Home Rule that the Devil himself could not have imagined'.[53] By threatening the use of force, they had won political concessions and the prospect of building a new political entity that was distinct and independent from its southern neighbour, one that was 'unlikely ever to be abolished without its own consent' and could not be 'altered except by the will of its own Parliament'.[54] But they were hampered by 'the turmoil of the new state's early years', which saw Northern Ireland forge its 'essential identity in bitter suffering and adversity'.[55] The new state was challenged in its physical security by an Irish Republican Army (IRA) campaign designed to make it 'impossible for the new government to function', one that, 'inevitably set in train ... [an] ancient sectarian war'.[56]

Despite the Government of Ireland Act laying the constitutional architecture for the formation of two states imbued with religious tolerance, the unionist government in Belfast did little to reach out to the minority Catholic nationalist community living in their midst.[57] Although it was subsequently characterised as a 'Protestant state for a Protestant people', a derogation on the boastful words spoken by Northern Ireland's first

Prime Minister Sir James Craig in a speech in 1934, this well-worn cliché underscored the political insecurity, intolerance and internal divisions facing unionist leaders as they sought to lay the foundations of a new state-based identity.[58]

In religious terms, the number of Protestants (those identifying principally as Presbyterian, Church of Ireland and Methodist) living in the new six-county state in 1926, when the first census since 1911 was carried out, was recorded as 762,929, while the number of Roman Catholics was 420,428. Importantly, the non-aligned population numbered 73,204.[59] Believing in safety in numbers, the unionist leadership played to the narrow sectional interests of the majority community. However, this overconfidence in the sectarian headcount and belief in the efficacy of their one-party system of government sowed the seeds of the unionist regime's ultimate political destruction. Not only did many Catholics opt out of Northern Ireland, but there were Protestants who were more socialist in their political unionism and who rejected all forms of parochial bigotry and elitism. The Stormont regime tended to play up the threats posed by physical force republicans, but the reality was that their greatest challenge came from independently minded and left-leaning people who believed in a more inclusive form of political union with Great Britain. The system the unionist leadership ultimately constructed was, therefore, based around a curious mix of attempts to manufacture consent while holding coercion in reserve, meaning it forever ran the risk of having to reconcile the logic of this mixed approach with the outlook and aspirations of a divided people. The fact that the unionist government spent much of its time looking for ways to stop its working-class supporters from voting for labour and socialist political representatives at election time – while also gerrymandering and discriminating against Catholics – said more about unionist fear, anxiety and uncertainty than it did about a systematic effort to repress the minority community.

By the mid-1960s, right-wing unionists and extreme loyalists saw a direct challenge to their way of life from three principal directions. The first was from the IRA, which, despite having failed to mount a successful armed campaign along the border in 1956–62, was continually represented as a security threat by rabble-rousers like the Reverend Ian Paisley. The second associated challenge was believed to emanate from the Irish government, which had opened dialogue with Northern Ireland's Prime Minister Terence O'Neill in 1965. Ever since the worsening of relations between North and South in the 1930s, irredentism was believed to guide Dublin's policy towards Belfast. A thawing of relations in the 1960s under O'Neill brought a rapprochement between the two jurisdictions, though some extreme loyalists believed it was a trap. Lastly, there were mild attempts by the Roman Catholic Church to enter into ecumenical dialogues with Protestantism aimed at promoting greater understanding between all the Christian denominations. Although fears of what might eventually accompany these changes – a unification of Ireland under Dublin rule – were largely manufactured out of paranoia, they were seen as real enough for some right-wingers within the Unionist Party to launch what amounted to a coup d'état, which eventually toppled O'Neill. This coup was to be driven by a cabal of right-wing unionist politicians, who presided over the formation of a secretive paramilitary group they called the Ulster Volunteer Force in homage to the earlier paramilitary force established to resist Home Rule.[60]

By the summer of 1969 the outbreak of serious intercommunal violence had shattered the façade that unionists and nationalists could live in harmony without the redistribution of rights amongst all those living in Ulster. In late March 1972, the British government finally stepped in to terminate what civil rights leader Kevin Boyle called 'an orange-unionist monopoly built through repression, jobbery and British apathy'.[61] Crucially, Boyle also characterised the unionist experiment as 'an artificial society they never did consent to'.[62] In reply, the Unionist Party MP for South Belfast, Rafton Pounder, urged unionists to enter a period of quiet reflection. He thought it important that the 'next year is spent in thinking deeply, positively and realistically about the form of regional government which we wish to see and indeed are determined to press for in Northern Ireland'.[63] A committed supporter of devolution, Pounder felt Stormont should return in more meaningful form – less a 'glorified county council' and more a regional legislature in its own right. 'No one disputes that Westminster is the sovereign parliament of the United Kingdom, and thus is all-powerful,' he observed. 'What rankles so bitterly has been the manner in which that power has been used, and the considerations which it is suspected weighed most heavily in deciding upon the exercise of that power.'[64]

After the collapse of the unionist experiment, Protestants generally diverged in their understanding of how regional government ought to make allowances for those who had withdrawn their consent to be governed by an 'orange-unionist monopoly'. On the one hand you had the Ulster British, who harboured a much broader and more inclusive idea of who formed part of their imagined community. They looked to the United Kingdom as a whole – and its four nations of Northern Ireland, Scotland, England and Wales – as their primary understanding of the state, with only a secondary regional identification with Northern Ireland.[65] They tended to be much more international in outlook and – through their commitment to liberty and tolerance – to see the potential for Catholics to form part of an organic political union with Great Britain.[66] Ulster loyalists, in contrast, tended to see Northern Protestants as 'their primary imagined community', while their 'secondary identification with Britain involves only conditional loyalty'.[67] In order to preserve their political union and identity, they saw domination over Catholics as essential.[68] The 'core assumption' of Ulster loyalism was that the 'only alternative to Ulster loyalist dominance is Ulster loyalist defeat and humiliation'.[69] Loyalists, therefore, interpreted the world in zero-sum terms. Their slogans reflected this: 'What we have, we hold.' 'Not an inch.' 'No surrender.' 'A Protestant state for a Protestant people' was, therefore, a natural outgrowth of such emotional sloganeering. For loyalists, after the fall of Stormont in 1972, the world looked and felt as if they were inhabiting a state of nature little different from what Hobbes had mapped out in the mid-seventeenth century. They yearned for a return to the 'artificial state' built by unionist leaders in the previous half-century in a way that jarred with the Ulster British sense of identity.

Throughout the 1970s and 1980s, unionist politicians proved particularly adept at exploiting these emotive slogans, even if they were 'all too exclusive and self-indulgent' and 'generally lacked a deep or ideologically sensitive reflection upon the character of the unionist tradition'.[70] In reality, the collapse of the unionist experiment meant that unionism could no longer rely on 'the same certainties which it had celebrated heretofore': its absorption and domination over devolved government, and its strength in numbers.[71] It required intellectual argument, reason and a vision for the future that could appeal beyond sectional interests. Few unionists were up to the task, with direct rule having had something of a discombobulating effect on those who found themselves in leadership positions. Few of them took Pounder's advice to spend their time 'thinking deeply, positively and realistically about the form of regional government which we wish to see'. Worse, they also failed to 'explain to others or even give their politics a second thought', leaving their opponents to 'fix upon unionism the label of an ideology of sectarian supremacism or to dismiss it as nothing but the flotsam or jetsam of Britain's imperial past'.[72]

As revolts began against ideological forms of political union across Europe in the 1980s,[73] in Britain, 'contentious assumptions about nation, state, identity and religion in Ireland' coalesced 'in the collective mind of Westminster and Whitehall'.[74] Unionism continued to live in a kind of groundhog day, stuck in a time loop, unwilling to let go of its belief in democracy as a form of majority rule, tethered to a fundamentalist notion of sovereignty as lying in a regional parliament with 'orange-unionist' trappings. Then, in signing the Anglo-Irish Agreement of 1985 behind the backs of unionist politicians, the British government left them with a 'dawning realisation ... that politics would not return full circle to those happier days before the autumn of 1968 when Stormont sat in magisterial splendour, when Orange marches filled the summers with the sound of Lambeg drums, and when politics still ministered to Protestant advantage'.[75]

By the early 1990s, the British government had forced unionists to accept its policy, carefully crafted and drip-fed into everything from the Northern Ireland Office's *The Future of Northern Ireland: A Paper for Discussion* (1972) to London's *entente cordiale* with Dublin represented by the Anglo-Irish Agreement (1985) and Downing Street Declaration (1993). To paraphrase Kevin Boyle, the days of 'repression, jobbery and British apathy' were over. Sovereignty, in a British sense, now had several new connotations. It meant forcing unionists to accept London's outlook that Northern Ireland would only continue to remain part of the UK until most of its people wished otherwise, countering any attempts to change this principle of consent by violence. It also meant a devolution of powers to local politicians in Belfast for as long as the arrangement was acceptable to both communities. And, finally, it meant addressing grievances, while demanding loyalists and republicans surrender to the rightful sovereign authority in the form of 'the mother of all parliaments' at Westminster.

However, this coercive approach would encounter problems during the emerging peace process. Both loyalists and republicans were reluctant to hand over their guns and, within unionism, a radical form of loyalism re-emerged to articulate a fundamentalist understanding of sovereignty, which saw the centre of gravity resting squarely with the Ulster loyalist people, rather than Westminster. This kind of narrow unionist outlook did much to perpetuate the myth of 'a people under siege', with 'its injunctions to close the gates and man the walls'.[76] Yet, paradoxically, the peace process also 'created new opportunities for meaningful political dialogue' and the enabling of 'more flexible definitions of Unionism'.[77]

Under the leadership of David Trimble, a politician long regarded by civil servants as an 'enlightened unionist', the Ulster Unionist Party (UUP) was persuaded to think positively and realistically by broadening its vision of who formed part of the political union. 'Ulster Unionists, fearful of being isolated on the island,' Trimble said in his acceptance of the Nobel Peace Prize, 'built a solid house, but it was a cold house for Catholics. And northern nationalists, although they had a roof over their heads, seemed to us as if they meant to burn the house down.'[78] Crucially, Trimble acknowledged what he saw as the imperfections and flaws of human nature that gave opportunities to fanatics who dreamt of 'forcing the Ulster British people into a Utopian Irish state, more ideologically Irish than its own inhabitants actually want', as well as those who dreamt 'of permanently suppressing northern nationalists in a state more supposedly British than its inhabitants actually want.'[79] Trimble found solace in battling these 'dark forces' in the teachings of the founding father of Conservativism, Edmund Burke, who saw parliamentary democracy as the vehicle that 'not local purposes, nor local prejudices ought to guide, but the general good resulting from the general reason of the whole'.[80]

Since the Good Friday Agreement (1998), the British and Irish governments have worked in lockstep to realise the Burkean ideal of the 'general good' by way of power-sharing between unionists and nationalists. However, the eclipse of the more moderate UUP and SDLP by the more extreme Democratic Unionist Party (DUP) and Sinn Féin in the 2003 and 2005 elections sent unionists and nationalists down a more divergent path, with a return to power-sharing in 2007 reinforcing 'local purposes' and 'local prejudices'. The DUP's dominant position – in terms of seats in the Northern Ireland Assembly – did little to resolve feelings of disaffection within the ranks of its supporters during these years. The so-called 'flag protests' in 2012–13 prompted the re-emergence of a populist form of Ulster loyalism, which slowly turned its grassroots supporters against dreams of a more inclusive future. Instead, this exclusionary form of political unionism induced nightmares populated by fear, anxiety and uncertainty. And it would soon have consequences in the real world when David Cameron's Conservative government held a referendum on the UK's continued membership of the EU in June 2016. In a significant swing in favour of Brexit amongst the unionist community, the loudest voices coalesced around a fundamentalist reading of sovereignty in the UK, which left little room for that kind of political unionism articulated by Hutcheson or Burke.

Although it might have been the case that, historically, debate on unionism has tended to be 'introverted and parochial, lacking any active sense of the wider history of political unions,'[81] it has certainly got much worse in the wake of Brexit. Nowadays, we find Enlightenment ideals like reason, science and progress readily replaced by emotion, quackery and populist nationalism. In Northern Ireland, unionists have become more insular again, resurrecting ethnic and nationalist notions of what constitutes the Union, rather than focusing on a form of civic unionism that offers a cosmopolitan political outlook which transcends, rather than erects, barriers between people. It is depressing and all too familiar.

In *A People Under Siege*, I offer an alternative vision for unionism and urge a return to the core values and beliefs of classic political unionism, arguing that this venerated tradition offers a more liberal framework for organising people in the early twenty-first century. Building on Francis Hutcheson's writings, this book offers a radical reinterpretation of unionism as a contract and set of relationships between individuals, their community and those who govern on their behalf in the common interest. This Hutchesonian unionism – 'with its emphasis on rationality, rational assent to moral principles and the improvability of mankind'[82] – offers a vision for political unionism that is more inclusive, progressive and benevolent. It places the greater good of humankind above and beyond narrow sectional interests defined by ethnic kinship. While Irish nationalism continues to reinvent itself as an extension of the 'enlightenment project' – with its accompanying bodyguard of millenarian republicanism[83] – it is time to map out the beginnings of a new political union that has the potential to offer a better future to all the people of Northern Ireland. But first we must return to the past to observe at close quarters how unionism lost its way and became so inward-looking and exclusive.

1

A State Born in Violence

> I am asked by Sir Edward Carson to convey to the people an expression of his earnest hope that they will give the authorities all possible assistance in quelling disturbances, whether by keeping away from areas in which trouble is likely to arise or, where it can be done, by using their influence for the prevention of disorder. Any other course would be simply to play into the enemy's game.
>
> Sir Edward Carson's appeal to loyalists to support the authorities, telegraphed from London to the *Belfast News Letter*, 24 July 1920.[1]

IN A PEN PORTRAIT OF the poet William Butler Yeats written in early 1920, the journalist and playwright St John Ervine departed from his biography of the great poet to observe the political context in which he was writing. There was nothing that made his 'Orange blood boil more', Ervine said, than the crudity of violence in Ireland. It was a land that gave birth to 'violent, crude plays', inevitable in a 'land of violent, crude beliefs'. Ervine singled out what he called 'Sinn Féiners' as the main source of this violence, for it was 'hard not to lose faith in human perfectibility when one considers how foolish are the political schemes they devise'.[2] He believed that the Irish people had lost the ability to think objectively about radical political schemes and that these critical faculties had 'decayed' and been replaced by 'emotional nationalism':

> For all sorts of reasons, political, social and historical and also religious, the critical faculty has rarely been employed and certainly has not been developed. Either you are for a thing or against it. Doubt

is treated as if it were antagonism. Reluctance to commit oneself to any scheme, however fantastic or ill-considered it may be, is treated as treason to the national spirit.[3]

Ervine had been born into a working-class community in East Belfast and was initially an early convert to Home Rule. He rejected Sinn Féin's obsession with forcing through Irish independence at the point of a barrel of a gun, and also unionist propaganda asserting 'Home Rule is Rome Rule'.[4] He observed how it had come to the stage where people were beginning to assert the belief – as if it were an article of faith – that an Irish Republic could only be established by force. In these tumultuous times, Ervine said, you were only really considered an 'Irishman' if you bought into this scheme wholeheartedly – there was no room for doubters, never mind dissenters. If you expressed views to the contrary, you risked being denounced as a 'West Briton, an anglicised Irishman, even, on occasions, as "not Irish at all", although his forebears have lived in Ireland for generations'.[5]

Ervine's reservations about the revolutionary change blowing across the island point to broader political challenges on the eve of partition. Cultural historian Connal Parr reminds us that Ervine is probably best remembered for his 'later incarnation as a pugnacious Unionist',[6] though his famous 1911 stage play *Mixed Marriage*, curiously, represented Orangeism 'as a divisive force within the working class'.[7] It might be observed that the Ervine of 1920 is, therefore, well-placed to offer us a window into the events surrounding the formation of Northern Ireland.

This was a period, according to historian Marianne Elliott, when the new political entity was 'born amid heightened violence' and a 'sense of siege'.[8] Elliott argued that one hundred years ago:

> [N]o one in Ireland wanted partition. Unionists would have preferred the entire island to remain with Britain. Nationalists, for their part, had been seeking a form of devolution in the return of the Irish parliament abolished in 1801. Why Unionists fought so hard against such a moderate measure has long been a matter of historical debate. Yet they did and were the first to threaten armed resistance.[9]

This much may be true. The threat of force certainly fused intent and capability, especially when the unionist leadership landed guns at Larne and Donaghadee in 1914. Despite its trappings as a mass movement, however, unionism was not a revolutionary force.[10] According to Irish nationalist historian Alice Stopford Green, a 'cynic might have suggested that it was the last bid of the aristocratic and superior classes, lay and ecclesiastical, in alliance with English Tories, to guide the people for their good'.[11] The outbreak of war with Germany, nevertheless, upended any extreme Ulster Protestant notions of switching allegiance from an English king to a German one and went some way to ensuring that the thousands of European guns landed in Ulster were never fired in anger. Nevertheless, from a political point of view, the 'position in which Ulster was now placed was … a very anxious one'.[12]

The absorption of an estimated 35,000 members of the UVF into the British Army soon followed, with unionist leader Edward Carson passionately informing the UUC on 3 September 1914 how, 'England's difficulty is not Ulster's opportunity: England's difficulty is our difficulty.' Ulstermen – and other Irishmen – joined up and were deployed in large numbers along the Western Front. However, while they fought and died in the trenches of Thiepval Wood, among other places, a small group of their fellow countrymen – who had ignored the call to join the firing line – was preparing for an organised insurrection against British rule in Ireland. In Easter Week 1916, some 1,600 rebels took over prominent buildings in Dublin, fortified them and defended them against soldiers 'whose superior numbers and firepower soon crushed their resistance'.[13] According to Dublin Metropolitan Police reports from the time, 429 people were killed and 2,582 people were injured in the skirmishes that followed, most of them civilians.[14] However, it was the execution of the rebellion's leaders by the British that was 'sufficient to effect a conversion to republicanism'.[15]

The Easter Rising 'forced the government to take the Irish question out of cold storage'.[16] In the aftermath of the attempted putsch, Prime Minister David Lloyd George wrote to Edward Carson proposing that they settle the matter of Ireland 'promptly', intimating that it was too distracting to the war effort. One aspect of the proposals was the exclusion of the six north-easterly countries of Ulster from any future settlement. The UUC deliberated before agreeing to Lloyd George's proposal. Unionists in Cavan, Donegal and Monaghan were said to have 'shed tears' on the occasion.[17]

More pressing war matters meant Lloyd George's proposals for Home Rule for Ireland, minus the six counties, were 'never implemented'.[18] The idea of dividing Ireland according to religious and, therefore, political majorities had by now moved centre stage. Yet, it was not until 7 October 1919 that the London government set up a cabinet committee to review proposals for Irish self-government.[19] By February 1920 the Government of Ireland Bill had been introduced into Westminster, which proposed the establishment of two parliaments, one in Belfast to preside over a six-county jurisdiction, and one in Dublin to govern the remaining twenty-six counties of Ireland.[20]

In the weeks prior to the introduction of the Government of Ireland Bill, much political activity in Ireland focused on the local and municipal elections held on 15 January 1920. Contesting 1,470 vacant seats, Sinn Féin ran 717 candidates, while Labour stood 595 candidates and the Unionist Party ran 436 candidates. A further 588 candidates competed under different banners.[21] In Belfast, the Unionists nominated 'a good selection' of candidates under the bannerette of the Ulster Unionist Labour Association (UULA), originally formed in July 1918 as a means of staving off electoral losses in the wake of an outbreak of intense class conflict across the United Kingdom. The Unionists used the UULA as a 'means of initiating a purge from the local trade union movement of "Bolsheviks"' and (what it saw as the same thing) republicans.[22] The UULA led a targeted campaign against what they called 'Sinn Féin trade unionism'. Fifty-five Official Unionist candidates were fielded against twenty-two Belfast Labour Party candidates, nineteen Nationalist Party candidates, thirteen Sinn Féin candidates, ten Independent Labour and three socialist candidates. The outgoing councillors consisted of fifty-two Unionists and eight Nationalists.[23]

Despite their negative campaign against Labour candidates, the Unionists lost fifteen seats, while a mix of thirteen Belfast Labour Party and Independent Labour candidates were elected. 'Unionist solidarity was broken in almost every ward of the city,'[24] with Labour councillors touting a progressive programme, including calling for the council to hold evening meetings so that working people could attend. This more transparent style of democracy was roundly attacked by the local unionist press, with the *Belfast News*

Letter moving at a brisk clip to smear the socialists for adopting a collective silence on political assassinations in Dublin. In the wake of Labour's electoral successes, the Unionist Party would scheme to reverse the British government provision in the Government of Ireland Act to hold local elections according to proportional representation. The prospective return to 'a simple majority system reinforced the traditional sectarian rivalries' and 'greatly hindered the development of the Labour Party in Belfast'.[25] Nevertheless, the combined total of 97 Labour and 153 Sinn Féin councillors vis-à-vis 329 Unionist seats made them a notable political force for the time being.[26]

While politicians in London debated the kind of new Ireland they wished to see established by the Government of Ireland Bill, tensions rose steadily in Belfast. A meeting was held by Protestant shipyard workers at the Workman and Clark south yard on 21 July 1920, attended by 2,000–5,000 workers. The speakers headlining the impromptu rally claimed that 'all aspects of the British administration had collapsed and Sinn Féin was in effective control'.[27] With the prospect of Sinn Féin subversion and – by extension – guerrilla warfare knocking on the door of the six counties, tensions boiled over. The speakers spoke of British duplicity and Catholic complicity, assuring those present that Ulster's position in the British Empire was in peril. A deputation of the Ulster Ex-Servicemen's Association (UESA) even went as far as to claim that Catholic Sinn Féiners were keeping loyal men out of a job. After the meeting ended, several hundred workers marched through the Harland & Wolff shipyard, 'ordering out all known Catholic workers and a minority of Protestants who were identified with the socialist movement. Some were beaten, kicked and pelted with stones and rivets; others, to escape, swam to the south side of the Musgrave Channel.'[28]

Within twenty-four hours, the expulsions had spread to other parts of industrialised Belfast, with the *Belfast News Letter* dubiously explaining these away by claiming that the 'outrages which have been committed by the adherents of the Republican party during the last two or three years are naturally much resented throughout the whole of Loyalist Ulster, and nowhere more so than in Belfast'.[29] So intense was the rioting between the two communities that the army had to be called in to reimpose order, resulting in the shooting dead of several rioters.[30] Violent confrontations between rival gangs soon escalated into a shooting war, with sniping particularly frequent in West Belfast. The situation in the Falls Road area was described as 'rioting having developed into guerrilla warfare on the part of the armed Sinn Féiners against the military'.[31] By the end of the week some 5,000 workers were out of work.

Some accounts of these expulsions see them as the result of sectarian bigotry and 'the inevitable reaction to the threat to the Protestants' national existence posed by the republican military campaign', while others see the real driver as being the failure of the industrial magnates to integrate former soldiers back into the workplace, thereby creating the conditions for the 'development of pogromist tendencies amongst the Protestant working class'.[32] The unionist leadership, aided and abetted by the unionist press, remained silent on the expulsions, beyond Carson's careful wording of a speech at the Twelfth celebrations when he 'warned against the "insidious" tactic adopted by Sinn Féin of tacking on the "national question" to the "labour question" to try and bring about disunity amongst the loyalist population'.[33]

Whatever the cause, the Belfast violence did not operate in a strategic vacuum and must be seen in the context of the IRA's guerrilla campaign throughout Ireland, which, in 1919–20, claimed the lives of 236 soldiers and police officers.[34] Unionists in the emerging jurisdiction of Northern Ireland feared an attempt by the London government to renege on the promise of locally devolved security under a new Unionist administration, particularly when subjected to pressure from the IRA. Ironically, the outbreak of the sectarian conflagration in Belfast in July 1920 initially met with a muted response from the IRA leadership in the city. Militant republicans 'remained aloof and resolutely opposed to any kind of participation in what they called "the usual fratricidal strife," fearing that their involvement would detract from their elitist perception of themselves as members of the key revolutionary force in Ireland'.[35] Understandably, this led to growing Catholic hostility towards the Belfast IRA at this time.[36] Some 70–75 per cent of the local nationalist population was estimated to have been against IRA activity, regardless of the myth of the roots binding the IRA and the minority community. As with much republican mythmaking at that time and since, the truth was much more mundane.[37]

Despite the fact that IRA attacks in the six counties in early 1920 were still quite rare, Ulster Protestants nevertheless felt vulnerable, organising defence committees and vigilante patrols. In Belfast and some smaller towns, 'working-class Protestants responded in their traditional way, by rioting, which in their eyes was a form of defence'.[38] Many loyalists were also deputised as Special Constables in the newly created Ulster Special Constabulary (USC) and, simultaneously, steps were taken to reactivate the UVF.[39] The consequence of drawing officers from a large pool, including several back-street thugs, meant some members of the USC became ill-disciplined. In February 1921 one platoon of Special Constables in Newry had to be disbanded following an official inquiry that uncovered corruption and the contested shootings of two internees in Ballykinlar, who were shot by USC guards for getting too close to the wire.[40] By early April 1921 the numbers killed in the IRA's revolutionary war had climbed to 363, the vast majority (270) being members of the Royal Irish Constabulary (RIC).[41] As one loyalist propaganda pamphlet noted at the time, 'the terrible tragedy goes on, gallant men are being killed, rebels equally, whose recklessness is often marvellous, are also being killed. Everywhere there is a feeling of insecurity and uneasiness.'[42]

Against this backdrop of violence, the unionist leadership faced the uphill task of building a new state in the six counties. 'Lacking the rich Anglo-Irish inheritance of the old metropolis,' wrote geographer Emyr Estyn Evans, 'the northerners had to create in Belfast not only the machinery of government and administration but the cultural centres necessary for a capital city.'[43] Amidst their truce with the IRA, the British government moved, in September 1920, to appoint a tax inspector, Sir Ernest Clark, as under-secretary to the chief secretary of Ireland in Dublin.[44] His task was to establish self-government in the North.

By the end of the month, Clark had ensconced himself in the Scottish Provident Building across from Belfast City Hall. Given the threat posed by the IRA, the local police erected steel shutters and posted an armed guard outside. Clark consulted regularly with Sir James Craig, the organisational brains behind Carson's public leadership of unionism, about the British government's plans for assisting in the creation of a new Belfast administrative centre. Given Carson's reluctance to assume the mantle of leadership in the new entity, Craig was duly elected leader of the UUC on 4 February 1921. Later that month Clark shared his plans for self-government with Craig, particularly on the future composition of the civil service departments to support a new administration.[45] By May 1921, Clark and Craig had succeeded in building the political architecture of the new Northern Ireland state.

They then turned their attention to the inaugural elections for a local parliament and an attempt to reach out to republican leader Éamon de Valera to resolve tensions between North and South. On 5 May Craig travelled to Dublin to meet with de Valera, displaying what the Chief Secretary in Ireland, Sir Hamar Greenwood, called 'magnificent courage'. Craig's reputation was 'enhanced by the episode', his biographer St John Ervine later wrote.[46] Newspaper coverage in the North proved favourable and Craig was greeted enthusiastically by supporters when he returned home.

In an address at Hillsborough shortly afterwards, Craig told supporters that they were 'engaged in a great historical campaign'. He continued:

> Never before in the history of their dear country had so much depended, not upon the leaders, but upon the people, and he was endeavouring by attending as many meetings as he possibly could himself … to bring home to all the people that the whole future of their six counties depended upon them receiving their votes on 24th of this month.[47]

The elections for the new Belfast Parliament were famously the first in Europe where such a body was elected using the proportional representation single transferable vote method.[48] Ten constituencies – Belfast North, South, East, West and Queen's University, as well as Londonderry, Antrim, Down, Armagh, and Tyrone and Fermanagh – were to elect between four and eight MPs each. The choice at the forefront of the minds of the electorate was the constitutional position of Northern Ireland within the United Kingdom.[49] This overrode everything else, including the testing of a new piece of legislation passed in 1918 enabling women to contest elections, though, intriguingly, not to vote in them. Earlier in 1921, the UWUC's president, Rosalind, 3rd Duchess of Abercorn, had expressed the view that the 'time was not ripe for this and the essential thing in the first Parliament was to preserve the safety of the Unionist cause', and that 'much organisation and construction work would be necessary for which perhaps women had not the necessary experience, and except in the case of outstanding qualifications, men candidates were preferable'.[50] In reality, neither the unionist leadership nor the UUC encouraged female participation because of the organisation's 'integral conservativism'.[51]

In the ensuing election, the Ulster Unionists, Sinn Féin and the nationalists contested the poll. While the Belfast Labour Party did not field candidates, five Independent Labour candidates did run in four Belfast constituencies and one in Down; all of them lost their deposits, winning less than 1 per cent of the total votes cast. 'The 1921 elections, therefore, provide a fairly clear-cut indication of the wishes of the Northern Ireland population on the border issue.'[52] Out of an impressive turnout of 89 per cent,[53] the Unionists won forty of the fifty-two seats, with the other two parties winning six each. Anti-partitionist candidates duly boycotted the first Parliament.[54]

The 1921 election was 'fought against a background of violence and intimidation', with the communal divide merely accentuating the outcome. 'Intriguingly, there had been a degree of acrimony over the selection of candidates for certain seats,' yet the unionist bloc 'held together in the manner of their pre-war Home Rule struggle; class, denominational and regional divides were transcended' as Protestants voted overwhelmingly for Unionist candidates.[55] However, the violence and intimidation were severely constraining and debilitating for those Labour candidates who had been brave enough to stand in the election. At Westminster, the Labour Party whip, Thomas Griffiths, MP for Pontypool, asked Hamar Greenwood if he could confirm the circumstances surrounding the allegation that shipyard workers had gate-crashed a rally at the Ulster Hall a few days before the election and threatened three Independent Labour candidates – James Baird, Harry Midgley and John A. Hanna – with revolvers. Greenwood replied:

> I am informed that the meeting in question, which was organised by the Labour Socialist party, was advertised as open to the general public, and that a procession of shipyard workers, availing themselves of the general invitation to attend, occupied the hall before the commencement of the proceedings. When the speakers arrived they

were offered a fair hearing, provided that no disloyal or seditious utterances were made, but they refused to accept this condition. The shipyard workers delegates and the police then advised them to withdraw as disorder appeared to be inevitable if any speeches of a seditious character should be made. This advice was not accompanied by any suggestion that the shipyard workers were armed and no revolvers were produced by them at any part of the proceedings.[56]

Whether a revolver was present or not, the three Labour candidates, one of them a former soldier, would hardly have departed so easily had intimidation and threats not been issued. The reality was that loyalist mob rule had descended upon the Ulster Hall in a concerted effort to intimidate non-Unionist candidates.

The organisation responsible for this intimidation was the UESA. It was one of several loyalist groups active at the time, particularly in the shipyards, that acted as a form of extreme right-wing unionist mob. Another group, known as the Ulster Protestant Association (UPA), had been formed a few months earlier in the autumn of 1920. Both were intimately involved in civil disturbances accompanying the election. According to one RIC intelligence report, the UPA attracted 'a large number of the lowest and least desirable of the Protestant hooligan element'.[57] The report concluded:

> For twelve months after that the city was in a state of turmoil. Sinn Féin was responsible for an enormous number of bombings, shootings, and incendiary fires. The work of the police against them was, however, greatly hampered by the fact that the rough element on the Protestant side entered thoroughly into the disturbances, met murder with murder, and adopted in many respects the tactics of the rebel gunmen. In the endeavour to cope simultaneously with the warring factions the police efforts were practically nullified. They were quite unable to rely on the restraint of one party while they dealt with the other.[58]

Sectarian assassination may well have raged between warring factions, but there was also a three-pronged fear amongst senior unionists – particularly in the country areas – that local 'hotheads' might take matters into their own hands, that the threat of IRA raids was rising and that some people in Ulster might turn to Sinn Féin.[59] As a way of channelling the violent potential of its supporters, the unionist authorities had formed the USC, with some thought also given to reforming the UVF as an additional force under the direction of the unionist leadership. Some 30,000–50,000 men eventually enrolled in the reconstituted UVF, poised and 'ready to meet the menace which is confronting them now, just as the original members of the organisation nine years ago were prepared to meet the menace which confronted them then'.[60] In the previous twelve months, the USC and UVF had been competing in the same recruiting pool, along with other groups like the Ulster Imperial Guards, which probably outnumbered the UVF's membership at the time. Other vigilante-style groups operated in rural areas too, with Fermanagh Vigilance, raised by future Prime Minister Sir Basil Brooke, and the Protective Patrol, led by shopkeeper John Webster in Armagh, being just two examples. The Northern Ireland government's relationship with loyalist paramilitary groups at the time was, therefore, close and binding, with some historians likening it to that between the Weimar government and the *Friekorps*.[61] The latter were groups of former soldiers mustered along paramilitary lines by German politicians wishing to resist attempts by Russian communists to overthrow their government in the wake of the First World War. In a similar sense, Unionist politicians were reliant on paramilitary groups to shore up their emerging administration in the face of IRA incursions into the six counties.

The violence of the 1920–22 period in Northern Ireland is frequently characterised as a 'pogrom' against Catholics,[62] though this has been challenged as 'problematic' and one respected historian has called for a 'more sophisticated understanding of the conflict'.[63] Out of the 491 deaths in Belfast between the first fatality on 21 July 1920 and the last on 29 June 1922, some 83 per cent of the victims were male (with seventy-eight females killed); out of these deaths, 56 per cent were Protestant and 39 per cent Catholic. Thirty of the victims were children up to sixteen years of age.[64] One of the worst days of violence came on Sunday 10 July 1921, when sixteen people lost their lives in Belfast. Thomas McNally, the IRA's quartermaster in its 3rd Northern Division, was one eyewitness to events as they unfolded over that summer:

> During this period there were some gruesome happenings on both sides. If a trusting Protestant passed through a Catholic area and if there were no Volunteers in the area at the time, he was liable to be murdered and brutally butchered. The Volunteers took no part in these butcherings but acted purely in a defensive capacity for the protection of the area.[65]

According to McNally, IRA volunteers were motivated only to protect the Catholic community rather than to go on the offensive against Protestants. The reality was much more complicated. Due to a huge upsurge in violent attacks committed by both republican and loyalist gunmen,[66] a heavy death toll followed, which created a general feeling of the new state being born of armed insecurity.

Key to the establishment of the Northern Ireland state would be the Unionist leadership's ability to keep in check the violent tendencies of their loyalist supporters, while allowing the new security forces time to regain control and reassure the population of the new state that they could protect them. They were aided in this by the temporary cessation of violence in the South, with the Truce of July 1921 and then the talks from October 1921 which led to the signing of the Anglo-Irish Treaty on 6 December 1921. The terms of this Treaty fell short for republicans because, amongst other concessions, they did not include the six counties of the fledgling Northern Ireland state. Conversely, the British offer of dominion status also fell short of the full independence demanded by Éamon de Valera and other hardliners.

For Carson, too, there was little merit in the Treaty's provisions. Although the baton of unionist leadership had been passed to Craig earlier in 1921, Carson had continued to take a close interest in developments from the House of Lords. He told the Peers:

> [These] were passed with a revolver pointed at your head. And you know it. You know you passed them because you were beaten. You know you passed them because Sinn Féin with its Army in Ireland has beaten you. Why do you not say so? Your Press says so, and you may as well confess it. There may be nothing dishonourable in it.[67]

Carson believed that the Treaty had been forced on the government by the IRA's guerrilla campaign, and he feared the consequences for Ulster and the wider British imperial project:

> But when we are told that the reason why they had to pass these terms of Treaty, and the reason why they could not put down crime in Ireland was because they had neither the men nor the money, nor the backing, let me say that that is an awful confession to make to the British Empire. If you tell your Empire in India, in Egypt, and all over the world that you have not got the men, the money, the pluck, the inclination, and the backing to restore law and order in a country within twenty miles of your own shore, you may as well begin to abandon the attempt to make British rule prevail throughout the Empire at all.[68]

Drawing attention to the strategic weaknesses of the British position with respect to the political outcome of the Anglo-Irish War of Independence was one thing; squaring Ulster unionism's continuing apprehension of IRA violence amidst the challenges of building a new state was quite another. It was to Craig that the practical activities of state-building fell, his first responsibility being to provide security to all the people of the six counties, including those amongst the Catholic community who did not want to be included in this new state. As Craig told the Northern Ireland House of Commons on 10 October 1922, 'Let it be known now that we have secured peace in our midst, and that we intend to maintain that peace, no matter what it costs us.'[69] Maintaining the peace in the way he and his cabinet envisaged would, arguably, place Northern Ireland in greater not lesser danger.

2

The People of Independent Thought

> We all rail against class distinctions, but very few people seriously want to abolish them. Here you come upon the important fact that every revolutionary opinion draws part of its strength from a secret conviction that nothing can be changed.
>
> George Orwell, *The Road to Wigan Pier*[1]

THE SOUND OF TIN WHISTLES and the heavy beat of drums echoed around the narrow streets of tiny, two-up, two-down terraced houses along the Shankill Road as a local flute band playing 'party tunes' marched proudly ahead of one of the most respected politicians in the area. It was a bitingly cold autumnal evening in 1923, but to his 'immense crowd of supporters' the man they'd come to see was truly 'a friend of the working men and women' of the district and stood up for them against the vested interests of the most powerful and influential men of the city. The jubilant crowd came to a halt at the corner of Greenmount Street and North Queen Street where the man mounted a stage to address them. This was not the official candidate endorsed by the Unionist government, but he was an Orangeman and, as a member of the Order, had solemnly pledged to defend the Protestant faith and the Union. His name was Tommy Henderson, and he was a housepainter by trade and an up-and-coming Independent Unionist politician, who was serving as a councillor on Belfast Corporation. Henderson was seeking to contest the parliamentary constituency of North Belfast against the incumbent Thomas McConnell

CBE, the managing director of a cattle and horse-trading business and an alderman on the Corporation.

Henderson told his assembled supporters that he had consistently fought their corner on important issues like employment, rent and rates. He had first been elected to the Corporation in 1919 and, he reassured his audience, had never let the people of the Shankill down. Henderson's opponents, principally to be found in the Unionist government, 'could not say anything against him', Henderson told the crowd gathered to hear him speak; 'they could not say he was a Socialist. He was a friend of the working man … His Unionism and his Protestantism were as good as his opponent's.'[2] Henderson encouraged his supporters to resist giving their votes to a man like McConnell, who had been rejected by the electorate in South Belfast. 'There was no power which would beat me,' Henderson said optimistically, 'so long as I have the honest working men and the intelligent women of North Belfast at my back.'[3] In the Westminster election, held on 6 December 1923, Henderson won 15,171 votes, reducing McConnell's majority by 1,600 votes.

Independent Unionists like Tommy Henderson posed a major challenge to a Unionist regime obsessed with its own survival. Although the power of independent politicians was usually limited to a handful of constituencies and relied disproportionately on the charisma of solitary political figures,[4] their potential 'for turning Unionist supporters against "their" government and thus giving an impression of Unionist fragmentation was amply acknowledged'[5] by Sir James Craig's government. Another political challenge to this government came from socialists. Labour politicians such as Harry Midgley, Sam Kyle, Jack Beattie and William McMullen were popular in Protestant working-class areas.[6] Midgley had recently contested the general election in West Belfast, winning 22,255 votes and reducing the Unionist majority to 2,720 votes, with one 'fair estimate' indicating his total 'comprised some 12,000 Catholic votes, and some 10,000 Protestant votes'.[7] According to his biographer, Graham Walker, Midgley's impressive showing 'indicated that a substantial portion of the working class was responsive to the politics of Labour and not in thrall to the respective ideologies of Nationalism and Unionism'.[8]

In light of Midgley's challenge, the Unionist Party mobilised its fullest resources at the next Westminster election, held in October 1924, which included turning a blind eye to intimidation, threats and violence at the hustings – Midgley's election agent Jack Beattie even sustained an ugly head wound. Lord Carson, the totemic figurehead of unionism, had been duly wheeled out to 'proclaim that the election was Ulster's "most crucial hour"', informing Unionists that any wavering would likely hand victory to Sinn Féin.[9] Unionist anxiety was greatly animated by the lingering prospect of the Boundary Commission reporting back about the final route of the border that would divide the new jurisdiction of Northern Ireland and the Irish Free State. The uncertainty surrounding the border, perhaps more than anything else, dominated politics in the first half of the 1920s. It provided the dominant geopolitical music to accompany pre-existing unionist intransigence towards all their opponents, whatever their religion or political creed. It also magnified the unionist mantra of 'Not an inch', which was used by Craig as a rallying call in the April 1925 Stormont election. When a 'forecast' of the Boundary Commission's report was leaked to the *Morning Post* in November 1925, it provoked a political crisis, particularly in Dublin. Irish political leader W.T. Cosgrave immediately sought a meeting with James Craig and British Prime Minister Stanley Baldwin in London, where it was agreed to suppress the findings of the Commission's report, revoke the Commission's powers and transfer the powers of the Council of Ireland to the parliaments in Dublin and Belfast.[10]

With Craig perceived to have defeated a serious existential threat to Northern Ireland, his attention soon turned to internal challenges, including from Independent Unionists. It has been said that the 'most heated political cleavage in inter-war Northern Ireland was not the traditional unionist–nationalist battle line; it was instead the intra-unionist divide'.[11] The roots of this internal dissent can be traced to when T.W. Russell and Thomas Sloan were elected as Independent Unionist MPs for South Tyrone and South Belfast respectively. Both men challenged official unionism on the grounds that it was disproportionately animated by its own class interests.[12] To stem the tide of dissent, the Unionist Party formed the UUC in 1905. Over the next decade the UUC brought together all key interest groups under its umbrella, from unionist trade unionists to the Orange Order. The Order's influence was judged so strong that it was duly allocated block seats on the UUC. It would come to 'play a crucial role in the fight against Home

Rule during 1912–14', after which 'Orangeism had become political capital within unionism'.[13] James Craig's determination to emphasise the national question in elections in the shadow of the Boundary Commission was, therefore, 'only half the truth', amidst the prospects of a fragile balance of power within his own support base, which promised to further fragment if left unchecked. The Unionist Party was 'by no means a classless party who simply stood for the Union; they were also a conservative party with strong vested economic interests (although they drew a large support from all classes)'.[14] Understanding how the party sought to stymie internal opposition is, therefore, crucial to understanding the character the state took in its formative years.[15]

By the mid-1920s the Unionist government had lumped all internal challenges from within the Protestant working class under the collective heading of 'disloyalists'.[16] Craig's regime duly moved to introduce legislation in the form of the Local Government Bill (1922) with the express intention of abolishing proportional representation, due to the helping hand it offered those in constituencies dominated by people who voted for Nationalist Party candidates. This action provoked embarrassment in the British government, which had initially made provision for religious equality under the Government of Ireland Act.[17] Royal assent was subsequently withheld for several months. Nevertheless, once introduced it led to a noticeable reduction in the election of Nationalist Party politicians. In the local government elections held in 1924, the Nationalist Party saw its control of councils fall from twenty-five in 1920 to only two of the eight bodies in Northern Ireland.[18] Despite their best efforts, however, the Unionist Party could not stop the haemorrhaging of support, with its MPs reduced from forty to thirty-three. Buoyed by the reduction of MPs on government benches, Nationalist Party politicians who had initially boycotted the new Parliament were persuaded to return to prevent any further encroachments on the minority's rights.[19]

Craig's concerns about internal challenges to the new state also extended to radical voices within the Protestant working-class community. Those in the unionist heartland of Duncairn, previously represented by Lord Carson, were particularly motivated to prevent Independent Unionists and Labour politicians from gaining ground. At the annual meeting of the Duncairn

Women's Unionist Association in early May 1925, one speaker, Mrs Hume OBE, told the audience how, 'they would always stand for their beloved country no matter what came ... Nothing would weaken them, and they would keep their beloved Ulster out of the Free State.'[20] Her comments were met with vigorous applause, followed by a rousing speech by Anthony Brutus Babington KC, the recently elected MP for Cromac and soon-to-be-installed Attorney General, who said that 'women were more continuously engaged in politics than men. Speaking more generally, businessmen only came into politics when there was some excitement' and the 'influence of women should be maintained continuously, and organisation should rest to a very large extent in their hands'. He encouraged those gathered to 'take a greater pride in the Parliament' for there were 'many who, though not exactly enemies of Ulster, would be glad to see the Ulster Parliament a failure'.[21]

Appearances by Unionist politicians at hustings like these were crucial in ensuring their followers were bound together by the fear of compromise with anyone other than themselves. While MPs like Babington urged their grassroots supporters to remain loyal and vote for the Official Unionist candidates, they also had to be alive to the challenge posed by those whom the government saw as attempting to sow division. Babington would soon be in an influential position where he could ensure the requisite legislation on law and order was passed to frustrate those who wished to directly challenge the Unionist regime, whether Independent Unionist, Labour or Nationalist.

By the mid-1920s rising unemployment was acting as an accelerant on an open fire of political disaffection amongst the working classes. Many out-of-work people had taken to the streets to protest the lack of assistance from the state. Responding to the promise of social unrest, the Inspector General of the RUC issued the following guidance to his officers:

> All persons causing an obstruction by taking part in the demonstrations are to be warned that they are causing an obstruction, and if they persist their names and addresses are to be taken with a view to prosecution and prosecutions are to follow. This will, of course, apply also to idlers who cause an obstruction by watching or following the demonstration, even though not actually taking part.[22]

The RUC had been greatly aided in its bid to outlaw protests by the Special Powers Act (1922), a major piece of legislation in the local state's armoury, which permitted the force to detain, arrest or keep under surveillance those who persisted in attempts to organise demonstrations. Some historians have labelled the Act as an 'authoritarian piece of legislation' that enabled the Unionist government to secure its position as the dominant political force in Northern Ireland.[23] Under the Special Powers Act, the Minister of Home Affairs, Sir Richard Dawson Bates, could and frequently did impose curfews and close bars, and he effectively undermined unionism's political enemies by drawing a sharp distinction between those they considered 'loyal' and those they labelled 'disloyal'.[24] Bates later told the Northern Ireland Parliament that the Special Powers Act 'only operates against the law breakers', who he defined as those judged 'disloyal' to the local state. There can be no doubt that those 'considered "disloyal" – primarily, but not confined to, Catholic, republican, and labour activists – suffered victimisation, repression, and employment discrimination'.[25]

Despite the willingness to enact such legislation, which was primarily designed to spike the guns of Independent, Labour and Nationalist opponents, the Unionist regime struggled to contain the challenges mounted against them. Throughout the second half of the 1920s, the government was plagued by chronic unemployment and increasingly relied on the British model of placing a Board of Guardians in charge of administering the Poor Law, which was designed to issue relief to those in greatest need.[26] 'The Unionist Government needed the Belfast Guardians,' wrote the author and Labour politician Paddy Devlin. 'They were an integral part of Unionist strategy to control votes for each election.'[27] Crucially, they were a sectarian tool that 'enabled the government to deprive the Catholic poor of relief by their powers of discretion'.[28] The Guardians were drawn principally from the Belfast business community, mostly Protestant, and, therefore, loyal men who could be trusted to distribute 'bones' to government supporters.[29] However, while unemployment remained at an average of 15 per cent in the years prior to the Wall Street Crash of 1929, in the years succeeding it the rate had almost doubled to 28 per cent,[30] precipitating the onset of a crisis for the Unionist government in the early 1930s. At that time there were some 72,000 registered and 30,000 unregistered unemployed in Northern Ireland, including 48,000 in Belfast alone.[31] The situation became desperate as only half of those people were entitled to benefits. On 29 September 1932, the unemployed workers decided to mount a protest march.

On 3 October 1932, 60,000 unemployed workers joined a demonstration to the Custom House steps, near High Street in Belfast. The next day, another protest march made its way to the workhouse on the Lisburn Road, where the Board of Guardians was meeting. In a bid to seek a greater distribution of relief, the protestors sought an audience with the Guardians but were rebuffed. Consequently, on 5 October, another march made its way to the workhouse, where it was met by a huge police presence. Later that night the police attempted to disperse the crowd by pushing them back along the Lisburn Road and into Bradbury Place and Sandy Row, precipitating a riot. Geordie Loughrey, who was on the march, recalled how 'things got a wee bit hot' when the marchers arrived at Sandy Row, with the police 'swooping on, trying to chase people away'.[32] Local people, seeing what was happening, opened their doors to the protestors. '[I]t didn't matter who you were, what you were – you were just brought into the house,' Loughrey recalled. 'The police didn't come into the houses. That was what really surprised me, to tell you the truth. They did it on parts of the Falls.'[33]

When the protestors subsequently emerged from the homes of working-class people in Sandy Row, they were baton-charged by the RUC, but this did not break the strikers' will and they vowed to continue their protests in order to secure food and other forms of relief. The RUC responded with further baton charges for the next two weeks. The protests only ended when Richard Dawson Bates met with the Board of Guardians and ordered them to concede to the strikers demands.[34]

In the wake of the outdoor relief riots, various bodies contacted the Unionist government to pledge their loyalty to the authorities or to register their grievances at the heavy-handed response to the protest marches. Writing to Craig, who had been appointed Lord Craigavon in 1927, Edward J. Clarke, the Honorary Secretary of the Loyalty League, a right-wing unionist grouping, proclaimed:

> That we the members of the loyalty league No. 1 outpost, heartedly congratulate the Minister of Home Affairs, in the vision, skill and

energy, with which his department met and dealt with the advent of organised forces of terrorism and disorder which for two days recently caused the destruction of life and property in the City and created a feeling of insecurity among the citizens of Belfast.

We are proud of our Police force whose loyalty to duty, bravery and success augur well for a peaceful future.

Ulster has in this matter we believe, set an example to other centres of population similarly menaced.

In our opinion, the cure for the spirit of hate thus active, under a false guise would be a vigorous appreciation of Britain's righteous laws against those who show disrespect either to the flag of Empire or our King.[35]

Meanwhile, Alex Gossip of the left-leaning National Amalgamated Furnishing Trades' Association, whose membership covered the whole of the UK, wrote to express his horror at the 'conduct of the Police in batoning and shooting the unemployed workers in Belfast last week, during their demonstrations against the infamous conditions under which they are suffering slow starvation'.[36] Internal correspondence between senior civil servants in Belfast reveals the extent of their contempt for such criticism of the RUC. 'You will see from Martin-Jones's letter that his first impression was to ignore the correspondence, and as you are probably aware, this is the policy we have adopted here in connection with any complaints that have been addressed to us in regard to the activities of the Police.'[37] As far as the Cabinet Secretary was concerned, the steps taken 'throughout the whole affair were justifiable and appropriate', and he stated:

> You might add that the action of the Police has earned the commendation of all the respectable elements of the community and that the Government is satisfied that the recent disorders were fomented and instigated by a gang of agitators who had no real interest in the unemployed persons in Belfast but who used their imaginary and alleged grievances as a means of fomenting disorder.[38]

To Paddy Devlin, the great chronicler of the outdoor relief riots, the upper echelons of the Unionist regime were now acutely aware that they had landed in a precarious situation. When all 'the smoke had blown away,' he wrote, 'the absolute necessity of returning immediately to the sectarian tactics of the early Twenties or of finding a new set of instruments to reassert control over the situation' became urgent.[39] While the Unionist regime may have been temporarily troubled by the brief sojourn of a class united by these riots, the harsh reality of inter-war Northern Ireland was that class and sectarianism were intertwined and a 'normal part of political life in Belfast'.[40] For the Unionist regime it was much more important to discredit Independent Unionists like Tommy Henderson, who posed a risk to their grip on their working-class supporters in Belfast.

A decade on from his initial entry into Northern Irish politics, and now an Alderman on Belfast Corporation, Tommy Henderson returned to the Shankill to renew his pledge to stand up for his constituents and to ask them to return him as their representative in the Northern Ireland House of Commons. He arrived on the Shankill Road on the back of a flat-bed lorry, plunking himself on an illuminated pedestal surrounded by a cloth shroud. When it was unveiled by his election agent, Henderson proceeded to address 'great crowds', causing something of a stir and disrupting tramcar traffic.[41] As a confident orator, he spoke plainly to ordinary people about bread-and-butter issues that directly affected them. Henderson boasted freely of having more supporters and more bands than his Unionist rival. One reporter who followed his progress along Agnes Street saw 'not only pipe, brass, fife, accordion, and flute bands, but on a horse van at the rear were two small boys beating minor models of the Lambeg drum'.[42] It was a theatrical performance worthy of a billing at the popular Empire theatre in central Belfast. And it was all designed to clearly illustrate his loyalist underdog credentials.

In contrast, Henderson's opponent, Captain Norman Fulton, could call on his accompanying loudspeaker, motorcade and 'winning smile', though he didn't have the rebellious streak the people of the Shankill admired in Henderson. 'They did not want Independents, who would promise the moon or any other impossible thing,' Fulton told his own supporters, in an attempt to rebuke Henderson. 'The people could not live on windy speeches. They wanted practical reforms.'[43] As far as Fulton was concerned, the people 'wanted work more than doles, and it was only by unity and co-operation on the part of employer and employed, [that] they could hope to achieve anything of a beneficial character'.[44] They were living in a 'fools' paradise' if they thought otherwise. Although calls to unity were heard loud and clear, the people of the Shankill preferred to hold the government to account. They wanted fair treatment, and Tommy Henderson offered them that. In the election held in December 1933, Henderson was returned by the people of the Shankill, unpersuaded by Fulton's attacks on their local hero.[45]

Henderson's victory did not go unnoticed within the UULA, the body set up to defend the constitution by sapping the political potential of opponents of the Unionist Party in predominantly Protestant working-class areas. UULA members believed there should be an active trade-off between class-based ideals and the 'wholehearted support and encouragement to those who are creating new industries and increasing employment', resolving to remain 'antagonistic to Socialists, Communists and other extremists with their pernicious doctrines'.[46] The UULA's membership rules permitted its members only to give backing to those political candidates and representatives who were committed 'to use their power and influence for the good of the community'.[47] The concept of the community was narrowly defined to include only those 'loyal to the Crown and Constitution'.[48] As the UULA's annual report for 1933 made clear:

> The need of such an organisation was never more necessary than to-day. What with Socialists, Nationalists, Republicans, and so-called Independent Unionists there are many disturbing elements in our midst, all striving to mislead the public and to gain the upper hand. These anti-loyalists whose efforts are as unscrupulous as their doctrines are pernicious must be vigorously opposed and exposed, and your Association in counteracting their efforts and spreading sound constitutional principles has rendered notable service. We rejoice that signs are not wanting of a revival of industry. The wave of depression is steadily if slowly passing away and the prospects for the New Year are much brighter. Already the linen trade has improved, and with orders for nine ships, our local shipyards are again becoming active.[49]

The UULA backed the views of Unionist candidates, like Fulton, who argued that employers and employees should be joined in harmony to ensure the safety of Northern Ireland's constitutional position.

By drawing such a sharp distinction between loyalists and disloyalists, the Unionist regime and its supporters attempted to impose an artificial world view on their opponents. In his memoirs, Thomas J. Campbell, the leader of the Nationalist Party and a respected barrister, recalled how:

> If the minority complained of discrimination they were upbraided as malcontents and malignants. What did this cold policy portend? The depression, the isolation and, if possible of accomplishment, the dispossession of one section of the community – an element forming 35 per cent of the population. In no other white-ruled territory is the like proscription enforced.[50]

In simple terms, Campbell reflected, the architects of the Government of Ireland Act were 'blind to the unwisdom of setting up Parliamentary Government in an area where there was the least chance of finding statesmen who would realise that one condition on which such a Government can subsist is that they must practice moderation and must not subvert the rights of minorities'.[51]

On 24 April 1934, in one of the most significant debates ever held in the Northern Ireland House of Commons on the position of the nationalist community and others branded disloyal by the Unionist regime, Campbell's party colleague Cahir Healy accused the government of blatant discrimination. The avowedly unionist daily newspaper, the *Belfast News Letter*, led with the view that Healy and 'his friends' were merely 'ventilating … imaginary grievances'.[52] Craigavon rebuffed the Nationalists, putting to them that the RUC had always kept the door open to one-third membership from the minority community. As the *News Letter* reported:

> Ministers draw a sharp distinction between the employment of Roman Catholics who are loyal to the State and those who are working for its downfall … The Prime Minister affirms the determination of the Government 'to make safe and sure what we have and what we intend to hold.' In the eyes of Ulster Nationalists that is the Government's real

offence. They are out, as they say, to do all that lies in their power to secure the political re-union of Ireland, which means the tearing up of Ulster's Constitution, and they regard it as a violation of their rights and liberties that any obstacle should be placed in their way.[53]

It was Craigavon's Minister of Agriculture, Sir Basil Brooke, who attempted to clarify who the government saw as 'loyalists' and 'disloyalists', explaining that 'disloyal men were men who schemed and plotted to destroy the country in which they lived'.[54] While those on government benches disputed the charges of sectarian discrimination, Craigavon had contradicted himself when responding to charges of being unduly influenced by his membership of the Orange Order. 'I prize that [being Grand Master of County Down] far more than I do being Prime Minister. I have always said I am an Orangeman first and a politician and Member of this Parliament afterwards.'[55]

Craigavon was at pains to highlight the appointment of the Lord Chief Justice, Sir Denis Henry, a Catholic, who was 'a man whom everyone respected' as evidence to the contrary of Nationalist claims. Craigavon said he had 'never known a country to prosper where the Judiciary was appointed on religious grounds, and so long as he had anything to say he would say that would never enter his mind'. During the three-hour debate, Craigavon appeared at pains to point out that the 'charges had been grossly exaggerated'. As he went on to argue, since his government had taken over office they had 'tried to be absolutely fair to all the citizens of Northern Ireland'.[56] Challenged by one Nationalist MP to explain why the Parliament had taken such a Protestant composition, Craigavon responded:

> The hon. Member must remember that in the South they boasted of a Catholic State. They still boast of Southern Ireland being a Catholic State. All I boast of is that we are a Protestant Parliament and a Protestant State. It would be rather interesting for historians of the future to compare a Catholic State launched in the South with a Protestant State launched in the North and to see which gets on the better and prospers the more. It is most interesting for me at the moment to watch how they are progressing. I am doing my best always to top the bill and to be ahead of the South.[57]

Craigavon and his colleagues entertained the mistaken belief that Northern Ireland could be governed like another part of the Commonwealth, without doing anything meaningful to overcome the sectarian divisions between Protestants and Catholics and by ostracising those they deemed 'disloyal'.

The last MP to speak in the debate on discrimination was Labour leader Harry Midgley, who observed how some elements of the proceedings ought to be deplored. 'So long as there were people in the community who are prepared to subordinate all public questions of policy and public life to the interests of sectarianism,' he told MPs, 'so long are we going to be precluded from obtaining the best we can obtain for the citizens under our control.'[58] Midgley argued that the Northern Ireland Labour Party (NILP) was the only organisation 'free from and untrammelled by any union or connection with any political or sectarian organisation in Ireland'.[59] For Midgley, there was much more of an onus on unionists to reach out to the minority community and those Protestants of a left-leaning disposition who rejected the exclusively Protestant complexion of the state. The political rhetoric on display in public and in private in these years pointed to the reality that Ulster Unionism essentially 'functioned effectively as a patronage machine for the needs of its supporters'.[60] Despite the points raised during this important debate, it led to no constructive changes in Unionist government policy.

And so, nine months later, on Saturday 5 January 1935, there was an air of triumphalism in the air as leading members of the UULA met to celebrate their organisation's 'coming of age' anniversary. It was a time of jubilation where they could celebrate the long, unbroken chairmanship of John Miller Andrews, who had led the association since its formation in 1918. He was the brother of the late Thomas Andrews, the famous designer of the SS *Titanic*, and a respected businessman who owned a linen mill in Comber in County Down.[61] Sending his apologies for non-attendance due to ill health, the UULA's president, Lord Carson, expressed his gratitude for the 'loyalty and assistance' the UULA had shown him 'in the fight they helped so much to win'.[62] Carson asked the UULA's Honorary Secretary, Sir Wilson Hungerford, to pass on his 'appreciation to Mr. Andrews who has led them with such unfaltering courage and such love and affection, particularly during the times of trial and distress from which all nations suffered so heavily'. Carson believed Andrews had shown particularly 'wise judgement' and 'unselfish ideals'.[63] Vice-Chairman William Grant grinned widely as he presented Andrews with a gift and a vote of thanks from the UULA's membership. 'It might seem paradoxical that a large employer of labour should occupy such a position, but the interests involved are not incompatible,' he said. 'Mr Andrews is essentially a worker. He is one of ourselves and has led us with unerring judgement. He has worked like a Trojan in trying to find employment for the working classes, in trying to raise their social status and in trying to lessen their hardships and distress.'[64] The paternalistic deception that Andrews was a big boss who nonetheless cared for the little men and women he employed was a façade. One would have expected Grant, a former shipwright, to have seen the deep irony in his empty words of gratitude, but that would be to underestimate Grant's abiding loyalty to the Orange Order, of which he and Andrews were prominent members. Andrews was duly re-elected chairman of the UULA to the raucous chorus of 'For he's a jolly good fellow'.

Beneath the bonhomie there lurked a darker, more exclusionary approach to employment adopted by the Unionist regime. In vast swathes of the public sector, including the civil service, for instance, Catholics were 'either absent or massively underrepresented', and the private sector was 'encouraged to discriminate'.[65] As the UULA annual report for 1934, read out to those attending the association's annual dinner made clear:

> [I]t is essential that the loyal workers should be well banded together and present a united front. The Socialists and Nationalists are strong opponents of everything held dear by Unionists, and in order that their attempts to destroy Northern Ireland, as a self-governing unit, shall be foiled there must be constant vigilance and fixed determination on the part of the loyalists.[66]

The report remonstrated with those who had given over to 'apathy and indifference', allowing two Belfast constituencies, Pottinger in the East and Dock in the North, to be lost to Unionist Party opponents in 1934. 'If Socialism and Communism with their wild cat schemes were to gain the upper hand, no section of the community would suffer more than the industrial workers,' claimed the report. 'The interests of Ulster must be safeguarded against those who are striving to destroy the State, and include all Ulster in an Irish Republic.'[67]

Unsurprisingly, perhaps, there was a rise of sectarian tensions against the backdrop of such rhetoric. One of the most extreme groups to take up the cause of maintaining the 'vigilance' talked up by the Unionist regime was the Ulster Protestant League (UPL). Formed in 1931, the UPL was dedicated to securing the election of militant Protestants to represent Protestant districts, seeking the dismissal of the Catholics from the police and government jobs, and denying them employment in Protestant-owned businesses.[68] The UPL's violent rhetoric imagined the group as the 'last line of resistance to Catholicism in Western Europe', and their outlook was 'apocalyptic', perceiving in the Catholic community an 'aggressiveness and a spirit of defiance which they felt was passing a government all too ready to appease the minority'.[69] Its outlook was considered even more extreme than that advocated by the Unionist regime, and it led to tensions between the UPL and the newly relocated Stormont administration. The Unionist regime needed to control and channel such sectarianism in a responsible fashion – in a way that emphasised more politically correct forms of exclusion that the loyalty-disloyalty distinction offered. The UPL was unpredictable in its unbridled extremism and did much to exacerbate the violent protest action that reached a nadir during fierce sectarian clashes in July 1935.[70] Although it was said that the UPL played no direct part in the riots, it did help to fan the flames of unbridled sectarianism, which centred on the York Street area but spread to Sandy Row and the Ormeau Road.[71] The Unionist regime's direct involvement in the violence was 'extremely slight', with much of the rioting the product of poverty, unemployment and ethnic insecurity made combustible by discontent over employment, housing and warm weather.[72] Interestingly, while some loyalists fell into line behind the regime, others resisted and, in time, would come to adopt a long-burning vigilante mindset which would develop independently of the state.

Not all elements of the Unionist regime were convinced of the need to maintain a controlled, populist sectarian strategy. As Andrews basked in the glow of his long tenure as a father figure for the UULA, he received a stern letter from retired Major General Hugh Maude de Fellenberg Montgomery, a former British Army officer who had served on the Western Front in the

First World War. Montgomery had long taken a close interest in relations between the two communities[73] and was not beyond taking Andrews to task on the record of the Unionist government. As the general noted:

> There is little to find fault with the expression 'a Protestant Government', which is a mere statement of fact when all the members of the Cabinet are Protestants; but, to use the words 'for a Protestant People' when referring to a population one-third of whom are Papists, is surely to incite to disloyalty every self-respecting Roman Catholic in the six counties.[74]

Montgomery's letter came in the wake of the most serious of sectarian disturbances in Belfast, in which thirteen people were killed and many hundreds injured. Much of the violence took the form of sporadic gun and bomb attacks, clashes between rival mobs and widespread looting in working-class districts. Only three years earlier these areas had been the scene of RUC baton charges against a broad coalition of Protestants and Catholics protesting at the lack of government relief for out-of-work people. Now, toxic levels of emotional loyalism had returned to stalk the streets, with suspicion and fear threatening to poison relations between the majority and minority communities in the same way they had done a decade earlier.

Observing the fracturing of communal relations in Belfast at this time was the poet John Hewitt. Hewitt was a radical, left-wing man of letters who liked to 'stir things up' even amidst the deadly ethnic rampages outside his window. In his poem 'The Bloody Brae', written in 1936, an elderly woman tells the story of an old soldier, Hill, who is confronted by the ghost of a Catholic woman and her child whom he had slain some seventy years earlier. When the soldier admits his guilt to a friend called Scott, Scott tells him the war is over. 'It is not over,' is the reply. 'There's a wolf in the heart of man, and violence breeds like the thistle blown over the world.'[75] In a powerful line, Hill observes: 'Hate follows on hate in a hard and bitter circle – / our hate, the hate I give, the hate I am given: / we should have used Pity and Grace to break / the circle.'[76] He continues that 'whenever the Irish meet with the Planter's breed / there's always a sword between / and black memories for both'. In reply, Scott observes, 'Black memories, John. You forget who began

/ the murder."[77] At a time when the northern state was taking an 'increasingly sectarian tone',[78] Hewitt's comrades in the labour and trade union movement faced an uphill struggle in building bridges between a divided community. Hewitt had the fighting outside his window in mind when composing 'The Bloody Brae'. It was a reflection of the new reality of divide and rule now operating at the heart of the Unionist government.[79] Hewitt, better than any other contemporary observer, reflected the reality of these divisions amidst the violent scenes engulfing Belfast. As an intellectual, Hewitt was nonetheless limited in what he could do to prevent the further descent into sectarian strife.

It was left to others inside the newly constructed Parliament at Stormont to take the political fight to Unionist government benches. With a recalcitrant Nationalist Party and a tiny coterie of Labour politicians, opposition politics was confined to Independent Unionists such as Tommy Henderson and the former RUC Inspector John Nixon. Henderson, more than any other MP, believed in holding James Craig's government to account in Parliament, even if this made no noticeable difference on the ground. As he once told Craig in a debate on the King's Speech in 1935, 'Ulster is not a paradise to live in,' with entire families 'trooping into the workhouses' and most living 'in utter destitution through unemployment'.[80] Henderson's dissenting streak endeared him to those who relished a more combative Belfast Parliament. In a visit to Queen's University Belfast in February 1937, Henderson recalled his reputation for long speeches in Stormont, in which he lambasted the Unionist leadership for its 'codology'.[81] Henderson instead thought of himself as a representative of 'the largest body of people in the Province – the people of independent thought'.[82]

By the late 1930s, a ramping up of rhetoric from Dublin, particularly around the state-wide plebiscite in favour of a new constitution, played into the Unionist government's hands. As a populist, Craig believed that by holding supporters in the grip of perpetual anxiety that they would be less inclined to vote for Independent Unionist and Labour candidates who enjoyed a reputation for defending Protestant working-class interests over and above their political masters. Under Articles 2 and 3 of this new constitution, Bunreacht na hÉireann, the Dublin government reaffirmed that its jurisdiction was to consist 'of the whole island of Ireland, its islands and the territorial seas'. It placed the authority for such a territorial reclamation project in the hands of de Valera and his deputies. Although it could not have been strictly described as a Catholic constitution,[83] the committee set up to draft the document included Fr John Charles McQuaid, a priest from Blackrock College and future Bishop of Dublin, who, along with his Jesuit colleagues, was intimately involved in drafting articles touching on family, education, private property, religion and directive principles on social policy.[84] The Church's influence on Irish constitutional matters also extended to individual rights and freedom of expression. With the two governments north and south firmly set on divergent paths, reflective perhaps of their own insecurities, 'any lingering hopes for dialogue between the two evaporated'.[85] Diplomatic relations between Belfast and Dublin reached a low point from where they would not recover for more than a generation.

3

Masters of Our Own House

> At no phase in history have the common people played a dominant part in the government of Great Britain, and in every phase the baronial oligarchy has prevailed.
>
> H.G. Wells, *The Fate of Homo Sapiens*[1]

IT WAS MID-OCTOBER 1938 WHEN a large crowd of several hundred people turned out for what was undoubtedly one of the biggest events in the history of Greencastle, a tiny working-class village on the northern outskirts of Belfast city. The opening of the new Orange Hall forty years after the founding of the local lodge drew several leading Unionist politicians and Orange Order dignitaries, including the local MP for Duncairn and Parliamentary Undersecretary at the Ministry of Labour, William Grant. Unusually for a Unionist MP, Grant was from a working-class background, having worked as a shipwright in Harland & Wolff prior to his election in 1921.[2] He was also a founding member of the UVF and had served as the vice-chairman of the UULA. Accompanying Grant was Sir Joseph Davison, a senator in the Northern Ireland Parliament who also held the dual role of grand secretary and deputy grand master of the Orange Order in Ireland.[3] In one of several speeches, Davison told the throng of people gathered around the entrance to the hall how the lodge responsible for erecting the new building, LOL 658, had 'put Greencastle on the map'.[4]

The main speech that day was delivered by the Minister for Finance, John Miller Andrews, who also served as president of the UULA. Andrews sat on the populist wing of the Unionist Party, which meant he favoured cultivating a close relationship with the Protestant working class in a way that was marked out by its adherence to a 'combination of sectarian and "democratic" practices, and by a high consumption of public funds'.[5] Amidst the backdrop of mass unemployment and a perceived weakening of the capacity of the Orange Order to bind together all classes in the Protestant community,[6] Andrews appealed directly to the people. 'We hear rumours,' he said, 'of conferences between Northern Nationalists and Southern Republicans with a view to adjusting their difference and hatching a plan for separating us from Great Britain and bringing us under a central Irish Government of some kind.' He continued, 'Such a plan is foredoomed to fail, because, as you all know, the loyalists of Ulster will never give up their citizenship within the United Kingdom and join a State of which his Majesty, our beloved King, is not the acknowledged head, and become part of an area over which the Union Jack does not fly.'[7]

Rumours of a dastardly plan by Éamon de Valera to pursue irredentism to its natural conclusion and force a weak British government to coerce unionists into a new Ireland had a familiar ring to them. On this occasion, however, they were grounded in fact. The Anglo-Irish Defence Agreement, signed in April 1938, ended the six-year economic war between Britain and Ireland, but crucially Britain also relinquished the treaty ports,[8] increasing the fears of unionists who believed this compromised their security within the United Kingdom. Andrews, utterly convinced of this, did not hold back on communicating his anxiety to the people around him. The Union was in peril, and the only way of insuring against an imminent calamity was to invoke the memory of their greatest saviour, Lord Carson, who, along with 'their esteemed Premier' Viscount Craigavon and those closely associated with them, 'won for them their Parliament, which it was their privilege and duty to defend and maintain'.[9] Andrews talked of nationalist boasts, plans and 'agitation' to undermine the Northern Parliament. 'They had got the Swilly now,' he reported as a boast made by de Valera's son. 'Derry was next.'

By now the crowd had been whipped into a frenzy and showed little inclination for compromise.[10] Many in the crowd would have been paid-up members of the UULA, who would have taken Andrews at his word – like Carson and Craigavon, he had led them through dark days before. 'Never,' they shouted. 'Ulster's reply and his today,' Andrews agreed, was 'Never'.[11] He continued:

My friends, I would remind you that our fate is of our own keeping. So long as we Loyalists remain true to our great traditions, united and strong, always putting the interests of the State first, we have nothing to fear. Our great Orange Order, as our first line of defence in the past, so is today and so it must ever remain.[12]

The crowd greeted his defiant words with rapturous applause. For the ordinary people in attendance, the opening of yet another Orange Hall was regarded as a major milestone in the building of their embryonic state,[13] but for their political leaders it was also an opportunity for senior members of the Northern Ireland Cabinet to reinforce the synonymity of unionism and Orangeism.

The Orange Order, formed in September 1795, was initially concentrated in East Tyrone and North Armagh, where the rapid economic expansion of the linen industry, population pressure and religious demography 'combined to produce a particularly volatile situation'.[14] Although Catholics were denied the right to bear arms under the Penal Laws,[15] some did nonetheless form militias. The local militia in this part of Ulster was known as the Defenders, and they came into open conflict with a local Protestant militia, the Peep o' Day Boys, in a skirmish known as the Battle of the Diamond, near Loughgall in County Armagh, on 21 September. In an exchange of gunfire, forty Catholics were killed and one Protestant.[16] At a meeting held in the aftermath at the nearby Loughgall Inn, a decision was taken by some of the Peep o' Day Boys to form an Orange Society, which would dedicate itself to the preservation of Protestant civil and religious liberties.[17] The society plagiarised some of its important rituals from the more tolerant Freemasons. As its 1933 constitution made explicit:

> The Institution is composed of Protestants, united and resolved to the utmost of their power to support and defend the rightful Sovereign, the Protestant Religion, the Laws of the Realm, and the Succession to the Throne in the House of Windsor, BEING PROTESTANT; and united further for the defence of their own Persons and Properties, and the maintenance of Public Peace. It is exclusively an Association of those who are attached to the religion of the Reformation, and will

not admit to its brotherhood persons whom an intolerant spirit leads to persecute, injure or upbraid any man on account of his religious opinions. They associate also in honour of KING WILLIAM III, Prince of Orange, whose name they bear, as supporters of his glorious memory.[18]

Interestingly, the Order retained firm rules on the behaviour and conduct of its members, ensuring that they were 'carefully abstaining from anything in word or behaviour which might unnecessarily give offence; and in all cases strictly obeying the law of the land, on pain of expulsion or suspension for any disobedience'.[19] Although the central event on the Orange calendar was the spectacle of 'commemorating the happy arrival of His Majesty King William III for the deliverance of the Nation' by parading on 12 July each year, the Order was also committed to holding an annual thanksgiving 'for God's gracious deliverance of the Protestant Parliament from the intended Popish Massacre by Gunpowder', with its members urged to 'keep in thankful remembrance, and celebrate the 5th day of November yearly'.[20]

In joining the Order, Protestants became champions of the British constitution and, therefore, the Union between Great Britain and Ulster. It was in bridging the gap between religious sectarianism and the constitutional connection that the Orange Order mobilised 'the mass of the Protestant population behind them'.[21] While it is accurate to see the Unionist political elite and the Order as 'organically linked', it is more accurate to speak of how the Order used the trappings of secrecy and ritualism in an ethnic community to build a 'stock of political capital' that helped it consolidate communal traditions.[22] Nevertheless, it was a relationship in need of constant management. Senior figures in the Order sought new members by reinforcing the ethnic myths of ancient enmity between Protestants and Catholics, which exploited anxieties and fears of encroachment on Protestant civil and religious liberties by the Roman Catholic Church in Ireland. The Order successfully maintained its position as a key interest group within the broader unionist community by equating its mission with that of the party. Its leading lights cleverly warned that any derogation from support for either would jeopardise the very survival of the unionist state.[23]

The synonymity of support for the Orange Order and Unionist regime was at the forefront of the mind of Deputy Grand Master Sir Joseph Davison, who told the *News Letter*: 'We are prepared to go to any length in defence of our hard-won liberties, and we back the Northern Ireland Government to the hilt. There is no change in our attitude. We are dead set against having anything to do with unity with Eire.'[24] Unionists tied to the governing party were acutely aware of the need to keep their constituents in the constant grip of a fear that their position was being constantly undermined by a range of opponents. Even an Independent Unionist like Tommy Henderson, who was a constant thorn in the side of the government, was a member of the Orange Order and recognised his duty to maintain the Union above all else. 'There is no doubt that we shall resist to the utmost of our power any attempt to coerce Northern Ireland,' he said. 'The people of independent thought are most anxious at any cost to retain their connection with Great Britain. It would be infinitely preferable for Northern Ireland to abolish its own Parliament and go back to Westminster rather than accept Mr de Valera's plan. Northern Ireland people will not give up the enormous benefits they have in the United Kingdom,' he added.[25] On the maintenance of the Union, Unionists of whatever shade of political opinion agreed with Lord Craigavon, who spoke of 'the loyalty and affection of the Ulster people towards the British Crown and Constitution', which he judged 'stronger than at any time in her history'.[26] Craigavon, like his party colleagues J.M. Andrews and Joseph Davison, took every opportunity to reiterate 'the old battle cry of Ulster: No Surrender!'[27]

In the closing hours of 1938, Lord Craigavon was satisfied that the Union was safe enough for he and his wife to take a long family holiday on a cruise to Ceylon and the Indian subcontinent via a short engagement with the newly established Northern Ireland Government Agent's office in London.[28] The office had been established by Craigavon to promote 'closer and ever-closer relations – trade and otherwise – with the Mother Country'.[29] Rarely one to pass on the opportunity to profess Ulster's loyalty, Craigavon told the press of how he and his countrymen were 'all very loyal, and we are all ready. We are on the leash, as it were, ready to spring to the giving of help that we could give in a national emergency. You could not keep our people back. Experience has proved that.'[30] The Craigavons embarked upon their voyage at a time when the storm clouds of war were gathering over Europe.[31]

Fierce fighting in Spain's Civil War, an upsurge in tensions in the wake of the German occupation of the Sudetenland, not to mention a worrying situation developing in Poland, all conspired to increase international tensions. With every likelihood of Britain being drawn into a fight, it was not yet clear from where the opening salvo would come. While Craigavon and his counterpart in London, Neville Chamberlain, were distracted by the allure of imperial interests and external threats, militants from the IRA were plotting to launch the internal challenge of insurrection at home.

A thick fog descended on London at 6 a.m. on 3 February 1939 as the morning commuters arrived into the capital's 116 underground stations. The still of the morning was rudely interrupted by a loud bang followed by several thuds and crashes as a bomb exploded at Leicester Square station. One wall was blown out, large pieces of brickwork being hurled many yards. The ceiling was stripped of plaster, and shattered wood and steel girders were left hanging down. A row of steel lockers crumpled like paper. Debris was strewn across the station floor. The scene was thick with dust. 'I was stunned and deafened. With my mate, I dashed into the street. There were showers of splintered glass, and I found that I had been struck on the left arm by a piece,'[32] one eyewitness caught up in the explosion told reporters. Meanwhile, at Tottenham Court Road tube station, a woman in the building opposite recounted how she was awakened by 'a terrific explosion ... There was a terrific lot of smoke coming out of the station entrance.' Another eyewitness said the 'pavement seemed to tremble and I saw a gigantic flash at one of the station entrances'. The left-luggage kiosk and several telephone booths were shattered and blown across the station.[33]

The events of that day took place two weeks after an initial round of explosions in London and three in Manchester, which had formally announced the IRA's new bombing campaign in England to the world.[34] Its aim was the withdrawal of British forces stationed in Northern Ireland, though the ultimatum duly published was greeted with 'derision or disbelief', according to historian Tim Pat Coogan.[35] With Sean Russell, the group's newly elected chief of staff, committed to attacking targets in Great Britain,[36] IRA volunteers were sent out to blow up electricity sub-stations, tube stations and other key infrastructure in the hope of causing maximum disruption to the British government at a time of international crisis.[37]

IRA bombs were also timed to coincide with a war of words between Éamon de Valera and Lord Craigavon. Their dispute had been running for some time, though de Valera had hardened his rhetoric in recent months, as he told the Seanad, Ireland's upper house:

> I can certainly say of myself that I have always realised that there was a difference of opinion between one section of the Irish people and the majority; that the section of the Irish people who opposed the majority view which wanted Irish independence had certain relations with Britain which made that relationship easier for them to bear, and which in fact, in some cases, made the continuance of that relationship a desirable one, but those views were not the views of the majority, and unless the minority is prepared to accept its part and to accept majority rule there is no way of settling that question that I know of except by force. Force naturally suggests itself as a means of solving problems that seem to be intractable otherwise, but there is no use in appealing to force if it is obvious that force cannot be effective, and in 1921, when the matter came up for consideration before the Republican Government of that date, as the Seanad was reminded here this afternoon, we came deliberately to the decision that force was not going to be effective, and was not going to be appealed to as a means of solving this particular problem. I think I can honestly say that I have adhered to that; I regarded that decision as a wise one at the time, and I have never retreated from that position in public yet, nor in private. I think it was a wise decision, and I put to those who think otherwise the question: 'How do you think that the method of force is going to be effective for this purpose?'[38]

Ironically, despite de Valera's uncompromising stance on partition, it was his government that introduced the draconian Offences Against the State Act on 14 June 1939, which would proscribe the IRA and ban it from holding parades.[39]

The legislation enacted to drive the IRA underground was judged insufficient by Craigavon, who believed de Valera spoke from two sides of his mouth on militant republican violence. In a speech delivered at the annual

Twelfth of July celebrations in Bangor in 1939, Craigavon sent de Valera a clear message that he and his government were to keep their 'hands off Ulster':

> The British Empire ... and all it stands for is the sun and air of our existence; British civilisation is the very breath of our life, and our resolve to remain within the United Kingdom is unshakable. Whilst there is breath left in us, we will fight to maintain the Union Jack over Ulster. We will never surrender our citizenship in the British Empire. We, for our part, would never surrender our citizenship in the great Empire, to which we are so proud to belong, for the narrow isolation of a Gaelic Republic, shut away from the world. Our destiny lies in the United Kingdom and the Empire, and no one could take this, our inalienable right, away from us.[40]

Orange Order platforms throughout the six counties were used to demonstrate the Craigavon government's opposition to de Valera's rhetoric. In Ballinderry, Lieutenant Colonel Sir Walter Smiles proposed a resolution promising 'our unflinching determination to maintain our position in the United Kingdom and to repudiate with all our power the widespread propaganda of misrepresentation, believing, as we do, that our welfare is extricably [sic] bound up with Great Britain' and in the 'hope that war clouds which threaten to break may pass away and that this Empire, together with all other nations, shall continue to enjoy progress, prosperity and peace.'[41]

De Valera was in no mood for compromise, as he indicated in an address to the Seanad on recent IRA attacks in England:

> There is a small community, occupying a very small area there, and they are insisting at the present time in holding in their area against their will people who have never wanted to be in that area. There are four counties adjoining ours, and if you were to take a plebiscite tomorrow in those four counties you would get a majority in favour of joining up here. Why should these people in Tyrone and Fermanagh be held and attached to the Northern Parliament and made become part of an area that they want to have nothing to do with? There are two sides to this, and I have been anxious to try to get at the bottom of

it: to try to build up good relations between the people of Ireland and the people of Britain by removing the present causes and difficulties.[42]

Throughout this time Unionists interpreted de Valera's talk of 'present causes and difficulties' to be the very existence of Northern Ireland. With Chamberlain's government distracted from Irish issues by tensions with Germany and by deep divisions on the constitutional question within Ulster's working class, the Craigavon government chose to neutralise threats by adhering to the principle of *divide et impera*.[43]

With this attitude prevailing within the Unionist political class, it was little wonder that nationalists felt disconnected from the northern state. By now a concerted policy of discrimination had become 'all-pervasive and deeply embedded in Protestant antipathy to imagined traits of Irish Catholic nationalism', which did not emanate from a 'desire to crush Catholics, rather to keep them in their place'.[44] This was not helped by what John Oliver, a long-serving civil servant in the Stormont regime, lamented as a 'tragic disregard which Catholic families and Catholic schools showed for the Northern Ireland civil service as a career', since in the 1920s and 1930s they 'could see no merit in sending their boys and girls to the service – with a small number of notable exceptions'.[45] The result was, he opined, 'an unhappy imbalance of religions in the service and a shortage of Catholics coming up through the ranks in the thirties and forties to occupy senior posts of responsibility and influence'.[46] This was replicated in the political life of the state, with a virtual absence of the Nationalist Party in Stormont's parliamentary debates.

With political nationalism conspicuous by its absence, Labour MPs emerged to represent the interests of a divided working class. In a special debate on the war with Germany, Craigavon professed his wholehearted loyalty to the London government's decision, telling MPs how there would be 'no slackening in our loyalty. There is no falling off in our determination to place the whole of our resources at the command of the Government in Britain.'[47] Anticipating an escalation in hostilities by the IRA in Northern Ireland, Craigavon announced the internment without trial of forty-five suspected members. 'There they will remain until the end of the war unless something justifies us in letting them out,' he said, to much tub-thumping support from government MPs. The Prime Minister continued:

> We must ensure that we are in complete control, that we are masters of our own house, and not here at the permission of anybody else. We are not here for the citizens to have their lives and property endangered by a lot of cowardly assassins, men who never hesitate to do what they can to destroy the State. Especially at this moment, when the Empire is at war and when every assistance is wanted, nothing should be done to put sand in the wheels of our defence here at home.[48]

They were stirring words, with few emerging from opposition ranks to counter them. Only Paddy Agnew, the NILP's MP for South Armagh and one of the most prominent Catholic politicians at Stormont, had the courage to countermand Craigavon's jingoism. Agnew spoke eloquently on behalf of his working-class constituents

> because I can speak on their behalf as a peace-loving people. They abhor war and all that it brings in its train. When I entered Parliament I had always foremost in my mind the great principle of advocating peace and goodwill amongst all men and amongst all creeds and classes. That is the same spirit that I hold today. I abhor war and aggression in no matter what part of the world it may be, at home or abroad. Where there is oppression of peoples or any member of society within this country or another, I feel we have a right to seek justice.[49]

Agnew's words proved prophetic, as low rates of enlistment in both communities jarred with Craigavon's jingoistic rhetoric.[50] Historian Yvonne McEwen has even suggested that of all army recruits entering the British armed forces, only 49,302 came from Northern Ireland, with some 50,644 others coming from Éire.[51] So much for Craigavon's earlier public boasts of Ulster Unionists being 'on the leash' and 'ready to spring to the giving of help … in a national emergency'.

Craigavon may not have been wrong in his characterisation of the majority of people not wanting to put sand in the wheels of Britain's defence, though he was delusional when it came to his methodology for achieving that objective. As a populist, Craigavon spent much of his time engaging in a 'paternalist indulgence of the most sectarian and parochial strands of loyalist opinion'.[52] He was sixty-nine in 1940 and in declining health, and so must have had one eye on his political legacy. As the founding-father figure of Northern Ireland, he had neglected to identify a successor or give serious consideration to preparing his beloved province for a future without him at the helm. With no long-term strategy for state-building and security in place from 1922, Craigavon's 'response to its deep sectarian divisions was to let matters drift rather than devise and implement policies directed towards its ultimate stability and survival'.[53]

Craigavon, therefore, spent much of this time placing 'the narrow interests of the six counties and the preservation of the union above loyalty to crown and empire and the crushing of fascism'.[54] As the Parliamentary Undersecretary in the Ministry of Home Affairs, Edmund Warnock, would later admit, this was starkly reflected in Northern Ireland's 'far too feeble' response to the war effort.[55] For Warnock, the Craigavon government's approach to civil defence bordered on criminal negligence, as the Prime Minister and his cabinet accepted the 'widespread conviction ... that the province would not be attacked'.[56] Deep down, Warnock may have resented the government's tardy response to the war effort, though the real reason for his energetic criticism of the Unionist leadership was his own political precariousness in his Belfast constituency of St Anne's. If the government did not act to protect the people from external aggression, Warnock would be held accountable and face a clear challenge from the NILP. After his death in November 1940, Craigavon's lackadaisical approach to governing would have profound repercussions for the Unionist Party.

4

Whipping Up the New Recruits

[I]f you live amongst them, as I do, you know that the patience of the Ulster Protestant in the face of official incompetence is matched only by the patience of the Ulster Catholic in the face of official persecution ... They frequently mention other incompetents in the Government and in the higher grades of the Civil Service. In other words, they have no illusions about their leaders: but they follow them all the same.

Ultach, *Orange Terror: The Case Against Partition*[1]

THE RUMBLE OF THE AIRCRAFT was closely followed by the piercing warble of sirens warning of an imminent attack by the German *Luftwaffe*. High explosive and incendiary bombs rained down on the industrial heartland of Belfast, pulverising its shipyards, factories, spinning mills and, horrifyingly, the homes of the great many people living in their shadows. One of the worst affected areas, located near a spinning mill in Greencastle, was hit by a high explosive charge, which brought down thousands of tons of masonry on small, working-class dwellings. These houses, many overcrowded, were deliberately targeted by the Germans to maximise casualties. Narrow terraced houses collapsed in on each other, the dead disappeared, swallowed up by the huge craters left behind. Survivors emerged from their battered shelters to a world changed – front doors blown up stairs, silk parachutes everywhere and unexploded ordnance strewn across the battered working-class districts of inner-city Belfast.

'The wantonness and ruthlessness of the attack was appalling,' reported the *Belfast News Letter*. 'Working-class and residential areas suffered most. Numbers of houses have been laid waste, banks, churches, a charitable institution, industrial buildings and cinemas, and schools were wrecked, and at one point trees bordering an avenue were uprooted and stripped of their branches by the force of the detonations.'[2] Panic-stricken men and women clawed helplessly at the endless rubble in a vain attempt to find their loved ones. One man carrying a small terrier dog said it was all he could find of his family. Three of his children had been taken to hospital, one of whom succumbed to wounds received in the attack. Residents fought the flames with small stirrup pumps. Debris balanced precariously as Air Raid Precautions wardens and firefighters grappled with the raging flames. Everything was wrecked, homes were destroyed and the bodies of local people lay dismembered, mangled and flattened.

Amidst the smouldering incendiary bombs and crushed bodies of civilians, there arose a display of patriotic fervour not seen in years. 'Beyond the great heaps of rubbish Union Jacks fluttered from gaping windows in proud defiance,' reported the *News Letter*. 'This spirit was characteristic of all the affected areas.'[3] Northern Ireland's unionist daily boasted of how 'Ulster could take it'. The 'viciousness of the onslaught, the repeated lacking in military objectives, evidenced a determination to break down the morale of the community,' trumpeted the newspaper. 'It has failed to do so. Northern Ireland is in this war to the finish, and will play its part even more resolutely because of this dire experience.'[4] Initial government estimates put the number of dead at 500 and the number of seriously injured at 420, with slight injuries totalling 1,142.[5]

In what must have seemed a world away, the *News Letter* also enthusiastically reported on 'society news', telling its readers how the Nazi-sympathising Marquess and Marchioness of Londonderry 'spent Easter quietly at Mountstewart' in the company of their daughter, Lady Mairi Keppel, and her husband, Captain the Hon. Derek Keppel. It was 'not the usual Easter house party' with the Marchioness of Dufferin and her children away to Montalto.[6] While working-class people picked through the burning wreckage of their lives, Ulster's aristocracy maintained a stiff upper lip by dabbling in societal soirées. Meanwhile, scores of bodies were rushed to

St George's Market where they would lie until claimed by survivors. The *News Letter* reported how those left unclaimed would be buried in reserved ground at the City Cemetery. At Stormont, John Miller Andrews, who had been appointed Prime Minister following the death of Lord Craigavon, expressed his sympathy for the ordinary people who had suffered so much in the attack:

> Our people, in my opinion and in the opinion of all in Ulster for whom I have any right to speak, have simply been magnificent. I have seen them at the funeral of their dear ones yesterday; I have seen them in their wrecked homes; I have seen them on the streets, and I cannot express the admiration which in my own heart I feel for each and all of those whom I have come across. Their morale is unbroken, they are strong and steadfast and true, and they are determined to see this thing through until victory, be it soon or late, comes. With all reverence I say God bless and protect them all.[7]

Andrews duly issued an appeal to all sections of the community to come together at this extremely challenging time. 'We all suffer with one another,' he said in his public statement. 'We are one in heart and purpose – united against a brutal foe. We will see this thing through to the end, so that we may rejoice together in the day of victory.'[8] It was marvellous rhetoric, aimed at stirring a divided community into pulling together and facing down the might of the Nazi war machine. However, it underplayed the structural deficiencies now eating away at the fabric of the Unionist state.

German bombers returned on 4–5 May, unleashing even greater destruction on Belfast. Amidst fascist bombs, the aloofness of Nazi-sympathising aristocrats and the obvious, patrician advice of middle-class politicians, labour relations between employers and workers broke down. Industrial unrest hinged on poor working conditions, the inexperience of management in dealing with trades unions, and a militant-minded Belfast Shop Stewards' movement. It led to 'remarkable strike activity', with walkouts rising from 114 in 1940 to 242 in 1941.[9] Tensions increased when ordinary people began to realise that their political leadership may not have had their interests at heart, with air raids revealing 'more glaringly the extent of the poverty and the deleterious social conditions which those thousands of working-class people of all denominations had to bear'.[10] In a meeting between Minister for Public Security John MacDermott, Minister for Home Affairs Sir Richard Dawson Bates, Minister for Finance Sir John Milne-Barbour and Head of the Northern Ireland Civil Service Wilfred Spender, MacDermott 'painted a very gloomy picture of public discontent in Belfast and said that he thought opposition demonstration would take an organised form and that he expected an attack upon the Stormont buildings by our population'.[11] This may have bordered on the hysterical, but Spender was acutely aware of the tendency of populists at Stormont to react swiftly to what they were hearing from their working-class supporters. 'I myself find it hard to believe that the Ulster people are so much more panic stricken than is the case with those in Great Britain and feel that if they were properly led they would respond just as well as their fellow citizens across the water,' Spender wrote in his diary. 'There is, however, very little direction on the part of most of the Local Authorities and the nearness of the Government to the centres of complaint undoubtedly encourages people to put forward demands which would not otherwise be presented.'[12] These demands included greater access to government socio-economic support as well as urgent assistance with re-housing.[13]

In total there were four Belfast Blitz attacks – the first on 7–8 April, the second on 15–16 April, the third on 4–5 May and the last on 5–6 May – which resulted in 1,100 people killed, over 56,000 houses damaged (which amounted to 53 per cent of total housing stock), 3,200 houses destroyed and 3,952 others badly damaged, rendering 100,000 people homeless and causing £20 million in damage.[14]

The regional economy in Northern Ireland had faced considerable strain before the war as unemployment skyrocketed, reaching 29.1 per cent of the insured industrial labour forces, the highest since the formation of the local state. Even after the outbreak of conflict, the number of unemployed 'remained well above the British average throughout the war, and, although it fell steeply from spring 1941, reaching its lowest point in autumn 1944, the regional economy never sustained "full" employment'.[15] Northern Ireland was not designated a 'special area' during the war, unlike other deprived parts of the United Kingdom. It also differed from the rest of the United Kingdom in two principal ways. First, military conscription did not apply, and, second, there was 'no compulsory general registration of labour and no policy of concentrating industry to make maximum use of labour factory space'.[16] The low recruitment numbers were disappointing, with only 2,500 men joining up each month at the beginning of the war, which quickly dropped to just 600 a month by December 1940, 'leading to some nationalist mockery of unionist claims of loyalty to Britain'.[17]

Objectively, Northern Ireland looked like the least mobilised of all the regions of the UK. Within fifteen months of war, Northern Ireland's rate of mobilisation and industrialisation in support of total war was 'negligible'. Sir Walter Smiles, the chairman of the Northern Ireland Area Board, in a letter to Harold Macmillan, the Parliamentary Secretary at the Ministry of Supply in London, observed how 'in this little corner of the British empire we hardly yet realise that the nation is engaged in a life and death struggle'.[18] The letter was composed on the day Belfast suffered its worst air raid in months.

Prior to the Blitz, the UUC, the Unionist Party's governing body, had taken the decision to suspend political activity for the duration of the war. However, this was not something accepted by their political opponents amongst the ranks of Independent Unionists and the NILP. The loss of Lord Craigavon's seat to Independent Unionist Thomas Dixon in February 1941 was a precursor of further electoral challenges to come. The next humiliation came in Belfast Willowfield, when the incumbent Unionist MP, Councillor Fred Lavery, was defeated by NILP leader Harry Midgley. Midgley's win, according to his biographer, 'constituted the biggest electoral upset in Northern Ireland's political history'.[19] Inside the Unionist Party there were stirrings of dissent. Wilfred Spender recalled how:

> Our newspapers are giving space to very outspoken criticisms of the Government in connection with the Willowfield Election and I fear there is no doubt the Unionist Party has stultified itself by the type of candidate it has selected. Lord Glentoran who in the Bangor Election pressed his Unionist followers to fight for an ex-Serviceman now finds himself confronted with the request to the electors to do the reverse at Willowfield. There is also very outspoken criticism of some of the

recent appointments in the Government, which, I am afraid, has some justification in fact.[20]

The Unionist Party duly responded with an attempted reorganisation, turning to sixty-two-year-old Herbert Dixon, otherwise known as Lord Glentoran, the party's Chief Whip, who was handed the task of revitalising creaking internal machinery. He had already expressed his concerns about the political challenge of Unionist Party opponents in a letter on 2 April 1941, where he acknowledged to a party colleague how 'purely political work would have to be begun again'.[21]

Dixon had first won the Westminster seat of Belfast Pottinger (later Belfast East) in 1918 and retained it in 1923, 1924, 1929, 1931 and 1935. He also held the Stormont seat of Belfast East from 1921–29 and Bloomfield from 1929 until his death in 1950.[22] A consummate campaigner, he wrote to all Unionist Association secretaries with an appeal to them to restart their local networks, most of which had been in abeyance due to the war. Reverend W. Martin of the South Down Unionist Association replied to Dixon's appeal rather glumly. 'While for Ulster Unionists the Border is indispensable,' he wrote, 'our young people will require … much wider opportunities and facilities than they have had in the past if we are to enlist their willing and hearty support.'[23] It was not the kind of response Glentoran was expecting. As he told Martin:

> I am much obliged for your letter and appreciate the fact that your Unionist Association, like all others in Ulster, accepted the Truce and turned their efforts towards war work. Unfortunately, our opponents have taken advantage of this to set out an extremely virile campaign against us. It is therefore necessary in order that we may help our position that we should set our Unionist Associations into motion again, and whip up as many recruits as possible to bring fresh blood and more activity.[24]

Glentoran believed Unionist Associations should take greater responsibility for energising the party's grassroots supporters. 'I am quite certain that it would not do for us to remain idle in the face of the activity now shown by our Opponents and, therefore, in one way or another we have got to keep going to meet this challenge.'[25] Glentoran's plea, however, was met with total resignation in areas like Larne, where the local Honorary Secretary offered a curious excuse. 'We have such a scattered area that I doubt if we should get many to attend a meeting at this period of the year, owing to rough weather, petrol shortage, etc. Personally I think our position is unsatisfactory, and I have thought many times of writing to you on the subject.'[26] It was a pathetic reflection of the perils of inertia, with the Unionist Party now in danger of becoming moribund.

In light of the internal difficulties in restarting Unionist Party activism amidst the political challenges launched by the NILP, the Minister for Commerce, Sir Basil Brooke, turned to the old populist playbook and made a direct appeal to what he regarded as the innate patriotism of working-class Protestants. With the country now facing physical destruction, Brooke asked all the 'workers of Northern Ireland, even though there may at times be difficulties, to let those difficulties be settled rather than to go slow or go on strike'.[27] He also raised the prospect of the damaging effects of strikes on Ulster's reputation, for, 'unless I can show that the output from the various tools and machines in Northern Ireland is as good as that in England I have no case when I go over to London to fight their battles'.[28] His words failed to have the desired effect. While Northern Ireland had managed to pay its way in economic terms, with its Imperial Contributions between 1922 and 1943 totalling some £76,000,000 – in contrast to the £32,000,000 paid by the Exchequer to Northern Ireland over the same period[29] – 3 million hours were still lost to strike action in the nine months to April 1943.[30]

With such a palpable 'lack of discipline' in the labour force, there was indeed a risk to Northern Ireland's status, with the London government freezing Stormont out of the decision-making process on the award of war contracts.[31] The peculiar nature of Northern Ireland – a patriotic British enclave whose workers frequently demonstrated an independent mind of their own by engaging in industrial militancy – provided a persistent headache for Unionist government ministers. As the defeated Unionist Party candidate in Willowfield put it in a letter to Andrews, a new 'feature of the election was the large number of the electorate termed Loyalist Labour, including many Unionists and members of the Orange Institution, who supported and voted Labour', which necessitated reorganising constituency branches throughout east Belfast.[32]

The Blitz had exposed a housing crisis, with many working-class families inhabiting slums without proper drainage or amenities. These dire conditions led the Moderator of the Presbyterian Church to predict 'solemnly that a revolution would ensue if these problems were not tackled'.[33] To compound matters, little had been done to address these issues in the two and half years since German bombers visited the city. When the Northern Ireland House of Commons was recalled from its summer recess in late August 1943 to debate a new Rent Restriction Bill, Jack Beattie of the NILP called it 'a disgrace for any Government which has been in power so long to allow these things to happen in the year 1943'.[34] Beattie was an impressive orator, who rivalled Tommy Henderson for the longest speeches delivered at Stormont. He was given to rhetorical flourishes in his criticism of government benches:

> The Members of this Government have done nothing since they came into power. They have found no respect for themselves in any quarter, and the people as a whole have less respect for them than for any Government that has existed since the setting up of this Parliament ... They can spend the money of the State in travelling; they can do many things, but they cannot do the things that matter. These include getting the work done, providing the people with houses, putting the landed and landlord classes in their rightful place in the life of the community, and making the people comfortable and happy.[35]

Along with Henderson and other Independent Unionists John Nixon and Thomas Baillie, Beattie made frequent interjections on issues of concern for working-class people. However, internal wrangling over NILP policy on the question of the constitutional position of Northern Ireland, to say nothing of the disparate views of the Independent Unionists, stymied any kind of co-ordinated effort against government policy. Despite this, Beattie's return to the West Belfast seat in a Westminster by-election in 1943 proved damaging to Andrews' position as Prime Minister. Backbenchers and junior ministers regarded Beattie's win as the final straw, and they openly called for Andrews' resignation. He caved in, handing the reins to Basil Brooke, who immediately set about checking the carping criticism of many within his own party as well as challenging more aggressively those in opposition parties[36] and setting about improving relations between Stormont and Westminster.[37]

These by-election upsets did little to encourage a rejuvenation of activism within Unionist Associations, but they did galvanise many younger people to join the NILP. One such person was David Bleakley, an apprentice electrician in the Harland & Wolff shipyard. 'The shipyard was tough but never rough,' he recalled. 'You formalise something you do informally. We were all in it together.'[38] Bleakley went to work at the shipyard, like so many other working-class boys at the time, to learn a trade. 'To be a labourer was a terrible thing and you didn't have a trade,' he recalled. Despite the war, the Labour Party's youth section thrived. Bleakley especially found it a supportive environment, and he was supported by other activists to seek to educate himself by attending the local technical college at night, where he studied English and economics. After reading a copy of the *Picture Post* in the barbershop one day, which featured the story of a miner who went to Oxford, Bleakley decided to seek a scholarship to the university. He would soon become one of a growing number of Labour activists who found education to be a radical way of challenging the status quo in a way that accorded with their moral outlook on life:

> One of things that attracted me to [the Labour Party] was the notion of service. No problem was utterly impossible if you got together on it. I regarded the Labour Party as a Keir Hardie party. I'd have been brought up with notions of Keir Hardie. My father was a trade unionist. He wasn't a political man, but I can remember he often quoted Keir Hardie. Keir Hardie was a figure up on the hill who we all looked to even though he wasn't one of our own people.[39]

Like Harry Midgley, Bleakley and other members of the NILP advocated an extension of all British rights for British citizens in Northern Ireland, though they emphasised a redistribution of these rights through the lens of democratic socialism. That meant that, while they supported the Union, they opposed the populist tendencies and sectarian rhetoric of the Unionist regime and, instead, articulated a more inclusive agenda. For these Labour activists, political change through parliamentary democracy was the only way Northern Ireland could be liberated from the social and economic ills that confronted it. It was something Midgley had been unequivocal about when he led the NILP. Rather cynically, Brooke countermanded the efforts of the NILP and other left-leaning groups when he encouraged Midgley – who had by now been expelled from the NILP and formed the Commonwealth Labour Party – to join his cabinet as Minister for Public Safety, a decision taken to create the impression that his government was 'broader-based and more representative of society'.[40]

For other left-leaning activists, such as the Communist Party of Northern Ireland's Sadie Menzies, there was now a pressing need to hold this broad-based government to account. In a letter she wrote to Brooke, Menzies proposed a new health ministry as 'the only answer to the inadequate health service both for children and grown ups'.[41] Her correspondence captured a reformist mood within the broader trade union movement, though it was not confined to it. The UWUC also reported that its members were attending regular meetings because they 'wanted to know what the Unionist Party was going to do for them'.[42] The UWUC had previously passed a resolution calling on the government to 'pursue without delay a vigorous and adequate housing policy'.[43]

In a speech to the House of Commons, Brooke remained cautious and non-committal in his promises to act in the interests of ordinary people. 'Regarding housing,' he said, 'I want to say that the Government look on this as a matter of the very highest priority.'[44] He compared the rebuilding of society after the war to the conquest of Everest, which he believed required 'team spirit', planning and effort. 'Without the work of all those on the route, the expedition will fail,' he told MPs. 'The Government has based all its plans on the maintenance of the Union of Great Britain', by which he equated the maintenance of the Union with the maintenance of a better standard of living for those who had sacrificed so much for the war effort. Refusing to concede the power of the people in forcing his government's hand on the need to improve their lot, Brooke instead emphasised the advantages of staying within the Union:

> The aim and end of the Government is to build a prosperous and progressive Ulster that can make her contribution in peace, as she has

done in war, to the well-being of the freedom-loving nations of the world. I believe that she can do that only in the closest association with Great Britain and the Empire. In this war we have taken our stand unequivocally on the side of justice and freedom. When the guns cease firing the march towards a free and better life for all will begin, and in that we intend also to take our place. To sever our connection with Great Britain would be to fall out of the great movement towards progress and prosperity.[45]

Brooke was cheered on by his MPs. Their new leader could do no wrong. It was left to Paddy Agnew to remind him of the challenges wrought by 'serious unemployment', which ran throughout 'the length and breadth of Northern Ireland'.[46] Agnew spoke for many beyond his own constituency when he said that for as long as they had a government based on the Unionist Party, they 'would never have prosperity ... [or] ... sound industry'.[47] In Agnew's view, there were 'people inside the Unionist Party to-day in Northern Ireland who do not care one iota about the returning soldiers'.[48]

As a former soldier himself and a cousin to Britain's most senior armed forces commander, Chief of the Imperial General Staff Sir Alan Brooke, the Unionist Prime Minister baulked at such criticism. Brooke nevertheless understood the dangers of the NILP's appeal to class-based interests within the government's traditional support base. He would have to stop their encroachment on his party's electoral fortunes or risk further political losses. A strategy to realise Brooke's vision of a 'prosperous and progressive Ulster' was now an urgent requirement.

5

Responsible Members of the Community

> Without civic morality communities perish; without personal morality their survival has no value. Therefore civic and personal morality are equally necessary to a good world.
>
> Bertrand Russell, *Authority and the Individual*[1]

THE DISTANT DRONE OF THE aircraft's engines could be heard high above the Royal Air Force (RAF) station at Long Kesh in Lisburn. Spectators waited patiently as the aeroplane came into view, shining silver-bright in the blinding sunlight, a pair of Dakotas accompanied by two squadrons of Mustang fighters piloted by Polish pilots alongside Warwick aircraft from the Air Sea Rescue Service. The Dakotas touched down on the runway at 4.39 p.m. on 17 July 1945, slowing to a crawl before taxiing to a halt. The door of the lead aircraft opened to reveal King George VI, Queen Elizabeth and their daughter Princess Elizabeth, who had made the short journey from RAF Northolt in Middlesex:

> A hush fell on the crowd of civilian spectators as the door of the great aircraft was flung back – a hush to be broken a minute later by a rousing round of cheers as the King, in the uniform of a Marshal of the RAF, came into view, followed by the Queen who looked radiant in a two-piece suit of dove grey and a matching hat with a royal blue bow.[2]

Princess Elizabeth was dressed in the uniform of the Auxiliary Territorial

Service, a symbol that everyone in British society had come to play their part in the war. The people cheered enthusiastically. It was a rousing reception, the first time the royals had arrived in Northern Ireland by air. They were then driven to Hillsborough Castle in Lisburn, where they were hosted by the Governor and Duchess of Abercorn. As they dined in the castle, the sound of Lambeg drums 'beat through the windows of Government House'.[3] The party adjourned to watch the drummers 'beat a message of welcome from Ulster to their Majesties'.[4] It was a joyous occasion on their two-day whistle-stop tour of Northern Ireland. People put out Union flags to celebrate, and the royal family was greeted everywhere by thousands of uniformed members of the armed forces and civilian well-wishers. Later the King and Queen would host one of the biggest garden parties ever seen in Belfast, with 5,000 workers invited to Botanic Gardens, where the royal family was greeted with the kind of adulation and deference a sovereign could expect from his loyal subjects.

Meanwhile, other elements of the working class were restive. Thousands of workers from the Shorts Aircraft manufacturing plant on Queen's Island in East Belfast assembled outside the factory gates and marched to Stormont. A colour party led the estimated 2,000–3,000 demonstrators, proudly carrying a Union flag alongside the Stars and Stripes and the flag of the Union of Soviet Socialist Republics. The protestors made their way up the long drive to Parliament Buildings, unfurling a banner that read 'Full Employment – Remember Your Promises of June 4'.[5] The workers were met by the newly elected NILP MP for Oldpark, Bob Getgood,[6] who later told the House of Commons how those gathered outside had only one demand: 'It was nothing less than full-time employment or full maintenance for themselves and their dependents during the period of redundancy, as it has been called, or during the period of unemployment.'[7]

Getgood appeared angry as he addressed his fellow MPs. He saw no 'tremendous sense or appreciation of the issues involved' as he looked across at the government benches: 'To my mind, our people are determined at all costs never again to go through the hellish times that they endured in the pre-war years. That is the hope of those demonstrators, and I take it what they had in mind was typical of the working class in Northern Ireland.'[8] Getgood spoke for an increasing number of ordinary people who believed Ulster should not depart from the rest of the UK in its pursuit of a fair deal for those returning from war. The Labour government in London saw welfarist policies as a monument to the sacrifice of many millions who died in the name of peace. Getgood shared this view, though he knew the Unionist Party would only continue to implement these policies step by step if held to account. Getgood and his only NILP colleague, Hugh Downey, resolved to turn their attention to harnessing persistent working-class disaffection in the cause of parliamentary socialism at Stormont.[9]

Britain's involvement in the Second World War had left the country on the precipice of bankruptcy. The exhaustion of its economic resources, only buoyed up by the Lend-Lease Agreement with the United States, saw London fall into Washington's debt. On the domestic front, Winston Churchill's stoic leadership may have led his country to victory, but it was soon scorned by an electorate tired of a Tory-led national government and eager for change. During the election hustings, Churchill boasted of seeing off the Labour opposition. At a huge rally at the Walthamstow Stadium in London attended by 20,000 people, he was heckled by Labour supporters. His response was to belittle them, threatening that they were soon to experience 'a thrashing such as their Party has never received since it was born'.[10] When the election came in July 1945, the threats failed to materialise. The Tories were roundly defeated by Labour in a landslide victory. Into the hands of the new Labour Prime Minister Clement Attlee was put the monumental task of building a country fit for their returning heroes. Attlee promised to build a National Health Service that would provide a battered and bruised population with a new system of healthcare from cradle to grave. He also pushed through legislation on welfare and education as part of his government's commitment to fighting social injustice.

Basil Brooke saw how easily a great wartime leader like Churchill could be swept from power for underappreciating the intense feelings of social transformation experienced by those who fought for freedom. Brooke recognised that Conservative policies no longer held sway and conceded the principle of having to sacrifice his own government's self-help doctrine in favour of Attlee's progressive socio-economic policies. As a key member of the Unionist cabinet during the war, Brooke knew that the working class in Northern Ireland were demanding change and had dispatched Unionist politicians during wartime by-elections who were judged not to hold their interests at heart. The Unionist regime's appeal to sectarianism had fallen flat. It was the Irish nationalist historian Alice Stopford Green who observed in the aftermath of the First World War how Catholic workers were less infected by Marxian socialist ideas than their Protestant counterparts who were 'riddled with it'.[11] Stopford Green believed that at times when the Irish question lay at the back of people's minds, Protestant workers were likely to 'turn anti-capitalist and renounce the Unionist politicians who saw themselves as the "natural leaders" of democracy'.[12] Brooke's experience as Minister of Commerce during the opening years of the Second World War confirmed the presence of militant tendencies. It likely motivated him to give 'a solid commitment on which the Unionist Party could base its pledges to take Northern Ireland into the new British welfarist and socially transformed era'.[13] Without these pledges, Brooke knew his party risked losing political ground to the opposition, many of whom were concentrated in the ranks of the NILP.

Brooke was fortunate to have some qualified civil servants grappling with the question of how to implement the new welfare state policies emanating from Westminster. John Oliver had entered the Northern Ireland Civil Service in 1937, working first in the Ministry of Finance before moving to the Ministry of Labour and then to the newly created Ministry for Health and Local Government. In his memoirs he recalled his 'exceptional experience to be able to play a part within government in helping to set up the administrative systems needed to alleviate the ills we have discerned'.[14] Oliver was proud of the work he had done in creating what he regarded as 'a better and above all a happier health service than was done in any other part of the kingdom'.[15] So immersed in the mechanics of extending the welfare state to Northern Ireland was he that he undertook a PhD on the topic of 'Pre-Supposition and Implications of the Welfare State'. Oliver adopted a rigorous academic approach to his work, building on what he learned while he completed his doctoral studies at Queen's University. His 'plan was to try and trace some philosophical thread of concern for the weaker members of society and of the obligation of others for them'.[16] He had in mind the basic idea of what constituted 'the good life' and from there worked out 'the role of society and of the state in fostering the good life'. Was it 'the job of the state to make people happy?' He was unsure, but he knew it had a role. Perhaps it was 'a matter of the state helping to create the conditions within which the individual can achieve his own fulfilment?'[17] Oliver had few answers, but he knew that the Unionist government must do something to meet the expectations of its supporters or risk political ruin.

Oliver's ideas were at root socially conservative and reflected the prevailing mood within Ulster's political elite to ensure they did everything they could to remain in power. However, they were also concerned with protecting the Union. The editor of the *Belfast Telegraph*, Jack Sayers, an influential member of the Unionist establishment, explained how the overriding aim of the Unionist Party was to 'preserve in the provincial House of Commons a majority in favour of the Union, and it has become instinctive among the people to safeguard the unity, not to say the singlemindedness, that makes this possible. All other matters are secondary so long as there is any attack upon the right of self-determination.'[18] This preoccupation had long blinded unionists to all attempts at accommodation with those critical of their majoritarian understanding of democracy. Indeed, the protection of the civil and religious liberties of Protestants underscored the entire system. The Unionist Party, consequently, stood 'a little less urgently for the economic advantages of free trade within the United Kingdom, and the raising of the standard of life to the highest national level'. While these objectives were, to borrow Sayers' words, 'at once idealistic and pragmatic', they were 'not to be derogated'.[19] Working out how to square the circle of parochial social conservative principles with the welfarist agenda in London now took on a sense of urgency.

In return for this outward compliance with its welfare reform agenda, the Labour government was 'broadly supportive of the Unionist leadership and responded with genuine sympathy to its requirements' for much of the immediate post-war period.[20] At a meeting between Attlee and Brooke at Chequers on 20 November 1948, the men discussed the serious matter of Éire's intention of repealing the Executive Authority (External Relations) Act of 1936, which had abolished the King's representative in Dublin but still retained a foreign policy role for the British government. The Irish Taoiseach, John A. Costello, had recently raised the prospect of repealing the Act at a meeting of the Commonwealth representatives. Brooke raised concerns that Costello's government still retained a policy of reuniting the hole island under Dublin rule. In seeking an assurance from Attlee, Brooke said his 'immediate anxieties would [only] be allayed if he could be given assurance that the constitutional position of Northern Ireland would not be prejudiced by Éire's ceasing to be a member of the Commonwealth'.[21] Attlee told him that 'the constitutional position of Northern Ireland would be fully safeguarded' in such an eventuality, suggesting that Brooke would be 'at liberty to say publicly that he had received that assurance'.[22]

Following this meeting, Brooke returned to London where he gave a speech to Conservative politicians at the Junior Carlton Club in Pall Mall. This was a time when the Tories took their Conservative and Unionist Party title seriously, supporting Brooke as they sought to maintain the Union amidst secessionist rhetoric in Dublin. 'The reason there are two political systems in Ireland,' Brooke told those gathered, 'is because there are, to all intents and purposes, two different peoples north and south of the border. Our historical associations are different, our religious beliefs and our political principles. These are fundamental and irreconcilable differences, and symptomatic of them is the attitude of the two peoples to the Crown.'[23] Sitting alongside Brooke was his cousin, Field Marshal Viscount Alanbrooke, his guest for the occasion and a man for whom many Tories had high regard. Brooke believed retention of the King as head of state in the island of Ireland was 'the touchstone of loyalty', though he could only speak for Ulstermen and women who remained steadfast in their belief that '[n]either difficulty nor danger will alter our allegiance to the Crown, or be allowed to undermine our position within the United Kingdom'.[24] A few months later Brooke won the argument by securing the support of both parties at Westminster in ensuring the passage of the Ireland Act (1949), which reaffirmed Northern Ireland's constitutional position within the UK. He saw the securing of the Union as a 'matter of strategic importance',[25] despite the rumblings from some nationalist-leaning parliamentary Labour Party backbenchers.[26]

In seeking to capitalise on the political concessions from London, Brooke called a general election in February 1949. It was designed to strengthen his hand in negotiations with Attlee. In order to maximise the Unionist vote, Brooke turned to his predecessor, John Miller Andrews, now Grand Master of the Orange Order. It was an enormous success, with the Unionists winning back four seats, including taking those occupied by Getgood and

Downey. The election proved that the Unionist–Orange alliance was still strong and binding. The Orange Order provided a centre for social activity that channelled its members, their families and supporters in the direction of maintaining the political status quo.[27]

Brooke would call on the support of Andrews and the Orange Order in the next two elections. Andrews even went as far as to issue a declaration cementing the alliance at a Central Committee meeting of the Grand Orange Lodge of Ireland on 10 October 1951:

> We desire to impress upon our Orange Brothers and Sisters the great importance of all Orangemen and Orangewomen voting in the present election for the Imperial Parliament for the democratically selected unionist candidates.
>
> Our opponents have given priority to the Boundary issue and it is for us to meet the challenge by returning our Unionist candidates with triumphant majorities in order to prove that the loyalists of Northern Ireland are as resolutely determined as ever, never to surrender their cherished birthright as citizens of the United Kingdom and the great British Empire.
>
> All we hold dear is at stake – our civil and religious liberty, the security of the Protestant faith, our social, industrial and agricultural wellbeing.
>
> Our duty is clear.[28]

Andrews' declaration was signed by all senior members of the Order. It gave an important guarantee to Brooke that they would do all in their power to prevent any encroachment on the Unionist Party's position. This meant keeping their members on a tight leash and ensuring they did not embarrass the government. On one occasion it was a Unionist MP, Nat Minford, who made the error of saying 'to hell with the Pope' at one political rally. At a special meeting of the Orange Order's Central Committee held on 7 November 1951 in Sandy Row, Andrews told his senior officers that he had become 'greatly distressed' by Minford's remarks. Andrews sought 'repudiation of the remarks attributed to Bro. Minford' and urged the Order's senior officers to censor the MP. They duly issued the following edict:

That the Central Committee of the Grand Orange Lodge of Ireland deplores the irreverent and insulting references to Roman Catholics in a speech made at a public meeting in Clifton Street Orange Hall, during the recent Imperial Parliamentary Election, by Bro. N. Minford M.P. This institution stands for civil and religious liberty and any departure from this fundamental principle is to be strongly condemned.[29]

The incident demonstrated how the Order held tight control over elected MPs. It also demonstrated how the Unionist–Orange alliance was anxious to preserve its image as tolerant even if, beneath the surface, it was nothing of the sort. Like Andrews, Brooke knew that it was wise to conceal the narrow sectional agenda of his party at a time when they were under scrutiny by the Labour government and their supporters in Northern Ireland.[30]

Basil Brooke could at times appear to be politically astute and forward-leaning on policy matters. In August 1948 he had taken the progressive decision to appoint a woman, Dehra Parker, the Unionist MP for South Londonderry, to his cabinet as Minister of Health and Local Government. Parker, who was born in northern India in 1882 to Anglo-Irish parents, moved to Ulster after the First World War. She was duly elected an MP for Londonderry in 1921 and 1929, representing South Londonderry after 1933, and was appointed Parliamentary Undersecretary at the Ministry of Education by Craigavon in 1937. Married originally to Colonel Robert P.D. Spencer Chichester and then Admiral H.W. Parker,[31] she was an influential member of the Ulster societal elite who held sway with important establishment figures in Northern Ireland and England. In a letter from Viscount Charlemont, the former Minister of Education at Stormont, to Basil Brooke at the time of Parker's appointment, her former boss was quick to point out how 'the Govt has obtained the services of a first class administrator[,] a tireless worker and a charming personality; moreover the appointment will be a popular one both for those in and away from Stormont'.[32] As a dyed-in-the-cashmere establishment figure, Parker's 'background and upbringing, indeed her personality made her an unlikely champion of the people'.[33] She was socially and politically conservative to her core, once telling a debate on Housing Trust rent increases that 'the country must face the hard facts and reconcile itself to the thought of some advance in rents of subsidised housing'.[34] Parker, however, was prepared to appoint individuals to public health bodies on the basis of merit, rather than because of pressure from the party's grassroots.[35] This sometimes infuriated local Unionist Associations, who were anxious not to see a reduction of their influence over central government.[36] By maintaining a degree of independence of action, Parker became a powerful force within the Unionist Party. It was no surprise, therefore, that her deep-rooted conservative views on community values would be reflected in the huge welfare state projects undertaken by her department.

By the mid-1950s, 'against a background of economic gloom in the Province's traditional industries', the Unionist Party nevertheless appeared somewhat detached from working-class concerns and, 'even more damagingly, insufficiently equipped to deal with problems'.[37] The party once again risked falling out of favour with its grassroots supporters in the Protestant working class, who were often more preoccupied with bread-and-butter issues – how to earn a wage, feed their families and live comfortably – than constitutional matters. With clear political challenges now emanating from the NILP, which had confirmed its commitment to maintaining Northern Ireland's constitutional position within the UK at its annual party conference in April 1949, the Unionist Party once again returned to its populist sectarian roots. The NILP, by way of contrast, chose to present a more inclusive alternative to maintaining the Union. In the spirit of inclusivity and maintaining its links both with the Labour and trade union movement throughout the UK (most trade unions in Northern Ireland were British), the NILP began to articulate a vision for the future that would better maintain the Union in the long term. For the NILP, the bedrock principle of the Ireland Act left the argument over the maintenance of the Union in the hands of the majority of MPs at Stormont. As the party made clear in its 1953 Stormont election manifesto:

> This, then, is our answer: we are ready and anxious to support the present constitutional position of Ulster against every attack save that through the ballot-box. This we do because we wish to see Ulster well governed and reconstructed socially and economically. To do otherwise is to put the cart before the horse: constitutions exist as a means of good government, not as an end in themselves.[38]

The NILP would become a constant thorn in the side of the Unionist Party. Its key strategists sought to anchor their support base within the Protestant working-class community by choosing candidates like David Bleakley – who had by now returned from his studies in Oxford. Through the connections Bleakley made at Oxford[39] and the efforts of the NILP and British Labour general secretaries, Sam Napier and Morgan Phillips, Attlee's party was able to offer its local sister party greater political, logistical and financial support.[40] The NILP now sought to broaden its support-base beyond the Protestant working class in the mid- to late 1950s by deliberately reaching out to the Catholic workers,[41] and was the only political party making 'any sustained effort to attract support from both sections of the community'.[42]

In a bitter blow to the Unionist government's narrow political agenda, the NILP secured the return of four MPs in the Stormont election held on 20 March 1958. Tom Boyd was elected to Jack Beattie's old seat of Belfast Pottinger while Vivian Simpson won in Belfast Oldpark. Both men received strong cross-community support. David Bleakley won the seat of Belfast Victoria and Billy Boyd took a seat in Belfast Woodvale. Shortly after winning his seat, Simpson thanked his election team for their support with his campaign. 'Our victory was the result of a big team effort,' he told them. 'To have wiped out our opponent's majority of 2,800 and still have 155 to our credit was a wonderful achievement, and it marks the beginning of a new political future within the Oldpark Constituency.'[43]

On the same day Simpson thanked his comrades, the Northern Ireland Housing Trust was opening one of its flagship housing projects in the newly created town of Newtownabbey. Under the Newtownabbey Urban District Act (Northern Ireland), 1957, the new Minister for Health and Local Government, J.L.O. Andrews, attended an unveiling ceremony at Whitehouse Town Hall, less than a mile from where, twenty years earlier, his father had presided over the opening of Greencastle Orange Hall. Andrews praised his cabinet colleagues for 'always being interested in the housing situation, and particularly since the war', doing 'everything possible through subsidies which kept down prices and rents'.[44] He compared the economic situation to the rest of the UK, where, he claimed, constituents ought to 'appreciate how fortunate Ulster is in being able to continue them'.[45] After his speech, Andrews was presented to the all-male council, whose chairman,

Henry Robinson, told reporters that he and his colleagues would 'go forward, with God's help, determined to do its part in bringing peace, happiness and prosperity to the people of this community'.[46]

Whether they thought much about it or not, the Protestant and Catholic residents of the new housing development of Rathcoole – the largest population centre in Newtownabbey and the largest housing estate in Northern Ireland – were part of a social experiment. In many ways they were a model village of how post-war life under the Unionist regime was meant to be organised. This was a political attempt at social engineering envisaged by Unionist elites to bring about their vision of a 'prosperous and progressive Ulster', outlined by Basil Brooke towards the end of the war and turned into a workable strategy by Dehra Parker.[47] The first bricks were laid for the Rathcoole estate in 1953. Its architects conceived it as a self-reliant community which would have its own shops, bank, schools, post office and cinema. It was convenient to Belfast and would serve as the residential housing stock for equally self-reliant mill and factory workers in the greater Belfast area. In time it would provide the homes of the industrial workers who would drive forward the Ulster economy in the East Antrim area.[48] Although largely benevolent on the surface, this vision for a compliant workforce betrayed the reality that Rathcoole would be predominantly Protestant in demographic terms and unionist in political terms. In the eyes of the Unionist regime, there was little troubling about representing Protestant culture as 'the state's sole identity'.[49] In this sense there was little in the way of different political or cultural avenues for anyone who was non-unionist – whether nationalist or labour – to go down.[50] Anyone who thought differently or wished to profess an alternative identity or form of cultural expression was deemed a traitor for denying the patriotic fervour of the Unionist regime's broader state-building project.[51]

If Newtownabbey was the Unionist government's vision for a model loyalist community, in which old and young alike could live in peace, happiness and prosperity, then Rathcoole was 'the latest jewel in the crown', the epitome of the Housing Trust's ambitious, ten-year-old building programme.[52] 'Charming little bungalows are provided for the old – no stairs to be climbed. They are built in groups – no distance to be walked to visit someone of similar outlook.' It was an idyllic, almost picturesque sort of lifestyle. And these were the kind of homes fit for heroes of the war. In a total war where all the people had been mobilised, this was their reward. 'The men play darts and gossip about anything and everything, and, towards the end, with cups of tea and tasties provided by the women members, the whole gathering indulges in a hearty sing-song, with occasional solo contributions which, no matter their quality, are always warmly applauded.'[53] In full propaganda mode, the *Belfast News Letter* even decried how the oldest member of the club, Mrs Mary McKay of Armoy Gardens, 'is in her 81st year, but, unfortunately, is not in the best of health at the moment. The others, however, generally enjoy good health, and good times, which would put to shame many of the young people of the estate, and enter into all their activities with an enthusiasm which belies their years.'[54] Shamed into looking up to their elders, the youngsters of the estate were also busily being instructed in the value of Unionist community spirit.

The Alpha Boys Club was promptly formed by a retired tax inspector from Southport in England called John Peake, who served as its first chairman. 'Some of us were concerned that boys coming into their teens had absolutely nowhere to go and nothing to do in the way of recreation.'[55] Joining forces with others in the community – including skilled tradesmen, joiners, plumbers, electricians – the boys formed a club in the Ardeen Hall, the local community centre.[56] It was a classic self-help scenario, where they raised money to pay for the rent and even refurbished the centre themselves. The Trust agreed to lend support to 'putting the outside in order', if the boys and their families provided free labour. Some of the unskilled boys 'dug drains and trenches for gas and electricity supplies', building showers and toilets for football players taking part in matches on the field outside. They had ambitious plans to install a boxing ring and even a library, though initially they occupied themselves with football, table tennis, darts and arts and crafts. Samuel Allen, the owner of the Alpha Cinema in the estate, promised to sponsor the boys' football shirts. As a former professional player himself, Allen hoped to arrange regular fixtures with neighbouring clubs.[57]

Elsewhere in the estate a Girls Club was also formed. Although the girls took responsibility for its day-to-day running, they were not deemed responsible enough to manage their club's business and financial affairs. The

Trust duly appointed a man to chair the group and another to act as club treasurer. One of the organisers of the club, Mrs M. Neilly, was reported to have 'very definite ideas on how such an organisation should be shaped, not only to entertain its members, but also to equip them for the time when they will be wives and mothers and responsible members of the community'.[58] The mission of the club was to contribute to the 'mental welfare of about 50 local girls', though Mrs Neilly was 'keen to introduce "something on more practical lines"'. Her ideas included bringing along an expert from the local technical college to 'give lectures on the management of money'. As Mrs Neilly pointed out, 'The day may come when they may have to work on a tight budget, and while drama circles and arts and crafts are all well and good, we feel we would be doing better for the girls if we help to make life easier for them when they have to shoulder responsibility.'[59] The Girls Club also organised talks on 'personal hygiene and cookery lessons … towards the same end', mostly on a Wednesday evening. They were under the tutelage of a teacher from Belfast, Mrs M.E. Strain, who was 'so keen on her voluntary work that she makes the long journey every week to be present on club nights'.[60] In the margins of such traditional female roles, the girls were permitted time to indulge in 'physical training and folk dancing classes' with some aspirations towards standing up a 'drama circle' alongside 'arts and crafts classes'.[61] There was no mention of a library for use by the girls, though the *News Letter* signed off with some words of reassurance:

> This is a mere indication of the comprehensive and helpful activities undertaken by the girls of the club, activities which undoubtedly do a great deal to curb any tendency to juvenile delinquency, from which the young and heterogenous Rathcoole is remarkably free. The girls are being well nurtured there, but Mrs. Neilly is not yet content. 'I think the most important thing of all to get across to the girls is how to balance a budget,' she says.[62]

In reality, the Unionist government's plans for its working-class supporters amounted to little more than ensuring their energies were responsibly channelled in support of their socio-economic and political 'betters'. In her role as Minister of Health and Local Government, Dehra Parker set the tone for such a socially conservative agenda. However, it was her role as chair of the Youth Committee established under the Youth Welfare Act (1944) and Council for the Encouragement of Music and the Arts that enabled her to relate her own sense of national identity, which was a more 'refined Britishness', to a firm connection with Ulster loyalism.[63] In practice, it had a 'distinctly tweedy, west-Brit establishment feel to it',[64] like much of unionist high culture at the time.[65]

As readers of the *News Letter* eagerly digested the Unionist government's narrow community vision and plans for Newtownabbey, David Bleakley and his colleagues in the parliamentary Labour Party were busily enlarging the idea of community to build bridges across the religious divide. The Queen's Speech read at the opening of the new parliamentary session in April 1958 had set out Brooke's agenda along the lines of bringing greater peace and prosperity to the people of Northern Ireland. 'We of Her Majesty's Opposition will do all in our power to preserve law and order in our community,' Bleakley said, 'and we will observe every legitimate step taken to preserve law and in this place we call Northern Ireland.' Reacting to the tub-thumping speeches of Unionist and Nationalist MPs in the Stormont House of Commons, he chastised them for paving the way to violence. 'We have no time for those who reject the democratic way of doing things,' he said. 'Those who reject that method are contracting out of our political community.'[66] After demolishing Brooke's 'dangerous optimism' about the resurgent unemployment problem, Bleakley concluded by recognising the lack of talent on the government benches. He spoke for his three colleagues when he said they would 'try and make those limitations apparent to all throughout the Province'.[67] However, with such flagrant challenges to the unionist agenda came risks.

The NILP MP for Woodvale, Billy Boyd, frequently worked long into the night to help his constituents. Many of the issues crossing his desk included assisting local people with housing, jobs and benefits. One of those who worked closely with Boyd was his wife, Beatrice. She recalled how when they left the premises of the NILP advice centre on Wilton Street in west Belfast they would be greeted by 'Unionists standing on the other side of the Shankill Road laughing because they would have let down the tyres [of our cars] and we would have come out, we had to get the tyres fixed to get home'.[68] Beatrice found the Unionist Party and their supporters to be particularly hostile towards the NILP, especially at elections:

> When we would have gone round the Shankill Road to canvass, you know, you found it very difficult. The unionists didn't mind coming out and shouting, 'Get you away from my door!' For example, one lady stopped me at the door, and she said, 'Hold on a wee minute, till I get his election address, here.' And I waited and she came out and she spat on it and then she said, 'There you are,' and give me it back. Really, in those days the Unionist Party were very much the dominant [party], even though they [constituents on the Shankill] were working class and had all these rich people representing them. But, nevertheless, they were for King and Country. And a lot of the houses would have had photographs of the Royal Family up … And Patricia McLaughlin would have been one of the leading Unionist politicians there. And she would have wrapped herself round in a Union Jack. Those Unionist politicians didn't mind going to extreme measures to show that the Labour Party wasn't like that … Some of the nicer unionists would have taken pity on us and given us a cup of tea and a sandwich. Things weren't really that bad. There wouldn't have been the shooting and that sort of thing.[69]

Notwithstanding the absence of 'shooting and that sort of thing', unionist supporters in the Shankill walked a fine line between juvenile pranks, casual catcalling and intimidation, though for the moment this could be easily dismissed with a polite smile or a bowed head.

Although Beatrice Boyd brushed off the harassment facing NILP activists on the doorsteps, David Bleakley was in no doubt that 'the wives were the heroines of it all. My wife was the one who made the sacrifices. Believe you me we knew the sale rooms of the Newtownards Road,' he recalled, as he also spoke about the challenges facing the Labour Party at that time. He remembered how the four Labour MPs were greeted when they were first elected:

> When we went into Stormont we were objects of curiosity. The first thing we brought forward was the idea of a full-time parliament. And

no longer was Stormont an exclusive club. The first thing we did was appoint Tom Boyd as Leader of the Opposition. When we got four seats there was Oldpark that was very strong Nationalist. Woodvale and Victoria were always traditionally Unionist. And I think Terence O'Neill more than anyone saw the danger. That's why the Labour Party was feared. We were weak because we didn't wave the Union Jack or the Tricolour. We said it was demeaning of these flags. They debased the National Anthem a lot of the time. We had a lot of history to face down. And, for anyone who wanted a political career, the Labour Party wasn't the place to get a political career. That sent a shudder down the necks of the Unionist and Nationalist parties.[70]

The new Labour MPs lost little time in challenging the government on its social, economic and political policies. 'The programme for this Session of Parliament contains cold comfort for the weaker and more unfortunate members of our community,' Tom Boyd told the House of Commons, before continuing:

> We are here because the electorate wants to see that remedied and in so far as we can we will seek to remedy the omissions from the Government's programme and thus seek to establish a fairer and more just society, providing more opportunity for all and a chance for every man and woman to make the best of himself or herself and so add to the heritage which has developed during the past years.[71]

For Bleakley, this idea of a 'fairer and more just society' in which every man and woman could make the best of themselves could only be understood against the backdrop of the welfare state, which won many temporary converts in the Unionist government at the time:

> The Unionist Party was more than a party in the narrow sense of the word. It brought in all sorts of people and it would have been very difficult to find a high proportion of Unionist Party members who would have been opposed to the welfare state once it had been established … That's the way politics go. You get a small change and

a small change and, suddenly, you get a jump ... It wasn't a big deal when you first grasped the idea of a welfare state. A welfare state could become dangerous and interfere with your freedom but in fact it was an idea whose time had come.[72]

Bleakley, however, remained downbeat about the NILP's calls for reform of the political system ruling Northern Ireland. The party could make no headway 'against the uncompromising and ungracious opposition of successive Unionist governments', he later wrote.[73] The return of four NILP MPs to Stormont after several years without any Labour representation at Stormont was nonetheless seen as a triumph, even if it did little to alter the sectional interests of the regime or make it more responsive to the needs of the whole community, regardless of their religious or political creed.

The Unionist Party at Stormont had traditionally been dominated 'by the business and professional classes', though by the 1950s it had become 'more representative' by ensuring more occupational groups were reflected amongst its MPs.[74] Brian Faulkner, who was first elected in 1949 and served as government Chief Whip at Stormont in 1956–59, believed the party now reflected a broad coalition of interests. 'My family background and business experience in Ulster,' he wrote in his memoir, 'had instilled in me a dislike of class-based politics. The Unionist Party had grown up as a community movement rather than a political organization, and it had retained much of its democratic all-class character.'[75]

Bleakley and other NILP politicians remained unconvinced by this claim that the Unionist Party embodied a 'democratic all-class character'. As far as Labour was concerned, a much more inclusive, class-based unionism could be promoted in Northern Ireland, and they used every available opportunity to push this agenda. It was a threat acknowledged by Unionist MPs, like Belfast MP Edmund Warnock, who confided in a letter to a Unionist Party colleague at the time:

> I am just as anxious about the position in Belfast. The opposition [including the NILP and Republican Labour MPs] hold 7 of the 16 Belfast seats, and our people are not getting the vigorous leadership which I would like to see. We have had three serious industrial crises

> in the past two years. Ten thousand men paid off in the shipyard, the closure of several of our great textile concerns, the threat to Short and Harlands. The inactivity of the Government has left a vacuum and a group of shop stewards has filled the vacuum, and has assumed the leadership of the industrial workers. The last election showed they wanted to be led by the Unionist Party, but they have looked to us in vain. The threat of further redundancy in Harland and Wolff will be a powerful weapon in the hands of the Labour Party in the coming election in Cromac. It is most unfortunate that we should have let the initiative pass to the Labour crowd, and I only hope that we won't have to pay for our inertia.[76]

Although he recognised the potential for Northern Ireland Labour's political challenge, Warnock also knew that a groundswell of working-class support would be unlikely to transfer its allegiance to the NILP against the backdrop of a continuing IRA border campaign. The IRA's so-called 'Operation Harvest' was conceived as a means of ending partition.[77] Although republican violence was sporadic, it did enable unionists to call for support for their superintendence of the Union at all costs. By making their own sectional agenda synonymous with the Union, the Unionist Party prevented a more 'powerful weapon' – the bleak economic situation – from being used more effectively by the NILP. However, this regime strategy would have profound and unintended consequences as some loyalists turned towards more extreme measures to fight an IRA threat largely exaggerated by Brooke's government.

6

An Ulster Divided Against Itself

> Under civil government subjects ought not to continue violence after they are secured from present danger.
>
> Francis Hutcheson, *A Short Introduction to Moral Philosophy*[1]

THE UNIONIST GOVERNMENT HAD PROVEN resilient in the face of IRA attacks in the 1920s and had been quick to repress physical force republican activities during the Second World War. Even amidst a total war, the IRA remained dedicated to overthrowing the Stormont government, and intelligence obtained by the RUC in 1943 suggested that the organisation was planning attacks against air wardens and RUC officers. The RUC had other ideas, running agents inside the IRA and interning its principal organisers and supporters in Crumlin Road gaol.[2]

Nevertheless, the IRA remained unbowed. Within a decade, the group had resolved to launch a new campaign. On 12 December 1956, it began its border offensive in Northern Ireland,[3] initially blowing up the BBC antenna in Belfast and attacking several RUC barracks and Territorial Army centres. The IRA's chief of staff at the time, Seán Cronin, was a former Irish Army officer, who had formulated a strategy of guerrilla warfare that blended tactics from the ancient Celts with more recent armed insurgencies in Algeria and Cyprus.[4] Initially to the dismay of some of his subordinate commanders, Cronin's strategy avoided Belfast, but they were soon won over by older volunteers who recalled the sectarian reprisals visited on Catholics by loyalists three decades earlier.

The new campaign was not without its challenges. Tactically, the IRA failed to issue its volunteers with maps or sketches of targets, nor did it think through the logistical challenge of feeding and resupplying its men. IRA volunteer Mick Ryan recalled how his unit was sent initially to the Glens of Antrim, a hilly outcrop on the north-east coast overlooking the Irish Sea. The wintry weather soon sapped the volunteers' morale, lifted only briefly as they moved from one hastily organised safehouse to another.[5] The IRA campaign was beset by further problems when it came to the actual mounting of military operations. Leaders of IRA's 'flying columns' were largely ineffective, their men given to frequent bouts of insubordination. Six months into the campaign, the IRA had limited its armed actions to occasional skirmishes in the border counties of Fermanagh, Tyrone and Armagh.[6] Despite issuing propaganda statements declaring their latest campaign part of the 'age-old struggle of the Irish people versus British aggression', which, the IRA claimed, was 'the same cause for which generations of our people have suffered and died',[7] such emotive language about a 'struggle of national liberation' fell on deaf ears in the Catholic community in Northern Ireland.

Unionists had spent the best part of four decades haunted by the spectre of IRA reprisals, subject to the constant drip-feed of alarmist speeches by their leaders, who conjured up the IRA bogeyman to keep their followers in a state of perpetual political anxiety. These fears grew in the early 1950s when several IRA members were apprehended while raiding British Army barracks for guns and ammunition in Northern Ireland and Great Britain. While the British authorities were effective in apprehending known IRA volunteers, their capture did little to prevent the influx of new members.

Mick Ryan was one of those who had eagerly signed up to participate in this resurgent campaign. He recalled how the emphasis was on 'physical training and developing our stamina, rather than on weapons or developing our shooting skills, partly because of the shortage of arms'.[8] As Ryan moved through his IRA recruit training and graduated into a special intelligence section, his main mission was the surveillance of other dissident IRA groups.[9] Interestingly, by the summer of 1956, the IRA had shifted its focus to training its members to develop their general knowledge of weapons and physical fitness, though they remained 'abysmally ignorant of military tactics and politics', with 'few if any' understanding how physical force related to politics or might play a role in influencing the government in either part of Ireland.[10]

In an internal report on its activities written in 1956, the IRA's Army Council said it 'has not been able to pursue as full a programme as it would have desired, due to a lack of finance ... which had indeed been one of the most disturbing features of the year'.[11] The knock-on effect of ever-diminishing coffers was that the IRA could not 'carry on essential services and is actually in debt'.[12] Nevertheless, it could report well-attended training camps where at least one member each of the IRA's forty-seven individual units received instruction in anticipation of resuming activities, albeit without full-time organisers in each of the six counties.[13]

The RUC's Special Branch, which was responsible for running agents inside the IRA, estimated that between 1944 and 1955 the group had received $16,600 from supporters in the United States.[14] In theory this money was earmarked for arms and ammunition. Uniforms and kit were another matter. Individual volunteers had to buy British Army surplus uniforms and sow tiny tricolours onto the fabric. Their leaders encouraged them to think of themselves in the same light as those who had launched the ill-fated Easter Rising in Dublin forty years earlier. The reality was this self-funded attempt at martial re-enactment was far from being as well-organised or led as its much-feted predecessor. Although the IRA continued its sporadic violence, it could do no more than raise a passing interest on the world stage. Republican violence, however muffled, did play well to an audience of Irish-Americans who would hand over a few thousand dollars in tin collections in places like Boston and Chicago. This support increased greatly with the resumption of the IRA's armed campaign, and a few weeks after this Special Branch estimated that the IRA was raising approximately $60,000–$70,000 per month from supporters in the United States.[15]

Meanwhile, Sir Basil Brooke's government lobbied the London government for support to defeat this new physical force republican threat. At the outset of the IRA's border offensive, Home Secretary 'Rab' Butler acknowledged how 'a strong protest should at once be lodged with the Irish Republican Government'.[16] This was echoed by Conservative Prime Minister Anthony Eden, who expressed 'the greatest sympathy for the people of Northern Ireland in face of the recent outbreaks of violence to which they have been exposed', while paying tribute to the police and auxiliary force, who, he said, 'have borne the brunt of these attacks'.[17] Conscious of ongoing commitments across Britain's ailing Empire, Eden resisted calls for a sterner response from London. 'I think that the whole House will agree that we want to try to avoid, if we can, this matter becoming even more serious than it now is,' he told MPs.[18] For the most part, London kept the violence at arms' length, periodically lodging its views via official diplomatic representation with the Dublin government. However, it did back Brooke's launch of internment without trial for IRA suspects, which came in July 1957, particularly when the policy was simultaneously introduced by the Dublin government.[19] Within weeks an RUC intelligence briefing to Unionist government ministers observed:

> The present IRA campaign has evoked no reprisals. This is due in no small degree to the influence of the Northern Ireland Prime Minister and his colleagues who have consistently urged upon Government supporters the need to exercise restraint in the face of provocative attacks.[20]

The briefing concluded with the observation that 'the life of the community remains largely unaffected'.[21]

While the Foreign Office in London focused on diplomatic overtures to the Irish government, which resulted in internment, the War Office promised Military Aid to the Civil Power (MACP), which would see some regular army units ordered to support the RUC. The army's garrison in Northern Ireland at the time was small, numbering less than 2,500 troops. The three regiments stationed there were the 15th/19th King's Royal Hussars (KRH), the 1st Battalion Royal Northumberland Fusiliers and the 1st Battalion Royal Warwickshire Regiment. Captain Alan Wooldridge, a Warwicks officer, reflecting on his unit's deployment at the time, recalled how:

> A little was going on in Ireland but not much. I was asked by some local reporter 'had we heard any shots fired?' And I said, 'Yes, we had heard shots fired,' which was true, 'on about one occasion in two years.' And it came out in the press as if we'd been under fire for the whole

period, the whole two years ... It was on the border. And it was in the night and an officer on patrol heard shots fired. And that was it. I don't even think he was fired at [deliberately].[22]

These regiments saw little action in Northern Ireland. A squadron from the KRH, which was based at Lisanelly Camp in Omagh, arrived in January 1958 and was immediately tasked with liaising with police officers in Tyrone. It also detached a troop of soldiers to help the police in Fermanagh. Many of the operations conducted by the Hussars included undertaking mobile patrols along the Irish border day and night, 'giving assistance to the RUC in the searching of specific areas for arms caches, searching of houses for incriminating evidence, reinforcement of RUC stations, road blocks, ambushes and showing the flag tours around the countryside'.[23] These were fairly typical of the tasks completed under the army's MACP mission.

Apart from military patrols, the Joint Intelligence Committee (JIC) in London, the coordinating body for all intelligence and security taskings in the UK and overseas, dispatched Brigadier Bill Magan, a senior director of the Security Service, MI5, to Northern Ireland. He first visited the province in late 1956 to help co-ordinate operations between London, the Stormont authorities and the RUC. Magan was Anglo-Irish by birth and knew something of the IRA, though his expertise lay largely in Britain's vast Empire, where he was a senior liaison officer between MI5 and colonial Special Branches. Magan returned to Belfast again in November 1957, reporting to the JIC that there had been a 'considerable improvement in the Internal Security situation' since his last visit.[24] In the five months after this second visit, the War Office would record sixty-nine separate incidents in Northern Ireland, with only one attack on the army, fourteen on the police and an abortive raid at a military camp in Blandford. In correspondence between Magan and the Deputy Director of Military Intelligence at the War Office, the MI5 troubleshooter said he 'had considerable difficulty in persuading the Ulster authorities to produce this Review [of intelligence organisation] and give it external circulation', particularly because they were 'exceptionally sensitive about the security of their information, and rightly so in view of the fact that they have had agents murdered in the past'.[25] As far as British Military Intelligence was concerned, the biggest threat came not from IRA attacks in Northern Ireland but from republican sympathisers in the ranks of the armed forces. As one intelligence report concluded in June 1958:

> It is not wise to underestimate the IRA in their cunning and ruthlessness which they have proved on countless occasions ... The IRA consider that they are 'at war' with Britain and this amplifies the seriousness with which the matter should be regarded ... The IRA will be satisfied with nothing less than a United Ireland (32 counties) governed by Sinn Féin.[26]

Magan would return to Belfast for one further visit in May/June 1958, reporting back to the JIC how 'the re-organised Intelligence Organisation in Northern Ireland was working smoothly and efficiently. This has resulted in a greater coverage of the IRA than was previously possible.' By now IRA attacks had dropped to about half what they had been in the proceeding twelve months, but there were 'still enough IRA fanatics to pose a serious threat, especially in border areas'.[27]

Despite the low-level threat posed by the IRA, the Unionist government remained fixated on the looming prospect of persistent IRA violence. It drove Brooke and his cabinet to make increasingly illiberal decisions, like the censoring or banning of any activity – whether security related or not – that threatened to upset community relations. The east Belfast NILP activist and playwright Sam Thompson fell foul of censorship when he tried to bring his fictional story of IRA violence and festering sectarianism within the shipyards to public attention. After accepting his play *Over the Bridge* for production in 1958, the Ulster Group Theatre company dramatically dropped it just two weeks before its original opening night in May 1959 because it was felt that its backdrop of the ongoing IRA campaign marked it out as too controversial. There were also fears within the Group Theatre's hierarchy that the play would foment sectarianism, the very issue it was attempting to highlight and challenge. The original director, James Ellis, resigned from the Group Theatre and together with Thompson opened the play at the Empire Theatre on 26 January 1960 to rave reviews and critical acclaim. 'It is a forthright, stimulating play that makes no concessions to delicate palates. In condemning bigotry it makes it clear it is a two-way traffic which, when it gets a grip, spreads and grows like a forest fire,' wrote the *Belfast Telegraph*'s theatre critic in the wake of the opening night.[28] Some 42,000 people flocked to see *Over the Bridge* in the course of its six-week run at the Empire.[29]

Against the backdrop of general anxiety felt by those who had come to see the IRA campaign as a real threat, Unionist MPs at Westminster were on hand to alleviate some of the fears by claiming that the IRA's campaign had been 'a dismal failure'. The Unionist MP for South Down, Captain Lawrence Orr, thought this was attributable to three principal reasons:

> First, it has not had the broad support of the Nationalist minority in Northern Ireland, and, secondly, it has been condemned by the Christian Churches. Thirdly, the Unionist majority has been calm and steady, and throughout the whole campaign there has not been one single act of reprisal. Therefore, the picture is not as someone reading casually the odd report of an incident from time to time might suppose. It is not a picture of widespread civil disturbance. It is not a picture which ought in any way to deter any man who is thinking of investing capital in Ulster.[30]

Responding to Orr, Rab Butler acknowledged the improvement in the security situation as well as the co-operative approach that Britain was receiving from the Dublin government. 'There is a great deal more improvement yet to achieve,' he told Orr, 'although we must recognise a welcome decrease in the number of terrorist attacks last winter. I hope that this will indicate the signal failure of the terrorist efforts.'[31] Butler rounded off his statement by paying tribute to the security forces.

As the year drew to a close, Bill Magan and his colleagues in British intelligence were convinced that 'existing tensions' within the IRA pointed to a fracture in the agreed direction of the campaign, with 'older and more responsible members' looking at ways to 'opt out of an active programme if this could be done without a loss of face'.[32] With 'no shortage of recruits or arms' and the 'majority of the IRA' continuing to believe that 'violence is the best policy', Britain's spy agencies remained cautious.[33] They viewed the imminent release of Seán Cronin from prison in Dublin at Christmas as a possible catalyst for an escalation in the IRA's violence, with hardliners seizing the initiative and ratcheting up the flagging campaign. It failed to transpire, even though some IRA hardliners, like Seán Mac Stíofáin, 'publicly supported the national leadership's decision to continue the campaign and called for an all-out effort by every Republican'.[34] Mac Stíofáin, who spent much of the IRA's border campaign languishing in an English prison, was so committed to the IRA that he took an extended leave of absence from the organisation after his release in August 1961 and was still on leave when the IRA's military campaign fizzled out in February 1962, with newly installed Chief of Staff Ruairí Ó Brádaigh ordering his volunteers to dump arms.[35]

Mac Stíofáin came to accept that the IRA 'would not have ended the campaign if there had been a chance of carrying on with any hope of success'.[36] With sixteen people dead (six RUC officers and ten IRA volunteers) and dozens of people wounded, the IRA were left 'exhausted and demoralized'.[37] Even Seán Cronin, its principal architect, believed it had failed to obtain its strategic objective because of an inflexible military mindset that was totally fixated on physical force, without recourse to the political realities of the 1950s.[38] Over the next few years the organisation became consumed with internal debates over the role of religion, Marxism and the future of physical force,[39] with Ó Brádaigh opposing the IRA's shift to the political left under his fellow Army Council members Cathal Goulding and Seán Garland.[40] Although the IRA's border offensive was seen by unionists as a failure, these periodic campaigns were regarded by republicans as physical manifestations of their perpetual struggle against Britain's occupation of Ireland – they 'kept the faith, offered example, and so were not in vain even if military failures'.[41]

The IRA's border campaign did something else too. John Oliver recalled how people in the countryside, where IRA attacks were common, continued to harbour suspicions that it would resume. 'The attitude of many people in positions of authority or influence across the country was becoming negative and defensive,' Oliver wrote in his memoirs,[42] suggesting they shared the views of their constituents. In some areas this caused consternation and panic, especially as the Minister for Home Affairs, Bill Craig, an MP who represented the loyalist stronghold of Larne at Stormont, began to close police stations on the border. The Order's Grand Master, Senator Sir George Clark, wrote to Craig in early July protesting at his department's decision to close rural stations. Craig's private secretary responded:

> The Minister stated that he considered the maintenance and security of Northern Ireland as his prime duty as Minister of Home Affairs, and where a Station was closed after a most searching enquiry, the centralisation of the R.U.C., and the use of Mobile Patrols was not to jeopardise the effectiveness in maintaining law and order, and that he was confident that any future activities of the I.R.A. could be adequately dealt with by the R.U.C.[43]

Clark thought the ministry had, nonetheless, along 'with the Inspector General of the R.U.C. and other advisors, gone carefully into this matter and he did not think that at this stage we could do much more. There was no further discussion.'[44] The Orange Order may have been a powerful interest group in Northern Irish society, but it could not force its will on Unionist ministers. Nevertheless, some members of the Royal Black Preceptory, an Orange Order offshoot, were not shy about using the closure of RUC stations in places like Middletown and other parts of Tyrone as a key plank in managing their own local constituency politics. 'It was not too late to realise that the peace was kept because the police were here,' Brian McRoberts told his local lodge in South Armagh, 'and it was no good pretending that the "eyes and ears" of the police were as good from a fast-moving patrol vehicle as they were from a resident police force.'[45]

This defensive attitude found a champion in the millenarian preaching of a little-known agitator called Reverend Ian Paisley who, on 28 September 1964, threatened to lead a Protestant mob into Divis Street to remove the Irish tricolour from the office of the Sinn Féin candidate and Belfast IRA leader William 'Billy' McMillen. The intervention provoked a firm response from the RUC, who pre-emptively raided the constituency office to seize the flag in a bid to defuse intercommunal tensions. The intervention, however, had the opposite effect. Tensions between the unionist authorities and the nationalist community soon reached boiling point. Several days of rioting broke out at the end of September 1964 in the Divis Street area, with the *Belfast News Letter* reporting on 2 October that this was the 'worst in the city for a quarter of a century' and 'went on for hours', with several police officers injured by an 'angry crowd which scattered in the face of police baton charges only to reform and attack again'.[46] A sizable number of the thousands of people who converged on the streets were children. The crowd seemed remarkably well-prepared for the arrival of police, throwing petrol bombs and hijacking and burning a bus. 'The scene according to bystanders, was reminiscent of the [early] "Troubles" – without the gun play.'[47] The violence was so bad that one RUC officer told reporters that 'things were clearly beyond R.U.C. control and the Army might be called in'.[48] Only the quick-witted decision by the senior police officer on the ground to block adjoining roads leading to the Shankill averted the spread of the violence into the neighbouring community.

'The threat of a return to the Troubled Twenties increased last night in Belfast as the Divis Street area of the Falls Road erupted for the third consecutive night into a battlefield. Blood flowed freely as casualties fell under a hail of missiles, and as shop windows crashed looters moved in,' reported the *News Letter*.[49] The newspaper's photographer, David Liddle, was confronted by one man in his forties who waved a gun at him. 'I'll look after you if you take pictures of this for the English papers,' he said menacingly. 'I would like the Queen to see what we are up to.' The man offered to set fire to a bus or arrange a 'better picture' if necessary. Liddle ran off, only to be set upon and beaten and kicked and his camera smashed.[50] The general atmosphere was one of pandemonium.

As the clear-up of burnt-out buses, broken glass and debris began, a handful of unionists and loyalists were convinced they had seen the stirrings of republican violence. It did not bode well with the fiftieth anniversary of the Easter Rising on the horizon. Over the next few months some loyalists contacted likeminded individuals in other parts of Northern Ireland, forming a right-wing unionist conspiracy that would give birth to a new paramilitary threat from within the ranks of Ulster loyalism. This time reprisals were firmly on the agenda.

Augustus Andrew Spence was a former soldier who had recently been released from a short prison sentence in Crumlin Road gaol for falsely claiming overtime in his job as a postal worker.[51] Spence enjoyed a reputation as a hard man in the bars around some parts of Belfast. According to one RUC file on him, Spence's father, Edward, had been convicted for indecent exposure in 1943 and his mother Isabelle was believed to be a 'notorious pickpocket'.[52] Spence's stint in prison had equipped him with a network of criminal contacts. It also equipped him with a personal introduction to his local MP, James Kilfedder, when Spence's brother, Billy, who acted as Kilfedder's election agent,[53] brought up the case in conversation. Kilfedder had been persuaded to lobby on behalf of Spence, helping him get his conviction quashed. After his release, Spence proved himself useful to Kilfedder by leading gangs of personators, who stole identities from dead people in order to 'vote early and vote often' and secure the return of the MP.[54] Spence's new-found connections with the Unionist Party placed him in a key position when 'certain Unionist politicians' conspired with others to raise a paramilitary gang for use in a wide-ranging conspiracy to bring down the liberal Unionist Prime Minister, Captain Terence O'Neill.[55]

O'Neill had taken over from Basil Brooke in 1963 and set out a bold and imaginative modernising agenda, which would see his mission 'literally to transform the face of Ulster'.[56] O'Neill had previously served as Finance Minister in Brooke's cabinet and knew the value of ensuring the economic viability of the state, particularly as Harold Wilson's Labour Party had promised to 'make far-reaching changes in economic and social attitudes which permeate our whole system of society', with a transformative agenda 'forged in the white heat of ... revolution'.[57] O'Neill also conceived his programme as a counter-weight to the challenge exhibited by the NILP, which he criticised for spouting 'hot air'. 'You cannot secure orders in competitive conditions by organising protest marches,' he told his party's ruling UUC.[58] It was a positive Conservative economic agenda, though it would also extend into other facets of life.

O'Neill, like Brooke before him, recognised the utility of renewing the social contract between the government and the people of Northern Ireland. However, they disagreed on the nature of these reforms. O'Neill favoured toleration, while Brooke opted to defend the sectional interests of the Protestant community. 'As I see it the tragedy of his premiership was that he did not use his tremendous charm, and his deep Orange roots to try and persuade his devoted followers to accept reforms,' O'Neill later wrote of Brooke. 'In twenty years as Prime Minister he never crossed the border, never visited a Catholic school and was never received or sought a civil reception in a Catholic town.'[59] O'Neill's vision was of an Ulster that was more liberal, tolerant and unionist – albeit not socialist and labour-leaning like that offered by Wilson to the remainder of the UK – particularly after the Labour Party was returned to power in the October 1964 Westminster election. It was a vision for the future that commanded support but it also invited criticism and, ultimately, conspiracy.

In November 1965 Spence and several other men travelled to Pomeroy in County Tyrone where they were sworn into a secret right-wing militia which took its name from the original Ulster Volunteer Force. This new UVF had little in common with its predecessor, except that it was formed with the explicit intent of undermining O'Neill.[60] Spence and other loyalists returned to Belfast imbued with a confidence in their secret mission. By the New Year they were ready to embark on their campaign of violence.

Through its network of intelligence officers and informers, the RUC Special Branch had been keeping a close watch on this growing militancy amongst loyalists in Belfast.[61] At meetings held under the auspices of Ian Paisley's church in East Belfast, it became clear that he and his followers were especially worried about the planned commemorative parades for the Easter Rising. Although these passed off peacefully in April 1966 – surprising even the Paisleyites – the relative peace did little to placate extreme loyalists like Spence. The new UVF had begun a twin-track campaign of intimidation, daubing sectarian graffiti on walls outside Catholic homes and firing bullets through the windows of Catholic properties. Matters became much more serious and violent when they firebombed the home of an elderly Protestant woman, seventy-six-year-old Matilda Gould, who lived next door to a Catholic-owned pub in the Shankill area. Mrs Gould was targeted on 7 May but did not die of her horrific injuries until 27 June. In the meantime, the UVF carried out a drive-by shooting in the Beechmount area on 27 May, killing forty-four-year-old John Scullion, a man walking home drunk from a night in a pub. On the day Matilda Gould died, the UVF was back in action, shooting several young Catholic men who were drinking in the Malvern Arms on the Shankill, a pub frequented by Spence and other members of his gang. One of the young men shot was eighteen-year-old Peter Ward, a former British soldier like Spence, who died of his injuries.[62]

Terence O'Neill was leading a pilgrimage to commemorate the heroic sacrifice of soldiers at the Somme when he heard the news of the shootings and promptly returned to Belfast where he announced the banning of the UVF. He was saddened by the emergence of this new terror group using a 'revered name in Ulster' to 'get support from unthinking, militant Protestants'.[63] O'Neill's government gave its full backing to the RUC in their attempts to combat the threat now posed by loyalist extremists who were taking the law into their own hands. By that point Spence and some of his co-conspiracists were in custody. The disorganised element of the right-wing coup, however, would soon give way to a more concerted effort to challenge O'Neill's authority.

Although he avoided becoming directly involved in the coup against O'Neill, Ian Paisley was busy swimming in the larger sea of subversion against the Unionist government. He was the figurehead of a new movement that would seek to fuse the religious and militant politics of loyalist extremism. Paisley founded a party, the Protestant Unionist Party, as a means of opposing O'Neill's liberalising agenda. According to loyalist pamphleteer Clifford Smyth, the Protestant Unionists were 'revamped' as a 'scarecrow party' to 'frighten the unionists of Glengall Street into adopting more right-wing policies in response to the IRA campaign and the propaganda of Irish nationalists'.[64] Paisley stepped up this 'scarecrow campaign' in the aftermath of a rapprochement between O'Neill's government and its Dublin counterpart, in which Irish Taoiseach Seán Lemass met with O'Neill in Belfast on 14 January 1965 and the two met again in Dublin on 9 February 1965. Paisley and his followers handed out flyers criticising the Orange Order's leadership over Sir George Clark's preference of an Irish name for the new city of Craigavon. The Lord Mayor of Belfast, William Jenkins, was openly criticised for inviting the Roman Catholic Bishop to a City Hall banquet on the Twelfth of July. His fellow Unionist councillors were equally lambasted for attending an event at a 'papist school' and hosting a 'papist' from the Dublin Parliament.[65] But much of the Protestant Unionists' hatred was directed at O'Neill personally, whom they criticised for inviting 'IRA murderer Lemass into Stormont'.[66]

Sir George Clark had been heckled by Paisleyites for supporting O'Neill at the annual Twelfth of July demonstrations in 1966. To his credit, Clark resisted the criticism by making the case that the Order had to adapt to the new political realities. At a meeting of the Order's Central Committee in Castlerock, Clark and other senior officials discussed the relaxation of their rules and regulations to bring them more into line with the O'Neill government's liberal agenda. The minutes from the meeting reveal that one of those who supported Clark was Brian Faulkner, a senior officer from the County Down district and the Minister for Commerce in O'Neill's cabinet. In a discussion on the possible revision of the rules banning the attendance of individual Orangemen at Roman Catholic Church services – such as at the weddings or funerals of friends or neighbours – Clark recognised it as 'a particularly difficult question, and one that would eventually have to be faced'.[67] For his part, Clark believed it was 'a question of individual conscience', feeling that anyone with a problem in fulfilling their duties and obligations of membership would have to withdraw of their own volition. Faulkner 'strongly supported the Grand Master's remarks', stating that 'in his own considered opinion there should be no change in the Laws of the Institution referring to the Code of conduct of an Orangeman', a vigorous middle ground that won him rapturous applause from other senior officers in attendance.[68] As Clark would subsequently tell those gathered to hear his speech at the Twelfth in 1967:

> We find there is a growing tendency for people to regard the words 'civil and religious liberty' as something which applies only to a section of the community, who feel that for some reason liberty is to be enjoyed only by themselves and that those who may be opposed to their particular ideals must be stopped from expressing their views no matter what the cost.[69]

Clark was again heckled, something he had grown accustomed to over the previous two years. Much of the opposition to the Orange platform came from Paisley and his followers.

In a poll undertaken by BBC Northern Ireland's *24 Hours* programme that same month, out of 720 people surveyed some 31 per cent approved of Paisley while 64 per cent did not. Complementary to this were the 72 per cent who approved of O'Neill's rapprochement with the Irish government. Intriguingly, only 55 per cent of those surveyed thought religious discrimination was a problem in Northern Ireland.[70] These changes in politics and society pointed to a thawing of community relations. Paddy Devlin, the chairman of the NILP's organisation committee, later recalled somewhat optimistically in his memoirs how 'for the first time in forty years there was a spirit of compromise in the air. People from the two communities were more prepared than ever to live together in harmony, and the old shibboleths that had for so long been sources of division were being closely questioned.'[71]

However, beneath the surface, sectarianism bubbled away like a half-dormant volcano, ready to erupt when conditions were right.[72] Ever since the RUC's decisive actions in early October 1964, there was perhaps more likelihood of clashes within the unionist community than between unionism and nationalism, but that would soon change. In a separate development within the Catholic community, nationalists and republicans met under the banner of the Wolfe Tone Society in Maghera, County Londonderry, on the weekend of 13–14 August 1966.[73] A few months later, in February 1967, many of these same people came together to form the Northern Ireland Civil Rights Association (NICRA). NICRA drew its inspiration, though not its model, from civil rights activism in the United States.[74] The movement immediately raised suspicions amongst right-wing unionists and extreme loyalists, who saw it as a new variant of IRA activity. But while IRA members were 'active in influencing the direction taken by NICRA as well as in its creation',[75] they were not the only people involved in the movement.

Despite the mounting challenge posed by this emerging group, some Unionist politicians known for their hard-line attitudes were beginning to think about how to meet the concerns of the Catholic community in terms of political solutions. One of those was Edmund Warnock, the former Attorney General and an influential backbencher. The Nationalist Party's grandee Cahir Healy wrote a letter to Warnock to congratulate him on writing an open letter in the *Belfast Telegraph*, which he said was a positive goodwill gesture towards the minority community.[76] Healy had found himself in the company of several unionists who were agreed that Warnock's comments reflected a prevailing mood of conciliation within the Unionist establishment. Warnock himself was surprised at the positive response and hoped it would lead to a more constructive exchange of views between unionist and nationalist politicians at Stormont and within the broader community. As he observed in his reply to Healy, 'no one knows better than you that tolerance, in Northern Ireland, is a very tender heart and will have to be carefully nurtured.'[77] Despite Warnock's plea for moderation, there was a mounting opposition to the Unionist government's gradual redistribution of rights from nationalists, which saw many of them 'abandoning old deference and seeking change by peaceful protest'.[78]

Within a year of Warnock's plea for conciliation, NICRA's leaders were readying themselves for street-based protest action to raise the issue of civil rights, particularly in relation to jobs, housing and employment.[79] In August 1968 civil rights marchers clashed with police officers in Dungannon, and on 5 October a march ended with a baton charge by the RUC in Duke Street, Derry. There was a sense that these clashes owed more to 'the *évenéments* of May 1968 in Paris, for example', than they did to 'the Penal Laws or the Battle of the Boyne'.[80] Mass protest was a key feature of the political landscape in Belfast and Derry, just like it was in London, Paris and Washington, but the changing demographics suggested that the younger people now marching in large numbers were 'too young to have any possible realization of the nature and consequences of previous Irish troubles'.[81] The vast majority of those who had pushed their way onto the streets were, therefore, nurtured in the relative calm of intercommunal relations. They had no collective memory of the 1920s and were less persuaded by the argument made by Unionists and the NILP that reform rather than revolution offered the best way to realise a fairer society.

Prominent Derry Labour Party activist Eamonn McCann recalled the divergence in those younger radicals prepared to put their feet on the street and those who were alarmed by the potential for confrontations like those witnessed in the early 1920s, in 1935 and in 1964. For McCann:

> The whole civil rights thing alarmed many people in the NILP. I mean … the party had supported civil rights in 1966, 1967, 1968 and so forth. It had in principle been progressive. Even before that – in the early 1960s – the Northern Ireland Labour Party was sending delegations to London … about fair allocation of housing, one person one vote, about the Special Powers Act and so on … [They] took a progressive view in relation to the sectarian setup here. But it is true that once violence started, I remember meetings in Belfast of the Executive of the NILP in which you could see that people were frightened; they were alarmed. Not that this was going to be a civil war zone, but just

about the idea that they might be associated with people who were in conflict with the cops. There were a number of people I remember who couldn't tolerate that; they couldn't fit that into their minds, because they believed in law and order.[82]

Electorally, the NILP had been rewarded for this commitment to parliamentary democracy, winning a significant proportion of votes at both Stormont and Westminster parliamentary elections in the 1950s and 1960s. The high point in the party's electoral fortunes came in 1964 when it won an astonishing 100,000 votes at the Westminster election, placing it second to the Unionists in Belfast. Within a year of the result, O'Neill's liberal modernisation agenda was costing the NILP votes, and David Bleakley and Billy Boyd lost their seats. Despite the reversal, Tom Boyd and Vivian Simpson continued to push a moderate agenda, believing the losses were only temporary. The party's 1966 position paper 'Citizens' Rights' became the policy basis for its commitment to a gradual redistribution of rights to all the people of Northern Ireland.[83] It was not enough to prevent the party's younger members like McCann from abandoning their ideals of forcible change via protest action.[84] The NILP was well-represented in NICRA and on civil rights marches, with McCann, Anne Devlin and Erskine Holmes being the most prominent members to serve on the NICRA committee.

Although the NILP had long made the case that all citizens in Northern Ireland, irrespective of religion, class or creed, should enjoy the same rights as other citizens in the UK, the party found it difficult to push these issues outside of Northern Ireland. With no NILP representation at Westminster, the Unionist Party could effectively insulate the province from prying political eyes. That was until the election of Republican Labour Party politician Gerry Fitt to the West Belfast seat in 1966. Fitt's difficult relationship with the NILP meant they could have no influence on the new MP, who was something of a maverick. He had resolved to overturn the convention at Westminster that prohibited the discussion of Northern Ireland matters. On 5 October 1968 Fitt led a delegation of Labour MPs to observe the banned NICRA march in Derry, which had departed from the railway station on the Waterside to walk along Duke Street. The RUC baton-charged the protestors, injuring Fitt, Nationalist Party politicians Eddie McAteer and Austen Currie, and the

NILP's Paddy Devlin in the process. Images of the frantic scenes were caught by television cameras and beamed around the world.[85]

In the wake of the Duke Street clashes, students and recent graduates of Queen's University Belfast came together to form the People's Democracy (PD), a loose association of members with a 'faceless committee' that intended to operate within the NICRA. The PD pulled together an eclectic mix of left-leaning, nationalist and republican individuals who were inspired by the kind of revolutionary language edifying protest movements around the world. In early January 1969 the PD led a 70-mile-long march from Belfast to Derry. The so-called 'Long March' – inspired by the more left-wing PD members who looked to Mao Tse-Tung's revolutionary Long March in 1930s China – ended in turmoil as demonstrators were attacked and badly beaten by loyalists. Some trouble erupted along the route, with the RUC doing all it could to protect the marchers, a diverse mix of male and female students who braved bitterly cold weather and bruised feet to make the trip. However, as they arrived at the Guildhall in Derry, Ian Paisley's counter-demonstrators again attacked the marchers with sticks and clubs. Forty people, including RUC officers, were injured. Some civil rights protestors toppled the nearby Christmas tree and used its lightbulbs as missiles. A car belonging to Paisley's right-hand man, Major Roland Bunting, was overturned and set on fire. Crowds of shouting, screaming people stood and watched as the fire brigade fought the blaze.[86] The prospect of sectarian confrontation that had so worried the NILP had come to pass.

'Ulster stands at the crossroads,' Terence O'Neill had told the Northern Ireland public in a televised broadcast a few weeks before the 'Long March'. O'Neill was a great reformer who had tried to broaden the appeal of Ulster Unionism beyond those who believed it should serve to keep Catholics in their place. 'For more than five years now I have tried to heal some of the deep divisions in our community,' he said in his broadcast on 9 December 1968. 'I did so because I could not see how an Ulster divided against itself could hope to stand. I made it clear that a Northern Ireland based upon the interests of any one section rather than upon the interests of all could have no long-term future.'[87] O'Neill's vision for the future, of a Northern Ireland which was a progressive part of the UK that paid its way and brought together all its people in harmony, was, despite his best instincts, falling apart. At first he refused calls for an election, which would have been 'utterly reprehensible ... against a background of bitterness and strife', but after the events of the march it was clear he had lost the support of key MPs inside his own parliamentary party. On 3 February O'Neill caved in to political pressure for a snap election, which was set for 24 February. He had hoped to shore up his position after an earlier vote of confidence. In a Declaration of Principle, issued to coincide with his announcement of fresh elections, O'Neill set out his programme for reform, much of it plagiarised from documents submitted to his government by the NILP:

> The Ulster Unionist Party believes in an Ulster in which the obligations and rights of all citizens will be fully recognised. It expects of all citizens that loyalty towards the State which is due when the institutions of that State have the expressed support of a clear majority. It seeks from every individual a proper sense of responsibility and wholehearted participation in the life of the State.[88]

O'Neill's hopes for a united community, however, had been exposed as an unachievable aspiration as tensions on the streets continued to mount between Catholics and Protestants. Despite claiming his policies were 'designed to ensure that all Ulster citizens continue to enjoy the benefits of the British connection – not just in high standards of services, but in high standards of fairness, tolerance and justice',[89] it was clear he had lost his political and moral authority. He resigned in April 1969, after a rejuvenated UVF terrorist campaign began bombing key utilities such as water pipelines and electricity substations.

By the summer of 1969, tensions had increased markedly within Northern Ireland's divided community, particularly in areas where unemployment was high and poverty and deprivation impacted on people most acutely. Trouble erupted in Lurgan after a Union flag was flown within sight of a Catholic area. Hand-to-hand fighting ensued and the police struggled to contain the violence. In Derry, police fired warning shots at rioters wielding petrol bombs at Butchers' Gate. Meanwhile, arsonists attacked Dungiven Orange Hall. This provided a hostile and antagonistic backdrop to the Apprentice Boys of Derry annual parade on 14 August, which prompted the outbreak of severe rioting in the walled city. On the same day a shooting war began between rival gunmen in Belfast, leaving five people dead in one night. The RUC Inspector General, overwhelmed and under pressure from Stormont ministers, finally relented and requested Military Aid to the Civil Power, a constitutional contingency to deploy troops in support of police only used in the most extreme of circumstances. It was the first time it had been activated since the IRA's border campaign.

As 1969 ended, the IRA was slowly re-emerging as 'necessary defenders' of the Catholic community in the North.[90] Yet, republicans nonetheless remained divided over how to advance their position. Some believed that they should avoid attacking the Unionist community; others, who went on to form the nucleus of the PIRA, believed that was the only route now open to them. What united them was the view that the British Army could not be seen as a neutral actor in the conflict now engulfing the streets. This was a tipping point from where the fabric of the state itself began to unravel and where communities that had lived together in relative harmony slowly began to pull apart from each other. The fear and anxiety that had largely been felt by right-wing Unionist politicians and their extreme loyalist followers – most of whom feared change – was now manifesting itself in a physical threat to Unionism in ways they could scarcely have thought imaginable.

7

A Regime Under Fire

Majority rule is not the same as unanimous consent. Northern Ireland is a society in which party loyalties reinforce discord rather than allegiance to the regime.

Richard Rose, *Governing Without Consensus: An Irish Perspective*[1]

ON THE EVENING OF 7 January 1970, Northern Ireland's Prime Minister Major James Chichester-Clark held a reception for high-ranking members of the British Army at Stormont. In attendance were General Officer Commanding (GOC) Lieutenant General Sir Ian Freeland, the top military commander in Northern Ireland, and several of his senior officers, including Brigadier Peter Hudson, the man in charge of British troops in Belfast, and his subordinates in charge of those battalions now deployed on the streets to keep an uneasy peace between what they saw as 'warring factions'. Also in attendance were senior RUC officer Harry Baillie, the Director of Intelligence and MI5's top spy at Stormont, Christopher Herbert, the Minister for Home Affairs, Robert Porter, and other members of Chichester-Clark's Cabinet. It was a night of celebration after the trials and tribulations of the past few months, which saw the army sent into Belfast and Derry to assist the police in the maintenance of public order. There was a spirit of mutual respect in the air as they sat down that evening to a sumptuous dinner and fine wine. Freeland wrote to Chichester-Clark the next morning to express his thanks: 'It was extremely generous of you to entertain so many soldiers and I know it was greatly appreciated by them all,' he said. 'I am afraid many of us stayed on longer than we should have done, but this was because we were enjoying ourselves so much and meeting new people!'[2] The reception was the high-water mark of bonhomie between the Stormont administration and the army, for the next few months would see a fracturing of relations, resulting in the mismanagement of the security situation, an increase in deaths and injuries on the streets and, crucially, the end of the honeymoon period up to then enjoyed between the soldiers and the Catholic community.

The army had been deployed onto the streets on 14 August 1969 due to a formal request by the RUC, which was not equipped for responding to large-scale civil disturbances. Although the British Labour government in London saw the army as impartial peacekeepers who had performed similar duties on the UN peacekeeping mission in Cyprus since 1964, this reputation was soon challenged by events on the ground. Stories of British troops enjoying cups of tea and sandwiches in predominantly Catholic areas were certainly based on fact, though this also tended to mask an undercurrent of ideological antipathy expressed towards the troops by some of those who began to swell the ranks of the IRA. Richard O'Rawe recalls how, as far as he was concerned, 'they were an occupation army',[3] a point reiterated by Tommy McKearney who sensed a breakdown in relations by the summer of 1970.[4]

Many nationalists became hostile because of the perception – later confirmed by coercive military operations – that the army was fixated on shoring up the Stormont regime, particularly as the military failed to adhere to its well-worn doctrine of minimum force.[5] There is certainly something in this, as many of the middle to senior ranks of commissioned and non-commissioned officers who deployed onto the streets in 1969–70 had previously served in far-flung places like Malaya, Kenya, Cyprus and Aden, where there was a philosophy of employing the 'minimum use of maximum force'.[6] However, while perception may have been everything in Belfast at the time, the reality was that most soldiers deployed in the city had quickly come to see the Protestant community as the aggressors. One of the biggest riots in Northern Ireland's history took place on 11 October 1969 and saw soldiers pitted against members of the predominantly Protestant community on the Shankill. Two local men, George Dickie and Herbert Hawe, were shot dead by soldiers. In retaliation, the UVF shot dead the first RUC officer to die in the Troubles, Constable Victor Arbuckle, in the same fracas.

Within two months of the 'Battle of the Shankill', soldiers were back on the streets, this time on the other side of barricades, in Catholic areas. As one former soldier recalled:

> Just after the New Year we were back in West Belfast again patrolling the now Catholic areas because the Catholics had now changed against us. We'd busted all the Protestant marchers ... and knocked all the barricades down and everything else ... So, '70 starts coming about and we were more or less getting the situation under control. At least there was no mass burning and murdering going on and we were in the middle of it. The B Specials were being disarmed, although I know for a fact that they weren't. It went from over the big raincoat to under the coat ... The Catholics were still feeding us up until Christmas ... Then, after Christmas, it went all pear-shaped where the Catholics weren't allowed, cos the IRA were infiltrating in now and getting a bit stronger. They were saying, 'the Army aren't doing a very good job of protecting the Catholics so we will protect the Catholics'. So that's how they gained strength. And the food stopped. They were frightened of their own people ...[7]

Ian Freeland held what the army euphemistically called a 'study day' for his senior commanders on 5 December 1969, which took stock of the serious rioting facing troops in Belfast and Derry. It concluded that the army's 'previous experience, training and the techniques given in the pamphlets, do not fully cover this situation' and that it had to respond to the situation 'with one hand tied behind its back'.[8]

The year 1970 was a time of new departures in Northern Ireland. For republicans, January signalled the launch of Provisional Sinn Féin following the IRA split (into the Official and the Provisional IRAs) of December 1969. For loyalists, the UVF had embarked on yet another bombing offensive and there were the first stirrings of vigilantism within what would later become the Ulster Defence Association (UDA). As far as the military was concerned, this was a time of deeper entrenchment in the conflict. The initial deployment of troops in August 1969 added some 500 additional personnel to the 2,500 already stationed in Northern Ireland. By January 1970 that number had doubled to about 5,500 troops, with some 500 additional RAF personnel deployed in an 'internal security role',[9] mainly at Aldergrove in County Antrim. Within a few months the numbers had doubled again. Some 11,000 troops from ten major units and the new, locally-recruited – and mostly part-time – Ulster Defence Regiment (UDR) were deployed by the summer of 1970. The UDR had recruited several thousand troops in its first six months.[10]

As manpower increased it became necessary to expand the number of army brigades. 39 (Infantry) Brigade, based at Thiepval Barracks in Lisburn, had been in charge of garrison forces since the 1950s. Its commander in early 1970 was Peter Hudson, a rifleman who had served in Kenya and Malaya in the 1950s. His opposite number in the newly formed 8 Brigade, based at Shackleton Barracks in Derry, was another rifleman, James Cowan, who had also served in Malaya.[11] The senior GOC was Ian Freeland, who had commanded the 2nd Battalion of the Royal Inniskilling Fusiliers in Cyprus in 1954–56. Much of the day-to-day management of military operations was left to Freeland's deputy, known as the Commander Land Forces (Northern Ireland). Between January and December 1970 this role was filled by three Major Generals – David Toler, Thomas Acton and Anthony Farrar-Hockley – who were amongst the army's most operationally experienced officers.

While the army was staffed by seasoned tacticians, the real problem was strategic and political. The Unionist government at Stormont was responsible for enforcing law and order; however, London was responsible for deploying the troops to accomplish this task.[12] Chichester-Clark repeatedly urged London to take a tougher line, particularly in terms of arrests,[13] but Defence Secretary Denis Healey disagreed and instead urged caution. By 22 April, Chichester-Clark was expressing the views of his government to Freeland. He made clear that the security situation, as he saw it, 'could only be improved on the basis of quick and firm action (especially in terms of numbers of arrests) against troublemakers'.[14] The army's failure to establish a firm presence in Catholic areas placed it at an operational disadvantage and enabled both wings of the IRA to build up considerable support amongst the people. British Army Headquarters Northern Ireland (HQNI) had been instructed to 'go softly' by their political masters in London and took the operational decision to remain outside 'no-go' areas. Behind the barricades, republican paramilitaries established mini-fiefdoms, making the old 'ideological inheritance of past upheavals available to explain what had happened now' and how the IRA could fill the gap left by the growing disillusionment with the army.[15] This would set the army on a collision course with its old nemesis and, eventually, lead to an escalation of violent conflict on the streets.[16]

Under pressure from its most powerful interest group, the Stormont government agreed to permit Orange Order parades in late March 1970. This decision shattered the tense, fragile peace that had existed between the majority Protestant residents of New Barnsley and the majority Catholic residents of Ballymurphy since the civil disturbances of the previous summer, which had prompted the deployment of the army across the city. The two estates were separated by the Springfield Road and had experienced a reduction in the number of Protestants living in both. The senior Orange Order member in the area lived in the New Barnsley estate and insisted that the parade should set off from the estate on Easter Tuesday, provoking residents in Ballymurphy to lodge a protest, as the parade would pass along the Springfield Road. In the last three weeks of March, the local army unit commander attempted to find a compromise between the two communities but failed. On 31 March, flute bands gathered in large numbers in New Barnsley and, despite agreeing not to play 'party tunes', immediately struck up as they left the estate. Ballymurphy residents were enraged and young people began to riot. The local MP, Gerry Fitt, later relayed to MPs in the House of Commons how events unfolded:

> When it was known that the Orange parade would traverse the Springfield Road which bisected the two estates, the member who represents that constituency at Stormont, the Peace Committees, both Protestants and Catholics, made representations to the Army commander in the area and to the police not to let this particular parade take place because the [sic] was a danger it would bring about violence. Whether it was the Stormont Government, whether it was General Freeland, whether it was the police authorities or not, a disastrous decision was taken to let that parade continue. When the parade was passing, many insults were hurled at the Catholic Church; many insults were hurled at the residents of the Ballymurphy Estate; many derogatory things were said – and I should make it clear, because this did incense the Catholic people – about the blessed Virgin Mary.[17]

The army could do little in the face of Chichester-Clark's government's decision to allow the parade to go ahead. As with the civil disturbances on the Shankill six months earlier, both communities were determined to go for each other's throats.

Although Official IRA commander Jim Sullivan and the local Stormont MP, Paddy Devlin, arrived on the scene to appeal for calm, tensions escalated.[18] The dynamic of conflict between the stone throwers of Ballymurphy and the army took a more serious turn when soldiers from the 1st Battalion Light Infantry and the 2nd Battalion of the Queen's Regiment appeared in Ballymurphy 'wearing gas masks and carrying clubs and shields, and supported by Saracen armoured cars and more troops carrying rifles, [and] launched another invasion of the estate'.[19] The limited numbers of troops available at the time forced the army into making a poor tactical decision, one that would have a profound strategic effect. By firing CS gas to disperse the crowd, it inadvertently radicalised the community. The PIRA now began, 'in the Army's apparent abnegation of its responsibility, to put itself forward more earnestly as the protector of under-pressure Catholic communities'.[20] With the spread of the use of CS gas, the army also choked off moderate political leadership in areas like Ballymurphy. 'During that spring of 1970, Provisional-IRA-inspired rioting spread through the Flax Street, Tiger's Bay, Lower North Street and Clonard areas like an epidemic,'[21] Paddy Devlin later wrote in his memoirs. For ordinary unionists there was a growing feeling of physical insecurity, and their demands for Stormont to do more increased in volume.

By June 1970, violence between Catholics and Protestants was reaching a crescendo. Further provocative marches on the Springfield Road on 26 June would lead Brigadier Hudson to deploy his soldiers in increasing numbers in the area. Tensions again rose and violence spread across the city like a contagion. In Short Strand in East Belfast, IRA gunmen sniped at Protestant civilians from St Matthew's Church, killing two men and wounding several others. A total of six people were killed and sixty-one were wounded in the clashes.[22] The army was now being confronted by gunmen, who were increasingly using the riots for cover. A report by the British Army later estimated that 1,629 shots had been fired from Catholic areas and a further 264 shots from Protestant areas across the city on 27–28 June 1970. Considerable restraint by the soldiers meant they only fired thirty in response.[23] However, it was the 1,600 CS gas canisters fired by soldiers wearing respirators that hung heavily in the air of working-class areas.[24] The *Guardian* correspondent Simon Winchester watched the trouble in Belfast unfold at close quarters. He spoke to PIRA commander Martin Meehan, who told him, 'and has told me since, that the first gunfire came from the loyalist streets, and that his "boys" merely returned like for like, in their mindless Ulster fashion'.[25] Regardless of who fired first, the net result was the same. 'The city was going berserk before our eyes,' Winchester later wrote.[26] One soldier caught up in the street battles remembered how the rioting went on all day long. 'All the business premises on the Crumlin Road were burnt out, including garages,' he remembered. 'Palls of black smoke hung in the air over the city, giving it the appearance of a blitzed town from World War Two.'[27]

Winchester believed the PIRA was 'responding to, rather than initiating, a desperate military situation',[28] while other eyewitnesses, such as Paddy Devlin, saw the more aggressive military tactics now in play as symptomatic of a change in political strategy following the UK's general election, which saw Edward Heath's Conservative Party achieve a surprise win over Harold Wilson's incumbent Labour government. Devlin was of the view that the Labour government's preference for 'containment' and 'playing for the hearts and minds of the people' was being replaced by 'one of outright suppression of the violence, which was only one symptom of the Troubles'.[29] Devlin and other locally elected politicians could do little to prevent the trickle of 'queues of young people, boys and girls, formed outside the houses of the leading Provisionals, all seeking to join up'.[30]

The violence continued into July 1970 and saw the army use increasingly heavy-handed tactics in its attempts to counter the republican threat, which unionists had judged to pose an existential crisis. A massive search operation and accompanying curfew centring on Balkan Street in the Falls Road area on 3–6 July ended with four dead and sixty-eight wounded, and when the army finally withdrew, the noxious CS gas they had fired still lingered. This was also the moment when deeper mistrust was sown between the Catholic community and the UDR, who manned roadblocks on the 'outer cordon' enabling regular units to conduct their large-scale search of the Falls.[31]

Frank Kitson, who had replaced Hudson as commander of 39 Brigade, would later claim that the riots in Belfast gave the IRA an opportunity to 'play on Catholic fears of the Protestants and they also had to discredit the British Army as a force that could defend them'.[32] It was certainly the case that the PIRA moved swiftly to capitalise on the rioting of 1970. However, by its coercive drive to disarm an enemy that had not gone on the offensive, the British Army must share some of the responsibility for escalating the conflict. Had it continued to practise restraint, then it might have helped de-escalate the deteriorating security situation. Of course, as Paddy Devlin rightly pointed out, such violence was symptomatic of a broader problem. Interestingly, Kitson shared the same analysis as Devlin about the best way to deal with the trouble, and that was through reform of the Northern Ireland state. As Kitson himself admitted, 'Obviously the best answer is to prevent the insurgents from becoming established in the first place by governing in such a way that they have no cause to exploit.'[33]

Amidst the drama being played out on the streets, Prime Minister James Chichester-Clark was attempting to govern in a more even-handed way. He had succeeded in making a 'series of courageous declarations of a civic-minded Unionism to his party and to society at large, and a raft of reforms the commendable and forward-looking character of which was in effect neutered by the mayhem in the streets'.[34] In one particularly heated debate at Stormont, Chichester-Clark contested the notion 'that a gun is the most useful weapon in the hands of the police'. In his view, far more could be 'achieved through public co-operation'.[35] Only when the problems of unemployment, poor housing, lack of amenities and the defeat of paramilitary groups in marginalised areas were dealt with could peace be returned to Northern Ireland.[36] In Chichester-Clark's view, a 'united effort ... [was required] against the subversive or disorderly elements in Northern Ireland'.[37] Shortly after his remarks of conciliation, violence would reach a significant new junction when the first soldier was shot and killed by the PIRA on 6 February 1971. After the death of Gunner Robert Curtis, Chichester-Clark announced that 'Northern Ireland was at war with the Irish Republican Army Provisionals'. Soon afterwards two RUC officers were gunned down in Belfast city centre. On 10 March three off-duty soldiers were murdered by the Provos in Ligoniel, leading to a huge public outcry. After a failure to secure 3,000 additional troops, Chichester-Clark resigned on 20 March 1971. It was left to his replacement, Brian Faulkner, to attempt to build a broader-based cabinet acceptable to London and the bulging ranks of those opposed to unionist rule.[38]

Faulkner took the helm at a time when Northern Ireland should have been celebrating its fiftieth anniversary. Yet, it was far from a joyous occasion for unionists, as much of public life was dominated by the escalation of violence on the streets. One of the formidable critics of the local regime, Gerry Fitt, took to the pages of *Fortnight* magazine to lament the continuation of partition, which he regarded as a 'frankly sectarian "solution" to the problems now to the forefront of people's minds'. Partition, he argued, not only divided the people of Ireland, it also 'divided the working people inside Northern Ireland on the basis of religious bogeys'. Fitt continued:

> People who have known those long, bitter and sometimes sad years of political activity, especially in the Labour movement, endeavouring to overcome the curse of sectarian-orientated conflicts, came to the conclusion long ago that normal or healthy political development was impossible within that framework.[39]

Fitt regarded the antagonisms between ordinary people to be 'unnatural'. 'The "common man" in Ulster,' he observed, 'has nothing to cheer about over the jubilee occasion.' He singled out the Orange Order as an 'intrinsic element of the administration and government of the place, leading to the widespread practice of religious discrimination as a matter of accepted policy'.[40] Fitt had long campaigned on the most pressing social issues that affected ordinary people, regardless of their religious creed. He believed they could never truly be united while they remained 'indoctrinated with the ideology of their political masters' and saw 'everything through a cloud of Vatican smoke'.[41] Fitt's criticisms were well founded, but he could not make working-class Protestants see the truth as they rallied around the Orange–Unionist state they had vested interests in defending:

> Without realising it, they become slaves to their own exploiters, so that you can see Orangemen carrying banners dedicated to the very employers and landlords who have battened on [sic] themselves and their families. Because of their sectarian blinkers, however, they

cannot see it that way, just as they cannot grasp the fact that the Orange Order has played a malevolent role throughout its history on the side of every reactionary cause, against every stage of progressive and democratic reform, and in defence of every sort of established parasite, from rack-renting landlords to greedy employers of slave-wage labour.[42]

Fitt was no fan of the Catholic state in the South either and thought there 'very little for the ordinary working man to celebrate in either' jurisdiction.

One of those who saw the merits in what Fitt was saying was David Bleakley. Although he lost his Stormont seat in 1965, following a concerted effort by Terence O'Neill to break the back of the Labour opposition, Bleakley nevertheless remained politically involved and believed the only way to change the system was by reforming it from within. As fate would have it, he received a telephone call in March 1971 from a civil servant at Stormont inviting him to a meeting with Brian Faulkner. '"David, you're always talking about the community working together," Faulkner told Bleakley when they met. '"Would you work with me?" And he says, "I'll bring you in as a full member of the cabinet."'[43] Bleakley recalled how he 'never had the slightest problem in co-operation. We were making a surprising gesture then that nowadays would be taken for granted. But it's the first step in the journey that's important.'[44]

It was difficult in practice, although, as Bleakley maintained, 'There is more difficulty in Northern Ireland in fighting and breaking the rules together than there is working together.'[45] Bleakley believed he was promoting the idea of the fairer and more inclusive society that the NILP had always advocated. He set to work with the overwhelming support of his party conference in April 1971, though his appointment was not universally welcomed. Johnny McQuade, the Unionist politician who had unseated Bleakley's colleague Billy Boyd in Woodvale, questioning Faulkner's motives. 'How can we have government of the people, by the people, for the people when we will have a man rejected twice by the people – Mr David Bleakley – on the Government front bench?' he asked. 'Mr Bleakley belongs to the same party as Eamonn McCann. The only thing missing from the Faulkner Government is Mr. Eddie McAteer, Nationalist leader, as Minister for Home

Affairs.'[46] Even some members of Bleakley's own party saw the appointment as a betrayal and called for his expulsion.[47] Quite apart from the fact that all his appointees were men, Faulkner said he had sought the 'best qualified' to 'create a broadly-based Government'.[48] Under the Government of Ireland Act, the Prime Minister announced that Bleakley would only be appointed for a six-month term.

Bleakley had publicly confirmed the NILP's acceptance of the Union between Great Britain and Northern Ireland in a public appeal to the electorate on the eve of the 1958 Stormont election.[49] He was a man of charm, charisma and intellect and, importantly, widely regarded as a good constituency politician. He was also an ardent Christian socialist who believed in protecting the spiritual and moral values of the working class.[50] Bleakley's trade unionism was arguably stronger than his Ulster unionism, a point that angered many unionists when he decided to walk in the annual May Day parade organised by the trade unions in Belfast. On the eve of the march, Bleakley released a statement praising the trade union movement, which, he said, had 'consistently and courageously preached the message that sectarian violence is the common enemy of Protestant and Catholic alike'.[51] Walking alongside 200 other members of the NILP and surrounded by fellow trade union members, Bleakley was jeered by housewives waving Union Jacks as he passed Shaftesbury Square, close to Sandy Row.[52] He continued as Minister for Community Relations until Faulkner's decision to introduce internment without trial on 9 August 1971, which made it impossible for him to stay in the role, particularly in light of the NILP's support for civil and religious rights and the protection of all citizens from the more egregious emergency legislation such as the Special Powers Act.[53] It was only the second time the Unionist government had appointed a non-Unionist Party member to the cabinet, with Harry Midgley appointed Minister for Public Security during the Second World War. It was a short-lived experiment that seemed to confirm Gerry Fitt's belief that the system was incapable of reform, only adaptation and self-preservation.

Violence had now bedded down in working-class communities on sectarian lines, despite the best efforts of well-meaning individuals like Bleakley. An accelerant poured on the open fire of disorder on the streets was the decision by the Unionist government to impose the policy of internment, which Faulkner announced as a way of returning security. While 'the manner in which the initial arrest operation [internment was launched on 9 August 1971 but would continue in stages until 1975] was undertaken was a mistake', argued historian Martin McCleery, the operation was 'not based on poor intelligence; it would be closer to the truth to say it had been based on limited intelligence', nor did it 'amount to an indiscriminate attack on the nationalist community'.[54] It has been widely held that internment was politically 'disastrous'.[55]

Belfast Telegraph journalist Kay Kennedy took a stroll along the Shankill Road in the week after internment was reintroduced. There she encountered a strange air of normality despite the increasing abnormality of life amidst the daily riots. Union Jacks, graffiti proclaiming loyalty or 'No Pope Here' were matched with a new state of mind. 'Down the side streets, bedecked with gaily fluttering Ulster flags and Union Jacks, a stranger is viewed with deep suspicion.'[56] A sea of eyes watched her as she walked along the road. 'Question someone and you will be asked: "Are you one of us?"' She noted an accompanying feeling of fear all around. 'It is a saddening and depressing experience but the truth is that these people feel genuinely threatened, although they are Protestants living in this most Protestant of Protestant strongholds.'[57]

Kennedy came across one couple, Ellen Forsythe, the caretaker of St Saviour's Church, and her husband Harry, who were busy arranging makeshift accommodation for Protestants who had fled their homes after being intimidated by Catholics. In an interview he gave to the *Evening Herald* at the time, David Bleakley estimated that around 10,000 Protestants and Catholics had been left homeless in the wake of the ongoing violence. Kennedy reported how the people on the Shankill were 'angry at what they consider the over-emphasis on the Roman Catholic refugee'. 'You'd think no Protestants were ever intimidated out of their houses,' Kennedy was told on several occasions. 'Imaginary fears and rumours became fact overnight and absorbed into the bitter folk lore of one side or another,' she wrote.[58] This febrile atmosphere enabled loyalist paramilitary organisations to flourish, forming vigilante units that would come to directly challenge the authority of their government at Stormont. Bleakley was in no doubt about how grave the situation had become. 'Our country is now very close to a terrible civil war, of this I am quite sure,' he said.[59]

The intimidation now plaguing many working-class districts peaked in the wake of the huge Vanguard Unionist Party rallies first organised in January 1972 and ramped up after the collapse of Stormont in March 1972.[60] Vanguard was formed in early February by the former Minister of Home Affairs Bill Craig, who had been sacked by Terence O'Neill for his hard-line views. He remained a party member until accepting the leadership of Vanguard in March 1972. Ulster Vanguard was conceived by Craig to be an umbrella organisation, rather than a political party, with the aim of ending division within unionism and conjoining its right wing to more extreme forms of loyalism. Vanguard, therefore, enjoyed close connections with loyalist paramilitary groups, including the UDA.

In the Rathcoole estate in North Belfast, the model estate built as an experiment in 'religious mixing' by the Housing Trust in the 1950s, Catholic families experienced high levels of threat and intimidation. The loyalist Rathcoole Defence Association (RDA), formed in mid-1971, had erected barricades at the entrances of the estate as a response to the IRA bombing campaign now underway across Belfast.[61] Although the barricades had since been removed, the vigilantes continued to patrol the estate. An anti-intimidation committee comprising representatives of both religious groups in Rathcoole was formed in early 1972 to counter intimidation and to help those families targeted. However, the group found it almost impossible to continue its work when the RUC and army refused to introduce more resources into the area. As one report from the time concluded, the RDA 'had virtually taken over control of these Estates [sic] and a collapse of communal order was evident'.[62] From the imposition of direct rule later in March 1972, some seventy-five families would be confirmed as victims of intimidation. David Bleakley's Community Relations Commission reported a similar situation in Monkstown estate, two miles along the Doagh Road from Rathcoole, and in Greenisland, an estate near Carrickfergus.

In all cases it was the poorest families that were suffering the most. Working-class Catholics were being intimidated by neighbours whom they had lived alongside for years in harmony. Some families reported slashed tyres on their cars, smashed windows and slogans daubed on their property, while others spoke of the physical harm inflicted on their children and of being shunned by neighbours at local shops. Most believed the security forces had effectively abandoned them. It was clear the RDA were behind the planning and orchestration of much of this intimidation in Rathcoole, though the group left low-level intimidation to the Tartan gangs, a particularly violent youth movement springing up in loyalist areas. 'I have no faith in the Police,' one victim told the Community Relations Commission. 'Very little. At the finish the Tartan gangs really and truly took over Rathcoole.'[63]

This victim and his family had originally moved into the estate in 1958, when it was touted as a model of peace and prosperity. They paid their rent regularly and were good, upstanding members of the community. But by the early 1970s they were being put through a living hell by the local Tartan gang. Although the victim and his family reported this intimidation to the police, all they received was 'tea and not very much sympathy'.[64] The situation worsened when their daughter was taken to hospital with severe headaches and blackouts, and their eldest son placed on a course of Phenobarbitone, a particularly strong medication used on patients suffering from extreme anxiety.[65] With the Unionist regime's vision of a model unionist community – living in peace and harmony according to conservative values – now engulfed in flames, unionists began to retreat further in on themselves.

Brian Faulkner continued to push an agenda for liberal reforms, though it was not enough for the Conservative government in London. Faulkner and his cabinet refused to rescind security powers, triggering a constitutional stand-off between both governments. Following a mid-week meeting between Faulkner and Ted Heath in Downing Street, the British government announced the suspension of the devolved institutions and prorogation of the Stormont Parliament on Friday 24 March 1972.[66] Power was now returned to the government in London, which established a Northern Ireland Office (NIO), with a cabinet minister to preside over it, to effectively govern Northern Ireland by way of direct rule. The army that had come to save them was now occupying loyalist as well as republican areas. Working-class housing estates effectively became armed encampments as vigilante groups roamed unimpeded, looking for victims. Violence soon spiked. Unionist insecurity returned as this once-dominant community confronted a Hobbesian 'state of nature' in perpetual conflict.

8

A Very Loyalist Coup

> Sovereignty is always shaped from below, and by those who are afraid ... No matter whether we are talking about a covenant, a battle, or relations between parents and children, we always find the same series: will, fear, and sovereignty.
>
> Michael Foucault, *Society Must Be Defended*[1]

THE UNIONIST PARTY WERE NEVER comfortable with being challenged on a political level. The decision by the British government to suspend the devolved institutions came as a complete shock. Brian Faulkner's party had built up what they regarded as an impregnable political position. While they acknowledged the persistent challenge from nationalists and republicans, they could never really come to terms with opposition from within their grassroots who gave their votes to Independent Unionists and the NILP. At the 1969 Stormont election the NILP had managed to win a seat in the predominantly Catholic constituency of Falls under the slogan 'British Rights for British Citizens'. The politician who secured the electoral success was the former IRA and Irish Labour Party member Paddy Devlin.[2] Devlin was an ardent socialist, and as he told his fellow Stormont MPs, 'I am a layman, a working-class man with nothing but instinct. I do not have a clue about economics although I have read a bit. My approach is purely and simply that of a working-class man. However, I can see clearly that we have two fundamental problems – too few houses and not enough jobs.'[3]

One of Devlin's first acts as an NILP MP was to bring a Private Members motion on world poverty.[4] He had bitter memories of his parents' struggles to put food on the table and, as soon as he reached adulthood, therefore, dedicated himself to ensuring people did not have to endure the same hardships. Devlin was an early opponent of the UK's pursuit of European Economic Community membership, which he said would see 'decision-making ... taken away from us. Indeed, because of her remoteness Britain will not have the same control over affairs.'[5] Despite his own private convictions on Europe, Devlin followed NILP policy on the matter, which was pro-European.[6] Devlin was proud of his labour roots and believed the broader movement played a vital role in founding and implementing the welfare state that lifted millions of working-class people out of grim living conditions.[7] As an implacable opponent of the old Unionist government, Devlin embodied an ethical socialism that placed opposition to sectarianism at the forefront of his political life.

Living in Andersonstown in West Belfast, Devlin saw the descent into violence at close quarters. He soon found himself drawn into street politics and became a leading member of NICRA, which dedicated itself to fighting discrimination in jobs, housing and employment. Devlin abhorred the sectarian clashes between the two communities and tried to use his influence in places like Ballymurphy to prevent an escalation of tensions. He was at a loss as to why the army was taking such a heavy-handed approach. The army's imposition of a three-day curfew on the Falls Road in June 1970 infuriated Devlin, and he lobbied the authorities to have the coercive measures lifted. However, by the time this extreme security measure was lifted it had radicalised younger people within the community, driving them into the arms of militant republicanism.[8]

By the end of that year, the PIRA had successfully increased their support 'in direct proportion to the weight of the British military presence in nationalist areas'.[9] The situation now saw the PIRA 'move from defensive mode into retaliation and attack'.[10] Tactically, this took the form of open gun battles between IRA volunteers and the security forces as well as the orchestrating of rioting. Despite the Provisionals' meteoric rise, Unionist Prime Minister Brian Faulkner was claiming by the end of 1971 that Belfast was almost free of IRA activity and that the organisation's morale was low owing to the effects of internment.[11] Indeed, the army had been boasting of the IRA's demise since October, despite the organisation contributing to some thirty bomb attacks and a startling rise in the death toll a few weeks later.[12]

On the other side of the sectarian divide, the UVF, which had been responsible for a litany of bombings and shootings since 1966, was joined in the paramilitary arena by the UDA, a mass organisation formed in September 1971 from local vigilante groupings. The UDA's motto was Cicero's *cedant arma togae* – 'let war yield peace' – chosen to reflect the organisation's rather ironic desire of seeing the reintroduction of law and order under a Unionist government in Northern Ireland.[13] The UDA's aims were to 'establish an organisation that would be able to take over in the event of a complete breakdown of law and order' and to operate as a pressure group to ensure that its policies were 'kept to the forefront of political activity'. For historian Thomas Hennessey, the growth of loyalist paramilitarism 'was related to the increasing levels of violence and the perception that the security forces could not contain violent republicanism'.[14] The number of casualties incurred by the security situation by the end of 1971 was 174 dead and 2,592 injured, an increase from 25 dead and 811 injured in 1970.[15]

The coercive thrust of the army's counter-insurgency strategy would soon prove disastrous. On 30 January 1972 British paratroopers opened fire on a civil rights protest march in Derry, killing thirteen people. Simon Winchester captured the mood best when he reported how:

> The tragic and inevitable Doomsday situation which has been universally forecast for Northern Ireland finally arrived in Londonderry yesterday afternoon when soldiers, firing into a large crowd of civil rights demonstrators, shot and killed 13 civilians … After the shooting, which lasted for about 25 minutes in and around the Rossville Flats area of Bogside, the streets had all the appearance of the aftermath of Sharpeville.[16]

In the wake of the killings, Ted Heath's government came under enormous international pressure to find a way forward and resolve the law-and-order problem without further loss of life. Faulkner recalled a telephone conversation with Heath in which, he claimed, the Tory leader did not seem to regard the crisis as any different from others they had faced.[17] Faulkner was prone to believing every word uttered by Heath, whom he famously said he 'trusted like a brother'.[18] Around this time the recently elected MP for

South Antrim, James Molyneaux, went to Faulkner and recommended he call a general election so as to strengthen his hand against Heath's plans to take back control of law and order.[19]

There can be little doubt that the devastation wrought in the Bogside by the Paras prompted London to seek the return of all security and policing powers from Belfast. Brian Faulkner regarded his relationship with Heath as a strong one and had even asked his party to have confidence in the Prime Minister. He did not believe the London government meant what was being reported in the press at the time about a 'package' of measures, including a proportional representation government, an end to internment and the transfer of security powers to London. 'I believed that the Prime Minister would not send me meaningless and misleading reassurance,' he said in the face of such intense speculation. Three weeks later, at Downing Street, Faulkner felt that 'the rug was pulled from under my feet', which 'came to me personally as a bitter blow'.[20] Heath announced the shift in government policy to the House of Commons on 24 March 1972:

> The United Kingdom Government remain of the view that the transfer of this responsibility to Westminster is an indispensable condition for progress in finding a political solution in Northern Ireland. The Northern Ireland Government's decision [to oppose the transfer of responsibility of law and order to London] therefore leaves them with no alternative to assuming full and direct responsibility for the administration of Northern Ireland until a political solution to the problems of the Province can be worked out in consultation with all those concerned.[21]

Heath spoke of a temporary, one-year suspension of Stormont, regular plebiscites on the border question and the beginning of the end of the policy of internment. While the operational responsibility for ending the violence rested with the army on the ground, the political responsibility for the region was now firmly in the hands of London.

The fall of Stormont was greeted with fury by unionists. For the first time in fifty years, their own politicians were no longer in charge. Fearing for their political future, loyalist paramilitaries mobilised onto the streets. Bill Craig threatened to form a provisional government.[22] He was joined by Ian Paisley, MP for North Antrim and the leader of the newly established DUP, who had recently cross-examined Heath in Parliament about his government's intentions in proroguing Stormont. Paisley asked the Prime Minister for assurances on the future of the devolved institutions and, crucially, that the Dublin government would not be consulted on the future of Northern Ireland. While assuaging Paisley's concerns about the security situation, Heath sidestepped the issue of the Irish dimension.[23] This would have serious repercussions in the coming months, as loyalists attended mass fascistic rallies presided over by Paisley and Craig, in which the latter arrived in 'an ancient limousine, complete with motorcycle outriders'.[24] At the end of May 1972, thousands of masked men formed up and organised into companies, three abreast, all displaying well-disciplined order, and paraded up the Shankill to a huge rally in Woodvale Park. Explosions could be heard in the distance as those lining the streets cheered on the men in combat fatigues and dark glasses. The reality was that in the absence of locally devolved institutions, an escalation of IRA attacks and intercommunal strife, loyalist paramilitary groups moved to embed their shadow authority in working-class unionist areas.

Meanwhile, in London, Heath's belief that direct rule would only be a temporary measure until a political solution was worked out was soon tested. Talks were convened in Darlington on 25–27 September aimed at delivering on that policy. However, they were limited. Only Unionists, the Alliance Party and the NILP participated, with the SDLP boycotting talks after withdrawing from Stormont following the killing of two men in Derry in July 1971 and the implementation of internment without trial in August. After Darlington, *The Guardian* newspaper led calls for a power-sharing settlement between unionists and nationalists:

> [The] army alone cannot win peace. The attitude of the Catholic community remains crucial. For that reason alone internment must be ended as soon as possible. But it is even more important to demonstrate positively to the Catholics that they are to have a guaranteed and effective role in the new politics of the North. In a community as divided as this, coalition administration is needed.[25]

The Guardian bemoaned the fact that unionists had been uncooperative on the matter, though noted it was important not to discount the psychological trauma that the fall of Stormont represented for them.[26] Unionists did not believe they needed to compromise majority rule to accommodate minority aspirations. The Guardian's suggestion that unionists trade power for security was a moot point, especially considering the mass mobilisation of loyalist paramilitaries now underway.

An example of how powerful the UDA was becoming at the time can be seen in the minutes of a secret meeting held between Tommy Herron, its leader in East Belfast, and the British Army's new GOC in Northern Ireland, Sir Harry Tuzo, the senior British Intelligence Officer, Frank Steele, and the former Secretary of the Northern Ireland Cabinet, Sir Harold Black. The meeting at Stormont was convened to address complaints about the deterioration in relations between the army and loyalists. Tuzo refuted allegations that the army had been deliberately provocative towards the local Protestant population. 'It must be understood', he told the loyalists, 'that the Army could hardly be to blame for the recent incidents since it simply was not in their interest to be engaged in East Belfast when they could be better employed dealing with the IRA.' In his opinion, he 'would be prepared to withdraw from East Belfast entirely were it not for the need to protect isolated Catholic communities which saw themselves as being under continual threat of violence from their Protestant neighbours'.[27] Herron challenged Tuzo to prove that the army was truly 'impartial', making the case that one of the Royal Green Jackets battalions based in the city had 'behaved in a fashion more appropriate to the area from which they had come and, behaving like conquering heroes, had over-reacted to the relatively slight disorders they had encountered from the Tartan gangs'. As Herron made clear to everyone present at the meeting, it would be 'unprofitable of these two forces to confront one another as enemies'; rather, Herron believed, the 'UDA and the Army should be seen to be getting together again and talking'.[28]

Earlier in the summer Tuzo had been open to the possibility that the UDA might be 'discreetly encouraged in Protestant areas to reduce the load on the Security Force'.[29] Although it was an attractive proposition for both parties, the meeting in October confirmed that the army had gone cold on the idea for one reason or another. 'The security forces remain responsible for law and order in this area, but it has been agreed that unarmed U.D.A. men may come and go provided they do not interfere with the local population or with the security forces.'[30] Nevertheless, although many Catholics and moderate unionists lived in close proximity to loyalist paramilitaries, it quickly became apparent that the British government was turning a blind eye to their violence and intimidation and, in some cases, even colluding with them.[31]

Despite loyalists killing 117 people in 1972 (republicans were responsible for 263 deaths, with British security forces killing 87 people),[32] the UDA remained legal. Many of the group's violent actions, including a spate of horrific stabbings and mutilations, were subsequently carried out under the banner of the UFF so as to square the UDA's public commitment to law and order with local pressures exerted upon its leadership to defend Protestant communities. According to one of its founding members, John White, the UFF was formed to 'take the war to the IRA', to 'put pressure on the IRA', particularly inside the Catholic community, which loyalists believed was giving popular support to both wings of the IRA.[33] Many of the murders carried out by the UDA/UFF at this time were motivated by both a deep insecurity and feeling of abandonment by the British government and a turn to sectarianism. Against the backdrop of 10,631 shooting incidents and 1,382 bombings – as well as 471 devices neutralised by army bomb disposal officers – UFF violence took on a grotesque logic. This turn of events, not to mention the 'souring of relations with army and police as conflict grew between loyalists and the state, gave violent men a simple, practical advantage: leeway for their actions.'[34]

Meanwhile, the Provisionals had become a force to be reckoned with on the streets. They divided their attacks between hitting security forces targets 'on the float' and carrying out scores of assassinations of Protestant civilians in North and West Belfast.[35] In many ways, the Provos represented a Faustian bargain between the conciliatory stance taken by leadership figures like Ruairí Ó Brádaigh[36] and a 'rampant Northern Republicanism deeply inlayed with sectarianism'.[37] The PIRA found it difficult to reconcile the contradictions and tensions inherent in its ideology and those members deeply imbued with an anti-Protestant bias.[38] What they also found difficult to understand was the essence of the so-called 'Protestant backlash', which was far from 'purely responsive or reactive to IRA actions'.[39]

In 1973 the British government turned its attention towards thoughts of creating a local political solution to the ongoing security situation. The publication of *Northern Ireland Constitutional Proposals* on 20 March, in which a Northern Ireland Assembly was proposed, was followed by elections on 28 June. The SDLP won the majority of seats in majority Catholic constituencies and later in the year would be persuaded to attend talks with Willie Whitelaw in October at which they disagreed on issues of law and order and internment but agreed to participate in further talks regarding devolved government and an 'Irish dimension'. The main parties agreed to the formation of a power-sharing Executive on 21 November. Faulkner's position as Chief Minister in the Executive was by now being challenged by his old party colleague Bill Craig, whose Vanguard Party had joined forces with the DUP to oppose power-sharing. Nevertheless, Faulkner persisted with his attempts to seek a return of the devolved institutions. At a subsequent conference convened between the British and Irish governments, Unionist Party, Alliance Party and SDLP at Sunningdale Civil Service College in Berkshire on 6–9 December, an attempt was made to finalise a political solution as envisaged by the *Constitutional Proposals*.

The resulting Sunningdale Agreement proposed one of the SDLP's key political recommendations of a Council of Ireland, which would give Dublin a consultative role. Loyalist paramilitaries stirred up by the dire warnings of Paisley and Craig were deeply concerned by the prospect of joint authority and promptly formed an Ulster Army Council, which brought together representatives from the UDA and UVF. Interestingly, the Sunningdale Agreement included nine clauses relating to security matters designed with the explicit intention of bolstering British attempts to contain the violence. Apart from entertaining notions of an 'all-Ireland court', which would enjoy jurisdiction over both parts of the island, the agreement also envisaged scaling back the military's role while returning the six counties to 'normal policing'.[40] In their rush to stop the violence, the British government sought to place power-sharing and an attendant Irish dimension at the core of its political approach. The recently appointed Secretary of State for Northern Ireland, Francis Pym, outlined this new policy in Parliament on 13 December. 'Throughout these difficult years,' he told MPs, 'it has always been said that a solution lay in a two-pronged approach: a vigorous onslaught against the terrorists, coupled with political advance. That political advance will shortly be a reality ...'[41] However, by increasing the anxiety of right-wing unionists and loyalist paramilitaries, the government left itself open to attack from a community unconvinced that the Agreement would make them safer.

The newly constituted Northern Ireland Executive met for the first time on 1 January 1974. 'Many people in the community saw the Executive as a useful experiment,' remarked the SDLP member and Executive's Health and Social Services Minister, Paddy Devlin, which, in his view, presented 'a real alternative to violence ... Nevertheless, a large number of loyalists were quite indifferent to the phenomenon of having people who were regarded as Catholics on an Executive and in charge of Government Departments.'[42] However, Faulkner's position as chief minister was severely weakened when the UUC voted to oppose the Council of Ireland on 4 January. Faulkner duly resigned as party leader but remained as chief minister. On 14 May, the Executive commended the Sunningdale Agreement to the Assembly, which defeated an anti-power sharing motion by forty-four votes to twenty-eight. Loyalist Assembly members present reportedly jeered Faulkner with shouts of 'No to a united Ireland – never' and 'No Surrender' as Faulkner beat a hasty retreat from the chamber.[43] In the wake of the vote, Harry Murray, the chairman of the previously unknown Ulster Workers' Council (UWC), issued a statement calling for a general strike to begin with immediate effect. The UWC had originally grown out of the Loyalist Association of Workers, a group based around the state's heavy industry, with close connections to loyalist paramilitary organisations. Its main aim was to oppose the Council of Ireland.

The strike was slow to start. The security forces noted a relatively quiet night with no reports of loyalist paramilitaries mobilising on the streets.[44] Despite the UWC repeating its calls for a strike the next morning, the trade union movement countermanded the demands by moving quickly to keep what it regarded as 'destructive politics off the shop floor'. However, the powerful emotional rhetoric by loyalist politicians calling on workers to down tools and walk out contributed to a fraught situation. Andy Barr, the district secretary of the Sheetmetal Workers and Coppersmiths Union, pleaded with his 2,500 workers to report for work.[45] Most did until lunchtime, when workers at the Harland & Wolff shipyard were threatened by loyalist paramilitaries that their cars would be burned if they did not walk out immediately. Nevertheless, unlike half a century earlier, many Protestant workers – as well as their nationalist counterparts – refused to be intimidated and continued working. Later that day the UDA sealed off the port town of Larne after warning that they would become 'a virtual occupation force'.[46] As in other parts of Northern Ireland, the UDA threatened those going to work. The initial refusal by ordinary working-class people to back the strike left the UWC with a strategic choice – either they could mobilise all those at their disposal, including paramilitaries, or risk the stoppage becoming a failure before it even got off the ground. The UWC immediately issued a statement making reference to electricity supplies, implying that these could be affected if their demands were not met.

Anyone who picked up *The Times* newspaper on 16 May 1974 would have been greeted by a mix of international and national headlines, from Israeli troops in action in Lebanon to the uncertain future of Rhodesia. Clydeside workers defied their trade union by continuing to build ships for the fascist junta in Chile. On the right-hand side of the front page, however, was a dispatch from the newspaper's correspondent in Belfast, Robert Fisk, noting how a strike called by a shadowy organisation known as the UWC was threatening to bring Northern Ireland to a standstill. Fisk informed his readers how it 'seemed last night as if the loyalists were intent on creating once again the old illogicality of threatening the British authorities in order to ensure that they remained British'.[47] Responding to national reporting on the UWC's threats, the Minister for Manpower, Robert Cooper, told local reporters he thought a strike would 'rebound on Loyalist leaders who give it support. They will lose support as a result of this.'[48] Later that evening, the UWC ordered those who had joined their stoppage to come 'off the drink' following an intervention by the wives of those on strike who said their husbands were losing money by spending too much time down the pub. Consequently, pubs in areas like the Shankill and Newtownards Road were closed; interestingly, pubs in Catholic areas reported a brisk trade.

The British Labour Party had come out against the stoppage and used all its power and influence on the Northern Ireland Labour movement to persuade workers not to back it. Indeed, a local branch of the NILP in Newtownabbey even called on the police to arrest Vanguard leader and UWC supporter Bill Craig. The Newtownabbey Labour Party thoroughly condemned the intimidation of workers, asking people to come forward with information. However, when television cameras interviewed a female employee of Carreras Cigarette Factory in Carrickfergus, she told reporters that when she did just that, the RUC said she should 'accept a certain amount of intimidation'.[49] Newtownabbey Labour said that if the strike continued into the following week, the RUC and army should be present in force outside the gates of all industrial sites.[50] For its part, the new Labour government led by Harold Wilson resisted the temptation to use force to break the strike, believing that such a move would provoke a bloodbath.

Despite this, blood did flow. On the evening of 17 May, reports began to filter into newsrooms across Ireland of a series of explosions in Dublin and Monaghan.[51] No warnings were issued prior to the bombings. Both wings of the IRA, as well as the UDA, were first out of the stocks to condemn the explosions. The UVF remained silent. Interestingly, republican spokesmen said that it bore all the hallmarks of an 'SAS-style operation'. There can be no doubt that those involved in the bombings had been ex-servicemen now in the ranks of the UVF.[52] Republicans such as Ruairí Ó Brádaigh of the PIRA and Malachy Toal, the press spokesman for the Republican Clubs, which were linked to the Official IRA, were quick to link the explosions to the ongoing strike in the North in their statements to the press.[53] Meanwhile, the UWC was still threatening a full shutdown of the power plants, which would have plunged Northern Ireland into darkness. Due to the walkout of power workers, only one section of the Ballylumford power plant in East Antrim remained operational, while the Coolkeeragh plant in Derry closed altogether. A bomb blast at the cross-border interconnecter on 8 February had still not been repaired, thereby disrupting electricity supplies further and leaving the ball firmly in the UWC's court. Nevertheless, Francis Pym's successor as Secretary of State for Northern Ireland, Merlyn Rees, was adamant that he would not negotiate with the strikers.[54] As he told a press conference: 'The Provisional IRA has tried to bomb its way to the conference table. Now people are trying to strike their way to the conference table. Either way, it's not on.'[55] The UDA's spokesman and leading figure in the UWC strike Glenn Barr called Rees' stance 'utterly irresponsible', suggesting that it was 'absolute nonsense to suggest that the UWC was trying to blackmail the Government'.[56]

By 20 May electricity output had dropped to one-third across Northern Ireland. Wilson and Rees responded by authorising the deployment of an additional 500 troops. It was a sign, perhaps, of the clear political challenge now facing London's plans to foist the Sunningdale Agreement onto the unionist community. For *The Times* newspaper:

> The strike called by the Ulster Workers' Council is explicitly political in its purpose. The strikers' demand is that new elections be held for the Northern Ireland Assembly in the immediate future. The politicians backing the demand argue that without fresh elections the will of the people is being frustrated, and their constitutional means of securing them have been exhausted without avail.[57]

The will of the people. It was an odd phrase given that the British government – in strict constitutional terms – claimed to speak on behalf of the will of the people. As the public face of that authority, Harold Wilson decided to personally reprimand those loyalists who thought they could usurp Westminster's authority. In his televised address broadcast on 25 May, Wilson referred to the strikers as 'spongers'. It was a huge miscalculation and only served to inadvertently radicalise those loyalists who had emerged as self-appointed protectors of their people. Despite further troop deployments, the Labour government proved unable to enforce its will on the UWC and on 28 May Unionist Chief Minister Brian Faulkner resigned, triggering the collapse of the power-sharing Executive and a return to direct rule. The UWC called off their strike on 29 May, having secured their objectives.

On the morning of 31 May, Merlyn Rees sat at the head of a press conference in Parliamentary Buildings at Stormont. Although he denied that the stoppage commanded the overwhelming support of the Protestant community, he did acknowledge an emerging spirit of loyalist defiance – framed politically as a kind of Unilateral Declaration of Independence (UDI) from Great Britain, a course of action taken in former colonies like Rhodesia – which was gaining traction within the UDA.[58] A few days later Rees was back in London for a special emergency sitting at Westminster on 3 June. He was in a combative mood. 'On 14th May the Ulster Workers' Council called a strike in the Province,' he told MPs. 'This group is a non-elected body of men that sought to subvert the expressed wish and authority to this Parliament through unconstitutional and undemocratic means involving widespread intimidation.'[59] One Conservative MP likened events to the miners' strikes, which Rees refuted on the basis that the miners never 'used guns'. Concentrating his gaze on attacks on three pubs and a fish-and-chip shop, not to mention the murders of two Catholic brothers at the Wayside Halt pub near Ballymena, he said the murders clearly 'demonstrated the violent forces which emerge, and are a consequence of, a strike of this nature'.[60] In reality there was a clear divergence between loyalists' understanding of the security situation and unionist views rooted in the constitutional arrangements approved by Westminster. The strike usurped Westminster's authority in setting up local power-sharing institutions, removing Brian Faulkner's ability to strike a deal with the SDLP.

Paddy Devlin was clear about what he thought was happening:

> The strike was never a strike in the sense that we in the Labour Movement would understand. It was in reality a coup organised for political purposes and carried into operation by armed men behaving as a paramilitary force and acting in accordance with a pre-ordained plan.[61]

Devlin might have disagreed with this very loyalist coup, but as Minister for Health and Social Services during the stoppage he still authorised the payment of social security benefits to the strikers and others out of work.[62] Intriguingly, the events of those fourteen days in May saw loyalist paramilitaries come to prominence in a civil society space hitherto dominated by non-sectarian trade unionists who would, in normal circumstances, have backed the NILP. For decades the NILP had been the one pro-Union party with the genuine concerns of working-class unionists at its heart. It had even pushed the agenda based around the greater extension of 'British Rights for British Citizens' to Northern Ireland. Yet the UWC strike trounced this more inclusive banner idea. The NILP could not continue to function without the support of working-class Protestants, who began to see sovereignty resting in themselves rather than in the hands of their political leaders in Belfast or, for that matter, 500 miles away in London. Ironically, by destroying the power-sharing Executive, loyalist coup leaders handed power back to the very politicians they believed threatened their place in the Union.[63]

For prominent DUP member Clifford Smyth – who would be elected to the Constitutional Convention a year after the UWC strike – the idea that Protestants were acting out of fear in opposing British policy on power-sharing indicated 'a very strong whiff of irrationality'.[64] He preferred to substitute the word 'fear' for 'distrust'. Smyth's analysis was rooted in the religious fervour of Protestant revivalism and what he saw as the Roman Catholic Church's 'determination to conquer Ireland',[65] though it was also based on the persistence of IRA violence. 'There is a vicious continuity at work in the war against the Protestants of Ulster,' he argued.[66] Smyth's deeply conspiratorialist beliefs found ready adherents within the upper echelons of the DUP in the mid-1970s. He may have even helped Ian Paisley to deduce 'from the constitutional stoppage the lesson that extra-parliamentary action such as a strike could succeed against the British Government'.[67] However, in Smyth's view, Paisley 'failed to appreciate the need to maintain a united loyalist approach and to ensure that future militancy would command the tacit sympathies of as wide a section of the public as possible'.[68] Paisley's conversion to a sectional world view was deeply imbued by a religious fervour but it was also shaped by his own self-belief that he alone could lead Ulster Protestants back to the promised land of majority ethnic rule.

In seeking to forge his path as the leader of Protestant Ulster, Paisley had to contend with the emergence of a 'new group of working-class loyalist leaders who had a proven capacity for carefully considered, direct action'[69] and, it might be added, a mind of their own. Amongst these leaders was Glenn Barr, the UDA member from Londonderry who was returned as an elected representative for Bill Craig's Vanguard Party in the 1974 Assembly and 1975 Constitutional Convention elections. Barr remained loyal to Craig after he shifted from the agreed policy of the United Ulster Unionist Council – formed by the DUP, Ulster Vanguard and Official Unionists, who were led by Harry West, to oppose Sunningdale – to seeking a return to majoritarian government and the removal of proportional representation in favour of a voluntary coalition with the SDLP. Barr expanded upon this position by remaining uncompromising in his views of a return to local government without the interference of the Irish government, though he believed in co-operation on agricultural policy and tourism. Barr's views brought him into conflict with Paisley when news leaked of the DUP leader's plot to organise another mass strike akin to the one Barr had helped to lead in 1974.[70] Although Clifford Smyth was made the scapegoat for the leakage of Paisley's plans, the reality was that Barr's colleagues in the UDA had informed the NIO in secret meetings they had attended with government officials in a safe house in Laneside, County Down.[71]

The Laneside talks had been facilitated by British Intelligence officers who reached out to loyalist paramilitary leaders in April 1974, with eleven meetings held with the UDA and a further seven with the UVF between then and the end of the year.[72] The NIO's intention was to gather political intelligence that could be exploited to help contain the volatile security situation. One of the regular visitors to Laneside was Glenn Barr's close friend and the UDA's Supreme Commander Andy Tyrie. Many of Tyrie's discussions with government officials centred on practical matters, including bus services for the wives and girlfriends of UDA members in prison. At other times, such as in October 1976, the NIO sought further detail on rumours of 'various independence proposals recently being discussed in some [UDA] circles'.[73] For David Middleton of the NIO, the British government welcomed these sorts of political proposals from loyalists on the future of Northern Ireland, even if they did not believe a UDI agenda commanded much support within the broader unionist community. 'The UDA's present attitude was that independence could well be a step closer to a united Ireland because the new state would inevitably become increasingly reliant on the Republic,' Middleton reported to his political masters. 'Mr Tyrie therefore thought that a better deal for the Loyalist population could be had by staying in the Union.'[74]

The NIO seemed concerned about the political and security implications that might flow from militant loyalism backing radical political agendas. A few weeks later *The Irish Times* broke a story suggesting these plans were intersecting with thinking within the Official Unionist Party policy. The former Unionist cabinet minister John Taylor was reported to have been building up an alliance with loyalists to oppose direct rule and for the return of the Stormont Parliament. 'Whether it's a strike or some other means I don't know,' he told reporters.[75] The NIO were anxious to find out what

Tyrie's own thoughts were on the matter, especially after he was quoted in the press as stating that it was 'time for us all to stop messing about and get on with the job of opposing direct rule'.[76] Did Tyrie mean the UDA supported a return to the status quo that existed prior to the prorogation of Stormont in late March 1972 or something more radical, like UDI? And, importantly, did it mean that loyalists would engage in violence to help radical Unionist politicians obtain these broader political objectives? Tyrie denied that his remarks carried any significance. As a political intelligence clearing house, Laneside had proved its worth, though it is thought its operation was run down by the time Roy Mason succeeded Merlyn Rees as Secretary of State for Northern Ireland.[77]

The UDA did not speak with one voice as it entertained the fanciful notion of a UDI. Prominent UDA leader John McMichael had formed the Ulster Loyalist Democratic Party (ULDP), which, within a few years of the UWC strike, had turned its attention to the question of Northern Ireland's constitutional future. In October 1981, in a letter to recently appointed Secretary of State for Northern Ireland Jim Prior, McMichael set out the UDA's proposals for an alternative 'viable political package' to the ongoing violence from loyalists and republicans. In sum, the 'aspiration' of the ULDP was to 'achieve Ulster National sovereignty by the establishment of a democratic Ulster parliament, freely elected by the Ulster people, whose authority will be limited only by such agreements as may be freely entered into by it with other nations, states or international organisations for the purpose of furthering international co-operation and world peace'.[78] It was a lofty ideal that evidence suggests was discussed in detail within the NIO, even if the civil servants who had engagement with loyalists believed it was some way off winning favour amongst the divided population. The trouble with the UDA's thinking was it wanted the best of both worlds. McMichael outlined how UDI would work by retaining 'a constitutional arrangement within the United Kingdom', negotiating 'a constitutional arrangement with Eire' and, finally, negotiating 'an independent Ulster state'.[79] Tyrie and McMichael had been influenced by Barr's ideas, which he helped to collate in an earlier UDA policy document, *Beyond the Religious Divide* (1979).[80] These ideas for UDI were bold and, perhaps unsurprisingly, failed to win broad support; nevertheless, they heralded a clear split with the DUP's political thinking.[81] There was undoubtedly some new thinking going on within loyalism, shaped by Glenn Barr's views on power-sharing with nationalists, albeit without an explicit Irish dimension.

Three weeks after the NIO received McMichael's correspondence, a senior civil servant in the NIO, David Blatherwick, sought a meeting with the ULDP candidate Billy Elliott. Elliott asked if he could bring McMichael and the UDA's West Belfast commander Tommy 'Tucker' Lyttle. Blatherwick refused the request and a follow-up request to meet Tyrie, despite the previous Laneside arrangements that saw Tyrie lead many delegations. Instead, Blatherwick met with Elliott and the ULDP's secretary, Mary McCurrie.[82] McCurrie 'did most of the talking', accepting the government's position that the involvement of the UDA in serious street violence 'could only divert the security forces from their proper task and undermine the Government's credibility', yet they reiterated the ULDP's view that 'Ordinary people from both communities wanted to live in peace together', ideally 'in a sovereign state of Ulster, which could express a separate Ulster identity acceptable to everyone'.[83] Intriguingly, it was the ULDP's position that a local assembly be formed in this new state, with a bill of rights and a system of checks and balances included to ensure no one was subject to discrimination. In articulating the UDA's political aspirations, Elliott and McCurrie echoed the views of those loyalists who did not believe that the government was on top of IRA terrorism, but seemingly 'as concerned with keeping Protestants under control as defeating the IRA'. They likened the position of 'Northerners' to 'children excluded from a discussion about their interests'.[84]

9

Prisoners of the IRA's Strategy

> I join with those brave and responsible leaders, clerical and lay, in Northern Ireland who have said to the Unionists and Loyalists: 'Do not become the prisoners of the Provisional IRA's strategy. Do not respond as they have intended and planned that you should do – in anger and in a manner that could escalate violence to new levels of horror and ultimately undermine your rights and liberties.'
>
> Irish Taoiseach Garret FitzGerald speaking in
> Dáil Éireann on 17 November 1981[1]

ROBERT BRADFORD HAD A PREMONITION that he would be killed. It haunted him. And then one day it came true. Bradford was one of Northern Ireland's most high-profile Unionist MPs. A married man with a young daughter, he liked to spend as much time with his family as he could in between frequent trips to Westminster. As the MP for South Belfast from February 1974 until his death in November 1981, Bradford had been a committed politician who put his constituents first. He was 'a very, very generous person', recalled his friend, Methodist Minister Jim Rea. 'He knew the struggles and difficulties that working people had.' Bradford had been a preacher before he became a politician. He was dedicated to public service and to helping those less fortunate in society. He was incredibly generous towards those he liked and even kinder to strangers in need. But Bradford could be bruising towards his opponents. As a politician, he didn't mince his words. He quickly earned a reputation for tough talking on the security situation. As a result, he became an implacable enemy of the PIRA.

In some of his more animated speeches in the House of Commons,

Bradford warned his fellow parliamentarians of the danger posed by terrorism. 'We must destroy the morale of the IRA,' he said in a speech in July 1981. 'We must put its objective beyond its reach, its touch and its attainment.'[2] On another occasion, he even lobbied for the return of capital punishment for convicted IRA terrorists, whom he accused of treason. Bradford would have been well aware of the reception his views received amongst republicans; after all, he made the most of his hard-line public statements in the immediate context of the hunger strike by IRA prisoners in HMP Maze. One after another, the prisoners refused food and water – their objective was to ensure they remained political prisoners in the face of British attempts to designate them as common criminals. Captured IRA volunteers had been down this road before. Every generation had resorted to the tactic of hunger striking since the days when Cork's Lord Mayor, Terence MacSwiney, turned his body into a weapon to fight against what he viewed as British injustice during the Anglo-Irish War of Independence.

Almost sixty years on from MacSwiney's prison protest, the IRA reluctantly endorsed its prisoners' decision to turn to hunger striking as a way of forcing concessions from the British.[3] One of the founding members of the PIRA, Tommy Gorman, had been involved in the so-called 'No Wash' or 'Blanket' protests in the late 1970s, which preceded the 1981 strike. 'On the blanket, we were so focused,' he said:

> You'd this paradox. Just physically, like. You were surrounded by shite but your mind was crystal clear. Because you'd no distractions. There was no TV. You were just fucking concentrating on the one thing: beating these bastards! We beat them by the old Terence McSweeney [*sic*] thing. We were suffering. We were suffering in silence. You know. 'It is not those who can inflict the most, it is those who can suffer the most who will conquer.'[4]

'Beating the bastards,' as he put it, was the way to do it. For the Provisionals the hunger strike was one of several tactics to be deployed in their armed struggle against the British.

In his prison writings, Gorman's friend and fellow IRA prisoner Bobby Sands recalled a story his grandfather told him of a lark that was imprisoned by a man who tried to force it to sing on command. The bird refused. The man threw a blanket over it, denying it the pleasures of its natural habitat and still it refused. The bird subsequently died from this harsh treatment. For Sands, the lark symbolised freedom and resistance; the story was a kind of parable that contained within it the idea that the prisoner should never conform to the whims of the system that imprisoned him. 'Eventually, if incarcerated long enough, he becomes institutionalised, becoming a type of machine, not thinking for himself, his captors dominating and controlling him.' It was, therefore, essential that the IRA prisoners not only endure the legal privations imposed upon them by their captors, but also incur more by refusing food and water, while their comrades beyond the prison walls remained open to more extreme, extrajudicial measures. Despite their moralising about absorbing judicial and physical punishment, republicans were always prepared to 'inflict the most' on their enemies.

Over the next few months, comrades of Gorman and Sands on the IRA's General Headquarters Staff decided to 'beat the bastards' by plotting against those who had traded blows with them in public. People like Robert Bradford. Of all the Unionist politicians on the IRA's hit-list at the time, only Ian Paisley rivalled Bradford for the top slot. In recognition of this danger, senior police officers in the RUC designated the South Belfast MP as a 'key person' and assigned him a bodyguard.

The IRA chose Saturday 14 November 1981 as the date for Bradford's assassination. They knew he held a regular weekend surgery in a community centre in Finaghy for his constituents and had a reputation as a reliable MP who never missed an appointment. A few days earlier the IRA dispatched one of its volunteers to carry out reconnaissance on the centre. He had noted the layout of the building, the access doors and, most importantly, the location of the office used by Bradford in his weekly surgeries. The recce was invaluable and added to the IRA's meticulous planning. On the day selected for Bradford's death, three IRA volunteers arrived outside the community centre by car. They were dressed in white, paint-spattered boiler suits, and two of them carried a plank of wood. It was an elaborate ruse designed to allow them to bluff their way into the building. Bradford's RUC bodyguard suspected as much and promptly broke off his conversation with the caretaker, twenty-nine-year-old Ken Campbell, to challenge the men, whereupon they quickly produced guns, shouting, 'Freeze.' The policeman tried to draw his pistol but was restrained by one of the gunmen.[5] The two other gunmen then entered the community centre, one armed with a Thompson sub-machine gun. They made their way through to the back office, where they shot Bradford as he sat behind his desk.[6]

One eyewitness had been standing in the hallway outside the office when he heard the first shot. He reacted instinctively and quickly ushered people into a public toilet for their own safety. 'Then there was a flurry of gunfire,' he recalled:

> A lot of screaming and shouting and what have you. When I came out, I don't think they'd actually left when I came out because I could see the backs of them. And I don't know what it was, I walked into the room where Bradford was and seen he'd been shot somewhere about the face, in the chest and, I think, in the eye because his glasses were sitting, you know, at the bottom of his nose.[7]

Before they left the centre, one of the IRA members shot dead Ken Campbell. The three gunmen piled into a getaway car, which then sped off. Robert Bradford and Ken Campbell were the latest victims in a conflict that had taken the lives of almost 2,500 people since 1966.

Bradford's death was discussed in the House of Commons two days later. Enoch Powell, Bradford's party colleague in South Down, was among the first to pay tribute to him.[8] Prime Minister Margaret Thatcher spoke for those on both sides of the House when she said that the government would 'pursue with the utmost vigour those who committed this wicked crime and we shall persevere in our duty to rid our country of the evil of terrorism'.[9] Gerry Fitt, who had left the SDLP in the late 1970s and served as an Independent Labour MP for West Belfast, called Bradford 'a man of rich humanity and compassion' and said his murder would 'bring the contempt of us all on those responsible for this callous deed', calling it a 'carefully calculated and meticulously planned murder' by people 'trying to drive the Northern Ireland community into total conflict and civil war'.[10]

But it was Ian Paisley who was both vociferous in his condemnation and cryptic in his belief that there might well be further empty seats in

Parliament before the end of the year. Paisley's prophesy came in the wake of the Provisionals' murder of retired speaker of the old Stormont House of Commons Sir Norman Stronge and his son James at their mansion, Tynan Abbey, near Middletown in County Armagh earlier that year. He also spoke from a personal perspective as, almost five months earlier, he had himself narrowly escaped an assassination attempt when the police car he was travelling in through Belfast city centre was targeted by a republican gunman who fired several shots from the Markets area. The group responsible blamed Paisley's 'incitement to hatred against the nationalist population', which made him 'a legitimate target and his security can be easily breached at any time'.[11] They threatened to return to finish the job. After the incident, Paisley's wife, Eileen, told reporters that her husband had been targeted before, though never by bullets fired directly at him. 'We had shots fired at the house at one time and someone also put a bomb outside our house before we moved in and destroyed the bay window,' Mrs Paisley said. 'This sort of thing will not deter him,' she continued. 'Whenever your life is in God's Hands nothing can harm you, except by his will.'[12] Within a matter of weeks of the attempt on Paisley's life, the PIRA had reportedly hired an assassin to kill Paisley's deputy, Peter Robinson, while on a visit to the United States. The FBI raided the temporary address of a twenty-seven-year-old Englishman in New York, arresting him on suspicion of plotting to murder the East Belfast MP. The man was in possession of a sub-machine gun, a revolver and ammunition at the time.[13]

It was a tense time for Unionist politicians as militant republicanism now threatened their personal safety. Two months before Bradford's assassination, UUP leader James Molyneaux met with the new Secretary of State, Jim Prior. He had a blunt message for Prior and proceeded to outline recommendations to 'avoid falling into the trap of searching for political solutions [to the violence]. There were none. The political vacuum in Northern Ireland should be filled by restoring Stormont, not necessarily exactly in its pre-1972 form but still based on the Westminster model.'[14] Molyneaux believed matters like education, health and, in time, law and order should be devolved. 'The SDLP were in disarray [due to their decision to stand aside for Sinn Féin in the Hunger Strike election, which saw a reduction in their vote share] and he did not envisage the emergence of a new cohesive minority party for ten years,' he told Prior. The Secretary of State was surprised at Molyneaux's demand for the restoration of Stormont and took the opportunity to reiterate the Conservative Party's policy that there 'could be no kind of devolved government without adequate protection for the rights of the minority and without their being able to participate in it'.[15] It was clear from a later NIO meeting with Frank Millar, the UUP's parliamentary researcher in London, that Molyneaux was testing the water with Prior before reporting back to the UUP's Executive Committee on the viability of devolution. In reality, the UUP's hierarchy was busy formulating a new slogan of 'British Rights for British Citizens', which sought to offer an integrationist alternative to the DUP's calls for devolution modelled on the collapsed Stormont system. According to Millar, the 'devolutionists were now being forced by the strength of this argument to float power-sharing concepts'.[16] It was reflective of tensions now manifest within the UUP, with the main fault lines being between those who favoured devolution and those who wanted greater integration with Great Britain.[17]

In consultation with grassroots UUP members, the NIO found 'disenchantment with the Molyneaux style of leadership'. One UUP councillor in Lisburn, Billy Bleakes, referred to some of the more affluent members of the party as the 'old fur coat brigade', which he said 'cut less ice nowadays with working-class Unionists'. Bleakes believed this was a challenge to the UUP's core support base, whom, he cautioned, might find themselves better aligned with the DUP, who were quite effective in managing their policies, so they better reflected the class interests of the loyalist community in both urban and rural areas. According to those political sources feeding the NIO information, there was something of a renewed urgency in some grassroots districts for a form of 'devolved government within a framework which secured their Britishness but left them with their own Ulster identity'.[18] The NIO believed there was now a shift in views within the party. 'Unionists have long had a deep mistrust of Westminster's commitment to the union, to the fight against terrorism and to the well-being of Ulster's economy.' One senior civil servant reported that 'ordinary working-class Protestants are increasingly convinced that the two main Unionist parties ignore the real issues, such as unemployment and housing'. Astonishingly, the NIO thought that many 'paramilitary groups have long wanted to do away with the sectarian divide and come to terms with the Republican [*sic*], e.g. in an independent Ulster. They have no hang-ups about links with the South, so long as each neighbour keeps to his own side of the garden fence.'[19] For senior NIO officials, this all spoke to 'the possibility of an honourable settlement between unionist and nationalist'. It was a sign, perhaps, that unionists were becoming more inclusive in their political outlook. One NIO official, however, warned of the dangers of trying to 'take the movement over, or channel it', which would 'expose it to Paisleyite attacks (as a tool of Westminster) and kill it'.[20] As a close friend of Ian Paisley, Bradford was perceived to have been flirting with more hard-line DUP positions on security. His death, therefore, removed another implacable opponent to rapprochement between unionists and nationalists.

A few hours after Bradford's murder, Molyneaux led a delegation, which included Harold McCusker and Councillors Billy Bleakes and Ken Maginnis, to register their revulsion at the killing with senior officials in the NIO. They were received by Jim Prior's parliamentary colleague and deputy, Kenneth Scott MP, and the senior civil servant in charge of the security side of the NIO, John Blelloch. 'There was a strong feeling of discontent amongst loyalists in Northern Ireland and a widely held view that security policy was not working,' Molyneaux told both men. McCusker believed the low level of confidence in the government was such that public representatives were now 'speculating about who would be next to be killed'. Maginnis recalled an earlier meeting he'd had with RUC Chief Constable John Hermon, which resulted in the Fermanagh unionist telling Hermon how best to deal with the terrorist problem. Tellingly, Maginnis 'warned that if nothing was done or was seen to be done by the Chief Constable and GOC, then Protestants would be forced to look to their own defences'.[21] It was clear from the meeting that grassroots unionists believed Northern Ireland was 'rapidly approaching a civil war situation'.[22] Scott cautioned against talk of vigilantism, which he told the UUP delegation, 'would merely have the effect of making the job of the security forces far more difficult than it might otherwise be and of diverting attention away from the real problems'.[23]

Despite the lofty pragmatism urged upon the UUP by Scott and Blelloch, there could be no doubting the reality that Bradford's murder – and the attempted murders of other Unionist politicians – rapidly increased the fear of mortal danger for many unionists. It also made them less likely to respect any political decision that threatened their position in the Union with Great Britain. As Molyneaux told the writer Padraig O'Malley in the wake of the Bradford murder:

> If 51 percent of the people of Northern Ireland in a free and open election opted for some form of unification, my party would have to accept it democratically. When you say 'accept,' presumably you're asking whether we would take up arms to resist it. As a political party I don't think that we would. But then you're leaving out of account the people who wouldn't be under the influence of any politicians – and there would be a growing number of them in those circumstances who would, if they felt that they were being pushed into a united Ireland against their will, without adequate safeguards and all the rest of it; then I think you'll find the strength of the paramilitaries vastly increased.[24]

Such language, whether uttered privately or in public, reflected a hardening of unionist views. They would not be coerced or cajoled into accepting any political arrangement that left them in what some of their leaders construed as a halfway house to Irish unification. Over the next few months, Prior and the NIO continued to press unionism to accept the concept of power-sharing, though only with explicit safeguards for the minority community. This had been a central plank of the NIO's agenda since 8 March 1982. Molyneaux condemned this in an address to the UUC on 11 June 1982, reiterating his party's objections to government proposals.[25] Basking in the afterglow of British military victory in the ten-week Falklands War, Molyneaux talked up his belief that Britain was a 'nation which is only at the beginning of the adventure of discovery. It is a greatness in which Ulster shares, for greatness is indivisible.' Ulster, he said, stood 'braced and ready to serve the nation of which we are and will remain an indispensable component'.[26]

It was around this time that Molyneaux felt the NIO were looking for ways to replace him by courting his rival Harold McCusker, the MP for Mid Ulster, who met regularly with civil servants. Molyneaux even joked with one of his parliamentary researchers at the time that 'McCusker wants my job. He's been promised devolved government with assurances for unionism.'[27] Interestingly, the possibility of McCusker mounting a leadership challenge had first been mooted in a meeting with an NIO source inside the UUP, David Trimble, who told one official on 9 April 1981 how 'he did not rule out an attempt to unseat Mr Molyneaux as OUP leader if the party did badly in May'.[28] Later that year Trimble sounded out the NIO on his own views on devolution, which he was beginning to form and push inside the UUP. As far as Trimble was concerned, 'there was considerable grass-root support for devolution', though this was principally for 'an unreformed Stormont'.[29] The NIO official thought such optimism would present 'Trimble and his friends' with some difficulty if they managed to convince their party of the merit of the proposal, only to see it unravel on the finer points of negotiation with the SDLP, which was considered to be enabling Provisional republicanism's turn towards electoralism at the time. Although Trimble and those NIO civil servants who met with him later denied he was 'an informer of any kind', matters did come to a head following a damaging disclosure of one civil servant's indiscreet comments to a PhD student who also worked as a parliamentary researcher for Jim Molyneaux.[30]

It was Molyneaux's close supporter and MP for South Down, Enoch Powell, who brought his fellow MPs' attention to the comments of that civil servant, Clive Abbott, who had given two interviews to a PhD student from the University of Keele. In the student's notes, Abbott allegedly pointed to the possibility of devolved powers being handed back 'progressively' to a Northern Ireland Assembly, which, he claimed, 'would be accepted by enlightened Unionists like Derek [sic] Trimble of Queen's University'.[31] The postgraduate student said Abbott told him that Trimble was 'a personal friend' and had 'kept us well informed about what is going on inside Jim Molyneaux' [sic] party for a number of years'.[32] In his disputed comments, however, Abbott is alleged to have said he believed 'integration will only guarantee more violence here and in Northern Ireland', continuing:

> Roughly speaking, one bomb in the United Kingdom is worth 100 in Northern Ireland. We cannot allow further violence in the UK. In the end I think that there will be a confederal Ireland, one could

call it an honourable draw, in which a package would be put together whereby Protestant rights would be guaranteed. There would be some re-alignment with the Commonwealth and the Irish Republic and a defence agreement would also be made. There is less certainty than there has been in the past about the strategic irrelevance of Southern Ireland. You know that a submarine can be used for more functions than the launching of missiles! The Americans would sleep easier in their beds if the Irish Republic was a member of NATO. The Irish Republic will not enter into any defence agreement until the issue of partition is resolved.[33]

When interviewed by the Cabinet Secretary Robert Armstrong about his dealings with the student, Abbott denied it was 'an even remotely accurate account of his meeting'. The NIO backed him, referring to 'absurdities in the document'.[34] Armstrong arranged for the student to be interviewed by senior MI5 officer Denis Payne, whom he recommended as 'one of the panel of people whom we use for the purpose of conducting investigations into leaks of confidential information'.[35] Payne was a skilled interrogator who had served in Northern Ireland and was amongst a few trusted heavyweight troubleshooters renowned for getting to the bottom of scandals.[36] While the furore over the episode was soon forgotten – though not by Trimble, who threatened to sue the student – it nonetheless drew attention to the heated debate between the sharp contrast of views about the future of Northern Ireland, between the entrenched positions of power-sharing devolved government with an Irish dimension, and the further integration of the province into the United Kingdom.

A few months after the 'Abbott Affair', Jim Prior mapped out the government's position that there could be no form of devolution without cross-community support:

> Any scheme that is to work in Northern Ireland does have to be a bit of all things to all men. It has at the same time to enable protestant Unionists to maintain an association and identify with the union, while it has to enable nationalists to have an identification and feel that they can fully identify with the Republic.[37]

Writing at the time, the historian Charles Townshend observed how 'Pragmatic politicians, as distinct from idealists, must take facts as they are.'[38] This was probably a good reflection of the British government's outlook, which was ever-mindful of how the 'history of British rule in Ulster during the last decade is littered with the debris of "political initiatives", as the history of British government in Ireland before 1922 is littered with the wreckage of political reputations. A more forgiving, or less demanding, British Parliament,' Townshend wrote, 'may now permit Irish Secretaries to enhance their reputations in coping with a tiresome, incomprehensible problem of little apparent relevance to the British polity.'[39] By now the way forward was clear. Unionism would have to abandon any notion of a return to its heady Stormont days of domination and its daydream of political integration with Great Britain. A middle road was now a more realistic alternative.

Two years to the day that the PIRA murdered Robert Bradford, one of its 'volunteers' was crawling under the family car of Charles Armstrong, the UUP's chair of Armagh City and District Council. The PIRA's modus operandi of skulking around family homes and looking for opportunities to kill unsuspecting politicians and off-duty security forces personnel was by now well-established. It meant their tactic of planting an under-car booby trap device with a mercury-tilt switch, the same sort of device that had been used by the INLA to kill British Shadow Secretary of State for Northern Ireland Airey Neave in March 1979, afforded them comfort and safety in distancing them from their targets. They rarely engaged armed opponents for fear of return fire. Armstrong, like Neave, died instantly, despite the brave attempts of an SDLP colleague to pull him from the burning wreckage.

Armstrong was targeted because he was seen as a 'perfectly legitimate' target, being a part-time member of the UDR.[40] Despite being a military man, Armstrong was also a liberal unionist who held a minute's silence for the brother of a Sinn Féin council member after his death. 'All human life is sacred,' he told the council chamber on that occasion. 'Murder, for whatever reason, must be condemned.'[41] It reflected the values Armstrong stood for, in contrast to his fanatical killers. John Taylor, the UUP's MEP at Strasbourg, told reporters, 'Until we have a Government at Westminster which both supports the Union and has the will to defeat terrorism, the best of our men will continue to be killed.'[42] Ian Paisley, who had frequently prophesied such assassinations, challenged the government to 'move onto the offensive after the recent murders', concurring with his late colleague Robert Bradford that the authorities should reinstate the death penalty.[43]

The public condemnation of these murders had little discernible effect. A few weeks later the PIRA was stalking another Unionist politician, this time in South Belfast. Following a reconnaissance of Queen's University, they murdered Edgar Graham, a law lecturer at the university and the member of the Northern Ireland Assembly for South Belfast. Graham had been as outspoken on physical security from IRA attacks as his constituency colleague Bradford. Indeed, he had found himself embroiled in a heated debate in the Assembly about the political segregation of paramilitary prisoners. Graham alleged that 'an approach had been made earlier this year by a republican terrorist organisation to a loyalist terrorist organisation with the objective of asking the loyalist group to "eliminate" a leading member of the Official Unionist Party'.[44] Graham declined to name the politician but said he 'would have been "more accessible" to the loyalist grouping'. He continued, 'It was agreed that an attempt would be made in that direction. That agreement did take place, and I thank God that the attempt proved fruitless,' he told the Stormont debating chamber.[45]

Twenty-four hours after his allegations were published in the *Belfast Telegraph*, the UDA challenged Graham to name names over his allegation of a joint assassination plot.[46] Graham declined. At the UUP annual conference in October 1983 – together with party colleagues Robert McCartney, David Trimble and leader Jim Molyneaux – Graham helped secure the passing of a motion demanding that the authorities should provide a more credible deterrent to terrorism, including supporting the security forces in their bid to act 'effectively and confidently' against the paramilitaries.[47] Graham, like Bradford, was far too outspoken for the PIRA, who were still determined to 'beat these bastards', even if that meant targeting democratically elected politicians.

In mid-November 1985, Prime Minister Margaret Thatcher and Taoiseach Garret FitzGerald met in Hillsborough to sign the terms of the Anglo-Irish Agreement between their respective governments. Although the Agreement gave Dublin a consultative role in the government of Northern Ireland, neither government believed that it would undermine the unionist position. However, unionists rejected the Agreement, which they regarded as treachery and a betrayal. From a Conservative government perspective, the Agreement offered an opportunity to prevent the PIRA from using the Irish Republic as a 'safe haven' for launching attacks in Northern Ireland. Security of the state was, therefore, paramount, even if it excluded unionists from the negotiations and included the Irish government in matters pertaining to the internal affairs of the British state. From FitzGerald's perspective, the Agreement helped to guarantee the rights of northern nationalists, who, he told his colleagues in Dáil Éireann, 'found themselves part of a State with which they could not identify and the institutions that were alien to them and appeared in so many ways to be designed to make them strangers in their own land – in the island in which their ancestors had lived for millennia'.[48] He highlighted their second-class citizenship, paying particular attention to the history of discrimination they suffered in housing and employment. FitzGerald surmised that this oppression 'drove many of them to withhold their allegiance from the system of Government and others to emigrate, who might, in different and more equitable circumstances, have been able to remain in their own land'.[49]

FitzGerald thought about these historical forces with an erudition that eluded most other Irish politicians. He could be objective when the situation demanded it, going as far as to ponder how unionists felt about this situation. He acknowledged that their control over the levers of power had once enabled them to maintain dominance:

> That this happened reflected however – and we should have sufficient insight to understand this – *a sense of fear leading to a siege mentality*, arising from finding themselves in a corner of an island in the greater part of which the Nationalist population, after centuries of subordination to external rule, *were at last accorded the power to which their numbers entitled them*. In a sense, unlike many people in this part of Ireland, the Unionist population of Northern Ireland never really accepted the division of this island; *they never felt secure about this division*, or accepted in their heart of hearts that it afforded them the protection which they felt they needed against an ethos which to them was alien, and appeared threatening. *These fears diminished them; they*

led them into ways of thinking and of acting, that did less than justice to the fundamental generosity of spirit which they share with those on this island who belong to the other, Nationalist, tradition.[50]

FitzGerald, however, underestimated how insecure unionists felt because of the Irish government's poor record of pursuing IRA members using the Irish Republic as a safe haven. A decade earlier he had observed in *Towards a New Ireland* (1972) how 'the British connection is no longer the crucial factor in the Irish problem. The issue now is whether and how the fears of the Northern Protestant majority about their role within a United Ireland, in which Catholics would have a three-to-one majority, can be allayed.'[51] FitzGerald did not deny that there were two types of people on Irish soil and that both had to be accommodated politically in a way that respected their identities. He knew that identity could be both fixed and yet retain the power to change. While there could be a softening of the dominant national identity, some groups were reticent about severing the apron strings and forging a new comprehensive identity that respected sovereignty and the rights of everyone, even in a divided place.

For hardliners like Ian Paisley, troop deployments along the border counties, in places like South Armagh, Fermanagh and East Tyrone where the Provisionals were particularly active, reinforced his conviction that the Irish government was complacent and did not have the interests of unionists at heart. The day before FitzGerald commended the Anglo-Irish Agreement to the Dáil, Paisley described it as 'document of treachery and deceit',[52] while, in contrast, SDLP leader John Hume believed it was 'an opportunity to make progress towards peace and reconciliation' for it provided 'recognition of the validity of both traditions'.[53] Hume was conciliatory, not triumphalist, and he saw the world in less stark colours than Paisley. Hume had told his party conference in the run-up to the Agreement that no solution to Northern Ireland's problems could be found on the basis of seeking to 'destroy or crush the Protestant heritage in Ireland'.[54] In a statement to the House of Commons, Hume concluded that his party 'and those who support me do not believe that there will be any resolution of the conflict in Northern Ireland which involves in any way the crushing or the defeat of the Protestant heritage there. Not only would that be unthinkable; it would be impossible'.[55] Such rhetoric did little to placate unionists who used the Northern Ireland Assembly to vote forty-four to ten in favour of rejecting the Agreement. The Unionist motion described it as 'an intolerable derogation of British sovereignty'.[56] Feelings of physical insecurity now fused with unionist political anxiety to produce a febrile atmosphere ripe for radicalising Ulster loyalists.

10

The Duisburg Formula

> Every shot that is fired, every bomb that is exploded, whether at the British or at the Ulster loyalists, further hardens the determination of the northern loyalists to have nothing whatsoever to do with a union with the south.
>
> Brigadier Bill Magan, former senior MI5 officer[1]

BELFAST CITY CENTRE GROUND TO a halt at 2.30 p.m. on 23 November 1985 as tens of thousands of unionists converged on the City Hall. The crowd swayed as they waited for their political leadership to take to the stage erected in front of the historic landmark. They had come to voice their anger at the Anglo-Irish Agreement. 'Many unionists,' the *Belfast Telegraph* reported, 'said it was the biggest rally ever held in the province, certainly since the days of the Home Rule protests 70 years ago.'[2] The newspaper called it an 'unprecedented show of loyalist strength' organised by 'the two unionist leaders'. Ordinary loyalists and unionists were joined by members of the Orange Order and Apprentice Boys as well as flute bands and the odd flag-waving skinhead. 'As ... loyalists swarmed around the City Hall the sea of bobbing heads stretched back along Royal Avenue, Wellington Place, Chichester Street and Donegall Place as far as the eye could see.'[3] Some loyalists carried placards: 'Iron Lady Be Warned – Your Iron Will Melt in the Heat of Ulster', while another read: 'Wanted – Maggie Thatcher for Treason'.

Rapturous applause rang out as Jim Molyneaux and Ian Paisley took to the stage, raising their clasped hands aloft in a gesture of solidarity. Many protesters looked on, adorned with rosettes, scarfs and badges proclaiming their loyalty, and some wore 'Ulster Says No' badges on their lapels.

Molyneaux warned of the dangers of the British and Irish governments establishing a system of joint control for Northern Ireland. 'It's a one-way deal in which we are the losers. The scheme will not work because there is no consent. There's even less consent for the agreement than there was for the Sunningdale Agreement.' He spoke also of a 'cruel deceit'. It was a calm and considered speech, typical of Molyneaux's mild manner and grey man persona. The flamboyance and theatrics were left to Ian Paisley whose booming voice pierced the cold air with a guttural intensity. 'It is a battle of the unionist family. It is the battle of the loyalist people of Ulster,'[4] Paisley roared at the crowd. He had by now established a reputation for raising the spectre of armed resistance, even if he always avoided responsibility for its commission by rougher men. Paisley had once countenanced the overthrow of the old liberal Unionist government and was now reconstituting himself as a human battering ram ready to smash the Tory government's designs for Northern Ireland. The DUP leader was mindful of how such militant narratives resonated with loyalists and sought to exploit their fears in a way that heightened his own profile and rewarded his party with further electoral returns.

Much of Paisley's rhetoric was forged in the fires of religious extremism. It was a curious American style of fundamentalism that he adapted to local circumstances.[5] Paisley also sought refuge in the Scriptures, paying particular attention to the Covenanting tradition and even visited key sites associated with it in southwest Scotland while on holiday. He held the 'commonplace modern position that the state should protect the citizen and the citizen should be loyal to the state' and so long as 'the state delivers, the private citizen has no right to use violence for political ends'.[6] If the state abandoned the citizen, so the logic of Covenanting ran, then the citizen was 'released from his obligation and may do whatever is necessary to protect himself, his family and his country'.[7] Crucially, as one of Paisley's biographers, Steve Bruce, emphasised, this did not extend to supporting loyalist terrorism.[8] Despite his bloodcurdling public speeches, Paisley dissociated himself from those amongst his followers who took the law into their own hands. Nevertheless, in the mid-1980s, as in the 1960s, he helped create a climate which 'led to a reinvigoration of the memory of militant resistance to the third Home Rule Bill within Unionist culture' and an 'effort to recapture the spirit and strategies of 1914'.⁹ The actual practical turn towards violence and the threat of violence was left to loyalists.

One of those loyalists who stood amongst the 100,000-strong crowd at the City Hall that day was Matthew. He had made his way into the city centre from his home in North Belfast, eager to stand shoulder-to-shoulder with other unionists and loyalists as they registered their anger at the negotiation of the Anglo-Irish Agreement over the heads of their elected representatives. He recalled early morning scenes as the car in which he was travelling made its way through the centre. 'It was about 8 a.m. and there must have been 400–500 skinheads in the town carrying Union Jacks.'[10] Matthew and his friends made their way to the City Hall hours before the speeches were scheduled to be delivered. They were all on the fringes of loyalist paramilitarism and shared the views of their leaders, such as prominent Belfast UVF commander John Bingham, who believed the Agreement posed a direct threat to the unionist community. A few months after the City Hall rally, Bingham told reporter Emily O'Reilly how loyalist paramilitaries 'have harnessed the frustration of the young men. We don't want to bring anarchy but if you think of the harness as being held up by a number of buckles then the unbuckling could begin tomorrow.'[11]

The reality was that the 'unbuckling' had already begun. The British Army's top agent inside the UDA, Brian Nelson, had been ordered by UDA leaders to obtain new weapons from South Africa. He visited Durban in June 1985 to arrange a shipment, all under the watchful eye of his security force handlers.[12] Although Nelson left Northern Ireland for Germany in October 1985, the loyalist conspiracy to import arms from the apartheid state continued in his absence.[13] Two years after Nelson's South Africa trip, the UDA, UVF and a new group known as 'Ulster Resistance' were busy finalising plans for a major shipment of arms, which would be funded by the robbery of the Northern Bank in Portadown on 8 July 1987.[14] Sometime in late 1987 or early 1988, a huge consignment of vz.58 assault rifles, Browning 9mm semi-automatic pistols, tens of thousands of rounds of ammunition, hand grenades and RPG rocket launchers were smuggled into the UK from Beirut.[15] These weapons were later described as 'a Godsend' by leading loyalist paramilitaries, one of whom detailed the significance of the firepower. 'Our organisations did not have an assault rifle, and it wasn't until these weapons came, this shipment came in, that the UDA, UFF, then took control of assault rifles. With that armoury of weapons and stockpile of weapons came confidence to the men.'[16]

To Thatcher and the upper echelons of her government, the Agreement provided an assurance from Dublin that it recognised the validity of the unionist position. In commending the accord to the House of Commons back in November 1985, she rebuked DUP attempts to spread fear within the wider unionist community, which she believed were groundless. The Agreement, in her eyes, would, instead, be instrumental in 'calming the fears of the Unionists and reassuring them that change would come about only by the will of the majority in Northern Ireland'.[17] For Paisley it did nothing of the sort, and he spent the next few years building on the 'Ulster Says No' campaign to highlight the dangers it posed to the unionist community.[18] Intriguingly, republicans rejected it for other reasons, with Gerry Adams claiming in 1986 that the Agreement copper-fastened partition.[19] At the time, the Provisional Republican movement believed it was just another attempt to reinforce British imperialist rule in Ireland.

Beneath the bombastic language, the truth was more benign. By the 1980s, unionism no longer formed part of an unbroken aristocratic lineage to the British establishment, with its political leaders struggling to get access to the Secretary of State for Northern Ireland in the wake of the PIRA's campaign of assassination against its politicians. Nor was Northern Ireland a 'training ground' for the armed forces of British imperialism, with some senior operational commanders seeing it as a 'sideshow' in the greater struggle against communism. Rather, the real reason why the British state remained involved in its troublesome province was due to successive governments respecting the wish 'of the overwhelming majority of Northern Ireland Protestants to remain British citizens', and 'because the Irish Republic's governments since the 1950s have never seriously wanted the British to withdraw', and, vitally, 'because neither state has wanted the submerged civil war to become a full-scale holocaust'.[20] The threat of civil war felt real to those unionists who lived close to the borderlands and who witnessed IRA atrocities on an almost daily basis as much as it did to those ordinary nationalists who were increasingly bearing the brunt of loyalist atrocity. By the late 1980s there was palpable fear in unionist communities along the border that the PIRA posed an existential threat. It was hard for them to square this with the conciliatory tone struck by the leader of northern nationalism John Hume.

Colm Tóibín discovered just how fearful ordinary Protestants had become at this time when he hiked the full length of the border. 'People are just living,' one Protestant in Castlederg told him, 'wondering who is going to be next, what's the next move, whose funeral is going to be the next one.'[21] This general feeling of anxiety fed an insecurity within the Protestant community in places like Fermanagh, Tyrone and Armagh that could only really be addressed through political pressure on the British government to dedicate more military resources to protect a people who felt increasingly under siege. The military, however, did not enjoy unfettered access to the highways and byways of rural Ulster, as events were soon to prove.

'At first we thought we had a massive accident, and we'd hit something. There's a weird smell, because you can smell all the burning diesel and burning oil, and everybody is screaming and shouting – you're just shouting for all your mates.'[22] It was a cold and wet night on 20 August 1988 when the IRA detonated a roadside bomb along the A5 at Ballygawley killing eight soldiers from the 1st Battalion of the Light Infantry and injuring another twenty-eight. Two hundred pounds of Semtex was used in a device that was remotely detonated as the coach carrying the thirty-six soldiers passed by. 'I have never seen anything like it in my life,' one local farmer who rushed to the scene recalled, 'and please God I never will have to see it again.'[23] Bodies were strewn all over the road, some were crushed by the mangled shell of the bus. People were running around stunned, screaming and bleeding. 'My whole memory of the scene was the absolute carnage. It was like driving into hell,' one eyewitness later recalled.[24] The bomb left a huge crater 12 feet wide and 6 feet deep in the road. The blast threw parts of the coach over a 100-yard radius, dropping its mangled remains 20 yards from where it had been positioned on the road when the blast happened. One soldier had crawled 500 yards to a cattle-shed where he bled to death. Another soldier's remains were wrapped around a road sign, his face badly mutilated and a family photo album not far from his body.[25] A local flute band returning from a parade in Portadown saw the explosion and immediately stopped their bus and ran to the scene to help the injured. Despite the lashing rain and falling temperatures, they took off their coats, jumpers and shirts to cover the victims.[26] It was a compassionate act that the soldiers who survived would never forget.

One of the first on the scene was local MP Ken Maginnis, who broke down in tears as he described what he encountered. It was an 'utter act of callousness', he told reporters. 'I want the Government to recognise that the law is inadequate to deal with terrorists and to introduce selective internment,' he said. Shortly afterwards, Maginnis boarded a flight to London for an urgent meeting with Margaret Thatcher, where he put forward his personal recommendations for dealing with this resurgent IRA threat. After the meeting at Downing Street, Maginnis told the *Financial Times* that he didn't 'seek selective internment as an alternative to justice. I see it as an alternative to the unimpeded march of the IRA through the lives of people in this community.' The newspaper reported how the Fermanagh MP was 'well qualified to talk about Northern Ireland's security crisis',[27] given his previous experience as a former officer in the UDR. Maginnis told journalists after the meeting that the RUC knew the identities of those responsible for the Ballygawley bomb attack. He also estimated that for 92 per cent of the killings in his Fermanagh and South Tyrone constituency – 160 out of 174 murders, including those of the eight British soldiers – no one was ever likely to be brought to justice.

Maginnis would later claim that he gave Thatcher a 'detailed plan [for dealing with the security situation in Fermanagh], which she had implemented to the last letter'.[28] He expected her to act on the information by ordering the detention of key PIRA leaders.[29] However, Thatcher or her advisers had other ideas. Within days the security forces ambushed three of the PIRA members suspected of direct involvement in the Ballygawley bus bombing. All three were killed instantly. 'While nobody can take comfort from further death,' Maginnis said at the time, 'in this situation one has, nonetheless, got to be grateful that security forces, by pre-emptive action, have saved further innocent people from death.'[30] Offering his own analysis to the press, he pondered how it had been 'a pity that it took the bus bomb to bring about this sort of action. What a pity that the pre-emptive action did not come two weeks before that tragic event.'[31] Maginnis had demanded action from the government, and he got it. As he later recalled, he was 'used to facing up to my responsibility'.[32] Having escaped assassination bids on at least two occasions, Maginnis knew how PIRA terrorists operated. He harboured little sympathy for those who engaged in terrorism, believing that the British government ought to live up to its responsibilities in the administration of justice, even if that meant a stark trade-off between individual liberty and collective security.

Incidents like Ballygawley understandably fed into the siege mentality shared by many unionists in border areas. Yet, they generally resisted the urge to take the law into their own hands. The PIRA's violent campaign along the border between 1969 and 1975 clearly demonstrated that the organisation 'carried out sectarian murders'.[33] The killing of Protestants took the form of no-warning bombs, shooting of unarmed civilians and torture – a consistent pattern of killings 'over several years', which indicated that the Provisionals 'tolerated sectarianism within its ranks, and suggests that such actions may have been sanctioned'.[34] Despite the mortal dangers due to the widespread perception that he was a unionist hardliner, Ken Maginnis remained deeply committed to a peaceful political solution to the violence. A few weeks after the Ballygawley bus bombing, he was to be privy to a new initiative designed to de-escalate violence in Northern Ireland and find a solution to the kind of insecurity felt by many of his constituents.

In late 1988 a middle-aged German lawyer, Dr Eberhard Spiecker, approached Maginnis' party leader, Jim Molyneaux, with an invitation for him to attend secret talks in his home town of Duisburg, West Germany. Molyneaux duly authorised his party chairman, Jack Allen, to attend the talks, which were aimed at finding a peaceful solution to the conflict. Duisburg was hardly the kind of place that attracted much in the way of outside attention. A quaint town at the junction of the mighty Rhine and Ruhr rivers, it had long been the site of one of the busiest ports in the world. Nestled in the quiet, leafy suburb of Huckingen, the small, white single-storey Angerhoff hotel was a short, ten-minute drive from Düsseldorf airport. There was nothing historic or noteworthy about the venue other than it was close to the home and legal practice of Dr Spiecker.[35] Yet, it was here, on 14–15 October 1988, that Dr Spiecker hosted the first serious attempt to bring together representatives of Northern Ireland's main parties in a political dialogue about the future. Jack Allen was joined by DUP deputy leader Peter

Robinson, Austin Currie of the SDLP, Gordon Mawhinney of the Alliance Party and a priest from West Belfast, Father Alec Reid, who was acting as an interlocutor for Sinn Féin and the PIRA. With unionist hostility towards the Anglo-Irish Agreement at an all-time high and a refusal to countenance any re-engagement in the political process until it was scrapped, the talks had to be deniable. A central question considered – known as a 'riddle' amongst the higher echelons of the NIO who were briefed on the talks afterwards – was 'how to provide Unionists with enough to participate in talks, without compromising the integrity of the Agreement'.[36] Politically the SDLP was hostile to any suspension of the Agreement, and so a balance had to be struck to keep all participants on board.

Rather than using the emotive term 'power-sharing', the delegates talked instead of 'sharing responsibility'. This phrase had been used a few years earlier by the UVF-linked PUP in a document of the same name it had published in 1985. One of the principal points discussed was a return to devolved government and how powers for law and order – long controversial and removed by the British government from Stormont when it was prorogued in 1972 – might be returned to local hands. The British government assessment of the parties' positions on the talks was that:

> Alliance are anxious that this initiative should make progress. DUP would like it to, but 'won't run after the SDLP'; like the OUP (the Unionist panel tend to bind the two parties together), they might like to run with these Duisberg [sic] ideas in order to show to other unionists that they are willing to look at constructive ideas that are compatible with their manifesto commitments on the Agreement. But despite Currie's enthusiasm, Hume seems unenthusiastic, and even unsighted; the SDLP could well end up allowing the Duisberg initiative to run into the sand.[37]

Much of the Duisburg process relied on the personal approach taken by Dr Spiecker, who believed the talks 'could be a starting signal for the democratic process in Northern Ireland which will lead to a settlement where the people take greater responsibility for their own affairs'.[38] Spiecker was shrewd enough to acknowledge that political progress could only take place with the 'participation of both traditions in the government and in the working out of a Constitution for Northern Ireland'. The proposals agreed at Duisburg were ambitious:

1. A caretaker government and a constitutional committee will be called by the Northern Ireland Secretary of State according to the proportional representation and proposed by the political parties in Northern Ireland.
   a) The caretaker government would be responsible for all departments except foreign affairs and defence.
   b) The constitutional committee would prepare a constitution which must be agreed unanimously.
2. The constitution must be accepted by means of a referendum. This referendum is to be held in Northern Ireland and could be held nation-wide.
3. With the acceptance of the Constitution it may be possible that the Anglo-Irish Agreement in its present form would no longer be necessary.[39]

There is little evidence of direct NIO involvement in Duisburg, but the department was briefed by several of the participants upon their return from Germany. News of the secret talks soon leaked to the press in early February 1989, with the revelations bringing 'angry denials from Unionist politicians that they had agreed on the suspension of the three-year-old Anglo-Irish Agreement while attempts were made to reach a new constitutional settlement'.[40] The leaders of the parties represented at Duisburg were conveniently one step removed from the process, offering them a certain degree of plausible deniability. When asked about the significance of the talks by the BBC, John Hume described reports of the talks as 'nonsense'. Jim Molyneaux labelled the idea of secret talks 'crackers'. Meanwhile, Paisley was also quick to issue a rebuttal, saying there have 'never been any negotiations about the future government of Northern Ireland'.[41]

Disclosure of the Duisburg talks caused considerable problems for both Unionist parties, though there was a positive reception from local journalists. Chris Ryder reported that, despite grassroots unionist opposition to the

Anglo-Irish Agreement remaining intense, 'there has been a noticeable thaw in the attitude of the leaders over the past two years' attributable to the work of the churches, which had persuaded Paisley and Molyneaux into 'talks about talks'.[42] Twenty-four hours after news broke of the Duisburg talks, Peter Robinson decided to get ahead of the news agenda. 'Sadly, there's no agreement, there's no new dawn, there's no new era. We are not on the eve of a breakthrough,' he told the press.[43] One of Secretary of State Tom King's senior officials, nevertheless, wrote to Dr Spiecker to acknowledge how his minister had been 'encouraged by the occurrence of these talks' for he 'felt that the constructive approach taken by Northern Ireland's politicians showed a genuine and proper concern for the people of the Province'.[44] The government had long held the policy line that 'dialogue is an essential prerequisite to political progress and in the hope of building on any signs of a desire for movement the Government has said it stands ready to play its part'.[45]

As the Northern Ireland politicians returned from West Germany, they were greeted by colleagues eager to maintain the mantra of 'good fences make good neighbours'. Ironically, events in Berlin were moving in the opposite direction. On 9 November 1989, East German authorities opened the Checkpoint Charlie crossing, allowing free movement between both parts of the divided country. The following day people began to tear down the Berlin Wall that had scarred their city since the early 1960s.[46] Meanwhile, in Belfast, Unionist politicians were back outside the City Hall clasping their hands and arms together as they pioneered a new form of peaceful protest against the Anglo-Irish Agreement. Significantly, the UUP and DUP no longer seemed united, with the protest dismissed as a 'gimmick' by one DUP councillor. The Reverend Martin Smyth, who had replaced Robert Bradford as MP for South Belfast after his murder, nevertheless offered his party's rationale for the non-violent protest. It had grown out of the negative publicity generated by loyalist violence in the wake of a mass rally outside Belfast City Hall in 1987. 'Unionist people do not like violence and destruction against their own community,' he told reporters, with some 'elements [having] destroyed the media impact because of isolated violence'.[47] For now, protest would remain peaceful. 'I believe what the Government has tried to do is condition people that there is no objection to the Anglo-Irish Agreement now.' By then there was a belief within official unionism that if the government 'continued to disregard peaceful protest and argument, they [the government] would be responsible if some of the people believed that violence achieved change'.[48] Inevitably, some people did believe in the use of violence for political ends, and they would soon return to the streets to exact retribution for the denial of their legitimate concerns. Blood would be spilled.

The Anglo-Irish Agreement was interpreted by unionists and loyalists negatively. They saw it as a usurpation of their position within the United Kingdom. Some felt betrayed, others insulted by their own government, which they saw as perfidious in its political intentions. When placed against the backdrop of PIRA violence, particularly in the border areas, a general feeling of insecurity began to percolate through the broader unionist community. Some militant elements undoubtedly acted on this, with loyalist paramilitaries embarking on a renewed terror offensive against Catholic civilians and republican activists. Despite the ramping up of the loyalist terror campaign, some hard-line unionist politicians like Ken Maginnis were privy to alternative initiatives aimed at de-escalating the security situation. Duisburg was the most significant of these secret initiatives. In many respects, its exposure and ultimate failure would come to represent a missed opportunity for peace in Northern Ireland, for it laid the basic foundations of a cross-community dialogue. That it failed so decisively owed much to the fact that the British government did not recognise how unionist insecurity made this community much more defensive and incapable of compromise. It would take another few years before the unionist community felt confident enough to engage in constructive political dialogue with northern nationalism.

11

An Image Problem

> In Northern Ireland people are often physically attacked for who they are and what group they belong to, not for anything they have done themselves. Violence can spread from one incident in a chain reaction, or fester as an ongoing feud. For this process to work it is not necessary for people to agree with the violence done by their own community. They only have to understand what is happening and to be frightened by it. Then, however much they dislike the violence done by their own people to others, the other side's violence is seen to be more dangerous. This process can develop until communities end up accepting the protection of violent people in their own group, even if they know that these same people played a big part in starting it.
>
> Frank Wright, 'Northern Ireland and the British–Irish Relationship'[1]

'GUN GANG KILL MAN IN Rathcoole attack', read the headline in the late edition of the *Belfast Telegraph* on 4 April 1990. 'A man was shot dead in Newtownabbey's Rathcoole estate this afternoon. The killing happened at Armoy Gardens, in the sprawling estate, at about 1.30 p.m. Police confirmed that one man was dead, but were unable to give any further immediate details about the incident.'[2] To local residents it was yet another killing in a depressingly steady body count of Troubles-related murders. Beyond Rathcoole, there was a strong perception that this 'overwhelmingly Protestant' estate had become a killing field for Catholics, although the *Belfast Telegraph* carried a reminder of an earlier attempt by the nationalist Irish People's Liberation Organisation to shoot a leading loyalist paramilitary there.[3] That incident was a reaction to the UVF's murder of thirty-four-year-old Malachy

Trainor, a married man from Kilkeel in County Down, who had been shot dead as he arrived for work on a building site at Clonmore Green.

It soon emerged that the killing on 4 April was of a former republican prisoner, thirty-eight-year-old Roger Bradley, who one UVF intelligence officer later claimed had been targeted because of his alleged involvement in the Claudy bombing in 1972.[4] Bradley had recently been released from prison and had taken on some contract work. He was sitting in his van eating his lunch when two gunmen approached and shot him at point-blank range.[5] Although he was never convicted for Claudy, Bradley had been jailed for his involvement in a gun attack on a UDR patrol in Kilrea, later serving a fifteen-year prison sentence for attempted murder.[6]

In early 1990, the UVF's violent campaign across the six counties combined random sectarian assassination with selective targeted killing of republicans. In truth, these murders were little more than pyrrhic victories for loyalists as the publicity surrounding the violence only served to bring guilt, shame and, ultimately, greater insecurity into the lives of unionists and loyalists living in Rathcoole and elsewhere. Yet the estate's reputation for being home to bloodthirsty loyalists bore little reflection to the reality. Local clergy in the estate thought as much when they banded together to condemn the latest murder, releasing a statement that expressed their 'shock and sadness at the killing and denounced those responsible'.[7]

The impact of the Troubles on working-class life after two decades of violence was dire. It was impacting negatively on those who lived in estates like Rathcoole, built to such fanfare and opened as the Unionist regime's flagship housing estate in the 1950s. Then, Rathcoole was a model village for Protestants and Catholics alike to live in peace and harmony; three decades later the estate was suffering from an image problem, with local community activists at the time suggesting that the profile of 'the estate will improve as and when it is demonstrated that the estate is a good and worthwhile place to live, a place with hope, with prospects and with internal dynamism'.[8]

One of the centres of working-class life on the estate, the Coole Social Club, which originally started as a shebeen before officially registering for its licence in 1973, was closed by the RUC in the wake of the UVF killings in the estate. The club had aimed 'to promote the interests of the tenants of Rathcoole estate and to provide social intercourse and recreation for the members',[9] but it had become a frequent haunt for members of the UVF, ensuring the authorities took a close interest in the activities of its patrons. Paramilitary groups were exerting their influence on the estate's other social clubs too, with the old Alpha cinema having allegedly become the UDA's headquarters in southeast Antrim.

'Rathcoole Estate, one of the largest housing estates in Europe, stretching over three square miles and at one time containing 17,500 people, is in a state of rapid decline,' reported J.A. Steele, a local Northern Ireland Housing Executive (NIHE) representative, to his manager on 31 January 1991.[10] The one-time jewel in the unionist crown was suffering from several debilitating issues. The population had dropped to approximately 9,500 people, with 63 per cent of all 'heads of Household' in the estate in receipt of benefits and a startling 70–75 per cent of all residents in the estate in direct receipt of some kind of state benefits.[11] Six hundred people were having their tenancies terminated annually, and 300 empty properties had been seriously vandalised.[12] Steele's manager recommended that 'vandalism has reached such heights that the only option left to N.I.H.E. is demolition'.[13] For a housing estate that had once been a central component of the Unionist government's planning strategy, this was a savage indictment. In many ways, the dilapidated state of housing stock in Rathcoole, which had once held such promise, was a perfect metaphor for Northern Ireland, which had long since fallen into disrepair under direct rule.

Under the Conservatives, the NIO moved to cut grants awarded for the maintenance of buildings and machinery and towards support for equipping new entrants into the workforce – and those on long-term unemployment – with the skills necessary to help grow the economy.[14] In the Thatcherite rush towards curtailing the size of the state, Tories like Richard Needham, Under-Secretary of State for Northern Ireland, moved towards undermining the Action for Community Employment (ACE) programme, which he saw as a 'make work' scheme.[15] Ironically, the same Tory government attempted to tackle the scourge of unemployment through the very ACE scheme they were now criticising. With unemployment sitting at a high of 13.7 per cent in the summer of 1991, the ACE scheme provided much-needed employment for 9,600 people across Northern Ireland.[16] For people living in marginalised areas like Rathcoole – especially those lacking the education, confidence and life opportunities of their peers in more affluent parts of Northern Ireland – the ACE scheme was a genuine lifeline.

Politicians like Lord Brookeborough, Dame Dehra Parker and John L.O. Andrews, who had done so much to commission community housing projects like Rathcoole, had long since retreated to their family estates or died in comfortable obscurity. A generation on, their social legacy lay in tatters, in the refurbished model homes in Armoy Gardens where working-class people were shot dead in the street, in the 'concrete jungle' of Portrossi, and in the main graffiti-laden Diamond shopping precinct with its distinctive Black Lady statue on the side of its VG supermarket. From 'Up The Hoods' to 'KAI – Kill All Irish', the walls of this 1950s-style architecture spoke of crushing anxiety, low self-esteem and the self-destructive tendencies of local youth. Far from being a model village, Rathcoole was now serving as a reminder that unionists felt perpetually under siege by the structural inequalities and unmet needs that had only been worsened by the Troubles.

A few weeks before Steele reported on Rathcoole in December 1990, a report co-authored by Rathcoole Self Help Group (RSHG) members Mark Langhammer, Bill McClinton, Myna McCullough, Andree Wallace and her brother Roy noted how a 'legacy of unemployment, debt and hitherto unknown social malaise' had grown up in the estate and added to already existing tensions between unionists and nationalists. However, it had to be seen against the undercurrent of violence that the RSHG believed left 'too many young people … incarcerated as a consequence of our "Troubles"'.[17] The multiple deprivations identified by the group conspired against Rathcoole, though it was the long-standing problem of 'stigmatisation' or an 'image problem' that really impacted upon the morale of its residents and spurred on a collective sense of low self-esteem.[18] A generation after the estate had been built to resemble the beating heart of model village unionism, these community activists were reporting how the estate now faced terminal decline. The Diamond should have given the estate a focal point but, instead, created a 'dismal picture'. At the top end of the estate the most significant image problem came through the legacy of 'large-scale intimidations' in the 1970s, population movements and associated vandalism, which left many homes vacant. They had been abandoned, which gave parts of the estate the feeling of having been caught up in the sorts of ethnic conflicts ongoing in other parts of the world. Teenagers even referred to abandoned buildings as 'Beirut' or 'Bosnia'. The appearance of the estate spoke to the sense of the people of Rathcoole being 'under siege'.[19]

The socio-economic problems of the estate left young people with little sense of belonging to the British state and some naturally drifted into paramilitary organisations that offered them an alternative sense of collective identity. One of those who lived in the highly dilapidated top end of the estate was twenty-three-year-old Colin Caldwell, who joined the UVF in the late 1980s. On 16 September 1991, Caldwell and two other men were stopped by an RUC patrol in possession of a stolen car – the vehicle was searched and a .357 Ruger revolver, a .45 Webley revolver and a quantity of ammunition were recovered. When charged with attempted murder, UVF membership and possession of guns, Caldwell told a police officer that he was 'glad we were stopped when we were', indicating the seriousness of the UVF volunteers' intentions. One of those arrested with Caldwell was subsequently charged with the murder of youth worker Peter McTasney, who had been shot dead at his home in Bawnmore on 24 February that year.[20] Caldwell and another loyalist prisoner, Robert Skey, were later killed in an explosion in the Crumlin Road gaol, when the PIRA smuggled in Semtex explosives. The Provos said the blast was retaliation for a loyalist attack on a bus carrying their relatives to the Maze Prison.[21]

Loyalists like Caldwell found themselves joining loyalist paramilitary groups that were politically committed to overturning the Anglo-Irish Agreement, which they saw as jeopardising their position within the Union. Many young people in Protestant working-class areas felt abandoned by the British state for this reason. However, Conservative Party policies, like cutting the ACE scheme and moving sluggishly to regenerate deprived areas, further compounded the sense of embattlement. Nothing reflected this turn inwards better than an upsurge in vandalism across Rathcoole and other Protestant working-class estates. On 2 June 1992 the local education board voted to close Rathcoole High School at the top of the estate and consolidate and extend facilities at Hopefield Secondary School at the bottom of the estate.[22] In the weeks after Rathcoole High School was closed, it was severely vandalised. All the school's windows were broken in a tremendous spate of attacks that also took place at school sites in Carrickfergus, Newtownabbey,

Antrim, Coleraine, Ballycastle and Ballyclare. Some £275,000 worth of damage was incurred, with smashed glass accounting for over 80 per cent of the bills.[23] The Unionist MP for the area, Roy Beggs, dismissed the incidents as part of 'the sectarian situation in Northern Ireland', which, he argued, 'contributed in some way to the heightened nature of vandalism, particularly the wilful breaking of windows'.[24] Vandalism and antisocial behaviour became an everyday occurrence in Rathcoole, where the RSHG identified a subculture of 'indifference'. There can be little doubt that the vandalism reflected a broader feeling of despondency within the loyalist grassroots. However, all was not lost, the RSHG concluded, with Rathcoole being 'a lot less "atomised" than other Protestant areas'. There was a stronger sense of community than virtually any Protestant middle-class area, the group argued, as they judged the community to be less 'apathetic' but perhaps more 'dispirited'.[25]

Three years after co-authoring the report on the need for a proper housing plan for Rathcoole, Mark Langhammer was returned as an Independent Labour candidate with 813 first-preference votes. He had previously run as a candidate for Newtownabbey Borough Council in 1985, when he attracted only 203 votes, and in 1989 he ran unsuccessfully for the European Parliament.[26] As a committed socialist, he believed that the British Labour Party should organise in Northern Ireland as a means of breaking the sectarian mould of local politics and give working-class people hope amidst abject despondency and disaffection. This was not a position widely understood in Britain or Ireland at the time, with Langhammer having to write to the Opsahl Commission – an independent public inquiry chaired by Norwegian human rights lawyer Professor Torkel Opsahl – to protest at their filing of his submission under the heading of 'Integration/Other Unionist proposals'.[27] As he reminded them, he was 'neither a unionist nor an integrationist'.[28] In the 1993 local council elections, Langhammer was elected on a 'straight Labour ticket – not Republican Labour or Northern Ireland Labour, but Labour pure and simple, without any qualification, condition or reservation'.[29] He was not the only socialist and labour councillor representing Rathcoole's electoral ward, Macedon. R.J. 'Bob' Kidd had been a towering presence on the council since first being nominated in 1961, when he and several Labour councillors broke the Unionist Party's stranglehold over Newtownabbey Council. Kidd remained an NILP councillor until the mid-1970s, when he left the party to become an Independent Labour representative. Langhammer's electoral success built on his tireless grassroots work aimed at transforming the face of Rathcoole.

Conversely, at the same time as he was elected on a non-sectarian ticket, loyalist paramilitary groups were attempting to revitalise their own highly sectarian standing within the local community. After a local woman was mugged in broad daylight sometime in 1993, the UVF took it upon itself to cross-examine several eyewitnesses to the incident. The shadowy figures who asked local people pointed questions about what they had seen didn't wear uniforms, nor did they bear RUC warrant cards or carry their weapons openly. Back then Rathcoole had one part-time community police officer based in the nearby Whiteabbey Police Station. He and his colleagues spent much of their time cruising around in armoured Land Rovers, rarely dismounting from their vehicles to interact with the local community, and they showed little if any inclination to investigate everyday crime. In the absence of the legitimate forces of law and order, paramilitary groups tended to fill the void.

Within twenty-four hours of the mugging, an apology was issued and the community assured that the perpetrator had been summarily dealt with. The mugger's fate was decided by the UVF, who then proceeded to administer their own form of rough justice.[30] During the 'Troubles' these so-called 'punishment beatings' were an everyday occurrence in marginalised and deprived communities across Northern Ireland. Experts have concluded that paramilitaries generally engaged in such coercive activity for three main reasons: 'the absence of a perceived legitimate or adequate policing service; the rising levels of petty crime and "anti-social behaviour"; and the perceived failure of the formal criminal justice system'.[31] The high watermark of loyalist punishment shootings came in 1992, when the UVF and UDA shot and wounded seventy-two people.[32] Many people in Rathcoole – through misguided loyalty or fear – tolerated the actions of these groups and helped them embed structures that would last long into the future.

In his acclaimed novel *The Corner Boys*, Geoffrey Beattie writes about working-class life in a Protestant part of North Belfast very similar to Rathcoole. Beattie's main protagonist is James, a seventeen-year-old lad from a working-class family who has no significant father figure in his life after his father's untimely death. His mother tries to make ends meet by working in a mill, suffering poor working conditions and low wages. Her weekends are spent in the company of people who share a penchant for too much booze and a heart disease-rich diet. Their life expectancy is, therefore, severely limited in comparison to those in more affluent areas. Amidst such embattled circumstances, Beattie's characters – like the real people they are based upon – still find a remarkable way of surviving the massive structural forces that threaten to overwhelm them. When James meets a family friend in a local social club, he discovers that his late father was a member of a loyalist paramilitary grouping. In a heady mix of lager-fuelled banter, 'Kingo's da' tells the impressionable teenager: 'On our own, we're nothing. We're fuck-all. We have to act together. We have to depend on each other.' The man then tries to convince James that he should follow in his father's footsteps. 'I think you'll turn out OK like him, now that you realise all that fucking Latin and maths isn't for the likes of you. Or me.'

The Corner Boys captures the generational conflict between those older people who wanted things to continue as they were and those younger people who wanted them to change but were robbed of the life chances to make this possible. In the absence of hope they tended to stick close together. Some of the early recruits to loyalist paramilitary groups in places like Rathcoole had been 'well-meaning people motivated only by a spirit of patriotism and social responsibility', with many early UDA leaders coming from a trade union or community leadership background.[33] However, throughout the 1970s and 1980s, the demographic of people joining paramilitary groupings had shifted towards those who saw opportunities for 'easy money, excitement and vicious thrills', so by the 1990s there were two types of individuals inhabiting paramilitary groups and both groups now competed to 'define the ethos of the organisations'.[34]

In marginalised areas robbed of opportunities and hope, belonging was a powerful adhesive binding together the people living there. It gave them an emotional attachment and helped them realise their potential as social beings. It also gave them the self-confidence to act in ways that ran against the grain by engaging in activity that might otherwise have been interpreted as anti-social or criminal. The breakdown of community cohesion in Rathcoole may have been attributable to structural factors like unemployment and a sense of 'dispirit', but the reality was that twenty years after the imposition of direct rule, political anxiety still kept the community down. There was a sense in places where loyalist feeling was particularly strong that relationships within the community were somehow breaking down. That cohesion and a sense of neighbourliness was being jeopardised. In other loyalist heartlands like the Shankill, slum clearance and redevelopment came to represent a challenge to established ways of life that had endured years of violent Troubles. The respected sociologist Rob Weiner was one of the first academics to observe these changes in the Shankill community in the late 1970s. He interpreted relationships within this close-knit community to be based around 'family structures and long-standing friendships' where 'people of different ages were joined together'.[35] In working-class Protestant families, the 'grannie' represented the family matriarch, playing a central role in kinship connections that gave people a sense of belonging. These patterns of life in unionist working-class communities dominated until the forces of progress and redevelopment challenged them. Families soon became dispersed, with younger people eager to escape the trap of poor socio-economic conditions moving out of the estate and into surrounding new housing developments. In turn, this began to hollow out the strong sense of community, reinforcing feelings of embattlement.

Sir Edward Carson at the annual Twelfth of July celebrations in Belfast *circa* 1914. Carson is seen as the founding father of Irish Unionism, but the reality is the ideas behind political Unionism pre-date him by several centuries. © Edwards Collection

Sir James Craig was the organisational brains behind the opposition to Home Rule. Craig was an empire loyalist who built a form of state-based unionism that appealed only to one section of a divided community. © Edwards Collection

A bonfire built in the Rathcoole estate, depicting effigies of Sinn Féin and Alliance Party politicians. The exhibition of intolerance at some bonfires deepened the sense of loyalist alienation and feelings of victimhood. © Edwards Collection

John Miller Andrews, Northern Ireland Prime Minister 1940–43.
© Museum of Orange Heritage

Sir Basil Brooke, Northern Ireland Prime Minister 1943–63.
© Museum of Orange Heritage

Queen Elizabeth II pictured alongside the Duke of Edinburgh and the Northern Ireland Prime Minister, Sir Basil Brooke, on a visit to Northern Ireland on 2 July 1953. Queen Elizabeth visited Northern Ireland on many occasions during her long reign, demonstrating the strong bond between Crown and the unionist community.
© SuperStock/Alamy Stock Photo

Captain Terence O'Neill, Northern Ireland Prime Minister 1963–69, pictured with Taoiseach Seán Lemass on 9 February 1965. O'Neill attempted to reform the Unionist-Orange state according to his liberal convictions, but he was thwarted by a powerful right-wing populist conspiracy. © PA Images/Alamy Stock Photo

British Prime Minister Harold Wilson pictured with NILP leader Tom Boyd and his party colleagues at 10 Downing Street. Despite impressive election results at local, regional and national level, the NILP was unable to sustain its challenge to Unionism beyond the outbreak of the Troubles. © Laurence Galbraith

Ulster Defence Association (UDA) members and British troops pictured dismantling barricades in so-called 'No-Go areas' in Londonderry on 1 January 1972. The UDA began as a vigilante movement in the early 1970s and at its height boasted 40,000 members. © Keystone Press/Alamy Stock Photo

A mural depicting women cheering the fall of the Northern Ireland Executive in 1974. The UDA provided the paramilitary muscle behind the Ulster Workers' Council strike, with several of its key leaders, like Glenn Barr, going on to form the political cadre of the UDA. © Edwards Collection

Derek Smyth, Glenn Barr, Alan Snoddy and John McMichael at a New Ulster Political Research Group press conference in November 1979. The NUPRG was established to provide the UDA with political analysis. © Alain Le Garsmeur 'The Troubles' Archive/Alamy Stock Photo

Rev. Robert Bradford, UUP MP for South Belfast (top right). He was assassinated by the Provisional IRA a few days later. In front of Bradford sits John Taylor, the UUP's MEP. Beside them are DUP leader Ian Paisley and his deputy, Peter Robinson. All four men were targeted for assassination by republicans. © Keystone Press/Alamy Stock Photo

Huge crowds gathered to protest at the Anglo-Irish Agreement in November 1985. UUP leader Jim Molyneaux was joined by DUP leader Ian Paisley on the stage in a show of unity. Beneath the surface, however, both parties remained divided over how best to oppose the Agreement. © Pacemaker Press

Tánaiste Dick Spring meets with the PUP's Gusty Spence and Hugh Smyth on 23 October 1995. Loyalist paramilitaries previously engaged with the Dublin authorities via an intermediary in a bid to lift the siege they believed they were living under with respect to Articles 2 and 3 of the Irish Constitution. © PA Images/Alamy Stock Photo

Billy Wright, the former commander of the Mid Ulster UVF, was stood down by the group's Shankill-based leadership because of his vehement opposition to the Framework Documents and developing peace process. He believed that republicans were insincere about respecting the Principle of Consent. © PA Images/Alamy Stock Photo

UUP leader David Trimble and DUP leader Ian Paisley exhibiting triumphalism as Orange Order marchers are allowed to walk their traditional route along the Garvaghy Road. Billy Wright and the local UVF provided the muscle forcing the hand of the RUC. © PressEye

The PUP delegation immediately after the signing of the Good Friday Agreement. Billy Hutchinson (left), Hugh Smyth (centre) and David Ervine (right) were the party's most visible members. Billy Mitchell (over Smyth's right shoulder) was the PUP's key strategist. © PA Images/Alamy Stock Photo

RUC officers line the route of an Orange Order parade in North Belfast on 12 July 2001. A heavy police presence was a familiar sight during the annual marching season. © REUTERS/Alamy Stock Photo

Greencastle Orange Hall had the dubious honour of being attacked more than any other Orange Order building in Northern Ireland. Opened by the Unionist government in 1938, a rapid demographic change during the Troubles saw the hall fall into a contested sectarian space. © Stephen Barnes/Northern Ireland News/Alamy Stock Photo

Jamie Bryson, the social media blogger and influencer who came to prominence during the flag protests, would later be consulted by politicians about his ideas on loyalism, particularly in the wake of the Brexit referendum in 2016. His interpretation of unionism chimed with that promoted by the DUP. © Stephen Barnes/Northern Ireland News/Alamy Stock Photo

Julie-Anne Corr-Johnston joined the PUP at the time of the flag protests in 2012–13, won a Belfast City Council seat in Oldpark, and subsequently left the party for the UUP. Her vision for the union was much more inclusive than that articulated by Bryson. © Horst Friedrichs/Alamy Stock Photo

12

Lifting the Siege

> It made no sense at all for people who profess their loyalty to the union continuing to bomb and shoot when republicans had put their weapons aside, telling the world they were relying on democratic politics.
>
> *Belfast Telegraph*, 13 October 1994[1]

TWENTY-FOUR YEARS ON FROM HIS formal recruitment into the UVF in a windswept barn in rural Tyrone, Gusty Spence's mindset had shifted enormously. 'I am a Unionist. I want to continue the union with Britain because it is deeply ingrained in my psyche and people just cannot understand that,' he told a reporter from the Dublin-based *Evening Press* in an interview at his Shankill Road home.[2] The interview came only a few days after the organisation he helped to create shot dead thirty-nine-year-old Liam Ryan, a leading PIRA volunteer, at his pub, the Battery Bar, in Moortown on the shores of Lough Neagh. 'As one of those who has been through violence, I know it [to be] counterproductive. All of them, the IRA included, should grease up their weapons and put them away,'[3] Spence said. He was in no mood to breathe life into the old dog of loyalist paramilitarism, even if he refused to condemn those loyalists who continued to flock to the group he helped create. Interestingly, Spence also refused to renounce his own participation in the sectarian murder of Peter Ward on a street not far from his family home. 'I was [a] paramilitary, and Ulster Volunteer, and I have no apology to make for that. It would be senseless and pointless to apologise anyway but I will be saying that I have passed through that stage – and I hope I have reached a higher plane.'[4] Spence intended to carry a message of peace to a meeting of the Irish Association – an organisation that sought to promote communication, understanding and co-operation between all the people of Ireland, both north and south – in the Gresham Hotel in Dublin in late 1989, where he was to share a stage with former PIRA member Shane Paul O'Doherty.[5] He was anxious to condemn the bombings in Dublin and Monaghan in 1974, which he called 'reprehensible', but explained his actions and the actions of his fellow men of violence in the following terms: 'What men resort to is beyond belief sometimes – but when people know as much fear as we did, when they have to defend their families and friends – people will do anything.'[6]

Fear, anxiety and insecurity were so intoxicating that loyalist paramilitaries used these strong feelings to successfully bind their volunteers to a life of militancy. It had been what right-wing loyalists like Paisley had used to fire up the emotions of those who flocked to the loyalist cause in the wake of the Divis Street riots of 1964. By the early 1970s, Spence had begun to pull away from Paisleyism's powerful gravitational pull. After the arrival of UVF detainees in Long Kesh Detention Centre in 1973, Spence facilitated a series of informal seminars, which intensified in the mid-1970s.[7] He spent many hours encouraging others who fell under his spell in prison to challenge the very foundation of their beliefs.[8] Outwardly, his regime in Long Kesh was organised along British Army lines and designed to ensure UVF prisoners had a sense of self-discipline, order and camaraderie that would see them through their prison sentences.[9] Inwardly, it was designed to create a cadre of political warriors who would play a key role in shifting the UVF in a more strategic direction by laying the foundations for a nucleus of loyalists who could provide political leadership in their communities once they were released from prison. As the UVF's former Director of Military Operations, Billy Mitchell, explained:

> In the compounds we had these regular seminars. Gusty would have provoked a lot of thought. So, there would have been differences of opinion. There were people still locked in what we would call a 'DUP mindset'. Others were more progressive in their thinking. And, so, there was this melting pot of ideas and thoughts. But, generally speaking, people like Gusty, Hutchy [Billy Hutchinson], Davy Ervine,

myself, Eddie Kinner, the small core – Plum Smith – that formed that nucleus of the PUP after the ceasefires. (Even Davy and themuns before the ceasefires.) We came to a consensus that we had to redefine unionism. One, we had to understand what unionism was all about. A lot of volunteers were responding to republican violence ... So, none of us went into Long Kesh with an ideology. So it was in Long Kesh that we hammered it out ...[10]

The political ideology formulated by UVF prisoners in the compounds was of a 'liberal, left-leaning and working-class alternative to mainstream unionism'.[11] Eventually the political discussions hammered out in Long Kesh fed into the thinking of Hugh Smyth, a local Independent Unionist councillor for the Shankill area in Belfast, who was close to the UVF. Along with former members of the NILP, David Overend and Jim McDonald, Smyth established the PUP in the late 1970s.[12]

Under Spence – and with the help of Smyth, Overend and McDonald – the UVF's prisoners developed a 'more sceptical understanding of their own contractual relationship with the British state via its proxy administrators in the old Stormont regime'.[13] In 1978, after a few years of running political education classes, Spence stepped down from his role as commander of UVF prisoners in Long Kesh,[14] believing in doing so that he had also resigned from the UVF itself.[15] Giving up his paramilitary role, Spence's mind turned to his family and the prospect of his release. He had almost died of a heart attack in prison, which had prompted him to relinquish his command and made him anxious to secure his liberty. By this point Spence was thought to be the longest-serving life sentence prisoner in Northern Ireland's prisons. With these matters in mind, Spence's family wrote to leading politicians to gain their support for his release. According to Spence's biographer, Roy Garland, the politicians who wrote to the NIO on behalf of Spence in the early 1980s included the UUP's Robert Bradford, Harold McCusker and Jim Kilfedder, as well as the DUP's Ian Paisley and Peter Robinson, and Alliance Party leader Oliver Napier.[16] It was clear these politicians believed the UVF figurehead had been rehabilitated and might play a useful restraining role on paramilitaries if released. So prolific was the correspondence that the NIO began to explore the possibility of releasing Spence early from his life sentence. NIO officials turned to the RUC for an assessment of Spence's standing within paramilitary loyalism, with the force's Deputy Chief Constable, Michael McAtamney, believing the veteran loyalist had 'a certain prestige amongst paramilitary groups even if connections were more tenuous in recent years. Has relatives deeply involved in terrorism. If so minded, he could be a focal point and is capable of organising and directing others. Risk not considered acceptable at this stage.'[17]

In an interview with an assistant governor on 26 February 1982, Spence no longer came across as a hardliner and had mellowed into something akin to an 'elder statesman'. 'He is articulate and certainly not unintelligent,' the governor recorded. 'He makes his point concisely and with precision.' He continued, 'I do not see Spence, the individual, as anything other than a disillusioned, middle-aged man, who just wants contentment in the bosom of his family.'[18] As the question over Spence's future release from prison gathered momentum inside the NIO, the government sought the view of MI5, which reported:

> We have discussed the security aspect with the RUC and we are agreed that SPENCE, if released, is unlikely to reinvolve himself in UVF terrorism. Quite apart from his age, health and any lessons he may have learned he is out of touch with UVF leadership outside the compounds. Any work for the UVF would probably be confined to Prisoners' Welfare.[19]

Based on intelligence, presumably gained by way of prison surveillance, MI5's assessment of the UVF figurehead suggested it was 'obvious from his behaviour in prison SPENCE has never renounced his association with the UVF, and he is still regarded as something of a folk-hero on the Shankhill [sic]'.[20] Intriguingly, MI5 thought that early release for Spence 'would not pass uncelebrated, but although this might offer the UVF a much-needed boost in morale, it would not bring them any tangible or lasting benefit, and could not affect their steady decline'.[21] After granting Spence his first parole on Christmas Eve 1982, when he returned some hours ahead of his allotted time, the Permanent Under-Secretary at the NIO, Philip Woodfield, sought the views of the Lord Chief Justice, Lord Lowry, on Spence's prospective release on licence. Woodfield thought it

> unlikely that Spence – at his age and in view of the fact that he has been out of circulation for so long – will actively participate in UVF operations of any kind. On the other hand they are not confident that he will avoid becoming reinvolved with the organisation to some extent, and think that he could be used as a figurehead who might bolster UVF morale which has suffered considerably from recent police successes.[22]

Against Lowry's advice, the NIO decided to authorise Spence's release, judging it 'unlikely that he would take part directly in terrorist violence'.[23] The veteran loyalist paramilitary was duly released on medical grounds on 13 December 1984.[24]

On the outside, Spence had indeed become a folk hero for the UVF, though instead of channelling that status in the direction of fundraising, he took the opportunity to build up his network of cross-community contacts in Northern Ireland. By the late 1980s and early 1990s Spence was situated firmly in the ranks of the PUP, the UVF's political associates, becoming a key member of the group's 'kitchen cabinet', which included David Ervine as the other PUP representative and two or three of the UVF's most senior leaders.[25] Indeed, many of the discussions held by the kitchen cabinet took place at his home on the Shankill.[26] The first role played by Spence and Ervine was to scrutinise information coming in from 'various sources' at the time, including the UVF's connection to Protestant clergy who had links to Father Alec Reid and the PIRA.[27] They were to assist the UVF leadership in determining whether republicans were serious about ending the armed conflict and under what conditions.

Another function Spence and Ervine performed was to offer the UVF political analysis, built around the ideas they had developed in prison. This had culminated in the PUP's original 1978 policy document *Proposed Democratic Devolved Administration for Northern Ireland* (reissued in May 1979), which advocated an end to what they called 'sectarian powersharing', though they did not define how their proposals for a devolved government in Northern Ireland would deliver beyond what had already been engineered at Sunningdale.[28] Nevertheless, the PUP's document usefully defined a unionist as 'a person who irrespective of political or religious persuasion believes that the economic link with the United Kingdom is more viable and beneficial than any other system proposed'. They claimed the 'progressive' element of their party's name was borrowed not from any kind of Marxist ideology but from a sense of democracy denied by the domination of Westminster over regional affairs, which 'had not been in the best interests of Northern Ireland'. The PUP would later develop its ideas around devolved government in its 1985 policy document *Sharing Responsibility*, where it put a more emphatic case for a broadening of the areas for adjudication by the Assembly established in 1982. The PUP advocated 'sharing responsibility' rather than 'sharing power' because it offered an opportunity for wide agreement and because the party believed 'power should not be available to any political structure designed to meet the needs of a region of the United Kingdom'.[29] What the PUP proposed was nowhere near as radical as the UDI concept advanced by the UDA and the ULDP (subsequently rebranded the New Ulster Political Research Group); rather, it advocated the creation of a glorified county council. Contentious issues like housing, education and security would be left on the back burner. Nevertheless, the central committee, select committee system, a North–South co-operative committee and a Bill of Rights were ideas ahead of their time. It seemed like the PUP were taking bold steps to offer alternatives to the logjam created by the Anglo-Irish Agreement, and it was against this backdrop that Spence and those around him coalesced in the early 1990s.

In early 1993 an invitation was extended to Spence to speak to a group involved in conflict resolution in Dublin, but he was ill and instead sent David Ervine.[30] Ervine was accompanied by the UVF's then director of military operations, later given the codename 'The Craftsman'. At the event both men found themselves in conversation with Dublin-based trade unionist activist Chris Hudson, who would soon emerge as an unlikely intermediary between the kitchen cabinet and the Dublin government. Meetings between the UVF's representatives and the Irish government about the prospects for peace were held in Belfast and Dublin, which, according to Hudson's recollections, were fed back by the UVF leadership to its volunteers.[31]

As a 'respected intermediary' in Irish government circles, Hudson knew that the best way to sustain the secret dialogue between Dublin and the UVF was for Irish politicians to publicly reassure unionists that they respected their identity and rights. As the Irish Tánaiste and Minister for Foreign Affairs, Dick Spring, told Dáil Éireann two days after its signing, the Downing Street Declaration – also known as the Joint Declaration on Peace – was an attempt by Prime Minister John Major and Taoiseach Albert Reynolds to lay a charter for the peaceful resolution of the Troubles. While the British government reaffirmed that it had no 'selfish strategic or economic interest' in Northern Ireland, it also gave assurances that it would uphold the principle of consent that no constitutional change would take place without the overwhelming consent of the majority of people in Northern Ireland.[32] Major's government sought to realise the goal of 'peace, stability and reconciliation' by acting in a manner to 'encourage, facilitate and enable the achievement of such agreement over a period through a process of dialogue and co-operation based on full respect for the rights and identities of both traditions in Ireland'. What troubled unionists was their acceptance that 'such agreement may, as of right, take the form of agreed structures for the island as a whole, including a united Ireland achieved by peaceful means on the following basis'. As suspicions grew, loyalists sought assurances from the Irish government. This was reflected in Spring's comments to the Dáil:

> I know, not least from my recent contacts with Unionist representatives, that there is within that community a fear of change, a belief that all change and movement in the political situation can only harm them and in some way threaten their links with Britain. Since taking office I have tried very hard to dispel those fears. I have argued that political change need not be a zero-sum game. The position of Unionists is, in a sense, doubly guaranteed. The British Government has used this Declaration to restate once more its constitutional guarantee that there will be no change in the status of Northern Ireland unless that is the express wish of a majority of its people.[33]

Hudson's contacts with the Irish government were also publicly acknowledged by Taoiseach Albert Reynolds, who admitted during the same Dáil debate how:

> Throughout the last two months, I have made a determined effort to reassure the Unionist community by whatever means were open to me. When tension was running high and when murders of Catholics were virtually a daily occurrence, I conveyed through another respected intermediary messages intended for the Loyalist paramilitaries, making it clear that in seeking peace I was not seeking in any way to predetermine or prejudice the shape of a political settlement. I specifically refuted any notion that the Irish Government was involved in some way or another in a pact to deliver peace in return for joint authority. These private messages reinforced public statements to the same effect.[34]

Hudson was fast learning the art of shuttle diplomacy – and maintaining a double-edged line for private and public consumption. As he explained:

> For instance, the clear indicators [of the Irish Government's understanding of the loyalist position] were the Downing Street Declaration. That they [the UVF] saw some of their language, which was used in it. And particularly the comment that was used at a later stage by Dick Spring when he said that 'there can never be a united Ireland unless the majority of unionists want a united Ireland' … And when he was taken up in Dáil Éireann by Fianna Fáil – who were the main opposition at the time – Spring said, 'Oh, how silly of me. That was a very clumsy thing to say.' Now, Dick Spring had a noted legal mind and was a practising barrister. He didn't use language carelessly at all. So, he had clearly put that in to indicate – particularly to the loyalists and the general unionist community – that, irrespective of what's agreed, there is no sense of having a united Ireland, unless a majority of unionists wanted it. And that has become central to the thinking in Southern Ireland today. And that has become very calming. As 'The Craftsman' said to me, 'If you lift the siege then

you will see how we can respond.' So, the siege to them was Articles 2 and 3 because – you may remember the case that Michael and Chris McGimpsey took [against the Irish government] in Southern Ireland.[35] The judge noted that there was a constitutional imperative to act on those two aspirations – they weren't aspirations, they were a constitutional imperative to seek a united Ireland. And in a way what the McGimpseys proved was that there was some sort of – not legal – but some sort of constitutional justification to the Provisional IRA 'cos they could argue that they were acting out a constitutional obligation, because it is the will of the Irish people.[36]

Much of the nature of the kitchen cabinet's discussions on strategy and politics was making its way into Hudson's orbit as he held regular meetings with both UVF representatives and Irish government officials in Belfast and Dublin. For loyalists, the same logic of capitalising on the fear and anxiety they had used to replenish their ranks throughout the conflict was now being used in a kind of reverse psychology to persuade Dublin to dial down its rhetoric around Articles 2 And 3. As Hudson recalled:

That was [sic] perceived by the loyalists to be the siege. In other words, people like me could say that Southern Ireland is a friendly state, a bystander, but in reality it wasn't. The very nature of the Southern state through its constitution gave some sort of credibility [to those committed to a united Ireland] and was hostile to the unionist people of Northern Ireland. And it impressed me that loyalists understood that. You know, these are the people who are perceived as Neanderthals, and incapable of having intellectual thought, yet they were capable of working that type of thing out … And when I would meet them, we would discuss things on two different levels. We would discuss things on a level that would make things happen to bring around the peace, but we would also have discussions on a philosophical level as well. How Northern Ireland is viewed in the South [for example]. So those things were significant but essentially most of what we discussed was how we made this [violence] end up here. The first time I met them was with The Craftsman and the Chief of Staff [The Pipe] and David

> Ervine arranged that meeting. And what they indicated to me was – and that was in early 1993 – the biggest difficulty for them was they were getting signals from the other side [the PIRA] that there was a dialogue taking place. And something was happening. There was some type of movement in the nationalist consensus towards ending the conflict. And they were hearing that probably as well through people like Father Alec Reid. David Ervine quite rightly said that 'Every time we raise our head above the parapet to be part of this dialogue, we get fired at [by the IRA].'[37]

It would take four years of regular dialogue before Spence and the other members of the kitchen cabinet would finally persuade their comrades in the UVF to move towards 'greasing up their weapons'. In an interview with the *Sunday Tribune*, eleven days after the IRA ceasefire, one of the UVF leaders who sat on the kitchen cabinet said he was hopeful the process could 'lead towards a confidence in the community instilled by the British Government and then to peace'.[38] Engagement with the Dublin government was an essential part of this movement towards ending their armed campaign. 'There's a dawning within the Loyalist paramilitaries that it's over,' he told the startled reporter.[39]

On 13 October 1994, Spence, Ervine, Smith and Jim McDonald made the short journey from the PUP's offices on the Shankill to Fernhill House in Woodvale, the home of the Cunningham family, who had signed the cheque to pay for the guns run into Ulster for the original UVF in 1914. There they were joined by Gary McMichael, a twenty-five-year-old Ulster Democratic Party (UDP) councillor from Lisburn, John White, a founding member of the UFF's feared C Company, and Joe English, the commander of the UDA in southeast Antrim. The loyalists had something important to announce to the world. They were to 'universally cease all operational hostilities' and pay homage to their 'Fighters, Commandos and Volunteers who paid the supreme sacrifice', as well as their 'physically and mentally wounded who have served Ulster so unselfishly'. It was time to call a halt to their respective armed campaigns, for their main objective was accomplished. 'The Union is safe,' Spence assured the loyalist paramilitary constituency.[40]

The next day a thick mist descended over Fernhill House in Glencairn, which perches high above North and West Belfast. Lindy McDowell, a journalist from the *Belfast Telegraph*, travelled to Fernhill House to interview people about their initial reactions to the loyalist ceasefire announcement. She reflected on how 'the word deprivation could have been coined for areas like this. Boarded up windows, bruised and battered streets'. Fernhill House once sat amidst the splendour of a private aristocratic estate, but its gardens had long since passed into public ownership where the local authorities had presided over the building of working-class homes. It was 'the dividing line between privilege and poverty', McDowell observed. The venue might have been chosen by Spence in a bid to connect modern-day paramilitaries to their forefathers, though the reality was the paramilitaries had simply holstered a sword that right-wing unionists had unsheathed three decades earlier near the same spot. McDowell interviewed community worker Jackie Hewitt, who spoke for many loyalists when he urged them to 'reinforce this peace. If what is happening now were to fail, we all go down.'[41] They were wise words.

On 15 December 1994, two months after their ceasefire announcement, loyalist paramilitary representatives were summoned to Parliament Buildings at Stormont for their initial meeting with the British government. The first to arrive were members of the UDP, their delegation led by Gary McMichael and including David Adams, John White, Joe English and councillor for Rathcoole Tommy Kirkham. The UDP delegates were followed a few minutes later by members of the PUP's Executive Committee, led by Billy Hutchinson[42] and including David Ervine, Plum Smith, Jackie Mahood and Lindsay Robb. For the British government, their ceasefire was a welcome sign that loyalist paramilitaries wished to play a role in the developing talks. For its part, the NIO regarded the meeting 'as merely exploratory dialogue' and reiterated the point that it 'should not be mistaken for negotiations'.[43] They were firm-handed with the loyalists, seeing them, in Hutchinson's view, as 'one issue' parties with a small mandate.[44] The NIO civil servants who had convened the talks even rearranged the room in a way that was designed to send a message to the loyalists. In a well-worn psychological tactic in British diplomatic circles for attaining their strategic objectives, chairs were set out to maximise discomfort and to place loyalist negotiators in a subservient position to government representatives. The NIO told the loyalists that the 'continuation and completion of this dialogue depends on the CLMC's

[Combined Loyalist Military Command's] continued adherence to this in word and action regardless of other circumstances and on loyalist political representatives demonstrating a commitment to exclusively peaceful methods and showing that they abide by the democratic process'.[45]

The government believed that the disarmament of paramilitary groups was a crucial first step in returning Northern Ireland to 'the democratic process', making the case that since the loyalists commanded only a tiny electoral mandate, they needed to continue to seek political office. Only when this 'decontamination' – to borrow Prime Minister John Major's phrase from the time – took place would the government meet more regularly with their representatives, like they did with mainstream political parties. As the NIO made clear:

> The Government's fundamental approach to the future of Northern Ireland is based on the right of self-determination and the principle of democratic consent, as set out in paragraph 4 of the Downing Street Declaration. The Government reaffirms all its commitments in that Declaration, together with its obligations under international agreements and the guarantees which it has given, including Northern Ireland's statutory constitutional guarantee.[46]

The British government's understanding of the 'principle of democratic consent' became the cornerstone of its policy – laid down by the then Secretary of State Peter Brooke in November 1990 – that Britain had 'no selfish strategic or economic interest in Northern Ireland'.[47] Although the language was ambiguous and contradictory, given that in constitutional terms Northern Ireland remained part of the United Kingdom, it reflected the dominant mood in Whitehall that 'we did not have a "selfish" interest separate from the interests of the people of Northern Ireland'.[48] In 1993, Prime Minister John Major had come to see the creative possibilities of forging a new dispensation amidst the entanglements of the past:

> We were prepared to accept the democratic wishes of the people of Northern Ireland, and we expected that Irish Nationalists, including the Irish government and Sinn Féin, should do likewise. If a clear

majority of the people of Northern Ireland wished to leave the United Kingdom, we would not force them to remain, notwithstanding our deep attachment to the Union as a whole. But we could not push them out. It was democracy at its purest: the people would decide.[49]

The British government meant to appear flexible on any future political dispensation in Northern Ireland, though this nonetheless alarmed loyalists. Indeed, UUP leader Jim Molyneaux remained deeply suspicious of this developing new agenda, stating the previous summer that his party would not tolerate new structures which would lead to the 'severance of the Union'.[50]

Although not acknowledged by the loyalist delegations in public at the time or since, the NIO had explicitly asserted its intentions surrounding the future political development of Northern Ireland's constitutional status. Government officials pointed to 'a set of geographical, historical and political realities which give the Government of the Republic of Ireland an interest in relevant Northern Ireland issues as acknowledged in the Anglo-Irish Agreement'.[51] London reiterated its belief in 'a unique relationship between the peoples of the United Kingdom as a whole and of the Republic of Ireland', remaining 'firmly committed to the enhancement of that relationship and to continuing close contact, consultation and co-operation on matters of shared concern'.[52] The civil servants present that day were particularly patronising in the way they engaged with the loyalist delegations, and, naturally, they leant on them heavily because of the sectarian dimension of the respective campaigns of the groups they represented. However, the government did not seem to fully appreciate the socio-economic inequalities within and between the two communities, going only so far as acknowledging that 'there is evidence of alienation from Government in parts of the majority community on the grounds that the Government are alleged to pay insufficient concern to their legitimate interests and aspirations'.[53] For their part, the loyalist delegates misjudged the mood music too by coming armed with a shopping list of economic demands that failed to excite the interests of a government already using everything in its power to drain the swamp of disaffection in marginalised areas.[54] Indeed, some of the senior government ministers responsible for promoting Northern Ireland's economy, such as Richard

Needham, came to regard loyalist paramilitaries as 'mirror images of the IRA' who were 'also fascist'.[55]

Above all, the major strategic objective in the government's coercive dialogue with the loyalists was to demand that the UVF and UDA disarm. In seeking this outcome from its engagement with the loyalist delegates, the government was taking steps to roll back from the position it had adopted twenty years earlier when it effectively ceded its monopoly over the legitimate use of force to the same groups.[56] There could be no disputing the seriousness of the stark choice the government was putting to loyalist paramilitaries on illegal weapons. 'Their continued retention will call such commitments [to a peaceful resolution of the conflict] into question and will constitute a barrier to the PUP and UDP playing as full a part in normal political life as is consistent with their electoral mandates,'[57] the government warned. Billy Hutchinson later admitted to becoming somewhat intemperate over this aspect of the government's demands, telling reporters after the meeting that he felt that 'our mandate is the silence of the guns'.[58] Despite the assurances they had received from intermediaries – mainly Protestant clergy – who had been engaging with the British government on their behalf, many of the loyalists left the meeting with a question: had there been a sell-out? Understandably, loyalists were as anxious to get an assurance from their own government about the principle of consent as they were from what they regarded as a foreign government in Dublin.

The idea of the 'Principle of Consent' – where a majority of people in Northern Ireland would have to agree to end the Union with Great Britain – can be traced back to the fall of the old Stormont regime and the passing of the Northern Ireland Constitution Act (1973), which reaffirmed 'that in no event will Northern Ireland or any part of it cease to be part of Her Majesty's dominions and of the United Kingdom without the consent of the majority of the people of Northern Ireland voting in a poll held for the purposes of this section'.[59] The British government had earlier given a guarantee in the Ireland Act (1949) 'that in no event will Northern Ireland or any part thereof cease to be part of His Majesty's dominions and of the United Kingdom without the consent of the Parliament of Northern Ireland'.[60] The Principle of Consent was first articulated in its current form in the Downing Street Declaration of 1993, where the British government agreed that it was 'for the people of the island of Ireland alone, by agreement between the two parts respectively, to exercise their right of self-determination on the basis of consent, freely and concurrently given, North and South, to bring about a united Ireland, if that is their wish'.[61] Not all loyalists and unionists had yet come to accept the British government's policy of 'no selfish or strategic economic interest' or, indeed, that a return to local power-sharing required both a power-sharing dimension or direct involvement by the Irish Republic.

In its first meetings with loyalist representatives in December 1994, the British government was explicitly seeking to turn loyalist guns into ploughshares. However, to the loyalists, the government appeared anxious to play the role of umpire. While the NIO acknowledged the Principle of Consent, it went beyond this to discuss what it called 'the political and social realities in Northern Ireland'.[62] As far as the NIO civil servants who met with the loyalist delegates were concerned, they were governing a 'deeply divided community where the larger part of the population ... retains a strong sense of loyalty to the Crown, believing that its culture and ethos can best be preserved if Northern Ireland remains part of the United Kingdom'.[63] In contrast, they said, the 'minority community, in general, sees itself as Irish. Politically, many in that community aspire to the achievement of a sovereign, territorially United Ireland.'[64] Importantly, and in line with its position in the earlier Anglo-Irish Agreement and Downing Street Declaration, the government recognised a 'set of geographical, historical and political realities which give the Government of the Republic of Ireland an interest in Northern Ireland issues'.[65] This was a reflection of London's acceptance since 1985 'that an intergovernmental approach was necessary towards Northern Ireland' and the government was 'keen to act in concert with Dublin where possible'.[66] In concluding its dialogue with the loyalists, the NIO reinforced its view that it wanted to govern on behalf of all sections of the community, citing 'Parity of Esteem' as its model.

The PUP and UDP representatives left their meeting with the NIO with a clear idea about how London intended to facilitate these peace talks. For loyalists, decommissioning was the price they would have to pay in a trade-off for access to electoral mandates and political power. The representatives were not universally popular for adopting a new-found evangelism for what was fast becoming known as the 'peace process'. Even before the meeting at Stormont, David Ervine's public statements and his public shaking of hands with Irish President Mary Robinson had incurred the wrath of hardline loyalists.[67] There were still some influential loyalists who maintained a healthy scepticism of the strategic benefits of the ceasefires, with Mid Ulster UVF commander Billy Wright, a close associate of PUP delegate Lindsay Robb, harbouring deep suspicions of the motives of the PIRA. Another loyalist close to Wright, Clifford Peeples, believed the approach taken by the British government was part of the beginning of an appeasement of the PIRA. 'Billy had a broader strategic understanding of the Provo's Tactical Use of Armed Struggle,' recalled Peeples. 'There were people around him who looked at what was happening here and seeing [sic] direct comparisons with the ANC and its armed wing in South Africa.'[68]

While initially supportive of the Shankill leadership's decision to call a ceasefire, Wright began to change his mind in early 1995. When the British and Irish governments released the Framework Documents on 22 February 1995, Wright's suspicions grew.[69] The documents were jointly agreed by Prime Minister John Major and his Irish counterpart John Bruton as a means of laying the foundations for the future shape of a political dispensation, including agreement that Dublin would drop its territorial claims on Northern Ireland, that a new eighty- to ninety-member assembly would be created along with a North–South body to co-ordinate matters of common concern on both sides of the border.[70]

On the surface, these documents were little more than a set of principles by which the British and Irish governments would approach negotiations with the political parties in Northern Ireland. While the Downing Street Declaration had acknowledged the need to remove the causes of conflict and overcome the mistakes of the past, the Framework Documents informed the emerging strategy for attaining these shared objectives: 'A collective effort is needed to create, through agreement and reconciliation, a new beginning founded on consent, for relationships within Northern Ireland, within the island of Ireland and between the peoples of these islands.'[71] This was hardly a revolutionary vision for the future. Any peace process would be based around 'the consent of the governed', which was judged 'an essential ingredient for stability in any political arrangement'.[72] Underscoring the Framework

Documents was a belief that any future agreement 'must be pursued and established by exclusively democratic, peaceful means, without resort to violence or coercion'.[73] Crucially, the scaffolding erected around the peace process was designed explicitly for the 'protection and expression of, the rights and identities of both traditions in Ireland and even-handedly [to] afford both communities in Northern Ireland parity of esteem and treatment'.[74]

In line with the British government's talks with loyalist paramilitary representatives in December 1994, the Framework Documents appeared on first glance to be deeply imbued with a pragmatic approach towards the unfolding peace process, acknowledging how the two communities held divergent views on the constitutional future of Northern Ireland. Nevertheless, as far as the Official Unionist Party was concerned, this latest Anglo-Irish communiqué offered nothing of comfort to unionists. Initially, Jim Molyneaux had trusted John Major's assurance that the British government would not seek to implement any initiative without unionist consent. Ian Paisley, on the other hand, had been consistently warning about the dangers of trusting the Major government since the DUP rejected the Joint Declaration and referred to Molyneaux unflatteringly as a traitor.[75] Molyneaux now found himself in almost the same position with John Major as Brian Faulkner did with Ted Heath, a position he had himself warned against two decades earlier. The publication of the Framework Documents undermined Molyneaux's position. The UUP MP in Upper Bann, David Trimble, was quick to set out his stall against the initiative, telling reporters he felt 'absolutely sick'. So incensed was Trimble he even claimed he would 'almost have preferred that there was legislation for a united Ireland. At least we would know where we stood'.[76] What incensed Wright and others sympathetic to his fundamentalist understanding of the Principle of Consent – as it applied explicitly to unionists – was the British government's reiteration that it would

> uphold the democratic wish of a greater number of the people of Northern Ireland on the issue of whether they prefer to support the Union or a sovereign united Ireland. On this basis, they reiterate that they have no selfish strategic or economic interest in Northern Ireland. For as long as the democratic wish of the people of Northern Ireland is

> for no change in its present status, the British Government pledge that their jurisdiction there will be exercised with rigorous impartiality on behalf of all the people of Northern Ireland in their diversity.[77]

This kind of language, originally used by John Hume and appropriated by Peter Brooke, may have been an attempt to make London seem more impartial. However, to unionist politicians it was ambiguous and contradictory.

For militant-minded loyalists like Wright – who saw the world in black and white terms – the Framework Documents were nothing short of a sell-out. A few months after their publication, Wright found himself at a meeting with Chris Hudson. 'Before the framework documents were published we were assured the Irish government was seeking a fair, honourable and just settlement for all. Their actions since then do not support that,'[78] the Mid Ulster UVF commander told Hudson. Expressing the anger felt by many grassroots loyalists, Wright pointed to the 'deep disappointment at the unfair and imbalanced documents', reiterating his view that they 'were not consistent with the search for a fair and honourable settlement'.[79] In an interview with the *Belfast Telegraph* shortly after his encounter with Hudson, Wright outlined his thinking on where this left militant loyalists:

> The Irish government is building a siege mentality among unionists, highlighting that they are on their own, while republicans are in the other corner with Dublin, the SDLP and others. That is very dangerous. Loyalists have not behaved like the republicans, crying wolf and threatening protest when there is a wind of change. There has been no breach of the loyalist ceasefire, but there has been no reward. That is going to have to change, loyalists must be treated as equals in this process.[80]

Without a firm guarantee on Northern Ireland's long-term constitutional position within the UK, Wright's mind drifted back to his belief in the efficacy of violence. A widening gulf now opened between Wright and the UVF's Shankill-based leadership. As one high-level MI5 agent inside the upper echelons of the group subsequently told his handler, Wright had become 'a "loose cannon" whose impulsive nature may well result in the resumption of at least localised violence in County Armagh.'[81] It was a stark warning that would threaten to derail the emerging peace process.

Meanwhile, major change was underway within the UUP. By placing his trust in the Major government not once but twice, Molyneaux opened the door to a leadership challenge.[82] On 14 March 1995 Lee Reynolds, a virtual unknown member of the party's branch at Queen's University Belfast, issued a personal statement stating he would put forward his name in the leadership election a few days later. Reynolds blamed repeated failures in terms of Molyneaux's misreading of the Anglo-Irish Agreement and his further acquiescence to the Joint Declaration and Framework Documents as justification for his decision to stand against his party leader. Nevertheless, Molyneaux won the contest, though Reynolds managed to win 88 votes out of the 619 cast.[83] The long-serving UUP leader was bruised by the encounter and limped on until the defeat of incumbent Alan McFarland in the by-election held in June after the death of James Kilfedder. The UUP's seat was won by former UUP member Bob McCartney, who had been expelled for his ardent opposition to the Anglo-Irish Agreement. It was a disaster for Molyneaux whose leadership was by now fatally wounded.

A senior member of the UUP told Molyneaux that he had lost the confidence of the voluntary component of the party. It rattled Molyneaux, who had been known for his nerves of steel. As an RAF serviceman, he had landed in Normandy on D-Day and had even been one of the first to liberate the Belsen death camp. He was rarely seen expressing much in the way of emotion. 'I remember going to see him in Westminster one day and he was really upset,' recalled a former aide. 'I'd never seen him like that. He'd always impressed me with his cool. His nickname in the party was "The Iceman". He told me point blank, "I'm going to have to resign."'[84] The senior UUP figure then invited Molyneaux along to a lunch with David Trimble, who was by now perceived as the heir apparent to the UUP's leadership. 'Trimble did not show. And he was the guy who was the NIO's stool pigeon who was meant to be seizing the crown, yet he didn't have the balls to turn up to a final show down.'[85] Molyneaux would eventually step down at the end of August 1995, resigning from the leadership position he had held since 1979. He would be replaced by David Trimble almost two weeks later.

13

Ulster's Answer to Leaderless Resistance

A political fanatic is not someone who wants to perfect himself. No, he wants to perfect you. He wants to perfect you personally, to perfect you politically, to perfect you religiously, or racially, or geographically. He wants you to change your mind, your government, your borders. He may not be able to change your race, so he will eliminate you from the perfect equation in his mind by eliminating you from the earth.

David Trimble, Nobel Lecture, 10 December 1998[1]

IT WAS NEARING LUNCHTIME ON Sunday, 9 July 1995, when former UFF leader turned pastor Kenny McClinton received a knock on his door. His wife, Wendy, answered to find Billy Wright standing there with a smile on his face. She called her husband, who was intrigued to receive his visitor. McClinton had known Wright since the early 1980s, when the two men were serving out respective prison sentences in the Maze. It was in the H Blocks that McClinton had baptised Wright as a born-again Christian. They had been friends ever since. As the local UVF commander responsible for Portadown, Wright had gone to elicit McClinton's support after around 200 nationalists began a sit-down protest on the Garvaghy Road as a means of stopping the Orange Order's annual church parade from returning from Drumcree parish church to the centre of Portadown. The Orange marchers had been halted at Drumcree churchyard by the security forces fifteen minutes later.[2] McClinton and Wright travelled to Corcrain Avenue to mount a counter-demonstration of their own. The loyalists were promptly met by a long line of armoured RUC Land Rovers driving in haste to block their path. 'If a Republican rent-a-crowd can block the homeward bound route of the Orangemen then a peaceful Protestant rent-a-crowd can make sure that the road the authorities were trying to force the Orangemen to take would be blocked,' Wright told McClinton.[3] The tactic was designed to draw the RUC away from the Garvaghy Road so the Orangemen and their supporters could force their way down it on their return route. 'If the Garvaghy Resident's Group and their imported Republican cronies really wish to block the Queen's Highway,' Wright said, 'then they can remain blocked into their own area without access to Portadown town centre.'[4] The loyalist protest would last two days, when a deal was brokered by intermediaries between the Orange Order, RUC and residents' group. Five hundred Orangemen walked down the Garvaghy Road, thereby completing their march. Accompanying them were MPs Ian Paisley and David Trimble, flanked by Paisley's son Ian and McClinton.[5] McClinton recalled that the Order's local district master, Harold Gracey, greeted him with tears in his eyes. They were soon joined by Billy Wright. 'You weren't permitted a band to play you home to Portadown, Harold, but listen, listen to the sound of that old Orange flute that is playing the victory for you at the Bridge,' Wright told Gracey as he shook the Orangeman's hand firmly.[6]

Wright and McClinton saw their counter-demonstration in Portadown as a triumph. For their part, the authorities were determined not to be outmanoeuvred a second time. The following July, the RUC deployed in huge numbers alongside the army, who erected barricades around Drumcree.[7] Loyalists realised they might have to escalate matters if they were to overturn the renewed ban on the Drumcree parade. In practical terms Wright and those around him set out on a secret enterprise to form a covert alliance with other rogue elements of the UVF and UDA. Intelligent and well-connected investigative reporters had questioned Wright about the rumours of a breakaway organisation as early as August 1995, but he was dismissive. The reality was that these loyalists were not seeking to form a group but rather to foment a conspiracy within the ranks of the loyalist paramilitary fraternity, who were officially observing a ceasefire. One paramilitary, 'James', outlined the nature of this conspiracy:

That was the year [1996] that really brokered cover names and brokered backstreet ordnance as a way to battle for control of the situation. How do you deal with large crowds of police and army? You can't go head-to-head but you can put small devices in crowds and mount attacks. Pop up protests went everywhere. Word of mouth and mobile phone technology was utilised for the first time. It was all designed to draw as many police and army personnel away from the church at Drumcree. The act wasn't really as important as the copycat actions it spawned. It had to look organic. It had to look self-amplified. There had been no real co-ordination in 1995, no preparation and no determination if the RUC did not allow the parade through. However, once you had manipulated so many people in so many areas, loyalists began to hijack vehicles. Pipe bombs were utilised in greater numbers than ever before. It wasn't as if there was widespread support for violence but the fact that some loyalists copycatted was enough. The UVF and UDA leaderships were against any violent protest action and were deliberately trying to control the situation. So, you needed to manufacture a widespread protest movement that was against the police, army, and the NIO. We would eventually draw support into Drumcree from Belfast, North Antrim and Londonderry and other areas. It was all built around the premise of supporting the Orange Order but, really, it was about creating a popular grassroots movement in opposition to the peace process. There were large numbers of paramilitaries who did not like it. But there were people who did from places like southeast Antrim, who were working with Billy Wright and other people from the UFF in West Belfast. They were technically under the control of their leaderships who backed the NIO. They were being controlled and the ones who were not being controlled were being promised things that were never delivered. The one-time UFF Brigadier in Mid Ulster … led from the front. He was instrumental in controlling the flying pickets. He had gone to live in Scotland in the 1980s and then returned after the ceasefires were called. He was instrumental in Drumcree. He wasn't organised in a military sense but he was instrumental in running the protests. He brought Portadown to a standstill. The street protests, the proliferation of pipe bombings, the dissatisfaction amongst loyalist paramilitaries was rife. What was instrumental in this was a form of leaderless resistance. As soon as you have a structured organisation, that leadership can be bought down or brought under control. It can be dismantled. So, you have to set up four-man teams. You control them. It doesn't matter about tactics. Like the French resistance you just create havoc.[8]

The ideas that helped shape the thinking of loyalists like James who took on the authorities over Drumcree had come from the most unlikely direction. At a time when the United States was taking a close interest in the emerging peace process,[9] James was using his contacts within the American evangelical community to formulate a strategy to undermine the security forces who had been sent to Portadown to prevent a reoccurrence of the protests witnessed the previous summer. James claimed he had begun his education in this form of 'leaderless resistance' by reading books and pamphlets sent to him by contacts in a loose network of American evangelicals, right-wing activists and conspiracy theorists. Sometime in the early 1990s he visited the United States to train alongside Christian militias who believed fervently in the Second Amendment right of all citizens to bear arms. James found himself engaging in discussions with influential militia leaders about how the threat of force could be used to preserve cherished local identities and values that harped back to a golden era of the first Ulster Scots frontiersmen. However, what really impressed James was his discussions with far-right activists who looked to the teachings of, perhaps, their most influential leader, Louis Beam.[10]

Beam coined the term 'leaderless resistance' in 1983. When serving as a helicopter door gunner in Vietnam, he had studied how the Viet Cong (VC) utilised guerrilla warfare to challenge the United States, and how the US military's hierarchical, pyramidal structures proved cumbersome when faced with the cell-based hit-and-run tactics of the VC. Beam argued that in this 'so-called "pyramid" type of organization, an infiltrator can destroy anything which is beneath him in the pyramid of organization.'[11] The same could be said of the infiltrator who entered the organisation at the bottom – as he or she rose then they could betray those above and below them and destroy the group. The answer to this, Beam said, was to develop a cell-based system where 'numerous independent cells are created which operate completely isolated from each other and particularly with no knowledge of each other, but are orchestrated together by headquarters'.[12] In the world of the American far right, there had always been a deep suspicion of centralised authorities and an ideological rejection of federal and state authority,[13] and so this kind of alternative way of living and organising politically had significant appeal. For James, he could see how this kind of network thinking offered loyalist paramilitaries not only a way of operating under the radar of their own hierarchical organisations, but also an invaluable means of forging a sense of shared historical identity by offering those sceptical of the peace process a new sense of belonging.[14] On his return to Northern Ireland, James immediately began to put his ideas into practice, which received an enthusiastic reception from Billy Wright and other loyalist paramilitaries in Portadown, Belfast and southeast Antrim.

Despite UVF attempts to woo Wright back into their fold and away from his dissenting views on the ceasefire, the Mid-Ulster loyalist was becoming more and more hard-line in his attitudes towards the peace process. 'The crux of our problem is the fear over sovereignty. If the constitutional issue is settled then a lot of the problems our two communities face can be settled in a time of peace and generosity,' he told one *Belfast Telegraph* reporter who interviewed him in Portadown in July 1996.[15] 'If the fear of the IRA assassin is gone, and if the democratic rights of the people of Northern Ireland have been upheld, I believe loyalists will be very generous in a future political settlement.'[16] It was an interview tinged by a fundamentalist reading of sovereignty that held out the prospect of a return to the days of unionist domination. The reality, as the British government's views on the ceasefire and ensuing Drumcree protests demonstrated, was that loyalists would have to willingly accept the new reality of parity of esteem.

Wright slipped further into the bowels of despair as the PIRA stepped up its renewed armed campaign. As far as he was concerned, the Union was in peril and only armed resistance could possibly stabilise the situation.[17] Interestingly, around this time the Belfast-born Australian academic and UUP member Norman Porter published one of the most influential books on Ulster Unionism, in which he saw a fixation on the constitutional issue to the detriment of all else as a sign of abnormality. 'Wrestling with political issues of identity is not in itself a sign of abnormality,' he wrote, 'though wrestling with virtually nothing else is.'[18] Those loyalists who felt Wright was being far too alarmist remained convinced that the Union nevertheless was 'safe' and had moved on to outline how it was now necessary to address questions beyond those involving political identity and the constitutional question. Ironically, despite being labelled 'liberals' by the press, they were prepared to support illiberal means to censor or discipline those who disagreed with them.

Within a matter of weeks of Wright's comments to the press, members of the PUP had colluded with the UVF to secure the expulsion of Wright and his associates – the CLMC, the umbrella group which had announced the ceasefires in 1994, even sentenced him to death for good measure. Wright had become irreconcilable in his criticisms of the PUP and their engagement with the peace process. 'At the end of the day I cannot reconcile myself to the beliefs of this political party I'm at loggerheads with: my feelings are the same as 97pc of the Protestant population and I can't support the party,' he told the *Belfast Telegraph*.[19] One letter-writer from Portadown noted in the same newspaper, 'Thank God for someone like Billy Wright. At long last grassroots loyalism has given us a true visionary who has spotted the dangers in the false peace process and is prepared to stand up for Ulster. One has to admire his courage in refusing to run from the threats of death by misguided and blindfold loyalists.'[20] The Loyalist Volunteer Force (LVF), formed by Wright after his expulsion from the UVF, became the physical force embodiment of the ideal circulating amongst militant loyalists who saw themselves as a vanguard acting on behalf of the Ulster people in resisting the British government's policy concerning the peace process.

Although Wright and the LVF were active in killings and other attacks, much of their disaffection was channelled in the direction of subversion and agitation against the PUP, the party he remained at loggerheads with. Clifford Peeples, who shared Wright's disdain for the PUP, referring to them as 'communists', was a key architect of an ongoing campaign to undermine their pro-peace process message:

> As to the allegation that I led a propaganda campaign against those who would sell out the future of Northern Ireland to republicans – absolutely. You could call it a propaganda campaign or you could call it

an information campaign. Whatever terminology you want to use – yes, I did it! I distributed leaflets, information booklets, videos. All that ... would have taken place from '95 – probably late '94 but almost certainly '95 – right up until my incarceration in 1999. So, it was a four-year campaign of telling people what was actually going to be the future for them [if they remained on this course]. It was based around a booklet and a video called *Sell Out and Surrender* and it gave facts and details based on [how that would play out]. It also gave people information about the background of individuals who were now ... leading loyalists towards surrender. The allegations I made about those groupings have all proven to be correct. I stand by the campaign that people would say I led – there were almost certainly other people involved and if they want to admit their part then that's up to them – there was nothing illegal in it. We informed people ... about the [PIRA's] Tactical Use of Armed Struggle. Told them that the British government and the Irish government would promise anything. They would bring loyalists in. They would destroy the RUC. They would destroy the UDR. They would destroy loyalists' will to resist. And anyone who was willing to make a stand against that would be blackmailed, would be taken out. And everything we said came to pass.[21]

As far as Peeples and Wright were concerned, there was an alternative to what they branded 'sell-out loyalism':

The alternative programme was to make a stand, whether individuals wanted to use that as a term of a physical stance – that was up to them. But it was almost certainly a stance where you would vote against anything that came along because their whole argument was that they [the British government] would manipulate the populace into voting for this. It was seen as a democratic process. And we saw documents – and documents were released – from the Northern Ireland Office – about how they would manipulate the media structures within Northern Ireland to bring about a positive result in their view. And how they would use psychological manipulation to control 70 per cent of the population.[22]

Peeples, Wright and others like them began to share stages at rallies with leading members of the DUP in 1996, 1997 and 1998. These rejectionist loyalists came to share a conspiratorial mindset of 'sell out' and betrayal, which very quickly turned into an echo chamber. Wright, however, did not live long enough to lead the opposition to the emerging peace deal as he was assassinated in December 1997 in controversial circumstances while on remand in the Maze Prison for threatening a witness and her son. Peeples, nevertheless, continued the fight, explaining:

> The issue came down to one thing. And it came down to future guarantees. And it came down to one thing: The IRA's use of the Tactical Use of Armed Struggle where they would continue to use the threat of violence. They had a direct line to the government in Downing Street, and they had a direct line to Dublin. And it came down to a back channel to the Irish government. It would continue to use that threat of republican violence through splits and breaks. And the threat of violence became a more potent weapon and more potent tool. Once you come away from violence people will do almost anything to stop it occurring. That was their wedge to the British government and how they were able to keep murdering their people and how they were able to continue to manipulate the situation to make Northern Ireland a 'basket case', where they were involved in criminality, where they were involved in a classic subversive campaign, undermining of a democratic state. Where they were being funded by criminal activity, yet there was no sanction. And they were able to use that as a wedge. And where we see the Principle of Consent has been washed aside. And where one of those aspects of the 'Triple Lock'[23] has been washed aside and no one cares. As long as the threat of Provo violence is kept under wraps.[24]

Peeples' involvement in the information campaign revolved around a core of twenty-five people who ran off leaflets, booklets and other ephemera, which they distributed at parades and other large gatherings in loyalist areas across Northern Ireland. It was a large-scale operation, funded by Protestant businessmen, and intersected with the agitation spearheaded by the DUP and its most senior politicians, who added political top cover to the anti-peace process cottage industry now animating sections of the loyalist grassroots. 'It could never compete with the NIO and the government,' Peeples recalled, 'but it did a lot to destabilise their process.'

After several days spent reaching agreement, the UUP under David Trimble – along with the paramilitary-linked PUP and UDP – announced their support for the Belfast/Good Friday Agreement, talks for which had been ongoing between the British and Irish governments and the main political parties since 1996. Signed on 10 April 1998, the Agreement made provisions for a power-sharing Assembly and Executive, and North–South and East–West ministerial bodies. Despite his earlier opposition to the Framework Documents, Trimble now became a champion for a deal that had a significantly beefed-up Irish dimension and a mechanism by which a united Ireland could be brought about. The Agreement would be sold on the basis of 'creative ambiguity' around the thorny issue of IRA decommissioning. This would not take place in lockstep with the erection of the new institutions but would be pushed into the future along with other challenging issues such as parading, symbols and the legacy of past violence. The release of paramilitary prisoners and the replacement of the RUC with a new police service was to complement the withdrawal of British troops to barracks and a process of further 'demilitarisation' once paramilitary decommissioning began. It was envisaged that the UDR, which had been amalgamated with the Royal Irish Rangers in 1992, would have its home service battalions further decreased in time.

In a referendum held a few weeks later, 71.1 per cent of the electorate voted in favour of the Agreement. While Peeples and other loyalists may have failed in their bid to convince a majority of unionists to vote No, only 53 per cent voted Yes.[25] Despite only just being a majority, it was a victory of sorts for the UUP and the smaller PUP and UDP, and something they felt they could build on. For those unionists who opposed the Agreement, like Bob McCartney and Stephen Cooper of the UK Unionist Party, there was a feeling that 'the whole world was against us'. As Cooper recalled:

> The talks themselves, whenever we were being vilified for not going in, we heard cries of 'If we walk away they [the British government] are going to enforce it on us' … The key, simple objection was

how could any unionist go into talks curtailed and limited to the Framework Documents because the Framework Documents, don't forget, were rejected by all of us [unionists] even by those people who went into the talks knowing the best that they could achieve were the very Documents that we had all rejected prior to the talks. So, our frustration was [born out] of that and so our suspicions were aroused. [We asked], 'What is going on here? What have these people been promised? What is the driving force? Have they got something to hide? Have they been compromised?' I mean at the time it was a very intense period. And it was a time, don't forget, when we were just coming out of false ceasefires and government ministers trying to talk to us and trying to manipulate us and trying to coerce us and vilify us … So that was where we were. In fact at the King's Hall when the result was given I was actually spat on by [a member of the Alliance Party] … such was the venom and the hatred [directed at us] …[26]

Anti-Agreement unionists may have found themselves in an embattled political position after the referendum, though the DUP and UK Unionist Party still managed to secure twenty seats and five seats respectively in the newly elected Northern Ireland Assembly election held on 25 June 1998.[27] It was clear in terms of the first preference votes won that the unionist community was evenly split with regard to the merits of the Agreement, reflective perhaps of their position in the referendum.

The PUP's senior strategist, Billy Mitchell, saw tough times ahead, with considerable work needed to foster support for the Agreement. While recognising the potential for political crisis and grave danger, he also believed unionism stood on the cusp of a time of 'transition, of invitation and of opportunity'.[28] Where there was suspicion, fear and mistrust, he nevertheless also saw signs of a 'new era of hope and opportunity'.[29] Mitchell had made the personal transition from militant loyalism to a form of inclusive and open-minded unionism. His political outlook – shared by many others in the PUP at the time – privileged a form of democratic socialism ahead of the social conservativism that had long marked out Ulster unionism.[30] It was, therefore, much closer to the ideals of the NILP and trade union movement.[31] Thanks primarily to Mitchell's force of personality in the 1990s and into the early 2000s, the PUP retained Clause 4 in its party constitution, seeking to 'develop a just, equitable and pluralist society for all our citizens within the United Kingdom'.[32] Mitchell had read and reflected on many of the great political philosophers, including Francis Hutcheson, though it was the English historian R.H. Tawney who offered a working definition of democratic socialism that chimed with Mitchell's own ideas, and it was something that he and an increasing number of his colleagues sought to apply in some of the most marginalised parts of Northern Ireland.

The gulf between violence and politics, between war and peace, had haunted all shades of Ulster unionism since the formation of Northern Ireland, and it was reflected in the internal dialogue now underway within unionism and loyalism. David Trimble believed that the gulf could be bridged. As he told the Nobel Peace Prize Committee in Oslo on 10 December 1998:

> We have a few fanatics who dream of forcing the Ulster British people into a Utopian Irish state, more ideologically Irish than its own inhabitants actually want. We also have fanatics who dream of permanently suppressing northern nationalists in a state more supposedly British than its inhabitants actually want.
>
> But a few fanatics are not a fundamental problem. No, the problem arises if political fanatics bury themselves within a morally legitimate political movement. Then there is a double danger. The first is that we might dismiss legitimate claims for reform because of the barbarism of terrorist groups bent on revolution.
>
> In that situation experience would suggest that the best way forward is for democrats to carry out what the Irish writer Eoghan Harris calls acts of good authority. That is acts addressed to their own side.
>
> Thus each reformist group has a moral obligation to deal with its own fanatics. The Serbian democrats must take on the Serbian fascists. The PLO [Palestinian Liberation Organization] must take on Hamas. In Northern Ireland, constitutional nationalists must take on republican dissident terrorists and constitutional Unionists must confront Protestant terrorists.[33]

Considering unionists had 'not exerted much intellectual energy in constructing a vision as to where the [peace] process should be going,'[34] Trimble must have seemed somewhat exotic. Like Edmund Burke, the founding father of British conservativism, Trimble believed that humankind was a work in progress and had to be helped along to craft its political agreements according to a socially conservative outlook.

Five days after Trimble's Oslo speech, Bob McCartney of the UK Unionist Party proposed a motion in the Northern Ireland Assembly aimed at reinforcing a fundamental plank of the Mitchell Principles: that committed paramilitary-linked parties rejected violence. 'No democratic institution worthy of the name,' he told members, 'can exist if it contains the political representatives of an unlawfully armed organisation which is committed to bringing about change by the use or the threat of acts of terrorism.'[35] McCartney's motion was aimed principally at Sinn Féin, though, intriguingly, loyalist representatives entered the debate, with Billy Hutchinson reiterating the PUP's pragmatic position that the party would continue to influence the UVF and Red Hand Commando (RHC) towards decommissioning. David Ervine quickly moved to remind McCartney and other anti-Agreement politicians why he supported the peace process:

> Perhaps this is the right time to encourage people to examine why paramilitary ceasefires were called in the first place. Were the ceasefires not some form of acceptance by the paramilitarists that the war was futile, that it is was [sic] unwinnable? But being in a war that is unwinnable is not the same as being defeated. There are those who have no concept of the difficulties that we have been going through. We know about the pain, the blood and the brains on the pavements; we know about news programmes by the day; we know about the suffering before, during and after the ceasefires. We know about all that, but we do not seem to have a formula or any policy that can cross the religious and political divide and give the people an opportunity to believe that there is a way out or a light at the end of the tunnel.[36]

Ironically, Ervine, a one-time 'fanatic' in Trimble's eyes, was now riding to the rescue of an Agreement that placed other fanatics at the heart of government. For Bob McCartney the principle of including terrorists and their representatives in government structures contravened the very essence of democracy. In his closing remarks, McCartney paraphrased Winston Churchill about negotiating with Fascists: 'where was the point of compromise between the fireman and the arsonist?'[37]

There were those who shared McCartney's sentiment within Trimble's own party and wondered when the British government's concessions to Sinn Féin might stop, as it soon became clear they would not decommission on anyone's timetable other than their own. Lee Reynolds was the UUP activist who had challenged Jim Molyneaux as a 'stalking horse' candidate in the leadership contest in 1995. He had later been key in helping the UUP to secure its electoral victories under Trimble's leadership, though after the signing of the Belfast Agreement he saw difficulties emerge:

> Trimble mis-sold the Belfast Agreement. There are two types of peace agreement – instrumental and constitutive. Constitutive, you agree everything and everyone knows what they have to do, when and where and how. And if anything goes wrong then everybody knows who to blame. And then you've instrumental, which is basically where you have fifty things you don't agree about. We've agreed on twenty. We'll make a start on those and we'll try and deal with those as we go along. The Belfast Agreement was sold to unionism as a constitutive agreement when it was an instrumental agreement. So that was fine to get it over the line but, basically, 'Right, we are making those compromises and that's it. [We] don't like some of those things but we'll bite the bullet.' And you also had Blair's five pledges, which were basically lies [which] helped sort of get the unionist majority in the … referendum. The problem with that was it wasn't a constitutive agreement. Other things were going to come up and then you immediately started to hit up against a section of the unionist community who voted for the Agreement who were saying, 'Hold on, hold on, what are you doing? You've got what you've got. You're not getting anymore. That was supposed to be your lot.' … There were intrinsic problems with the Agreement itself. You know. Trimble had learned the lesson of the previous Agreement and you know …

'Sunningdale for Slow Learners' is a nice line but it's actually bollocks. Trimble fundamentally made sure that the North–South stuff wasn't anything like the North–South stuff in Sunningdale ... he fixed the old problem but the actual operation of the new Executive and Assembly was the new problem he had created. And that's what he wrestled with. There also wasn't such a strong team with the UUP.[38]

As doubt began to infect unionism, their political leaders had to redouble their efforts to keep their supporters engaged with the peace process. What complicated matters, according to political scientist Christopher Farrington, was the presence of four different unionist political positions on the Belfast Agreement. On the pro-Agreement side were those who voted Yes from a principled perspective and who saw it as a positive step forward for everyone in Northern Ireland. There were also pragmatists who saw it as a 'good deal' for unionism. On the other hand, there were those who were opposed to the Agreement because they saw it as a 'bad deal' for unionism and, finally, those who viewed it from a principled No perspective and saw it as inherently bad because it saw terrorist prisoners released while also allowing terrorists into government.[39] The latter category adopted a moral standpoint and would come to be associated with the DUP's rejectionist position.

Two years after the Agreement was signed, the principled No group had gained ground, especially as Trimble's attempts to deliver on Blair's pledge to secure PIRA decommissioning faltered. Trimble loyalist Esmond Birnie observed how the 'greatest threat to unionism may be those pessimists within the camp who perpetually talk of sell-outs and treachery, and so talk themselves into an abyss of despair.'[40] Clear demarcation lines were now becoming more accentuated between those pragmatic unionists who believed in securing the Agreement, come what may, including further concessions to nationalists and republicans, and those principally opposed to it. Over the coming months and years, the wider unionist community 'found it increasingly less persuasive that the gains justified the concessions.'[41]

14

The Changing of the Guard

> Rulers of Western democracies must learn the lesson that there cannot be dialogue with terrorism – for it is the lie incarnate. Its high priests and acolytes are unchangeable liars. They are hellish bloodsuckers, who in these crimes were prepared to knife young children to reach their heinous ends. Concessions have turned the monster into a greater monster, which now rages across the world and comes forward to torment us all. A new and terrible dimension has been added to the terrors of our unknown tomorrows. We must have firm faith in a sovereign God – the only true and living God – who will ultimately bring evil to the judgement bar and mete out his judgements on those who have committed such dastardly deeds.
>
> Ian Paisley, speaking in the Northern Ireland Assembly after the 9/11 attacks[1]

'I SAID AT THE VERY beginning of this campaign that I believe in this life you have to fight for the things you believe in. I believe in the Agreement and I believe in the people of North Down. I will fight for the Agreement and I will be fighting for the people of North Down.'[2] These were the triumphant words of Lady Sylvia Hermon, the UUP candidate who won the Westminster seat of North Down in the general and local council elections held on 7 June 2001. Hermon became the first woman to be elected to a Westminster constituency in Northern Ireland since Bernadette Devlin thirty-two years earlier. Later that day it was announced that Iris Robinson, the wife of DUP deputy leader Peter Robinson, had won the Strangford seat. They were soon joined by Sinn Féin's Michelle

Gildernew, who unseated Ken Maginnis by a slender majority of fifty-four votes in Fermanagh and West Tyrone. The election of more women MPs pointed to a renewed energy within the political parties to push for more equality of representation, which tended to undermine 'the male dominance of political and paramilitary structures'.[3]

Maginnis' defeat exposed serious problems with David Trimble's leadership of the UUP, which was coming under considerable strain from within his own party as it became ever more divided over the Belfast Agreement.[4] Once all votes had been counted, Trimble's party had lost three seats to the DUP. Trimble himself only narrowly retained his seat as he saw his majority tumble from 9,252 to 2,058 votes.[5] At a noisy count in Lisburn, Trimble was defiant, telling those gathered that he would get the Agreement implemented. 'We are not quitters. We will stick with this until the job is done.' But unionists were unsure, and the DUP's campaign had inflicted the first of many blows on its rivals that would culminate in the party's electoral demise over the next two years.

Later that day, at the Joey Dunlop Centre in Ballymoney, Ian Paisley had arrived to hear the returning officer announce his victory. 'This is a great day for this province. The unionist people have arisen with strength. You will never, never conquer us,' he told supporters who broke into an impromptu rendition of 'God Save the Queen'. Paisley, who was dressed in his trademark black pinstriped suit and Union Jack tie, continued: 'I believe in the power of the ballot-box, and today the ballot-box has spoken loudly across the province.'[6] The DUP had successfully made the election a mini-referendum within unionism on Trimble's handling of the peace process. The party singled out what it called the 'broken pledges of Tony Blair and David Trimble' that had 'allowed IRA/Sinn Fein to reap all the benefits of the appeasement process without giving anything in return – not even the decommissioning of a single bullet'.[7] The DUP manifesto had warned unionists against voting for the UUP, which it equated with a 'green light for a further raft of concessions' to what the DUP called the 'age-old enemies of unionism'.[8] The DUP painted a picture of Trimble's party wracked by division and dissent, which was contributing to a weak front in the face of what the DUP saw as further British government concessions towards Sinn Féin:

> Day by day our British heritage and way of life is under attack. The symbols of the State, including even the National Flag and the image of Her Majesty, are being torn down. Everything Gaelic, republican and Irish is promoted while everything British, unionist or Orange is derided and reviled. Traditional parades are banned and the Union Flag can no longer fly on most days from government buildings. The Agreement is being used to undermine every expression of British identity. If allowed to continue the Britishness of Northern Ireland will be totally submerged. Don't let it happen![9]

The DUP's brand of anti-Agreement unionism built on its thirty-year track record of oppositional politics, where dangers abounded for unionists and only a strong, united political leadership could offer an alternative. This disaffection percolated through unionism and loyalism, with academic Colin Irwin noting how, in a group of surveys conducted between 1999 and late 2003, the number of Protestants wanting to see the Agreement work dropped from 49 per cent to 36 per cent.[10] The core of the DUP's position in these years was attributable to their strategy of continuing to 'draw directly on ideological fears concerning the dilution of Unionist identity; political fears surrounding betrayal by Britain; and moral fears about political concessions to terrorism'.[11] This reflected an inability to see the peace process as offering any gains to unionism, despite securing the Union, ensuring the dropping of the Irish government's territorial claim in Articles 2 and 3 in its constitution, and the replacement of the hated Anglo-Irish Agreement.[12] Nevertheless, the DUP capitalised on loyalist fears around the failure of the peace process to deliver anything other than concessions to nationalism. One party within loyalism, however, was prepared to put forward a more upbeat, pro-Agreement case and challenge the DUP's position.

The PUP had been formed in 1979 by members of the UVF and RHC, as well as former members of the pro-Union NILP.[13] These individuals believed it was imperative to offer political analysis to militant loyalists in a bid to break the violent impasse since the collapse of the Sunningdale Agreement. The PUP's leading members became radical thinkers and set about offering an alternative to the DUP and other hard-line unionist politicians. One of those who campaigned tirelessly for a new approach was the former UVF bomber David Ervine. Ervine often asked himself if 'stinking, polluted politics came before paramilitarism?' He believed they did. His analysis was, therefore, designed to bring to the surface some inconvenient truths about the causes, course and consequences of the violence. In a talk delivered at University College Dublin, Ervine said the DUP's political project depended on their dismal vision that it was better to 'be defeated than to compromise':

> My community in Northern Ireland believes that conflict resolution comes in a plastic bottle that is to be found on the shelf in the chemist's shop, and you apply it like suntan lotion; or they believe that conflict resolution is an event. It is neither a suntan lotion nor an event. It is a process; and when you are a politician, process protects. Process allows you to manoeuvre and take forward the arguments and the circumstances based upon the protection that process creates. We have not educated the unionist community well enough. We in the loyalist community have educated our people and worked hard at it, but the larger unionist community has not been educated well enough on the issues of process. Indeed, I witness the potential difficulties around the corner for the peace and political processes, but remember these are not one and the same thing. It is only when the peace process and the political process converge that perhaps we will come of age.[14]

The spirit of compromise animated the PUP in these years and enabled the party to think creatively about how best to secure the peace process they had invested in since the ceasefires.

Ervine's colleague Billy Mitchell believed that it was right and proper to educate the broader unionist community and to carry a torch for conflict resolution, regardless of criticism from the DUP and other anti-Agreement forces. Mitchell said of the DUP at the time, 'I've just found that they've this mentality that we're terrorists in suits or we're the disreputable end of unionism and we are not worthy of being heard. Sometimes they are worried about our message.'[15] In the run-up to the 2001 elections, Mitchell wondered if the DUP was trying to block unionists from reaching their radical potential. 'I believe that if the people of Northern Ireland have human rights and social and economic rights and citizenship rights, that – particularly [for] a broad swathe of the Catholic middle class – this idea of Catholic/Nationalist and Protestant/Loyalist will disappear,' he argued.[16] Mitchell's words, like Ervine's, were laced with hope and optimism, of creative and imaginative political thinking about the future. He was articulating a future for political unionism and loyalism based on benevolence rather than competition, where people could harness the creative and intellectual potential of all in ways that tackled social injustice, fear and sectarianism:

> I'm an evangelical Christian and I would be opposed to abortion and homosexuality and stuff. Yet I believe that gays should have social and human rights. We shouldn't discriminate because we disagree with what they may do in private ... If the Brook [family planning] clinic wants to operate, you know, to provide advice to people who don't believe in my values and who believe that they need to address an end of an unwanted child or unwanted pregnancy, they should have a right to do that. So, there are a whole rake of rights there. I would love to arrive at a state where you didn't need a Bill of Rights – where people automatically respected each other and gave [each other] rights. But, unfortunately, we live in a world – a selfish world – so the rights are there to protect everyone, not just the Catholic minority ... I don't believe the inevitable will happen, in terms of being outvoted [by Catholics]. I believe that if the people of Northern Ireland have human rights and social and economic rights and citizenship rights, that – particularly [for] a broad swathe of the Catholic middle class – this idea of Catholic/Nationalist and Protestant/Loyalist will disappear ... Slowly but surely human rights have come to everyone. And I think it's a good idea to have it embedded in the constitution.[17]

A decade on from his release from prison, Mitchell spent much of his time formulating his thoughts on how best to realise this more benevolent form of unionism in a practical partnership between political and community activists, trade unionists and elements of civil society in Northern Ireland.

Mitchell's form of unionism – what he called 'Progressive Loyalism' – was calmer, more tolerant and outward-facing in its championing of equal citizenship within the Union. It sought to maintain the link with other parts of the UK as equal partners in a constitutional arrangement that subscribed to the idea of sovereignty lying in parliamentary democracy, although power would, ultimately, be concentrated in the hands of politicians at Westminster – Mitchell believed in the concept of Queen in Parliament – with devolved functions ceded to regional bodies where the people would have a greater say in their governance. For Mitchell, the 1912 Solemn League and Covenant provided a practical framework for the people to agree a constitution – underpinned by a Bill of Rights – between themselves and those elected representatives who were to govern on their behalf. Mitchell's articulation of Covenant unionism helped provide a radical redefinition of the relationship between the people in Northern Ireland and other unionists in the other parts of the UK. In *The Principles of Loyalism* (2002), he also called for a reinvigoration of the Union from a class-based perspective. Like Ervine, Mitchell was an advocate for a more liberal form of unionism that, ironically, he and his UVF comrades had done everything to destroy in the 1960s.

Despite a strong articulation of a positive way forward for unionists and loyalists, Mitchell and his colleagues in the PUP could do little to stem the haemorrhaging of electoral support from pro-Agreement unionism to the DUP. By 2003, the PUP's Billy Hutchinson had lost his Assembly seat and would soon be ejected from his council seat too. The ground beneath pro-Agreement unionism was steadily shifting, most notably when UUP politicians Arlene Foster and Jeffrey Donaldson and party activist Lee Reynolds left to join the DUP. This was not a shift confined solely to unionism, as parties like the SDLP, Alliance and Women's Coalition lost seats in the face of an electoral consolidation by the DUP and Sinn Féin in the 2005 elections. Although much of the shift in unionist politics owes more to the ineptitude of the UUP than to the strategic articulateness of the DUP, this pointed to a hardening of attitudes amongst unionists, who 'increasingly believed that the benefits of the Agreement had not been equally distributed'.[18] It did not coincide with a wholesale rejection of the Agreement, however, as a broader sub-culture of cosmopolitanism seemed to be reflected in areas such as sport. On 7 September 2005 the Northern Ireland football team played England at Windsor Park in a World Cup qualifier. Thanks to a seventy-fourth-minute goal by striker David Healy, the local side won. In its editorial the next day, the *Belfast Telegraph* reported how the result would 'go down as the night a new generation of Northern Ireland football fans were born. The magnitude of our victory over England at Windsor Park last night cannot be overstated. It was quite simply a breathtaking triumph of monumental proportions.'[19] It was in many ways a 'night to remember' – a truly David-versus-Goliath moment – and reflected a general mood within the pragmatic supporters of the Agreement that a brighter future beckoned for the troubled province.

Confidence seemed to return to Northern Ireland, though it would not last long. Within hours of the win, the *Belfast Telegraph* was running with the headline 'Drumcree comes to Belfast'. Tensions between the Orange Order and residents in the Springfield Road area, a parading flashpoint since the earliest years of the Troubles, were reaching a crescendo, with little prospect of a breakthrough in talks aimed at finding a compromise. That was not all. Loyalists were busy shooting one another in another feud between the UVF and LVF. The UDA, on the other hand, was meeting with Irish President Mary McAleese. Lindy McDowell complained about McAleese's warm embrace of loyalist Jackie McDonald: 'Does she not realise that most Protestants would regard McDonald and all that he stands for as repulsive?'[20] Worse was to come. After a second consecutive night of serious rioting from loyalists, which broke out in the wake of tensions between Protestant marchers and Catholic residents along the Springfield Road, loyalist gunmen opened fire on police and soldiers, with at least one blast bomb thrown at the security forces.[21] They responded with live ammunition and baton rounds. Police Service of Northern Ireland (PSNI) Chief Constable Hugh Orde blamed the Orange Order and the two main loyalist paramilitary groupings for the trouble, and there were calls on the Secretary of State, Peter Hain, to publicly state that the UDA and UVF had effectively broken their ceasefires.

Denigration journalism was now out in full flow, with the doyen of right-wing commentators, Max Hastings, finding a sympathetic readership in the apparently more liberal *Guardian*. 'It seems to dwellers on this side of the water an injustice that we should be obliged to govern, fund and police such a thankless fragment of historical flotsam,' he fumed, before continuing:

> Fanatics need enemies. If the IRA had not been bombing, it is hard to believe that militant unionism would be in such rude health. Northern

Irish Protestants have been able to sustain a sorry pantomime, conscious that they are unloved beyond their own streets. Thanks to a perverse community of consequences, if not of purposes, between the labours of Gerry Adams and those of Paisley, many Protestants see themselves as Christian martyrs, sacrificed to nationalist extremism and English perfidy ... The latest riots seem a manifestation not of Protestants' power, but of frustration and impotence. They see their tiny world decaying towards oblivion. The unionists' transfer of allegiance to Paisley and his kind, the extinction of David Trimble, represent a rejection of rational politics, a resort to absurdity such as only desperate people could entertain ... When unification comes, Northern Ireland's Protestants may be amazed by the wealth and happiness which accrue to their children, once they shed the baggage of Cromwell as icon, the Orange Order, mafia rule and institutionalised bigotry.[22]

Hastings liked to play a familiar tune in many of his articles at this time – a condemnation of unionists, a conflation of anti-Agreement unionism with political unionism generally and unrealised predictions of imminent Irish unification. He would return again and again to this form of political astrology as he rubbished the feelings of insecurity animating those who lived in a cycle of perpetual despair and had not found the answers to their problems in the form of unionist leadership offered by David Trimble. Loyalist efforts to put 'feet on the street' to register this anxiety, Hastings rightly observed, would not square this circle. Nor would the anger that flowed with it dissipate as the last of the broken glass, concrete and twisted metal was brushed from the streets.

The PIRA, which had been present at the riots in one guise or another, nevertheless took the bold step a few weeks later of announcing the end of their armed campaign. This decision, ironically, owed little to the violent flexing of muscles by loyalist paramilitaries, who could only speculate at their motives. Peter Hain moved quickly to try to rebuild shattered unionist confidence by announcing the appointment of a victims' commissioner, further financial backing for Ulster-Scots cultural initiatives and a rates relief for Orange halls.[23] Such moves made little difference to those who had flocked to the riots eager to register their anger and frustration at what they perceived to be a loss of their tribal rites at Drumcree. Geordie Newell, a community activist in East Belfast, spoke for many when he told a reporter how at 'the moment there's no future in communities like these. People feel they have nothing to lose,' he opined. 'People protest all over the world to air grievances but it just so happens that we come from a culture where people have seen the benefits of what violence brings.'[24]

By May 2007 the same 'absurd' fanatic whom Hastings had bitterly complained about, Ian Paisley, had agreed to sit down with his arch-rival Gerry Adams to agree the terms of a return to power-sharing. In an interview Paisley gave to the *Belfast Telegraph* in June 2007, he said he had 'done what is right' by going into government with the same people who once tried to kill him. It was a Damascean conversion few ever expected to witness. He was nevertheless at pains to emphasise that the agreement to work with Sinn Féin was going to be business-like. It was a 'work-in and not a love-in' for the benefit of 'our people [unionists], and indeed for the whole of the people of Northern Ireland and it has got to be done'.[25] Sitting in the same office once occupied by his arch-rivals Terence O'Neill, James Chichester-Clark and Brian Faulkner, he talked of 'better days' in Northern Ireland. Looking out across the well-manicured gardens of the Stormont estate, where he had once led huge rallies to protest one act of betrayal by the old unionist regime or the NIO, he was confident that he enjoyed the backing of the people. 'You have got to live and you have got to let live,' he said, 'but of course in a time of war things differ ... I may have said things a way that hurt people, but I think they needed to be said in that way, for if I hadn't have said them in that way, no-one would have listened.'[26]

Amidst an outburst of renewed optimism, Northern Ireland looked like it would defy denigration journalists and become a model for peace and reconciliation. There was even a move by loyalist paramilitaries to declare an end to their armed campaign, which was accompanied, eventually in 2009, with disarmament but, crucially, not disbandment. Unsurprisingly none of this really squared the circle of feelings of fear and anxiety – they would remain to haunt the political landscape.

15

A People Under Siege (Again)

[E]thnic-national identities are based not on what their members have in common – they may have very little in common except not being the 'Others'.

Eric Hobsbawm, 'Identity Politics and the Left'[1]

IT WAS A BITTERLY COLD night in early December 2012 as people gathered at the Christmas market outside Belfast City Hall. As the scattered showers subsided, revellers enthusiastically sampled the overpriced bratwurst and Belgian waffles while a large throng of men jovially congregated around the beer tent. Christmas lights illuminated the small wooden sheds crowded by those who had come to enjoy some festive cheer. At the rear of the building another ritual was being played out as loyalist protestors descended on one of Belfast's important landmarks and the seat of local authority in the city. The orange glow of the streetlights soon revealed a growing crowd, many of them dressed in tracksuits, quilted jackets and baseball caps. A few were carrying Union flags as they burst through temporary security barriers, pushing their way inside the rotunda in an attempt to storm the council chamber. A security guard responsible for protecting the building was injured as he attempted to block their entry. Police officers soon arrived to reinforce the security and hastily pushed back against the door to keep the protestors at bay. A window was smashed. A Union flag was unfurled and held up against it as one woman shouted, 'Shame on you!'

The loyalists had come to disrupt a vote in the council over planned restrictions on the flying of the Union flag over council-owned buildings. The protest represented a final attempt by ordinary men, women and children to register their grievances at what was transpiring inside the debating chamber. The motion the protestors found so abhorrent was originally moved by an Alliance councillor for Pottinger in East Belfast, Máire Hendron, and seconded by her party colleague, Mervyn Jones, a representative for the adjoining Victoria ward. Both constituencies were in traditionally working-class districts with sizeable loyalist electorates. The PUP's late leader David Ervine had held a council seat in Pottinger from 2001 until his death in 2007; with his party colleague Dr John Kyle subsequently co-opted into his seat. They were also, incidentally, constituencies that had at one time rejected Unionist MPs at Stormont and returned Tom Boyd and David Bleakley of the NILP, back in the 1950s and 1960s, before the Troubles. Changing demographics had long since left the cross-community Alliance Party as the middle ground within a divided city.

A few months prior to the outbreak of the flag protests, Billy Hutchinson was sitting in the PUP's offices on the Shankill Road complaining about the growing frustration of people on the ground in loyalist communities. He was of the view that there was a clear lack of a 'peace dividend' and that young loyalists felt left out by the process. He believed that political education was the only way to engage young people and take them off the streets, channelling their energies in more creative ways.[2] Hutchinson would have been well aware of loyalist views regarding Sinn Féin and their attempts to radicalise their voter base by convincing them they had somehow 'won' the war; the attempts to lower the Union flag had, therefore, become a key element in this attack on the unionist community's cherished symbol of its Britishness. Hutchinson's late party colleague Billy Mitchell[3] had first warned of Sinn Féin's strategy on Anthony McIntyre's blog *The Blanket* a decade earlier:

> Personally speaking, I believe that Sinn Féin's preoccupation with flags and emblems has more to do with wanting to remove any visible sign of their failure to break the link with Britain than it has to do with republican ideals. Having lost the constitutional battle they have resorted to agitating for the removal of the symbols that remind them of their failure. British symbols are a stark reminder that after a sustained campaign to break the Union, Northern Ireland remains British and that is hard for nationalists to stomach. The removal of

those symbols from certain public buildings may help alleviate the pain of failure but it is nothing for nationalists to be jubilant about or for unionists to be despondent about.[4]

In arguing that Sinn Féin's preoccupation with flags and emblems was a way to cloak their strategic failure, Mitchell also pointed to the debilitating effects that Sinn Féin's political actions would eventually have on his own community. His words would prove prophetic.

Although many loyalists still trusted the analysis of those in pro-Agreement parties like the PUP and their counterparts in the Ulster Political Research Group (UPRG), a think tank that grew out of the UDA,[5] an alternative view was emerging that chimed with that advanced by former DUP politician Jim Allister. Allister had left the DUP and formed the Traditional Unionist Voice (TUV) in the wake of the DUP power-sharing deal with Sinn Féin in 2007. Younger loyalists who had since come to the fore, like twenty-two-year-old Jamie Bryson, believed in Allister's reading of the peace process, rather than that offered by Hutchinson or Mitchell. 'Those were the years of the glory days of the peace process, you know,' Bryson recalled. 'Everybody was on the gravy train and things were good and it was not a popular viewpoint to have. It wasn't a fashionable viewpoint until probably the flags protests. And it found fertile ground then and has developed ever since.'[6] Bryson believed that anti-Agreement unionism stood a much better chance of preventing slippage towards a United Ireland:

> The flag protest was probably a symbolic turning point ... You see when you entwine peace and the process into this phrase 'the peace process' you conflate two different things, which is peace, which is just the absence of violence. And every sensible person is committed to an absence of violence but when you say, 'Well, that has to be predicated on this Agreement ... and you must agree with this and if you don't you can't have this.' And, I mean, that's the fundamental flaw at the heart of it. We need to disentangle those two things because you should be able to have peace without the process. Otherwise – and this makes my point for me in some respects – otherwise if you have to have the process then the peace is predicated on a veto of violence

to those who want to move the peace process along and that's probably what we have seen ... And because it's ... a process which is designed to, incrementally, ease Northern Ireland out of the United Kingdom and remove every vestige of Britishness; the longer the process goes on, the more it becomes more pronounced.[7]

As the flag protests gathered momentum over the next few months, one of those who believed in the efficacy of the peace process, despite losing elected office at the hands of those who didn't, Billy Hutchinson, decided to show his face at the protests outside City Hall. It was a bitterly cold Saturday morning when he gave an impromptu interview to reporters about what he thought was behind the agitation. Hutchinson complained of 'de-Britification', a shorthand for what unionists believed was a concerted Sinn Féin strategy of seeking the removal of all British symbols in an attempt to wind up unionists and radicalise their own support base.[8] Within a few months of this speech, the PUP leader was telling journalists how he had been saying 'since before there was a flags protest' that he believed a feeling of disaffection was 'bubbling underneath and that if Sinn Féin were going to do anything big in 2012 it was going to be around the union flag'.[9] Hutchinson was of the view that he and others in the PUP needed to offer grassroots leadership to young loyalists and set them on a path away from protest that would see them develop the political skills necessary to engage with republicans. 'Irrespective of all of that, what we need to do is we need to move forward,' he said.[10]

As a community development worker since his release from prison in the 1980s, Hutchinson knew that the gulf between perception and reality in Northern Ireland could be huge. He also knew that this gulf had become ever more cavernous since loyalists had turned back towards confrontational street politics in East Belfast in June 2011.[11] It was obvious to close analysts of the security situation that intense riots in the summer of 2011 were a by-product of deep structural inequalities in Protestant working-class areas, which had 'given rise to feelings of collective fear, frustration and anger'.[12] Poor educational attainment, long-term unemployment and a 'poverty of aspiration' had given way to a sense of belonging, where role models were more likely to be loyalist paramilitary figures than sports people.[13] Although some loyalists believed they were worse off than republicans (whom they frequently compared themselves with) in socio-economic terms, this was not borne out by the facts. In 2010 the Northern Ireland Neighbourhood Information Service reported that those in predominantly Catholic wards were actually worse off than those in predominantly Protestant wards, with East Belfast ranked nineteenth and West and North Belfast ranked first and second respectively in terms of the most deprived areas in Northern Ireland.[14] While deprivation itself was undoubtedly a key structural factor in feeding perceptions of inequality amongst loyalists, it was the construction of a victim identity by some loyalists themselves that was ultimately feeding these feelings of insecurity.

The media representation of the flag protestors continued to superimpose this victim mentality on them and also talked up the political anxiety felt by loyalists. If anything, however, loyalists' actions on the streets were counterproductive – offering them publicity but denying them political success – and only served to lower their self-esteem, arguably rewarding their defiance by keeping them out in the cold, harsh streets. Unsurprisingly, perhaps, loyalist protests led to a middle-class, business-orientated backlash. Curiously, unionist politicians found the protests to be little more than an embarrassment, despite having wound up those who were now on the streets by distributing leaflets warning of the dire consequences of limiting the number of days the council could fly the Union flag.[15] In the 1970s, 1980s and 1990s the unionist political class had depended on loyalists to help them bring a more muscular response to political protests – now they were abandoning them. What unfolded over the next few months was a perfect storm that mixed growing disaffection at the political process with the perpetuation of a victim mentality. As John MacVicar, the editor of *Shankill Mirror*, perceptively argued at the time:

> The protests are not about the flag, they never were just about the flag. There is a deep-rooted disillusionment within PUL [Protestant, unionist, loyalist] working-class communities that they have been left behind by those in power at Stormont. The myriad of issues have been well rehearsed repeatedly in the *Shankill Mirror* over the last ten years, job creation, inward investment, educational attainment, health inequalities, housing, to name just a few.[16]

Apart from Hutchinson's occasional attempts to provide a constructive alternative to those engaged in street protests, unionist political leaders were conspicuous by their absence. The DUP found themselves in a difficult position, for they had previously supported the flying of flags in certain council areas only on designated days.[17] One contemporary report on the flags protests found that the so-called '"designated days" policy was not anathema to all unionists', given that 'three councils with unionist majorities, Ballymoney, Lisburn and Craigavon, operated a designated days policy (with some additional days incorporated), and did so in the belief that this was in keeping with local government custom across the UK'.[18] Therefore, the DUP's position on the issue was far from clear, leaving some loyalist activists free to portray the move as little more than a dastardly republican agenda.

In the absence of strong political leadership, loyalist paramilitary groups stepped into the breach to exploit these grievances for their own ends. The East Belfast UVF, which had become more autonomous from the Shankill Road 'peace leadership' since the group chose to decommission its arms and explosives in 2009, used the protests to camouflage its criminal enterprises. One senior PSNI officer who had direct involvement in the security response to the group explained how the police tried to tackle the problem:

> We shifted from concentrating on their *ideology* to their *methodology*, which took us into their criminal activities. And whereas their ideology may enjoy some community support, more often than not their methodology did not ... We are concerned that there is going to be a Flags II – the anniversary of it – so we then come up with an operation, which becomes Operation Mors ... So, we then sat down ... and we looked at [how] we fundamentally have to undermine the East Belfast UVF or there will be a Flags II. Now, to challenge them, because they're bussing old ladies out to the seaside and buying them sandwiches and all this sort of stuff ... If we challenge them on the ideology it [wouldn't have worked]. No, we will get them for their criminal activities. And we targeted their drugs ... We found some of them involved in some very unsavoury things ... We got them for dog fights ... The other thing we did was we did a massive licensing review across the city because we knew they were running illegal

clubs and these clubs were feeding them cash ... So, we cancelled lots of licences ... That was to reduce their money. Now, coming out of that, we also did the whole stop and search, put the specialist teams in. We didn't actually get many arrests but we completely crumpled their ability to make money and that was one of their big [methodologies] ... And it was impressed upon them that this would continue to be the case all the way until we got through the anniversary of the flags protest ...[19]

Owing to a strategically imaginative policing response, alongside the work of NIO engagement teams and community relations activists, the protests fizzled out. It was a clear success for the PSNI, which was determined to ensure malign groups like the East Belfast UVF were degraded and unable to mount violent activity under the cover of spontaneous protest action.

Under Billy Hutchinson, the PUP managed to harness the energies of younger loyalists in a political direction. Within a year of the incursion in City Hall, loyalist protest action had subsided, and it had proved strategically ineffective, leaving loyalists in a greatly diminished position. Hutchinson's strategy to mop up disaffection and channel it in a positive political direction also carried with it diminishing returns. As a party, the PUP has always had two wings: one Ulster British, with some semblance of democratic socialism, and the other Ulster loyalist. Each strand periodically jostled for dominance in a party with a small membership. The influx of new members in the immediate aftermath of the protests saw the party grow exponentially, to around 500 members,[20] but while some of the new cohort were progressive, others were not.

Julie-Anne Corr-Johnston had joined the PUP out of an interest in helping the grassroots community to which she belonged. While she sympathised with those driven to protest, she was more interested in what the PUP historically stood for. 'More and more people came to join the party but they weren't suited to the party,' she recalled. 'They were very much disillusioned with the DUP and a lot of it was protest. Some came from the TUV. And they didn't join the party because of its policies, because of its vision for the future. They joined it because of its reaction to certain events and thought that it would give them strength in numbers.'[21] Corr-Johnston felt that the upsurge in numbers saw the party make a trade-off between its values and the interests of new party members:

> I felt that the upsurge in numbers gave people who I feel, in my opinion, were not necessarily right for the party. It empowered them. And it gave them more ammunition, it gave them more strength, it gave them more power, to move the party in certain directions ... Slowly you could see it moving to a more hard-line [stance] ... definitely moving away from those – Gusty Spence, David Ervine – moving away from that class of politician – the visionaries – moving away from that, and it was more reactionary ... I always remember using the line of 'promoting tolerance for a diverse society, rather than a reaction to a divided society' ... And the party had become that – it epitomised that. It knew what it was against but not what it was for. And conversations were always about what it was against and not what it was for.[22]

By attempting to harness the tribalism that had emerged from the street protests, the PUP did little to challenge the views of a hard core of anti-Agreement loyalists who had now emerged and believed that the peace process was rewarding republicans. The PUP simply side-stepped the issue. The party also emerged with a new mantra of 'putting country before party', though it did little to position its political project at the heart of UK politics by establishing a civic form of unionism with a more inclusive agenda.

For much of the 1980s and 1990s, the PUP represented a democratic socialist alternative to exclusivist unionist politics. Under the leadership of Dawn Purvis (2007–11) and Brian Ervine (2011–12), the party lurched first in a liberal direction and then a right-wing one. Only after the election of Billy Hutchinson as party leader did the PUP's left-leaning credentials return, though this was to be short-lived. The influx of new members in the wake of the flag protests included loyalists more in tune with 'The Sash' than 'The Internationale'. Disappointingly, the PUP failed to capitalise on its impressive showing at the 2014 local government elections, where it won over 12,000 first preference votes and saw four councillors elected in Belfast and Coleraine. The attempts to reconcile two increasingly divergent strands

– cultural loyalism and civic unionism – running through the party came at a heavy price. Outwardly, at least, the party made a trade-off, jettisoning some of its democratic socialist, pluralist and civic unionist ethos for the short-term political gains offered by tribal protest. A quick glance at the PUP's policies in 2014 suggested that, on devolution, for instance, the party had not bothered to define what it understood by unionism, retreating into a centre-right position on 'more stringent background checks' for economic migrants. On education, social development and justice the PUP did, however, appear to be more liberal and forward-leaning. On the surface, for that is all there really was to the PUP at this time, the party was trying to be all things to all people.

The 2016 Northern Ireland Assembly elections saw the PUP's new loyalist vanguard strategy come unstuck. Billy Hutchinson and John Kyle only managed to secure 5,955 first preference votes, failing to grow the party's electoral profile, seeing many DUP and TUV types return to their natural political homes. Meanwhile, the DUP reinforced its thirty-eight-seat lead, with Sinn Féin winning some thirty seats. Not all was lost for those now occupying a squeezed middle group, with the Green Party polling well in middle-class areas such as South Belfast and North Down and more than trebling its share of the vote from 6,031 votes to 18,718 votes, winning an additional seat. The anti-austerity People Before Profit Alliance (PBPA), which drew on strong support in the marginalised Catholic working-class areas of West Belfast and Foyle, won two seats, taking 13,761 first preference votes. It had polled only 5,438 votes in the previous Assembly election in 2011. Despite West Belfast and Foyle being predominantly Catholic in religious terms, the party's new MLAs, Gerry Carroll and Eamonn McCann, made the point of telling voters on the campaign trail that they were 'neither orange nor green', thereby seeking election on a cross-community basis. The PBPA's focus was on protecting the rights of working people, the unemployed and the disabled, many of whom felt marginalised by the traditional parties who had done little for them during the long years of austerity following the economic downturn of 2008.

The agenda of protecting the most deprived and marginalised people in society has a long tradition. Eamonn McCann was a founder member of the Derry Labour Party, a key constituency of the NILP, until his stance on civil rights led to a parting of ways in the early 1970s. After the outbreak of sectarian violence and the collapse of the NILP vote, the party's leading lights threw their energies into the Campaign for Labour Representation (CLR). The nucleus of the CLR pressure grouping wanted the British Labour Party to organise in Northern Ireland, but it was not until late 2003 that that party was forced to concede membership rights to people living in Northern Ireland. After the election of Jeremy Corbyn in September 2015, there was some speculation about whether the party would finally contest elections in Northern Ireland, as their Conservative rivals had repeatedly done. The speculation proved short-lived, as Corbyn resisted taking up the banner of democratic socialism in Northern Ireland and even went as far as to ban Labour Party members from contesting elections. Eight members defied the ban to run in the 2016 Assembly elections, though they polled only 1,577 votes. With the PUP now having jettisoned its socialism in favour of loyalism, the only real alternative for left-leaning unionists was to vote for the PBPA. This narrowing of the political bandwidth within unionism would have serious repercussions within weeks of the Assembly elections, when the British Conservative government led by David Cameron called a referendum on the UK's membership of the European Union.

16

Toppling the New Tower of Babel

> The country is very beautiful and if only I could deport the Ulstermen and fill their land with a populace of my own choosing, I should ask for no better place to live in. By the by it is quite a mistake to think that Ulster is inhabited by loyalists: the mountains beyond Newcastle and the Antrim 'hinterlands' are all Green.
>
> C.S. Lewis, All My Road Before Me[1]

AT THE CORE OF THE Northern Ireland conflict are two conflicting world views. There are unionists who are committed to the maintenance of the Union between Great Britain and Northern Ireland and who cherish their British identity above any Irishness. Then there are nationalists who wish to see Northern Ireland joined with the rest of Ireland, a thirty-two-county Irish Republic, free from Britishness. At the more extreme fringes of both political creeds are those loyalists and republicans who make prescriptions about the kinds of people they are prepared to admit to their respective British and Irish communities. These identities are mostly conferred at birth. They offer people who ascribe to them a powerful adhesive binding their respective 'imagined community' together during times of hardship and danger.[2] Experts inform us that these ethnic identities are forged in the 'myth of common ancestry, which usually carries with it traits believed to be innate'.[3] In deeply divided societies like Northern Ireland – where loyalists and republicans interpret the world around them in very different ways – these differences reflect core political identity concerns. The groups tend to place considerable emphasis on symbols of identity, customs and traditions, which often manifests itself outwardly in divisive ways that can inflame passions and emotions.[4]

It is uncertain how strongly these identities inform the people who adhere to them, but it is obvious that they can very easily differentiate between what is best described as their 'in group' and those they perceive as belonging to an 'out group'.[5] In ethnic conflicts like Northern Ireland, some people witnessing this conflict may place more emphasis on the religious aspects of what they perceive to be the primary identities, while others tend to play up deep demarcation lines over national identity.[6] The key point to note here is that despite being drawn to conflict with one another like moths to a flame, people do have the capacity to change the emphasis in their political identities or to reject them completely. They are not forever condemned to remain incapable of change. Northern Ireland, like many other places, has seen people shift their perceptions on how best to organise themselves and their communities in ways that have moved from moderation to extremism and back again, even if two-thirds of Protestants and Catholics remain committed to their core national identities of unionism and nationalism.[7] In order to understand this capacity for change it is, therefore, necessary to look beyond the view that identities are fixed and unchanging and, instead, consider how they are subject to dynamics of change.[8]

In the census held in 2011, of the 1.811 million people in Northern Ireland, two-fifths (40 per cent) of usual residents identified with a British-only national identity, a quarter (25 per cent) identified with Irish-only and just over a fifth (21 per cent) identified as Northern Irish only.[9] Eighty-one per cent of those who had declared themselves to be British also happened to be Protestant, with only 12 per cent who thought themselves British brought up in the Catholic tradition. In contrast, 94 per cent of people who described themselves as Irish were brought up as Catholics, compared with only 4.4 per cent who had been brought up as Protestants. Interestingly, of the people who described themselves as Northern Irish, 58 per cent of respondents were Catholics and 36 per cent of respondents were Protestants.[10] Overall, these three political identities – British, Irish and Northern Irish – appeared to dominate. In terms of those self-designating as British, there was a consistency across all age groups, with people aged sixty-five and older likely to feel more British than younger age groups.[11] Although the category of Northern Irish was more likely to have been consistent across all age groups, it nevertheless points to a growing third group of people for whom identity is changing.[12]

In Northern Ireland, as with other parts of the United Kingdom at the time, a growing number of people surveyed in the census had been born outside these islands. This demographic change had become particularly acute in those areas once regarded as traditional strongholds for Ulster loyalism. In South Belfast, the areas of the Donegall Road, Sandy Row and the Shankill were all noticeably ethnically diverse. This is a pattern that has repeated itself in other urban areas and, more broadly, in country areas too. The idea that Northern Ireland remained solely the preserve of those with British or Irish identities began to be called into question. And it would have considerable consequences for those working-class unionists who felt themselves out of sorts with the new transition. It was amidst this rapidly changing demographic context that Prime Minister David Cameron's call for a referendum on the UK's continued membership of the European Union must be viewed.

It is impossible to understand why most unionists voted in favour of Brexit in 2016 without placing the referendum in the context of eight years of austerity. The policies of these long years implemented by the Northern Ireland Executive on behalf of the British government in London would have far-reaching consequences for marginalised working-class areas which formed the core energy behind the DUP's campaign in support of the UK's exit from the EU. In many ways the working class in Northern Ireland were affected like their counterparts elsewhere in the UK, with the referendum giving 'full expression to much deeper divides in Britain that cut across generational, education and class lines'.[13] Typically, the vote in favour of Brexit was

> anchored predominantly, albeit it not exclusively, in areas of the country that are filled with pensioners, low-skilled and less well-educated blue-collar workers and citizens who have been pushed to the margins not only of economic transformation of the country over recent decades but also by the values that have come to dominate a more socially liberal media and political class.[14]

Understanding why those most affected by austerity could vote for a Brexit championed by the very people who made the cuts that impacted so heavily on working-class unionists may seem like a paradox at first glance. In a pioneering survey of referendum voters undertaken by Queen's University Belfast in the summer of 2016, a strong correlation was found between those who identified themselves as British and those who voted to leave the EU. In fact, 63 per cent of those holding a British identity voted Leave, compared to only 13 per cent of people who described themselves as 'Irish'. Those who identified themselves as Northern Irish tended to vote Remain, with almost two-thirds doing so. The overwhelming majority of those surveyed who were in favour of a United Ireland (85 per cent) were also Remain voters, while 60 per cent of those in favour of remaining in the UK under direct rule favoured Leave. Fifty-eight per cent of people who wished to remain within the UK in a devolved settlement wished to remain.[15]

One *Belfast Telegraph* commissioned poll published three days prior to the referendum on 23 June indicated that 38 per cent of Protestants surveyed were in favour of leaving the EU,[16] an increase on the last poll published on 26 May, which revealed 28 per cent of Protestants believed the UK would be stronger outside the EU.[17] The director of Vote Leave in Northern Ireland was DUP member Lee Reynolds. In comments published in the *Belfast Telegraph* on 20 June, he believed the increase correlated with 'the national pattern and it's clear that Vote Leave has the momentum to win'.[18] For Reynolds, the reason was simple:

> Remain just handed us voters. And they did it in ways that the elite doesn't get. Guess which event was the most successful for Vote Leave in Northern Ireland during the campaign? ... The best event for Vote Leave in Northern Ireland was when Tony Blair and John Major gave a speech in Magee. Absolutely. That is when unionism is going for Leave. Before then it was flowing to Leave. After then it was gushing towards Leave. We had a system in Leave where I would turn on the computer every morning and it would tell me how many people signed up or engaged with Vote Leave in Northern Ireland ... On a bad day or quiet day there would be thirty more people. On a good day I would basically get fifty to sixty ... When I turned on the computer on the day of

that speech I had 2,700 (roughly) people connected to the campaign or signed up to it or whatever, giving their data to the campaign. The only news story that day, locally and nationally, were those speeches. And it was just a wave. When I turned on my computer the next morning I had something like 350 new people signed up. And that was what told me that it was the reaction to this [speech] which was not the reaction we thought there would be. People viewed that, particularly in the unionist community as 'You are threatening us.' You are also saying that 'the peace process is the possession of nationalism' and they didn't like it.[19]

In their speech the two former prime ministers told their audience that leaving the EU would 'endanger not just the ongoing peace process, but also the very existence of the UK'.[20] Tony Blair reiterated his view that the Belfast Agreement was built on 'complex foundations on which we were able to make peace in Northern Ireland'.[21] John Major made a straight connection between voting Leave in the referendum and his long-held belief that it would open the door to Scottish independence and the end of the Union: 'A British exit from the European Union could reopen the whole issue of independence [for Scotland] and could tear apart the United Kingdom – the United Kingdom, outside the European Union and Scotland outside the European Union. The most successful union in world history would be broken apart.'[22] A vote for Leave, Major said, would 'throw all the pieces from the constitutional jigsaw in the air and no one would be certain where they might land'.[23] Blair also flagged up the prospect of a change in borders from external ones to a clear demarcation line within the British state itself. There would be 'either border controls on the border between north and south ... [or the] only alternative would then be to have them between Northern Ireland and the rest of the UK which would plainly be unacceptable as well'.[24] The problem facing both former prime ministers was that memories within the broader unionist community were famously long and their respective deals with the PIRA and their political associates in Sinn Féin was not easily forgiven, especially as a growing number of unionists believed their community had paid a heavy price for peace.

First Minister Arlene Foster echoed this sentiment when she reacted angrily to the Major–Blair intervention:

> It's all very well to talk about constitutional uncertainty in the United Kingdom but when we're handing away our sovereignty to Brussels all of the time, people need to reflect on that, and I do find it rather disgraceful for two prime minsters, who know full well the importance of the peace process here in Northern Ireland, to come over here and suggest that a vote in a particular direction is going to undermine that.[25]

Speaking in the House of Commons, Foster's deputy, Nigel Dodds, called the intervention by Major and Blair as 'very dangerous and destabilising, and it should not be happening'.[26] In an intervention in the letters page of the *News Letter*, the Northern Irish-born Labour MP for Vauxhall Kate Hoey rubbished Major's and Blair's claims as 'yesterday's politicians determined to spread fear in Northern Ireland'. Instead, she emphasised the state's economic prosperity, which was 'totally tied to its position within the UK', denying that Brexit would 'lead to border problems in NI' – 'if some documentation of freight trade is required in the age of the internet,' she counselled, 'this will not involve hold-ups at the border'.[27] Concluding her remarks, Hoey said the 'more Tony Blair talks about the need to remain the more the public will be persuaded to leave'.[28] In the final comment she was not wholly inaccurate. Many people across the UK had become more cynical about Blair's legacy, especially considering the debacle of the Iraq War.[29]

To understand the reasons why the DUP led calls for Britain to leave the EU, it is necessary to examine the party's unique views on sovereignty. As a loyalist party, DUP members are 'twice as likely as UUP members to identify as "Ulster" rather than have an identity with Irish in the label', according to one large-scale membership survey conducted in 2012–14.[30] They share with other unionists a strong sense of Britishness, but the DUP has always held to the belief that Protestantism is 'the basis for its Unionism'.[31] Inside the DUP, the Free Presbyterian sect constitutes the single most influential interest group and limits the ability of the party to transform itself beyond its confessional identity.[32] In this respect, the DUP continues to be guided by a highly localised idea of what constitutes sovereignty. By 2016, over 70 per cent of DUP voters supported the party's campaign to Leave the EU. The

DUP's position on the EU was articulated in its most classic form by the most Eurosceptic of the party's MEPs, Ian Paisley. In his farewell address to the European Parliament in Strasbourg on 4 May 2004, twenty-five years after being elected, Paisley expressed bewilderment at the 'rapid growth' of the EU, which he saw as the 'political mystery of the age':

> I do not believe it is to the best advantage of the European peoples. Enlargement has triggered the destruction of the cooperation of the sovereign states of Europe and brought about the construction of the sovereign superstate of Europe, the new Tower of Babel. The effects of the full battle between the voluntary cooperation of the European sovereign states and the dictatorial incorporation of those states into the European superstate have yet to be witnessed. In our history superpowers have always been detrimental to peace. The wars in the Balkans in recent years have been conveniently forgotten when fiery advocates of an almighty Europe tell us the new Europe has prevented and stopped wars. Some prevention, and some stopping.[33]

Paisley's scepticism must be seen in the context of the DUP's shared idea of what constitutes democracy. It is fundamentalist and traces its genealogy back to the Ulster people, with European integration ultimately 'understood as an existential risk to, rather than an opportunity to further their primary political goal: that of defending the Union and Northern Ireland's place within it'.[34] However, it is quite wrong to see Euroscepticism as a long-time 'feature of the political culture of Ulster Unionism', even if the DUP's 'unionist credentials' extend 'only as far as the borders of the British state and not beyond'.[35]

The DUP's Euroscepticism, therefore, remains based on a narrow interpretation of sovereignty fused with a broader political response to what it sees as a set of supranational institutions limiting the independence of its member states. In this sense, Euroscepticism is far from the preserve of religious fundamentalists or populist nationalists. Tony Benn, the long-serving socialist and Labour MP, for instance, sketched one of the most important Eurosceptic positions two years prior to the UK joining the EEC:

> A major constitutional issue lies at the heart of this question [about EEC membership]. We have talked about sovereignty, but what does it mean? Without referring to the old texts or the Treaty of Rome, it means that when people come to this Chamber we can point to the Treasury Bench and around the House and say, 'This is where your laws are made and your taxes are imposed. This is where policies are explained, and you can get rid of these men yourselves.' That is all there is in parliamentary democracy. Open debate plus a secret ballot is parliamentary democracy. It has nothing to do with Mr. Speaker's wig or the mace, or all the little things the tourists come to see. It is the combination of open debate and secret ballot, that is the basis of our system. Parliamentary democracy does not mean that we control our destiny. Our future could be decided in Brussels, Peking, in the Kremlin, the Pentagon or anywhere else. What it does is to guarantee that how we respond to the circumstances of our time is decided after open debate and by secret ballot.[36]

In a Northern Irish context, unionists believed in priority access to the institutions of the British state and for those in the DUP the European project placed a barrier in the way of that.

Loyalists who had previously supported the DUP over its rejectionist stance on the peace process prior to the return of power-sharing with Sinn Féin in 2007 also shared this fundamental belief in priority access to Parliament's sovereign authority. Clifford Peeples, a veteran loyalist activist, had earlier campaigned for a No vote in the referendum on the Good Friday Agreement. He now found himself becoming an ardent proponent of Vote Leave. Following the leave vote and during the UK–EU negotiations on the Withdrawal Agreement, Peeples believed that Brussels still intended to derail Brexit:

> The goal of the European Union is a second referendum. The whole game-plan is to limit the UK's room for manoeuvre so as to back the UK into a corner and force another vote. The thing you have to remember though is that Britain is a representative democracy. The Tories should have taken that into consideration. Half of them are

pro-Europe anyway. You see, whenever the people didn't want Europe, it scared them. Europe knows that financially and politically it is finished. Once that door is closed, they're finished. If Britain leaves Europe, their experiment is finished. The only reason why they're there is because of the UK's contribution. Once that support is pulled, it's finished. People want control over their own finances.[37]

Peeples was adamant that the EU project depended so much on the UK's membership that without it, it would break up the bloc. He was joined in his opposition to the EU by younger loyalist activist Jamie Bryson, who said he understood the anger now animating sections of anti-Agreement unionism and loyalism:

Nationalism made clear that any land border would see them take to the streets. Unionism/Loyalism would inevitably end up taking to the streets in mass numbers should any economic United Ireland be forced upon us. Once that genie gets out of the bottle, it would be very difficult to put it back in. We all want to avoid such an unpredictable situation.[38]

It seemed that while loyalists on the right wanted Brexit, they did not like the terms upon which the UK's departure was being negotiated. At a meeting held in the Carleton Street Orange Hall in Portadown on 24 November 2019, Bryson told a packed audience: 'We are in the final days of the Union if this withdrawal act goes through,' adding how, 'When it comes to regulations that would affect Northern Ireland on goods, the Dublin government would have a greater say over Northern Ireland than the sovereign government in Westminster. Is there anyone in this room, any unionist in NI who thinks this is acceptable?'[39] His words were met by applause and shouts of 'No!' Bryson then went on to blame the Belfast Agreement, which he said rewarded nationalism ahead of unionism.

Not all unionists shared this downbeat analysis of Brexit or believed the blame should be placed at the door of the Good Friday Agreement. Belfast councillor and deputy leader of the PUP John Kyle believed inequality was driving much of the disaffection in loyalist working-class areas:

> The people at the bottom of the pile, for them life is rough and tough. It's stressful, they're doing everything to keep body and soul together, to try and hold family together. There are these issues of mental health problems, of drug and alcohol addiction, welfare reform, problems around housing, anti-social behaviour, poor employment opportunities, a low wage economy that they're a part of. All that means that life is pretty grim.[40]

The PUP, he said, accepted and respected the outcome of the 2016 referendum, though in reality they preferred to sit on the fence over the issue and did not take a strong position on Leave or Remain. For Kyle's party leader, Billy Hutchinson, Brexit was largely 'a Westminster issue', even if they laid the blame of mishandling EU exit at the door of the DUP. The DUP's position on Theresa May's negotiation of the Withdrawal Agreement, in Kyle's view, caused considerable problems for subscribers to a more progressive form of unionism:

> What you have got is the DUP not just failing to promote the benefits and the value of the United Kingdom. They have presented a very self-serving, self-centred Little Britain image. It's all about preserving a backward-looking Northern Ireland governed by Unionists, rather than being part of a United Kingdom that enhances this country, that offers a good working relationship with the Republic of Ireland and is a context in which nationalists can live comfortably and happily.[41]

Kyle believed a more solidly liberal form of unionism that looked for the benefits in a difficult set of circumstances needed to be re-established. He saw the fate of unionism at stake because of the DUP's antics around Brexit. 'We need to promote and champion a progressive moderate unionist voice in terms of policies,' Kyle said, 'because I think the United Kingdom view us quite negatively now ... We need to discover those synergies because therein lies the security of Northern Ireland.'[42]

17

Circling the Wagons

> Northern Ireland teeters on the rim of history repeating itself. Surely after all the years of division even the slow learners have discovered that you cannot govern without consent. Residing in a state of self-induced denial will only prolong the agony.
>
> Peter Robinson, *News Letter*, 9 April 2021[1]

'THERE ARE CERTAIN CIRCUMSTANCES WHERE violence is the only tool you have left ... I am not sure if and when violence will be the answer. I am just saying that I would not rule it off the table.' These are the words of Joel Keys, a young loyalist activist speaking to the parliamentary Northern Ireland Affairs committee on 19 May 2021.[2] Keys' comments generated a social media storm, but they nonetheless encapsulated something of the essence of the embattled position younger loyalists occupied in the wake of violence in Belfast, Newtownabbey and other parts of Northern Ireland in early April that year. In an *Irish Times* column written in the wake of Keys' comments, veteran journalist Susan McKay blamed the influence of older loyalists for encouraging what she regarded as regressive thinking. '[F]ormer paramilitaries know they are perceived to be bitter and banjaxed – they need a new generation of young lads who look fit for fighting. Should it come to that,' she complained.[3] Keys was part of a delegation of the Loyalist Communities Council (LCC), which was formed in 2015 to represent the interests of the UDA, UVF and RHC. Much of the LCC's oral evidence to Parliament was highly defensive and reflective of the insecurity felt within these paramilitary groups. The deputy editor of the *News Letter*, Ben Lowry, complained that Keys was 'not a credible witness for MPs'.[4]

It was Good Friday, 2 April 2021, when young people first took to Belfast's streets. The violence had a 'multitude of factors', according to the *News Letter*. 'For loyalism, Brexit's Northern Ireland Protocol has undermined its place in the Union,'[5] though the spark for the unrest was the decision by the Northern Ireland Public Prosecutions Service not to charge senior Sinn Féin politicians for attending the funeral of IRA chief Bobby Storey, despite the breach of coronavirus legal restrictions. This provoked young people into a confrontation with the police.[6] As tensions mounted, bricks, iron bars and fireworks were thrown at police lines by loyalists. Injuries were sustained as the dynamic escalated to include a more concerted attack on PSNI officers, leaving several seriously injured. The trouble spread to towns and cities across Northern Ireland as cars were hijacked and petrol bombs were thrown. One *Belfast Telegraph* journalist was beaten in a sectarian attack. Matters soon came to a head as a public bus was hijacked by masked men and burnt out on Lanark Way in the Shankill. Pitched battles soon spilled out along the peace line, threatening to draw in younger members of the nationalist community. Loyalist youths attacked the gates between the two communities, throwing petrol bombs and attempting to make an incursion into the nationalist side. There was a real danger that if the violence got out of control, it risked derailing the entire peace process, so rival paramilitary leaders emerged on both sides of the divide to put a lid on it. It was only at this point that Prime Minister Boris Johnson belatedly responded to the violence by tweeting that he was 'deeply concerned by the scenes of violence in Northern Ireland, especially attacks on PSNI … The way to resolve differences is through dialogue, not violence or criminality.'[7] Johnson resisted calls for a British and Irish summit on the violence, likely motivated by the public link now being made between the Protocol and the 'febrile atmosphere' on the streets.[8]

The reality of the situation was reinforced by the fact that the violence had caught the police unaware. The PSNI's Chief Constable Simon Byrne had publicly stated a few weeks earlier that he did not 'see the prospect of a return to protest or violence'.[9] Ironically, Byrne had admitted to the Northern Ireland Policing Board on the eve of the trouble that 'the wider environment in which policing operates has experienced wide-ranging political, economic, social, technical, ethical, legal and environmental changes', with his force continuing to 'operate in challenging circumstances which increase the volatility, uncertainty, complexity and ambiguity (VUCA) of the environment'.[10] Yet, he did not foresee this leading to disorder. This, perhaps, spoke to the failure of police human intelligence sources to report to their handlers accurately, or at the very least to the inability of senior PSNI commanders to understand how dynamically the security situation had changed in recent years. The police may have also interpreted their successes against loyalist paramilitaries since the flag protests of 2012–13 as an indication of how unlikely these groups were to orchestrate trouble again. However, such groupthink resulted in an underestimation of a shift in loyalist mindsets on the ground, where there had been a noticeable disconnect between paramilitary groups and younger people – partly due to low levels of recruitment and partly due to the growth spurt of a new discourse of loyalist disaffection. Much of this disaffection was cleverly exploited by prominent loyalist grassroots activists in their uncompromising views on the Protocol, which were double wrapped in complaints of 'two-tiered policing'.

Joel Keys was one of those who came under the spell of this double-wrapped mantra when he was arrested amidst the violence in Sandy Row. He said he had been trying to deter younger children from becoming involved, something he later repeated to the Northern Ireland Affairs Committee:

> I understand that these young people are frustrated. They do not know the details of the Northern Ireland protocol. They could not quote you certain paragraphs or anything, but they know that, fundamentally, something is wrong. They know that, when they are out, even at the Shankill, at Lanark Way, and they are watching the nationalist youths on the other side of the fence, the police are not responding to them. The police are not arriving to control their side of the fence, but they are arriving on our side of the fence. Young people see on the ground that there is an injustice. There is a sort of imbalance in how nationalists and unionists are treated. The violent outbursts we have seen across the country are a reflection of that. It is a way for these young people to vent their anger and frustrations. While I disagree with the methods of doing so, I understand their frustrations.[11]

For more seasoned loyalist politicians like PUP leader Billy Hutchinson, the Protocol was a 'political problem' that could 'only be resolved by political solutions'. Hutchinson's party once prided itself on being close to grassroots loyalists and so should have had a ringside seat to judge the mood. Yet, even the PUP failed to anticipate the fast-moving situation, though, as Hutchinson went on to explain to MPs, he believed the high levels of anger revolved around an unhappiness 'about being a region in the UK and being treated differently to other regions'. He continued:

> Loyalists feel threatened at the moment and they feel threatened for a number of reasons, far too many to go through here. There are a plethora of them. Let us be very honest and frank: the protocols are a threat to business in Northern Ireland. The biggest threat is that we are sitting in the single market, as the only region in the UK that is. That means that all out autonomy would be aligned elsewhere and not to the UK. That is a threat to people's Britishness.[12]

Senior loyalists close to the thinking of the UDA concurred with this feeling of insecurity. Trevor Greer, a former loyalist prisoner who had worked tirelessly to calm tensions at the interfaces over the years, saw the recent violence as a consequence of the British and Irish governments having ignored the views of loyalist representatives:

> What I noticed was there were a few riots in southeast Antrim and a wee riot in Sandy Row. Not a word said until it hit an interface … If any sort of violence starts … the one thing I don't want to see is loyalists rioting in their own areas … The problem that I can see is people taking it to other areas and I mentioned interfaces. And then the Shankill happened. When it happened that night … it only took Boris Johnson two … hours to come out and make a tweet about what was happening in the Shankill … For a week and a half previously, there were riots in loyalist areas and he never said a word. But as soon as it hit an interface … then you've got a problem … This is the problem I can still see because if people notice that it works … One of the things I've said for the past 4–5 years is the rhetoric that was

coming out of Dublin about the North–South border saying 'There could be a return to violence' ... As I said to one reporter, 'What did anyone expect loyalists to do?' Dublin constantly said, 'There could be a return to violence.' Now, on a personal note with me, over those 3–4 years that all this talk was going on, I would have been in contact with republicans. And that would have been IRA, ex-IRA, INLA, ex-INLA ... and in that time I had never, ever picked up once that there would be a return to violence by republicans. And I started asking questions: Is the Irish Government and Leo Varadkar talking about dissident republicans? But, sure, they're already doing the violence anyhow so what would be the difference? If they expected to add another border – East–West – without anybody bringing violence into it, then they were stupid. If they thought they could do that without anyone kicking up a stink it was mad ... For two major [players] – a government and the EU – to not think about one half of a community – 800,000 people – there was something wrong with their heads ... Thankfully it was only the timing of the Duke of Edinburgh's death [that stopped that]. You have to break the back of it. You can have interface trouble. If you can stop it for two nights, then you break the back of it.[13]

Greer believed loyalist paramilitaries were finding it difficult to challenge the actions of the young people involved in rioting because of the growing feeling of disenfranchisement in working-class areas. He admitted that while the Protocol provided the necessary excuse, this disenfranchisement meant many young people were primed for violence against the state, even if they did not fully know why:

I think the context with the Protocol has changed a lot but even with that and with the riots that happened, were them young people out there rioting because of the Protocol or were they out rioting because they could? Because nobody was going to tell them not to ... The Protocol gave these young people a cause because even loyalist paramilitaries couldn't have gone out – even if they wanted to and stopped it – because they would have been called 'traitors'. Because in their eyes they were doing it to save Northern Ireland because of the

Protocol ... A large majority of them didn't know why they were there but I would say a few of them did ... They were there because they could be ... I have always said, in Northern Ireland terms, see when you mention the word 'protest', the next words that usually comes out of people's mouths is 'Where are we getting the bricks?' Some of those so-called protests is detrimental to loyalism and unionism. Most of these protests were set up by people who nobody knew.[14]

The riots in early April 2021 proved that the political instability around the Protocol was creating new avenues for growing militancy among the loyalist grassroots, while simultaneously breathing new life into old paramilitary structures.[15] How the effects of the violence played out within these loyalist grassroots was complex and multi-layered, and fed into a much broader rejection of the peace process amongst those who came onto the streets. As Jamie Bryson wrote in an article for *Belfast Live* at the time:

The Protocol – which many quite legitimately feel was imposed on the basis of the weaponisation of threats of potential violence should there be a land border – does not respect the fundamental plank of the peace agreement in Northern Ireland in so far [as] it demolishes the principle of cross community consent.

There is not a single elected unionist – at any political level – who consents to the Protocol.

The protests are not merely for protesting sake; there is a clear strategic objective – the rebalancing of the imbalanced 'peace process' and the removal of the unjust and unconstitutional Protocol.[16]

It was clear that a battle for the soul of Ulster loyalism was in play, with pragmatic proponents of the peace process now seemingly aligning with the views expressed by principled opponents.[17] Such a Faustian pact would have seemed improbable in the years prior to the Brexit referendum, and it would have serious repercussions for the PUP who, under heavy influence from their associates in the UVF, moved ever closer towards a rejectionist position on the peace process.[18]

Although much of the media and political attention focused on the exploding petrol bombs and burning buses on Northern Ireland's streets, loyalists were attempting to challenge the Protocol on legal grounds too. Clifford Peeples had initiated legal proceedings against the British government on the basis that London had breached the 1801 Act of Union. Peeples' legal team based their case on the following argument:

> It is submitted that for the above reasons, Articles 5–10 and 18 of the Protocol and the 2020 Regulations are ultra vires, unlawful, unconstitutional and are of no effect in domestic law. The Applicant says that if the impugned provisions of the Protocol are to have effect, they must first be consented to by the people of Northern Ireland through a plebiscite, not by a vote of politicians in the Assembly.[19]

The case was dismissed by the judge, who made it clear that the Protocol did not contradict the Act of Union. Reflecting on the verdict, Peeples observed:

> By sleight of hand a so-called Unionist and Conservative Prime Minister destroyed the very concept of a United Kingdom. His duplicity swept aside centuries of brotherhood that was forged with the blood of our forefathers in their quest for freedom. This has been facilitated by the ineptitude and cowardice of the current, so-called Unionist leadership, who have sat on the sidelines and cheered while the very precept of the Union was destroyed.[20]

In another legal case brought by Unionist political leaders, including TUV leader Jim Allister, the judge dismissed their case on the same grounds.[21]

The idea of betrayal animated the language used by loyalist activists, such as Jamie Bryson, who called on Boris Johnson's government to trigger Article 16 of the Withdrawal Agreement. He likened the legal attempts to challenge the Protocol to the insecurity of tenure that homeowners experienced when they realised their house has passed from freehold ownership to leasehold guardianship:

> I mean, all that's okay as long as you don't hand the deeds over officially. And if that is the case then the Belfast Agreement offers no protection

to Unionism because it can be incrementally dismantled. And it's only the last lowering of the Union Flag, as it were, the cutting of the last tie that's protected by the Belfast Agreement. So that should illuminate to people that if the Act of Union – the very fundamental basis of the Union – can be repealed and set aside without the triggering of protections of the Belfast Agreement, I mean, what protections actually are there for the Union, apart from the formality of handing the deeds over?[22]

Other loyalists, such as Stephen Cooper, a TUV councillor in Comber who spoke at a number of anti-Protocol rallies, believed that 'the damage to the Union is at its most critical stage' with the 'sea border ... in situ and the High Court has found that Article Six of the Act of Union is no longer in place as a result of the NI Protocol which has been foisted on the people of Northern Ireland at a huge financial cost'. The evidence for this conclusion has been mixed. As the academic economist and one-time UUP politician Esmond Birnie observed, the Protocol was 'likely to affect different sectors or industries in various ways. It may hurt sectors that are dependent on inputs coming to Northern Ireland from the rest of the UK but help those that buy from or sell into the Republic of Ireland or the rest of the EU.'[23] And that, for unionists opposed to any attempt to unite Ireland by stealth, is the fundamental point. As Cooper suggested:

> The Belfast Agreement and the Protocol are designed to have the same end objective and that is to subsume Northern Ireland into a united Ireland. And the Belfast Agreement does that by ... at every level ... having the whole island linked North–South and the [move towards greater] harmonisation ... The Protocol does the same thing but does it with economics. It diverges trade away from GB, obviously, and encourages the economic links to the Republic, and of course through that by extension the EU ... It's almost like a twin-track approach wherein the economic driver is going to get the island united in an economic sense. The Belfast Agreement, of course, which is thought upon by most unionists who were pro-Agreement as a settlement ... Sinn Féin/IRA have always said at the outset, 'This is not a settlement,

this is a transitionary phase to a united Ireland.' And that has been their position always. And some of unionism still have not grasped that to my eternal frustration.[24]

Regarding the Agreement and Protocol as two sides of the same coin, Cooper and other rejectionist loyalists have highlighted the British government's continued attempts to ignore and override 'our democratic right and insistence on our wish to remain within the UK on an equal and equitable basis with the rest of our citizens'.[25]

That loyalists came to see the Northern Ireland Protocol as the latest attempt to push them from the Union only led to a growing consensus that the Union was not safe and that they had lost out in the peace process. Nigel Gardiner, a PUP representative in the Waterside area of Londonderry, was concerned about the lack of leadership being shown by the mainstream Unionist parties over this issue. It had led to interface violence in the past, something Gardiner had been active in trying to prevent for over twenty years. Loyalists in Londonderry felt that their community was in disarray and suffering from collective low self-esteem. A former soldier and factory worker, Gardiner had been working in community development and community relations for several decades. 'People are apathetic,' he said. Gardiner was walking along Clooney Terrace as he spoke, pointing to the lack of infrastructural investment and generally dishevelled nature of the residential and commercial buildings lining both sides of what had once been the thriving economic heart of this local community. The architecture in this part of the city is Georgian but has been hollowed out by the various economic tsunamis that have engulfed deprived parts of the UK for decades. It was now a street lined by an assortment of pizzerias, tanning salons, burger bars and off licences. Gardiner pointed out flats that have been there for over thirty years. 'People think we are a majority on the Waterside. We aren't, we are a minority in our own city.'[26]

Gardiner was motivated by a spirit of public service, yet, like many working-class unionists and loyalists in the city, he failed in his bid to be returned to public office in local elections in 2011 and 2014. The PUP in the city had never attracted more than a couple of hundred votes, with the DUP and UUP typically winning most votes within the unionist community.

Gardiner was keen to articulate the reasons behind loyalist apathy. Things have gotten worse, he argued, in light of the Northern Ireland Protocol. It had caused the temperature to rise on the streets, and while one loyalist observed that the media was successfully keeping 'the heat' out of the news headlines, the PUP knew something was going to give. The COVID-19 pandemic restrictions – in terms of keeping people at a social distance and preventing them from mixing in households and in large groups – kept a lid on tensions until the end of March 2021, when loyalists in the Lincoln Courts estate rioted against the PSNI for four consecutive nights. Intriguingly, the violence in Derry predated trouble in Belfast, building on what one Unionist councillor referred to as 'frustration'. Although *The Irish News* believed the reasons for the riots were 'unclear', their reporter noted how 'anti-police and anti-Northern Ireland protocol graffiti ... [had] appeared in recent days'.[27]

Gardiner believed that one of the principal reasons behind this kind of spontaneous violent protest action in Londonderry was the lack of younger loyalist activists being prepared to come forward and make a positive case for the Union and the peace process. It is important to examine the failure of younger leaders to make a breakthrough. The PUP, like the UPRG, is too heavily dependent on paramilitary networks for support. These groups operate hierarchically and are uninterested in doing things on a co-operative basis. They have also had their structures hollowed out by years of criminal enterprising by some of their members. In recent years, paramilitary loyalism has drifted, nominally supporting the peace process but doing little to put a positive case for it by disbanding. In this sense, the peace process leaderships of the UVF and UDA have been seen as being increasingly out of touch with their grassroots supporters. The violence in late March and early April 2021 prompted a strategic rethink within these organisations, which were worried that factions in places like North Antrim, East Belfast and Mid Ulster would seek to seize their mantle in the event of blind support for the peace process, which had come to be regarded, along with the Protocol, as damaging to Northern Ireland's position within the Union.

On 8 November the PUP finally came out against the peace process. It was a seismic *volte face* for a party that had once laid the foundations for the transition away from armed conflict. For those who had observed the sea-change in attitudes amongst PUP members at close quarters, those bandsmen who had joined in the wake of the flag protests represented a right-wing rejectionist unionism inside a one-time left-wing, consensus-forming party. What was surprising was that the person left to announce the major shift in the PUP's position was the one figure who had been so closely identified with the leftist wing of the party, Billy Hutchinson. In a press release leaked to the *Belfast Telegraph*, he referred to the Principle of Consent as a 'deceptive snare'.[28] It was language redolent of that used by Jamie Bryson who moved from a once-derided position within loyalism to one of acceptance.

While it may well be the case that loyalism has moved in a more rejectionist direction, there are still some grass-roots unionists who believe in maintaining the pragmatic stance once occupied by the PUP. In the latter camp is Julie-Anne Corr-Johnston, who came into politics through the flag protests in 2012–13, but who left the PUP for the UUP. The former PUP councillor denied that a groundswell of opinion within grassroots unionism was now opposed to the peace process. In her view:

> Those minority voices that have been dissenters basically on it [Belfast Agreement] have got louder and louder and louder and the microphone has been turned up. So, we are hearing more of it. And we are hearing it louder, but I don't for a second believe it is wholesale consensus. In fact, I believe the majority are fed up to the back teeth of this perpetual cycle of constitutional dominance, of unmet need, of fear and division. I genuinely do. Look at the protest that was called in Lanark Way. There were about 500 people there. That's probably too generous a number ... The majority of those people came from other areas onto Lanark Way. There's 18,500 people that live in that Shankill ward alone and the majority of them stayed at home. Similarly with Twaddell and Woodvale, people came from all over ... I remember being in the thick of – genuinely believing – at each and every single election, believing, 'This is it. Big, big, big change here. You know. The DUP is going. The DUP is going. This is it. This is it. Big change here.' And then bang! And it was the same thing over and over and over again, feeling that people were hardened, that they were energised and motivated. And that they were coming out to keep the other side out. That that was the only thing they were voting for. And yet, for the last

four consecutive elections, unionism has circled the [wagon] train. It's lost a majority at every single election. And this may be the turning point.[29]

For loyalists in 2021, like their ancestors in 1921, there was a real danger of losing their sense of identity inside a fast-changing set of circumstances. One hundred years earlier, Northern Ireland's markets were tied to the broader British Empire, still at the height of its power and prestige, even after emerging from a Great War. Then the immediate danger to Northern Ireland's position was Southern irredentism and IRA violence. A century on, with the Empire long gone, the context had changed. Northern Ireland's access to the UK internal market was being impeded by a Northern Ireland Protocol that gave the EU a regulatory say in the UK's internal affairs. Loyalists were animated by what they saw as British government duplicity and betrayal and a resurgent Irish government irredentism. Only a few were prepared to break from this political anxiety and offer a more hopeful vision for the future.

18

Political Unionism and the Greater Good

Nay as the end of all political unions is the general good of those thus united, and this good must be subordinated to the more extensive interests of mankind.

Francis Hutcheson, *Philosophical Writings*[1]

WHAT IF PEOPLE LIVING IN Northern Ireland broke the spell of seeing everything in zero-sum terms and acted in the interests of the greater good, rather than in the sectional interests of their own respective community? How much happier and more self-confident would they feel when faced with the day-to-day challenges of providing for themselves and their families, while contributing to wider society? Suppose I witnessed someone being kind to another person. It made me so happy I, in turn, decided to prolong this positive feeling by being kind to a fourth person. My act of kindness was then, in turn, witnessed by two more onlookers, call them Person 5 and Person 6. They, in turn, paid that goodwill forward to others, and so on and so forth. In doing so we created a chain reaction and, thereby, a general climate of happiness that produced a virtuous circle, benefiting everyone whose life it touched. The Ulster-born moral philosopher Francis Hutcheson believed the extent of this virtue could be worked out according to a formula – simply put it was: 'in proportion to the *Number* of Persons to whom the Happiness shall extend; (and here the Dignity, or *moral Importance* of Persons, may compensate Numbers) and in equal *Numbers*, the *Virtue* is as the *Quantity* of the Happiness, or natural Good; or that the *Virtue* is in a compound Ratio of the *Quantity* of Good, and *Number* of Enjoyers'.[2] Much later, this process of extending goodwill in a benevolent and altruistic way to the greatest number of people possible would become known as utilitarianism.[3] Hutcheson was one of its early proponents, believing that happiness was preferable to its reverse, misery, which, logically speaking, could also be gauged by the number of people suffering as a result of its spread. In promoting the greater good, Hutcheson urged us to live our lives in a way 'which procures the *greatest Happiness* for the *greatest Numbers*; and *that*, *worst*, which, in like manner, occasions Misery'.[4]

Hutcheson, wisely and progressively, believed that human progress could be advanced unselfishly without making narrow judgements on a person's socio-economic background, their skin colour, religion or other ascribed identity. In other words, you and those around you could make decisions based on the words and deeds you witnessed by way of empirical observation rather than necessarily on the identity or appearance of the person performing those acts. Hutcheson preoccupied himself with studying human behaviour and what he saw as the human species' capacity for acting morally; Hutcheson referred to this as a 'moral sense', and he believed it accompanied the five basic senses of sight, smell, taste, hearing and touch.[5] Having built on the work of fellow philosopher Anthony Ashley-Cooper, the 3rd Earl of Shaftesbury (1671–1713), who was tutored by John Locke (1632–1704), Hutcheson then imparted his system of moral philosophy to his students David Hume and Adam Smith. They were values shared and promoted by other Enlightenment figures, including Immanuel Kant (1724–1805) and Jean Jacques Rousseau (1712–1778), who organised their ideals around the principles of reason, science, humanism and progress.[6]

Hutcheson's moral outlook imparted a powerful example of a more enlightened political path for subsequent generations to follow. In today's world it offers unionists a beacon of hope for shaping and influencing the kind of politics we ought to promote across these islands and further afield. Unionists in Northern Ireland have for too long been distracted from fulfilling the potential of their political philosophy to make the world a better place for everyone, regardless of their social class, ethnic, national, religious, cultural or other sectional identities or interests. Political unions ought to be inclusive and judged for the dividends they bring to those who live under them. In the case of those who were conquered to build a political union and who may not wish to live under these new constitutional arrangements, Hutcheson believed that an 'equitable plan of civil power, as sufficiently consults their future safety and prosperity' was essential for them to gain experience of it and be 'truly satisfied to submit to it' with their 'subsequent consent' becoming 'a just foundation' of the power 'and a sort of civil expiation of the injury done in the conquest'.[7]

The concept of the consent of the people is, perhaps, easier to achieve in homogenous societies where passions and emotions originating from ethnicity or tribalism are rarely excited. However, several centuries after Hutcheson wrote these words, we live in a world where counter-Enlightenment forces like identity politics retain a strong gravitational appeal. 'Identity politics thus engenders its own dynamic,' the American political scientist Francis Fukuyama has written, 'by which societies divide themselves into smaller and smaller groups by virtue of their particular "lived experience" of victimization.'[8] We can all see the dangers of our societies becoming even more divided. And, so, in creating a better world, we need to question the assumptions accompanying the '"lived experience" of victimization'. To be a classic unionist in the sense that Hutcheson thought about political unions, therefore, is to reject narrow identity politics and, instead, to strive to realise the 'greatest happiness for the greatest numbers'. The serious challenge for all of us who believe in less territorial, less nationalist and less ethnic forms of political union is how you achieve this amidst a deeply divided society like Northern Ireland.

North Belfast is a patchwork quilt of division, and its borders are, in the words of Susan McKay, 'dangerous places, and had continued to be volatile after the 1994 ceasefires had brought their "imperfect peace", as it became known'.[9] There is a real sense in which this area, having seen the worst of the violence during the Troubles, has continued to be pockmarked by the legacy of the conflict, rampant inequality and deprivation. For UUP political activist Julie-Anne Corr-Johnston, it is also an area of huge untapped potential:

> It's less about patriotism. It's about pragmatism. The Union is the only way I can provide for my kids, and quickly. The infrastructure is there. I look at it like a house. If you and I were going to look for a house, they

give you the big brochure as you are going through the door to have a look at the home. Taking a dander around the home, you'd imagine the furniture down and the estate agent is chirping in the background giving you all the selling points of the property. So, I imagine going into the Union and them saying, 'You've a free education system here. Your kids are going to get educated at nursery, at primary school and secondary school. It's all free. We have an NHS for you. We're going to look after you. And, listen, when you get old, we'll still care for you. You've got a pension. There's a welfare state. If you lose your job we've a safety net for you. You know, we care. We're compassionate. The Union is great.' And then you look at the United Ireland [option], and they're drawing it from scratch. 'What do you want? What do you want to see in this room and what do you want to see in that room? I don't want a new home. I want that house and I'm going to put an offer in on the Union. I'll put my offer in on that particular property and then the surveyor comes out and the surveyor takes a closer look at the property and thinks, 'There is subsidence, you know. Yes, there's a free NHS, but there are 350,000 people on the waiting list. Yes, your kids are going to be educated free but if you happen to be from this community, if you happen to be working class, with free school meals, then it's 150 per cent more likely your child is going to leave school with no employability qualifications. And then, yes, you've got a welfare state safety net but you're going to wait five weeks before you get a single brass penny in your pocket. And people are dying in the queue. And, yes, you will get a pension but we have the worst pension rates in Europe.' You know, we need to take that survey report – for me and for my brand of unionism is taking that survey report and saying right, 'The infrastructure is there – we can fix it but we need the political will to do x, y and z.' While other people are about 'no Irish language, no this and no that'. Almost like rearranging the furniture in that house and it's not fixing the fundamental problems in that property ...[10]

Corr-Johnston believes in the potential of the people of North Belfast and of the Union she holds dear to deliver for them. She is rooted in the area's many structural problems and in the claustrophobic sense of social injustice. She is well-placed to advocate for its political and socio-economic renewal. In this sense she conforms to a pragmatic unionism that believes in the benevolent good of the Union to deliver for everyone, regardless of their colour, creed or other deep-rooted beliefs.

Corr-Johnston was drawn into political activism by a curiosity to discover more about the dynamics of the street activism she witnessed amidst the flag protests a decade ago. 'Yes, I was annoyed about the flag,' she recalled. 'Maybe it's a maturing or evolution,' but that does not concern her to the degree it once did. Now, 'I'm a unionist who measures the strength of the Union on the basis of the socio-economic wealth of the people living here, rather than the parties.'[11] Corr-Johnston has a much grander vision for the political union between Great Britain and Northern Ireland, focused on securing the structural ties that bind the United Kingdom. She sees herself as a 'Covenant Unionist' who developed her political analysis by reading Billy Mitchell's *Principles of Loyalism* (2002). Mitchell regarded the Solemn League and Covenant as the 'birth certificate of modern Ulster', where its core principles of the material well-being of Ulster, civil and religious freedom, equal citizenship and, perhaps uncomfortably for many, unarmed resistance formed the basis of his commitment to work for the betterment of all the people of Northern Ireland.[12] For Mitchell, and now for Corr-Johnston, the whole point of unionism was to share both the territory and a vision for a future that was inclusive for everyone, regardless of their religion or sectional political identities. Corr-Johnston believes in human-to-human interaction and places value in those relationships. Not only does she believe in the structural foundations of the 'house', but also in the people who live in it. For her it is as much about security of tenure as the quality of life of its inhabitants. People who have problems paying their home heating bills, who cannot find enough money to pay their mortgage or rent, feel themselves less empowered and less part of a community. Corr-Johnston's vision for political unionism begins with the individual and their family and builds outwards into a community and civil society that works for everyone in the neighbourhood.

One academic expert on unionism, Graham Walker, has argued that we need to radically rethink the idea of the Union in a way that broadens the debate conceptually and politically.[13] It would seem logical and sensible to address this not only in a way that reflects connections between Northern Ireland and Great Britain, but also in terms of British–Irish relations within a broader international context. Cultural critic Edna Longley's influential characterisation of Northern Ireland as a 'cultural corridor' between Britain and Ireland is a persuasive one, articulating a vision where we do not have to brood over an Orange or Celtic 'dawn'.[14] Longley talked of unionists wanting to block off one end of the corridor and republicans the other, though maintained that 'Culture, like common sense, insists it can't be done.'[15] With 'Ulster Irishness and Ulster Britishness … bound to each other and to Britain and Ireland', she argues that it is far better for the Irish Republic to 'come cleaner about its own de facto connections with Britain' and admit the entanglement, across these islands.[16] In culture, as in politics, it is high time we recognised how the 'geopolitics of the British Isles is a product of a continuous history, both geographical and human'.[17] It is unrealistic to completely divorce one part of the British Isles from another in the way that extreme Ulster loyalists and extreme Irish republicans continue to advocate. The reality is that the geopolitics of Anglo-Irish relations continues to have a powerful 'conditioning influence' on political developments.[18] That Britain and Ireland are part of an intertwined archipelago is as indisputable as the truism that they form part of the region of Europe.

If those who judge the Union between Great Britain and Northern Ireland to be a success story, then it must be asked why that has been the case. According to a British government policy document:

> The Union between England, Scotland, Wales and Northern Ireland has proved its worth time and again, including in this pandemic. It is our greatest source of strength at home and abroad. Our country overflows with creativity in the arts and sciences: the wellsprings of unique soft power that spans the globe.
>
> Few nations are better placed to navigate the challenges ahead, but we must be willing to change our approach and adapt to the new world emerging around us. Open and democratic societies like the UK must demonstrate they are match-fit for a more competitive world. We must show that the freedom to speak, think and choose – and

therefore to innovate – offers an inherent advantage; and that liberal democracy and free markets remain the best model for the social and economic advancement of humankind.[19]

Senior British government ministers have been at pains to reassure Parliament that the government remains 'steadfast in its commitment to protect and promote the hundreds of years of shared history, beliefs and interests embodied in our Union – the most successful political and economic partnership the world has seen'.[20] It is encouraging to hear how the government has laid the sketch outline of plans to 'strengthen the Union' further, but a lot will rely on how unionists themselves – 'by hearty consent of the people' – respond in selling its benefits to those who would prefer to see their political future under a united Ireland.

Several hundred years ago Francis Hutcheson characterised political unions as an imperfect but necessary counterweight to living amidst the miserable circumstances thrust upon them by anarchy. There were greater prospects under a civil polity that governed on behalf of all its citizens. This was preferable to the uncertainty of the 'everyone for themselves mentality' that ran as an undercurrent of Hobbes' state of nature. In order to construct this kind of polity it required 'wise and good men' and women 'directing the conduct of a large body' of people, which would 'much more effectively promote the interest of all, than the same number could do while each one followed his own measures'.[21] He acknowledged, as Edmund Burke later did, how in much of humankind there was 'a sense of right and wrong in all, with a natural indignation against injustice'.[22] No one feels this more acutely than unionists in Northern Ireland today.

Unionists, therefore, have a responsibility to help everyone – including the people and their government – to work continuously to perfect their political union. It is natural for unionists to maintain a healthy scepticism about the constitutional designs of the British government that they feel have been thrust upon them over the past century. However, they hardly covered themselves in glory under the old Stormont majoritarian regime that did everything it could to deny those deemed disloyal the full British rights they were owed. That is why unionists must always ask how they can work to secure the general happiness and general interest of everyone in Northern

Ireland. It is the responsibility of all unionists to articulate a moral case that the 'pleasures or interests of one, or of a few, must always be subordinated to the more extensive interests of great numbers'.[23] This ought to be the guiding thread in all unionist interactions with other unionists and with those who maintain nationalist or republican designs for political organisation. As the great unionist thinker Norman Porter put it in his influential book *Rethinking Unionism* (1996), this kind of unionism 'does not start from the conviction that "the Union, the whole Union and nothing but the Union" is what matters most; it does not regard the Union as a sufficient end in itself but as one among other ends'.[24] What ought to matter most to unionists, argued Porter, is 'not the Union per se but the quality of social and political life in Northern Ireland'.[25] This kind of unionist vision of working together and sharing responsibility has been practically articulated by John Kyle and Julie-Ann Corr-Johnston, amongst others, as evidenced in this book.

Unionism desperately needs a vision for the future that can appeal to people right across the four parts of the United Kingdom. So far little thought has been given to how best to sell the Union to those who remain undecided or uninformed about its benefits in Northern Ireland or elsewhere. The truth is that the Union is more than a subvention between London and Belfast or London and Edinburgh or London and Cardiff,[26] more than access to participatory democracy or the NHS. It is also more than nostalgia and it is much more than an attempt to dominate 'the other', despite what nationalists argue. To truly sell the Union to a greater number of people, unionists in Northern Ireland need to abandon pretensions of governing on the basis of majoritarian democracy. The unionist community has long since lost its ethnic supremacy, and it is never coming back. Unionists need to articulate not only a vision for political union between Northern Ireland and Great Britain, but also a strategy that will secure their stated policy – laid down 110 years ago in the Solemn League and Covenant – of equal citizenship within the UK. While this objective has faced serious obstacles over the past decade or so, it should not be impossible to achieve.

To rebuild their faith in an honourable compromise, which was represented by the Belfast Agreement, unionists need to revisit their antiquated understanding of sovereignty and patriotism. Professor John Denham, a former Labour Party MP and government minister, has argued that we need to formulate a new form of what he calls 'progressive patriotism' in British politics, which is badly needed in light of the huge shift in globalisation, identity politics and the common bonds that bind the Union together.[27] For this to be successful, however, Northern Irish unionists will need to engage in a national dialogue with other unionists right across the UK. For Denham, who approaches progressive patriotism from a democratic socialist perspective, there remain serious questions about how those who believe in their country engage with patriotism, which is often conflated with conservativism. Denham suggests that a series of questions are posed ahead of party politics: 'Do these politicians understand me? Will they stand up for people like me on things I really care about?' He concludes that this is 'the most fundamental relationship in politics, and one that continually frustrates the left'.[28] As Denham notes, this has become a dilemma for the Labour Party when it has been misrepresented as unpatriotic. Under Jeremy Corbyn, Labour was stripped of its patriotism and lacked credibility in terms of its support for British institutions like the monarchy and armed forces. 'The rewards of patriotism will be thin,' notes Denham, 'unless it accompanies a more persuasive and inclusive story about nation and people that can give a richer meaning to the idea and symbols of the nation.'

As in England, so in Northern Ireland. Moderate unionists find the kind of 'flag shagging' displayed by Ulster loyalists to be a tribal-based relic of a bygone era, though the crisis ushered in by the DUP and Conservative Party's approach to Brexit has seen a return to 'flag shagging' not witnessed since the loyalist protests of 2012–13. It is impossible to dispute that calm, rational and moderate unionism has been drowned out amidst the rancour of boisterous flag-waving rallies on single issues like the Northern Ireland Protocol. People in Great Britain and the Irish Republic would be forgiven for believing in the representativeness of this stereotype. The reality, as this book has proven, is that a more inclusive form of political unionism does exist. This form of progressive, open-minded, UK-wide unionism is something that many Northern Irish unionists should seek to privilege in building an inclusive political union above their sectional interests, as it offers a positive vision for the future – one that is based on tolerance, reason and securing what is in the interests of all the citizens of Northern Ireland. For this is the only way for unionists to save the precious Union they hold dear.

EPILOGUE: EVERYDAY PATRIOTISM

> When we look after the people of Northern Ireland is when we secure the union.
>
> Julie-Anne Corr-Johnston[1]

Ballymoney, North Antrim, 12 July 2021

I'M BACK HOME AGAIN FOR the Twelfth, twenty years after my grandfather's lodge was refused permission to walk down its traditional route. This time a coronavirus pandemic has intervened to impose a whole new set of restrictions on Orange Order parades. On my early morning run around Ballyduff and Monkstown I'm greeted by the acrid smell of the Eleventh Night bonfires. They've become a much grander feature in working-class unionist housing estates than they were in 2001. Burnt tyres and thousands of pallets make me dry heave as the smell seeps into my pores. I return home to a morning of online teaching, to be greeted by students eager to hear about the state of the world and the effects of mega-trends like globalisation, pandemics, climate change, the rise of China and resurgence of Russia, ahead of the tribal rituals practised in a place the British Army has long since consigned to nostalgia-filled memories of 'Op Banner'. Peace has come to Northern Ireland in the years since Britain's massive security *cordon sanitaire* was lifted and troops ordered back to barracks, even if the news headlines occasionally make mention of the violence visited on marginalised communities like those I know only too well.

A few hours after it died out, the Ballyduff bonfire still smoulders in the distance, burning beneath the ash and metal rims of the odd car wheel, the last of the gigantic pallet fortress set alight less than twenty-four hours earlier. I am reminded of how loyalist culture now appears mesmerised by the ritual act of burning that it creates – it's a perfect metaphor for the wrecking of working-class areas and the burning of cars and a bus that proceeded the beginning of the Protestant marching season in 2021. Later that afternoon I make my way to Mossley West train station for an onward journey to meet some north Antrim loyalists in Ballymoney. Orange Standards, loyalist paramilitary flags and new Northern Ireland centenary flags line my route as I make my way through one working-class estate after another.

My train journey is much less eventful. There is a skeleton crew of passengers all heading home from a day watching the parades in Belfast and other parts of Northern Ireland. I half expect a throng of people making their way to and from the parades at Ballymoney as the train pulls into the station, but there are few people about – only a few stragglers as I make my way up the main street to the old hotel where I have arranged to meet the loyalists. As I get closer, I spot a senior DUP figure coming out and walking down the street. I make my way around the back, where a couple of bouncers stop me and ask me for a fiver to gain entry to the function room where my contacts are waiting.

The loyalists I'm here to see inform me that the DUP politician called in to discuss the Northern Ireland Protocol. It seems that the DUP is working hard to keep its supporters on board with their strategy, though it's clear to me that their patience is wearing thin. We're joined by a young Conservative Party social media campaigner who has come over to cover the Twelfth and report back to the Tory grassroots about the feelings of betrayal and disgruntlement with the party's leadership around Brexit. He's finding the emotional bouts of everyday patriotism overwhelming – as I know from my own years living in middle England, this populist dreamtime is how Tories imagine the entire UK once was. I'm reminded of George Orwell's observation about patriotism in *The Lion and the Unicorn*, which he saw, in England at any rate, as 'boasting and flag-wagging, the "Rule Britannia" stuff', 'done by small minorities'.[2] For ordinary people, patriotism was never 'vocal or even conscious'.[3] In Ulster loyalism it is often the opposite. It can be loud and overbearing, rough and ready, complete with tawdry flags and chest beating. In paramilitary circles it is even rougher, with respect for virility, black humour and an unhealthy appetite for the martial spirit trumping light conversation and, paraphrasing Orwell, talk of a nice cup of tea or the pleasures that come from a spell in the back garden. I am troubled by the hijacking of patriotism by Conservatives, though I am comforted by Orwell's other observation that patriotism has 'nothing to do with Conservativism. It is actually the opposite of Conservativism, since it is a devotion to something that is always changing and yet it is felt to be mystically the same. It is the bridge between the future and the past. No real revolutionary has ever been an internationalist.'[4]

The more I have travelled the world, the more I have become increasingly internationalist, which the late, great Christopher Hitchens observed is 'the highest form of patriotism'.[5] I became an advocate for change and making the world a better place not through some kind of idealism, but by the example I was set by role models like Mark Langhammer, Bill McClinton and Dougie Jamison from the Rathcoole Self Help Group, who offered an alternative to a tribal-based view of the world, as well as visiting places less fortunate and more troubled than where I grew up.

Here in Ballymoney, it's heading towards the afternoon and a ramping-up of loyalist festivities as people enjoy the craic while taking the piss out of each other. Oddly, I'm surrounded by an eclectic mix of people of all backgrounds, both male and female, young and old. It's predominantly white and poor, but there are a few who defy this stereotype. They are all welcomed at the table. There are no boundaries in this imagined community, except between those loyal to the UK and those who are not, none of whom appear to be in attendance. This is the closest thing to a holy day for loyalists.

I know that there is good in the people around me here in this heartland of loyalty. They want the same things as we all do. I have learned that even though we might disagree on how to politically achieve these things, it does not have to make us opponents. Too often I have seen loyalism self-destruct because of a clash of personalities or the cynically held view that one person – the 'man in the big picture' – has all the answers. Some of the biggest bluffers and chancers have come from the ranks of loyalist paramilitarism, and even more from the small crew of acolytes who flock to them. They have a selfish view of human nature and of their own interests. Few of them are as welcoming as the loyalists in front of me now, most of whom seem self-aware and conscious of their own limitations. Several of them tell me of another encounter with a senior member of the DUP who privately told them they 'have at best fifteen years before they ended up like Hong Kong', presumably in a transitional hand-over of power by London to Dublin and what Arthur Aughey calls 'sugar candy Ireland'. Brexit has given rise to an intense echo chamber of calls for a 'united Ireland' or a 'new Ireland'. The champions of this fundamentally utopian future typically give little thought to winning over unionists who have no time for it. They can't accept that unionists believe in the status quo and won't be moved. Not now. Not ever. It's not a conversation the 'new Irelanders' wish to have and it's unlikely those around me will accept willingly. These loyalists harbour deep suspicions that in that kind of eventuality, Northern Ireland will resemble Bosnia in the 1990s more than Hong Kong in the 2020s. It is a dismal vision of the future many journalists and academics find an essential characteristic of Ulster loyalism. To my mind, however, it is millenarian rather than utilitarian.

What I find lacking in the conversations around the table is a proactive case being put for the Union between Great Britain and Northern Ireland. Simply articulating a loyalty to a London government that seems somewhat distant from the everyday realities of the people in this part of Northern Ireland seems futile and unproductive. Earlier in the year distinguished historian Marianne Elliott observed in the *Financial Times* how Northern Ireland, a 'state created out of our disagreements 100 years ago has some way to go before its siege mentality evaporates sufficiently for constructive discussion to take place about its long-term future'.[6] There is more than a hint of this 'siege mentality' around the table in Ballymoney. It is like collective mourning for a loss not yet experienced – like a family struggling to come to terms with a loved one transitioning to palliative care after being diagnosed with a terminal illness. It has a familiar ring to it and reminds me of the tenor of those conversations I had in North Belfast twenty years earlier and have had with some unionists and loyalists every year since. As far as I am concerned, it is as if millenarian loyalism repeats its narrative of political anxiety and insecurity continuously so it can resist breaking free from the spell which uncertainty holds over its adherents.

A few months after the Twelfth, I'm at the Hammersmith Cultural Centre in central London to interview Dr John Kyle, then deputy leader of the PUP, on the topic of 'Understanding Northern Irish Loyalism'. I've known Dr Kyle for over sixteen years and have huge respect for the practical peacebuilding and conflict transformation work he has conducted. I was proud to work alongside him on some of these initiatives. He has a message to impart, one that is upbeat and optimistic and far removed from that shared with me by millenarian loyalism:

> I think we are in difficult times. Troubled waters. I think there is a lot of insecurity out there and I think some unscrupulous people want to take advantage of that – and exploit it. I think that there are genuine concerns ... Unionists, loyalists are concerned about a drift that, whereas GB heads off in this direction after Brexit, ... Northern Ireland, which is tethered to the EU, begins to move in this direction. And so there's a growing divergence between Northern Ireland and the rest of the United Kingdom. That is, I think for many people ... a real concern. I think that there are things that can be done to address that. But I don't think it's possible to have Brexit without there being some downside to it for Northern Ireland. And I think that politicians need to be honest and say that. You know, we can't go back to the days before Brexit. It is going to bring change that we need to work with. We need to look at what opportunities there are to see how we can build on it and benefit from it and not just see it entirely as a loss to unionism.[7]

I'm eager to get Dr Kyle's take on the future. As a physician, he is used to diagnosing an ailment and then offering his prognosis based on years of experience:

> In terms of the future, Aaron, I think there are difficult negotiations ahead. I think we can resolve the problems around Brexit. I've always believed that, but it will take some serious negotiations and some work in good faith from all parties. I think ... Brexit has destabilised Northern Ireland and there's a call for a border poll. And Sinn Féin are pushing for a border poll. There definitely has been – the opinion polls suggest that more people are more open to considering a united Ireland. Many of the middle-ground, middle-class community in Northern Ireland who would have voted Remain don't view a united Ireland with the negative analysis that they had maybe twenty years ago. So definitely the mood has changed. However, a border poll that results in 52 per cent in favour of a united Ireland and 48 [per cent] in favour of remaining in the United Kingdom, to my mind, would be an absolute disaster. It would plunge us into all sorts of problems

and uncertainties. However, for the situation in Northern Ireland, I think there is enormous potential for a future that, I think, David Ervine envisaged ... Seamus Mallon envisaged, that politicians in the past were confident could be achieved, and that is a Northern Ireland that is an inclusive Northern Ireland, that's based on mutual respect, that's based on consent where we learn to live together well, where a majority doesn't impose its will on a minority, where our traditions can work together, ... where the strengths of both communities can be synergistic in creating a Northern Ireland that is successful, that is peaceful, that is respectful, that is creative, that has expressions of its Irish members [who] can express their Irishness, the British component can express their Britishness and they can live together in a productive and effective way. But it does need us to work together to achieve that. There needs to be work in good faith. We need to work together in partnership. We need to work together – not brushing our differences under the carpet, but being able to disagree and to disagree in a good way. To be able to work together despite our disagreements. To be able to work together despite our different aspirations. And I don't mean to ... pretend that that – you know, let's all get along together type of thing – I realise that there are differences. I realise that politics is a competitive sport. I realise that, in terms of our political parties, we work together in an adversarial way, but we can also work together in an instructive and in a collaborative way. And I think that if our parties are prepared to do that, and prepared to address the injustices that are in our society, prepared to acknowledge the mistakes that were made in the past, then I think that the future, actually, is very positive for Northern Ireland. There's an opportunity to build in Northern Ireland, I think that can be something that everyone can be proud of. And everyone can have a place in.[8]

As far as Dr Kyle is concerned, there is a need to heal divisions. I couldn't agree with him more. The healing of those divisions, however, must start within the wider unionist community in Northern Ireland. For that to happen, we must have a greater understanding of the concept of political union. This book has been a contribution to that important goal.

ENDNOTES

PROLOGUE

1 Robert Greacen, *The Sash My Father Wore: An Autobiography* (Edinburgh: Mainstream Publishing, 1997), p. 34.
2 Malachi O'Doherty, *The Trouble With Guns: Republican Strategy and the Provisional IRA* (Belfast: Blackstaff Press, 1998), pp. 174–5.
3 *Belfast News Letter*, 20 September 1887.
4 Ibid., 5 July 1899.
5 Ibid.
6 Ibid.
7 Ibid., 6 July 1899.
8 Ibid., 8 July 1899.
9 Ibid.
10 Ibid., 12 July 1899.
11 Ibid., 19 July 1899.
12 *Sunday Independent*, 12 March 1922; *The Cork Examiner*, 20 June 1922.
13 Marianne Elliott, *Heartlands: A Memoir of the White City Housing Estate in Belfast* (Belfast: Blackstaff, 2017), pp. 167–8.
14 *Belfast News Letter*, 6 January 1973.
15 Ibid., 12 July 1976.
16 David McKittrick, Seamus Kelters, Brian Feeney and Chris Thornton, *Lost Lives: The Stories of the Men, Women and Children Who Died as a Result of the Northern Ireland Troubles – Revised and Updated* (Edinburgh: Mainstream, 2001), pp. 661–2. Condemnation was not confined to nationalist politicians, with the local unionist politician Captain Austin Ardill describing the murders as 'an atrocity carried out by sub-humans', *Belfast News Letter*, 12 July 1976.
17 *Belfast Telegraph*, 29 October 1983.
18 Ibid., 8 December 1983.
19 Journalist Susan McKay visited North Belfast in 2000, noting how 'Boundaries have been constantly shifting, house by house, street by street, identified by flags and painted kerbstones. The constant was that Protestants were losing territory, and Catholics were gaining it … These borders were dangerous places, and had continued to be volatile after the 1994 ceasefires had brought their "imperfect peace", as it became known.' Susan McKay, *Northern Protestants: An Unsettled People* (Belfast: Blackstaff, 2000), p. 53.

20 Elliott, *Heartlands*, pp. 166–7.
21 Dervla Murphy, *A Place Apart* (London: John Murray, 1978), pp. 179–80.
22 Brian Walker, '1641, 1689, 1690 and All That: The Unionist Sense of History', *The Irish Review*, 12, Spring–Summer 1992, p. 61. As Luisa Passerini has expressed it, 'It is the reference to the individual or the group that remembers that allows us to situate historically and make concrete what is remembered and what is not. The issues of forgetting and silence are indeed equally important for understanding the political reverberations of memory.' Luisa Passerini, 'Afterword', in Susannah Radstone and Bill Schwartz (eds), *Memory: Histories, Theories, Debates* (New York: Fordham University Press, 2010), p. 460.
23 Professor Ian McBride has noted that it is 'common to deplore the stubbornness with which Ulster Unionism remains mired in a siege mentality', given that the 'perpetuation of the siege myth, after all, depends on the plausibility of the narrative as a representation of contemporary circumstances'. Ian McBride, *The Siege of Derry in Ulster Protestant Mythology* (Dublin: Four Courts Press, 1997), p. 81. That day on the bridge in North Belfast, it seemed justified.
24 The *Belfast Telegraph* reported that 'fear gripped Ulster on a scale not felt since the aftermath of the Shankill and Greysteel atrocities'. *Belfast Telegraph*, 28 April 1994.
25 The concept of an 'Imagined Community' was coined by Benedict Anderson. He suggested that 'the members of even the smallest nation will never know most of their fellow-members, meet them, or even hear of them, yet in the minds of each lives the image of their communion'. Anderson formulated an understanding of imagined community that was limiting (not everyone in the world belonged), it was sovereign in so far as its adherents dreamt of being 'free' and it was imagined in fraternal terms as a community of people who are prepared to die for their imagined nations. Benedict Anderson, *Imagined Communities: Reflections on the Origins and Spread of Nationalism* (London: Verso, [1983], 2006).
26 McKay, *Northern Protestants*, p. 11.
27 Ibid., p. 35.
28 Max Hastings, 'This grossly misguided excavation of the past', *Daily Mail*, 17 June 2010.
29 Max Hastings, 'There will always be an England, but not a UK', *Bloomberg*, 14 February 2021.
30 Max Hastings, 'The last writhings of a society left beached by history', *The Guardian*, 15 September 2005. Hastings has since offensively called unionists 'grotesque', caricaturing them as 'tribal' and living in 'an oppressive sense of confinement in a ghetto' 'bestrode the dunghill'. Max Hastings, 'It's charming but, for me, addresses almost none of the dirty stuff', *The Times*, 21 January 2022. In this latter article, *The Times* altered the electronic version of the article's title, presumably following complaints.

INTRODUCTION

1. Francis Hutcheson, *A Short Introduction to Moral Philosophy in Three Books Containing the Elements of Ethics and the Law of Nature – Translated from the Latin – Second Edition* (Glasgow: Robert & Andrew Foulis, 1753), p. 273. My thanks to the staff at the British Library for access to the original works by Francis Hutcheson and to Dr Sean Brennan for introducing me to Hutcheson's ideas.
2. Francis Fukuyama, *Identity: The Demand for Dignity and the Politics of Resentment* (New York: Farrar, Straus and Giroux, 2018), p. x.
3. The Thirty Years War (1618–48) involved several powers in a religious conflict that devastated much of Europe and led to the deaths of 4–8 million people, a significant proportion of the continent's population at the time.
4. Thomas Hobbes, *Leviathan* (London: Penguin Books, [1651], 1987), p. 186.
5. Ibid., pp. 225–6.
6. Ibid.
7. R.F. Foster, *Modern Ireland, 1600–1972* (London: Penguin Books, 1988), pp. 50–9.
8. Ibid., pp. 59–60.
9. Patrick Buckland, *Ulster Unionism and the Origins of Northern Ireland, 1886–1922* (Dublin: Gill & Macmillan, 1973), p. xviii.
10. David Miller, *Queen's Rebels: Ulster Loyalism in Historical Perspective* (Dublin: University College Dublin Press, [1978], 2007), p. 12.
11. The Laggan Army would eventually break up and transfer its allegiance to Parliament after the execution of Charles I in 1649.
12. Lord Ernest Hamilton, *The Irish Rebellion of 1641: With a History of the Events Which Led Up To and Succeeded It* (London: John Murray, 1920), p. 297.
13. Ibid., p. 298.
14. Miller, *Queen's Rebels*, p. 15.
15. Ibid., p. 11.
16. The term 'dissenter' was used to describe all those Protestants who refused to accept the Book of Common Prayer introduced by the Episcopalian Church of England, which became the Established Church in the wake of the Restoration of the Stuart monarchy on the English throne in 1660.
17. Foster, *Modern Ireland*, p. 156.
18. William Robert Scott, *Francis Hutcheson: His Life, Teaching and Position in the History of Philosophy* (Cambridge: Cambridge University Press, 1900), pp. 5–6.
19. Ibid., pp. 55, 142.
20. S.J. Connolly, *Divided Kingdom: Ireland, 1630–1800* (Oxford: Oxford University Press, 2008), pp. 282, 374.
21. Ibid., pp. 258, 266–7.
22. Caroline Robbins, '"When it is that colonies may turn independent": An analysis of the environment and politics of Francis Hutcheson (1694–1746)', *The William and Mary Quarterly*, 11(2), 1954, p. 243.

23. Francis Hutcheson, *A System of Moral Philosophy in Three Books: Volume I* (London: R. and A. Foulis, 1755), p. 281. This volume is housed in the John Adams Library housed in the Boston Public Library.
24. Ibid., pp. 212–13.
25. Ibid., p. 213.
26. Ibid.
27. Garry Willis, *Inventing America: Jefferson's Declaration of Independence* (Boston, MA: Mariner Books, [1978], 2002), p. viii; Scott, *Francis Hutcheson*, p. 270. The second President of the United States, John Adams, for example, owned half a dozen copies of his books in several editions in his personal library. *Catalogue of the John Adams Library in the Public Library of the City of Boston* (Boston, MA: Boston Public Library, 1917), p. 125. Hutcheson's influence in Ireland extended to the rise of New Light theology and the reformism of Ulster Presbyterians. See Connolly, *Divided Kingdom*, pp. 374, 392; Daniel Carey, *Locke, Hutcheson and Shaftesbury: Contesting Diversity in the Enlightenment and Beyond* (Cambridge: Cambridge University Press, 2006), pp. 150–99.
28. Alvin Jackson, *Home Rule: An Irish History, 1800-2000* (Oxford: Oxford University Press, 2003), p. 12; Marianne Elliott, *Wolfe Tone: Prophet of Irish Independence* (New Haven, CT: Yale University Press, 1989), p. 3; William Drennan MD, *Fugitive Pieces in Verse and Prose* (Belfast: F.D. Finlay, March 1815), p. 193.
29. The Protestant ascendancy, which entered political discourse in 1791-2, is generally regarded as a 'slogan to defend the retention of privilege in Protestant hands; it represented a selfish, negative and reactionary concept, at odds with the "liberal" spirit which had entered Irish politics during the two previous decades'. Jacqueline Hill, 'The meaning and significance of "Protestant ascendancy", 1787–1840' in *Ireland after the Union* – Proceedings of the second joint meeting of the Royal Irish Academy and the British Academy, London, 1986 (Oxford: Oxford University Press, 1989), p. 2.
30. Drennan, *Fugitive Pieces in Verse and Prose*, p. 213. The Irish infant of '82 mentioned here by Drennan refers to the volunteer militias raised throughout Ireland in 1778 that met in Dungannon in 1782 to call for legislative independence from England. The most prominent advocate for this political course of action was the leader of the Irish Patriotic Movement, Henry Grattan. In a speech in April 1782, he reiterated the volunteer's call for legislative independence for Ireland. 1782 is generally seen as the origin year that gave rise to the spectre of paramilitary force in Ireland, which would eventually lead to the United Irishmen's rebellion of 1798.
31. Linda Colley, *Acts of Union and Disunion: What Held the UK Together – and What is Dividing it?* (London: Profile Books, 2014), pp. 98–9.
32. UK Parliament, Act of Union (Ireland) 1800. Archived at: www.legislation.gov.uk/aip/Geo3/40/38/data.pdf (accessed 23 January 2022).
33. Richard English, *Irish Freedom: The History of Nationalism in Ireland* (London: Macmillan, 2006), p. 89.
34. Drennan, *Fugitive Pieces in Verse and Prose*, p. 215.

35 English, *Irish Freedom*, p. 111. Nationalism is 'concerned with territorial politics, appealing inter alia to territory and polity, peoplehood and identity, democracy and self-determination, law, constitutionality and rights.' Jennifer Todd, 'Unionisms and the challenges of change', *Irish Political Studies*, 35(3), 2020, p. 337.

36 Liam Kennedy, 'One island, two peoples: Ethical perspective on ireland's constitutional future', *Irish Studies in International Affairs*, 32(2), 2021, p. 449.

37 Peter Gibbon, *The Origins of Ulster Unionism: The Formation of Popular Protestant Politics and Ideology in Nineteenth Century Ireland* (Manchester: Manchester University Press, 1975), p. 143.

38 Ibid., p. 136. Stephen Howe has pointed to the 'weakness of explicit support for a conception of Ulsterness as a separate nationality', though he points to Fred Halliday's idea that 'Unionism, nevertheless, defines a distinct community', choosing to 'exercise its right to self-determination not by demanding independence but by choosing to adhere to the UK'. Stephen Howe, *Ireland and Empire: Colonial Legacies in Irish History and Culture* (Oxford: Oxford University Press, 2000), p. 196.

39 Frank Wright, *Two Lands on One Soil: Ulster Politics Before Home Rule* (Dublin: Gill & Macmillan, 1996), p. 510.

40 Brendan O'Leary, *A Treatise on Northern Ireland: Volume 1 – Colonialism* (Oxford: Oxford University Press, 2019), p. 289.

41 Graham Walker, *A History of the Ulster Unionist Party: Protest, Pragmatism and Pessimism* (Manchester: Manchester University Press, 2004), p. 48.

42 Sydney Brooks, 'The new Ireland IX: The Unionists', *The North American Review*, 189(638), 1909, p. 116.

43 Ibid., pp. 116–17.

44 The Act gave rights to all women over the age of twenty-one to vote. They could become elected to political office in 1918.

45 *Belfast News Letter*, 19 January 1912.

46 Ibid.

47 Diane Urquhart (ed.), *The Minutes of the Ulster Women's Unionist Council and Executive Committee, 1911–40* (Dublin: Irish Manuscripts Commission, 2001), p. xxii.

48 Ronald McNeill, *Ulster's Stand for the Union* (London: John Murray, 1922), p. 280.

49 Ibid., pp. 280–1.

50 Ibid., p. 141.

51 For more on McNeill and his views on Ulster unionism, see Richard Bourke, 'Unionisms and partition', *Dublin Review of Books*, 1 October 2021. Archived at: https://drb.ie/unionisms-and-partition/ (accessed 16 February 2022).

52 Ivan Gibbons, *Partition: How and Why Ireland was Divided* (London: Haus Publishing, 2020), pp. 120, 127.

53 John E. Sayers, 'The political parties and the social background' in Thomas Wilson (ed.), *Ulster Under Home Rule: A Study of the Political and Economic Problems of Northern Ireland* (London: Oxford University Press, 1955), p. 59.

54 Ibid.
55 A.T.Q. Stewart, *The Narrow Ground: The Roots of Conflict in Ulster*, New Edition (London: Faber and Faber, 1989), p. 174.
56 Ibid.
57 Gibbons, *Partition*, pp. 127–8.
58 Michael Farrell, *Northern Ireland: The Orange State* (London: Pluto Press, 1976); Michael Farrell, *Arming the Protestants: The Formation of the Ulster Special Constabulary* (London: Pluto, 1983); Desmond Bell, *The Protestants of Ulster* (London: Pluto Press, [1976], 1987), pp. 65–72; Richard English and Graham Walker, 'Introduction' in Richard English and Graham Walker (eds), *Unionism in Modern Ireland: New Perspectives on Politics and Culture* (Dublin: Gill & Macmillan, 1996), p. ix.
59 Government of Northern Ireland, *Census of Northern Ireland, 1926* (Belfast: HMSO, 1929), p. 57. Archived at: www.nisra.gov.uk/sites/nisra.gov.uk/files/publications/1926-census-general-report.pdf (accessed 13 September 2021).
60 For more on the UVF, see Aaron Edwards, *UVF: Behind the Mask* (Dublin: Merrion Press, 2017).
61 Kevin Boyle, 'After direct rule: The opposition', *Fortnight*, 37, 13 April 1972, p. 7.
62 Ibid.
63 Rafton Pounder, 'After direct rule: The Unionists, *Fortnight*, 37, 13 April 1972, p. 7.
64 Ibid., p. 8.
65 Jennifer Todd, 'Two traditions in Unionist political culture', *Irish Political Studies*, 2, 1987, p. 11.
66 Ibid., pp. 14, 17. Todd sees the Ulster British as averse to discussing contentious issues around politics and religion. While this may have been the product of the Troubles adage of 'whatever you say, say nothing', it did not preclude the emergence of a more radical and honest strand of progressive unionism in the context of the peace process.
67 Ibid., p. 3.
68 Ibid., pp. 10–11.
69 Ibid., p. 3.
70 Arthur Aughey, 'The idea of the Union' in John Wilson Foster and William Beattie Smith (eds), *The Idea of the Union: Great Britain and Northern Ireland* (Belfast: Belcouver Press, 2021), p. 223.
71 Ibid., pp. 222–3.
72 Ibid., p. 219.
73 Tony Judt, *Postwar: A History of Europe SInce 1945* (London: Vintage Books, 2005), pp. 616–22; Timothy Garton Ash, *We the People: The Revolution of '89 Witnessed in Warsaw, Budapest, Berlin and Prague* (London: Penguin Books, 1999).
74 Aughey, 'The Idea of the Union', p. 221.
75 Richard Bourke, *Peace in Ireland: The War of Ideas* (London: Pimlico, 2003), p. 288.
76 McBride, *The Siege of Derry in Ulster Protestant Mythology*, p. 81.
77 Ibid.

78 David Trimble, Nobel Lecture, 10 December 1998. Archived at: www.nobelprize.org/prizes/peace/1998/trimble/lecture/ (accessed 24 January 2022).
79 Ibid.
80 Ibid.
81 Bourke, 'Unionisms and partition'.
82 Todd, 'Two traditions in Unionist political culture', p. 17.
83 Kennedy, 'One island, two peoples', p. 452.

1. A STATE BORN IN VIOLENCE

1   'Sir Edward Carson's appeal: Support to the authorities urged – The right course of action', *Belfast News Letter*, 24 July 1920.
2   St John Ervine, 'Some impressions of my elders – Yeats', *The North American Review*, 211(771), February 1920, p. 236.
3   Ibid.
4   Lauren Arrington, 'St John Ervine and the Fabian Society: Capital, empire and Irish Home Rule', *History Workshop Journal*, 72(2), 2011, pp. 52–73. As Arrington suggests, for Ervine, Home Rule was not a specifically Irish question but had profound consequences for Britain's Empire: see p. 56.
5   Ervine, 'Some impressions of my elders – Yeats', p. 236.
6   Connal Parr, *Inventing the Myth: Political Passions and the Ulster Protestant Imagination* (Oxford: Oxford University Press, 2017), p. 51.
7   Ibid., p. 55.
8   Marianne Elliott, 'Northern Ireland's uneasy centenary', *Financial Times*, 7 May 2021.
9   Ibid.
10 McNeill, *Ulster's Stand for the Union*, p. 141.
11 Alice Stopford Green, *Ourselves Alone in Ulster: New Edition with Notes* (Dublin and London: Maunsel and Company Ltd, 1918), p. 7; *The Times*, 9 May 1913.
12 McNeill, *Ulster's Stand for the Union*, p. 240.
13 Fearghal McGarry, *The Rising: Ireland: Easter 1916* (Oxford: Oxford University Press, 2016), p. 120.
14 Central Statistics Office, Number of persons killed and wounded during the Easter Rising. Archived at: www.cso.ie/en/releasesandpublications/ep/p-1916/1916irl/society/crime/ (accessed 30 May 2021).
15 McGarry, *The Rising*, p. 280.
16 Buckland, *Ulster Unionism and the Origins of Northern Ireland*, p. 104.
17 Ibid., p. 106.
18 Ibid.
19 Ibid., p. 113.
20 Ibid.
21 Arthur Mitchell, *Labour in Irish Politics: The Irish Labour Movement in an Age of*

Revolution (New York: Barnes and Noble Books, 1974), p. 123. The results were: 550 seats for Sinn Féin, 355 seats for the Unionists, 238 seats for the Nationalist Party, 108 seats for the Reform Party, 161 seats for Independents and 394 seats for Labour candidates. Conor McCabe, 'The Irish Labour Party and the 1920 local elections', *Saothar*, 35, 2010, pp. 7–20.

22 Paul Bew, Peter Gibbon and Henry Patterson, *Northern Ireland, 1921–2001: Political Forces and Social Classes* (London: Serif, 2002), p. 16.
23 Mitchell, *Labour in Irish Politics*, p. 125.
24 Ibid.
25 Ibid.
26 Ibid., p. 126.
27 Henry Patterson, *Class Conflict and Sectarianism: The Protestant Working Class and the Belfast Labour Movement, 1868–1920* (Belfast: Blackstaff, 1980), p. 115.
28 Ibid., p. 116.
29 *Belfast News Letter*, 22 July 1920.
30 Ibid.
31 Ibid., 23 July 1920.
32 Patterson, *Class Conflict and Sectarianism*, p. 117.
33 Ibid., p. 131.
34 Statement by the Attorney General for Ireland Denis Henry, House of Commons Debates (Hansard), Vol. 138, Col. 1795, 2 March 1921.
35 Robert Lynch, 'The people's protectors? The Irish Republican Army and the "Belfast Pogrom", 1920–1922', *Journal of British Studies*, 47(2), 2008, p. 381.
36 Brian Hughes, *Defying the IRA? Intimidation, Coercion, and Communities During the Irish Revolution* (Liverpool: Liverpool University Press, 2016), Chapter 5.
37 Lynch, 'The people's protectors?', p. 391.
38 Miller, *Queen's Rebels*, p. 125.
39 Ibid.
40 Statement by the Chief Secretary for Ireland Sir Hamar Greenwood, House of Commons Debates (Hansard), Vol. 138, Col. 93–94, 16 February 1921.
41 Statement by the Attorney General for Ireland Denis Henry, House of Commons Debates (Hansard), Vol. 140, Col. 463W, 7 April 1921.
42 TNA, CO 904/27, *Plight of Southern Irish Loyalists* (London: Duke of Northumberland's Fund, 1921), p. 5.
43 E. Estyn Evans, 'The personality of Ulster', *Transactions of the Institute of British Geographers*, 51, 1970, p. 15.
44 Bryan A. Follis, *A State Under Siege: The Establishment of Northern Ireland, 1920–1925* (Oxford: Oxford University Press, 1995), pp. 6–7.
45 Ibid., pp. 11, 25, 27–9.
46 St John Ervine, *Craigavon: Ulsterman* (London: Allen and Unwin, 1949), p. 410.
47 *Belfast News Letter*, 9 May 1921.

48 D.G. Pringle, 'Electoral systems and political manipulation: A case study of Northern Ireland in the 1920s', *The Economic and Social Review*, 11(3), 1980, p. 189.
49 Ibid., p. 190.
50 Urquhart (ed.), *The Minutes of the Ulster Women's Unionist Council and Executive Committee*, p. 123.
51 Ibid., p. xix. See also Rachel Ward, *Women, Unionism and Loyalism in Northern Ireland* (Dublin: Irish Academic Press, 2006).
52 Pringle, 'Electoral systems and political manipulation', p. 191.
53 Walker, *A History of the Ulster Unionist Party*, p. 57.
54 Pringle, 'Electoral systems and political manipulation', p. 193.
55 Walker, *A History of the Ulster Unionist Party*, p. 57.
56 Chief Secretary's statement on the Labour Socialists Meeting, House of Commons Debates (Hansard), Vol. 142, Col. 1257–8W, 2 June 1921.
57 Public Records Office of Northern Ireland (PRONI), CAB/6/92, Report on the Ulster Protestant Association, dated February 1923.
58 Ibid.
59 Tim Bowman, *Carson's Army: The Ulster Volunteer Force, 1910–22* (Manchester: Manchester University Press, 2007), p. 191.
60 Cited in ibid., p. 196.
61 Ibid., p. 199.
62 A useful Catholic nationalist account of the 'Belfast Pogroms' is G.B. Kenna, *Facts and Figures of the Belfast Pogrom, 1920–1922* (Dublin: The O'Connell Publishing Company, 1922).
63 Lynch, 'The people's protectors?', pp. 375–91.
64 Niall Cunningham, *The Social Geography of Violence During the Belfast Troubles, 1920–22*, CRESC Working Paper Series Working Paper No. 122 (March 2013), p. 7. Archived at: https://hummedia.manchester.ac.uk/institutes/cresc/workingpapers/wp122.pdf (accessed 12 May 2021).
65 Bureau of Military History, 1913–21, statement by Colonel Thomas McNally, quartermaster, 3rd Northern Division of the IRA, dated 18 July 1950, p. 20. Archived at: www.militaryarchives.ie/collections/online-collections/bureau-of-military-history-1913-1921/reels/bmh/BMH.WS0410.pdf (accessed 2 June 2021).
66 Cunningham, *The Social Geography of Violence*.
67 House of Lords Debates (Hansard) on the King's Address, 14 December 1921, Vol. 48, Col. 41.
68 Ibid.
69 Northern Ireland House of Commons (Hansard), 10 October 1922, Vol. 2, Col. 956.

2. THE PEOPLE OF INDEPENDENT THOUGHT

1 George Orwell, *The Road to Wigan Pier* (London: Penguin Books, [1937], 1966), p. 138.

2   *Belfast News Letter*, 30 November 1923.
3   Ibid.
4   John F. Harbinson, *The Ulster Unionist Party, 1882–1973: Its Development and Organisation* (Belfast: Blackstaff Press, 1973), p. 212
5   Walker, *A History of the Ulster Unionist Party*, p. 70.
6   Graham Walker, *The Politics of Frustration: Harry Midgley and the Failure of Labour in Northern Ireland* (Manchester: Manchester University Press, 1985), p. 33.
7   Ibid., p. 32.
8   Ibid., p. 33.
9   Ibid., p. 35.
10 Jonathan Bardon, *A History of Ulster: New Updated Edition* (Belfast: Blackstaff Press, 2001), p. 509.
11 Colin Reid, 'Protestant challenges to the "Protestant State": Ulster Unionism and Independent Unionism in Northern Ireland, 1921–1939', *Twentieth Century British History*, 19(4), 2008, pp. 419–45.
12 Ibid., pp. 421–2.
13 Ibid., p. 423.
14 Pringle, 'Electoral systems and political manipulation', p. 204.
15 Aaron Edwards, '"Signposts to the New Ulster?" Unionist Government Administration, the Labour Opposition and the Protestant Working Class in Northern Ireland, 1956–72' (unpublished MA thesis: QUB, 2002).
16 Farrell, *Northern Ireland: The Orange State*, pp. 81–3; Paddy Devlin, *Yes We Have No Bananas: Outdoor Relief in Belfast, 1920–39* (Belfast: Blackstaff Press, 1981), p. 113.
17 Farrell, *Northern Ireland*, p. 83.
18 Ibid., p. 84.
19 Buckland, *Ulster Unionism and the Origins of Northern Ireland*, p. 92.
20 'Duncairn Unionists: The influence of women – Let boundary question die', *Belfast News Letter*, 8 May 1925.
21 Ibid.
22 PRONI, HA/5/1427, Unemployed Workers' Meeting in Linenhall Street, Belfast, on 8 June 1926 – Obstruction of Traffic.
23 Christopher Loughlin, 'The moral economy of loyalty: Labour, law, and the State in Northern Ireland, 1921–1939', *Labour History Review*, 82(1), 2017, p. 8.
24 Ibid., pp. 5–6.
25 Ibid., p. 5. Despite the opposition to such legislation by the NI Labour Party between 1925 and 1929, the Special Powers Act remained on the statute books as a temporary measure until being made permanent in 1933.
26 Devlin, *Yes We Have No Bananas*, p. 2.
27 Ibid., p. 110.
28 Ibid.
29 Ibid, p. 178.

30 Ronnie Munck and Bill Rolston, *Belfast in the Thirties: An Oral History* (Belfast: Blackstaff Press, 1987), p. 18.
31 Ibid., p. 24.
32 Ibid., p. 28.
33 Ibid., p. 28.
34 Ibid., p. 33.
35 PRONI, CAB 9B/207/1, Edward J. Clarke to Lord Craigavon, 18 October 1932.
36 Ibid., Alex Gossip to Lord Craigavon, 22 October 1932.
37 Ibid., Cabinet Secretary to Sir Charles Blackmore, 9 November 1932.
38 Ibid.
39 Devlin, *Yes We Have No Bananas*, p. 136.
40 Ronnie Munck and Bill Rolston, 'Oral history and social conflict: Belfast in the 1930s', *The Oral History Review*, 13, 1985, p. 12.
41 *Belfast News Letter*, 28 November 1933.
42 *Belfast News Letter*, 30 November 1933.
43 Ibid.
44 Ibid.
45 *Belfast News Letter*, 2 December 1933.
46 PRONI, D1327/12/1, The Ulster Unionist Labour Association: What It Is (n.d.).
47 Ibid.
48 Ibid.
49 PRONI, D1327/11/1/5, Ulster Unionist Labour Association Report for 1933.
50 T.J. Campbell, *Fifty Years of Ulster, 1890–1940* (Belfast: The Irish News, 1941), p. 329.
51 Ibid.
52 *Belfast News Letter*, 25 April 1934.
53 Ibid.
54 In their analysis of Northern Ireland published in 1962, Denis P. Barritt and Charles F. Carter drew a sharp distinction between those unionists who 'lose no opportunity of thumping the Protestant drum', including evidenced by this debate, which they said was 'intended, not as an expression of religious bigotry, but as an attack on treasonable nationalists', and those 'in favour of justice towards Catholics'. Denis P. Barritt and Charles F. Carter, *The Northern Ireland Problem: A Study in Group Relations*, Second Edition (Oxford: Oxford University Press, 1972), p. 46.
55 Northern Ireland Parliamentary Debates (Hansard), 24 April 1934, Vol. 16, Col. 1091.
56 Ibid., 1095.
57 Ibid.
58 Ibid., Col. 1121.
59 Ibid.
60 Alvin Jackson, *The Two Unions: Ireland, Scotland, and the Survival of the United Kingdom, 1707–2007* (Oxford: Oxford University Press, 2012), p. 319.
61 Harbinson, *Ulster Unionist Party*, p. 67.

62 PRONI, D1327/11/1/5, Ulster Unionist Labour Association correspondence, Carson to Hungerford, 17 December 1934.
63 Ibid.
64 *Belfast News Letter*, 7 January 1935.
65 Bob Rowthorn and Naomi Wayne, *Northern Ireland: The Political Economy of Conflict* (Cambridge: Polity Press, 1988), p. 33.
66 PRONI, D1327/11/1/5, Ulster Unionist Labour Association Report 1934.
67 Ibid.
68 Graham Walker, '"Protestantism before party!" The Ulster Protestant League in the 1930s', *Historical Journal*, 28(4), 1985, p. 964; A.C. Hepburn, 'The Belfast Riots of 1935', *Social History*, 15(1), 1990, p. 77.
69 Walker, 'Protestantism before party!', p. 967.
70 Ibid., p. 964.
71 *Belfast News Letter*, 15 July 1935.
72 Hepburn, 'The Belfast Riots of 1935', p. 96.
73 David Murphy, 'Hugh Maude de Fellenberg Montgomery (1870–1954)', *Dictionary of Irish Biography*, October 2009. Accessible at: www.dib.ie/biography/montgomery-hugh-maude-de-fellenberg-a5903.
74 PRONI, D2661/C/1/A/1/1, Montgomery to Andrews, 3 September 1935.
75 John Hewitt, *The Collected Poems of John Hewitt*, edited by Frank Ormsby (Belfast: Blackstaff, 1992), p. 408.
76 Ibid.
77 Ibid.
78 Henry Patterson, *Ireland Since 1939: The Persistence of Conflict* (Dublin: Penguin Books, 2006), p. 9.
79 Bew, Gibbon and Patterson, *Northern Ireland, 1921–2001*, p. 60.
80 Northern Ireland House of Commons Debates (Hansard), Vol. 17, 20 November 1934, Col. 21–22.
81 *Belfast News Letter*, 10 February 1937.
82 Ibid.
83 Michael Gallagher, 'The constitution and the judiciary' in John Coakley and Michael Gallagher (eds), *Politics in the Republic of Ireland: Fourth Edition* (London: Routledge, 2005), pp. 73, 78.
84 Dermot Keogh, 'The Jesuits and the 1937 Constitution', *Studies: An Irish Quarterly Review*, 78(309), Spring 1989, p. 91.
85 Jonathan Tonge, *Northern Ireland: Conflict and Change: Second Edition* (Essex: Person Education Limited, 2002), p. 32.

3. MASTERS OF OUR OWN HOUSE

1 H.G. Wells, *The Fate of Homo Sapiens* (London: Secker and Warburg, 1939), p. 197.

2   Harbinson, *Ulster Unionist Party*, p. 190.
3   Museum of Orange Heritage, Belfast, Grand Orange Lodge of Ireland, Report of the Proceedings of the General Half-Yearly Meeting held in the Memorial Hall, Londonderry, 15 June 1938. My thanks to Dr Jonathan Mattison, Curator of the Museum of Orange Heritage, for facilitating my research in the Museum's archives and for permission to cite from the Order's official documents.
4   *Belfast News Letter*, 17 October 1938.
5   Bew, Gibbon and Patterson, *Northern Ireland*, p. 48.
6   Patterson, *Ireland Since 1939*, p. 10.
7   *Belfast News Letter*, 17 October 1938.
8   Paul Bew, 'The decay of the Union' in D. George Boyce and Alan O'Day (eds), *Defenders of the Union: A Survey of British and Irish Unionism Since 1801* (Abingdon: Routledge, 2001), p. 320.
9   Ibid.
10 Gillian McIntosh argued in her influential book *The Force of Culture* that the press overage in the 1930s was 'as comprehensive as it was dramatic', giving 'the masses … a sense that they were participating in the collective life of the community'. Gillian McIntosh, *The Force of Culture: Unionist Identities in Twentieth-Century Ireland* (Cork: Cork University Press, 1999), p. 36.
11 Bew, 'The decay of the Union', p. 320.
12 Ibid.
13 McIntosh, *Force of Culture*, p. 36.
14 Jim Smyth, 'The men of no popery: The origins of the Orange Order', *History Ireland*, 3(3), 1995, p. 51.
15 Ibid.
16 Ruth Dudley Edwards, *The Faithful Tribe: An Intimate Portrait of the Loyal Institutions* (London: HarperCollins, 2000), pp. 222–3.
17 Ibid., p. 223.
18 Museum of Orange Heritage, Belfast, Grand Orange Lodge of Ireland 1933 Constitution, Laws and Ordinances of the Loyal Orange Institution of Ireland, Revised and Adopted by the Loyal Orange Institution of Ireland, 14 June 1933 (1938).
19 Ibid., Rule 28.
20 Ibid.
21 Farrell, *Northern Ireland: The Orange State*, p. 16.
22 Eric P. Kaufmann, *The Orange Order: A Contemporary Northern Irish History* (Oxford: Oxford University Press, 2007), p. 21.
23 Ibid.
24 *Belfast News Letter*, 18 October 1938.
25 Ibid.
26 Ibid.
27 Ibid.

28 The Northern Ireland Government Agent was Major General (Ret'd) Sir James Cooke-Collis, a decorated war hero who had latterly been General Officer Commanding in Northern Ireland.
29 *Belfast News Letter*, 31 December 1938.
30 *Belfast News Letter*, 31 December 1938.
31 Ibid.
32 *Evening Herald*, 3 February 1939.
33 Ibid.
34 *Evening Herald*, 16 January 1939.
35 Tim Pat Coogan, *The IRA: New Edition* (London: HarperCollins, 1995), p. 126.
36 Farrell, *Northern Ireland: The Orange State*, p. 151.
37 Coogan, *The IRA*, p. 127.
38 'Question of partition – motion (resumed)', Seanad Éireann, 3rd Seanad, Vol. 22, No. 11, 7 February 1939.
39 Coogan, *The IRA*, p. 132.
40 *Evening Herald*, 12 July 1939.
41 *Belfast News Letter*, 13 July 1939.
42 'Bombing activities in Great Britain', Seanad Éireann, 3rd Seanad, Vol. 23, No. 9, 26 July 1939.
43 Liam De Paor, *Divided Ulster* (London: Penguin Books, 1970), pp. 103–4.
44 Marc Mulholland, 'Why did Unionists discriminate?' in Sabine Wichert (ed.), *From the United Irishmen to Twentieth-Century Unionism: A Festschrift for A.T.Q. Stewart* (Dublin: Four Courts Press, 2004), p. 206.
45 John Andrew Oliver, *Working at Stormont* (Dublin: Institute of Public Administration, 1978), p. 60.
46 Ibid.
47 Northern Ireland House of Commons Hansard, 4 September 1939, Vol. 22, Col. 1902.
48 Ibid., Col. 1907.
49 Ibid., Col. 1925.
50 Keith Jeffery, 'The British Army and Ireland since 1922' in Thomas Bartlett and Keith Jeffery (eds), *A Military History of Ireland* (Cambridge: Cambridge University Press, 1996), p. 437; Steven O'Connor, 'Irish identity and integration within the British Army forces, 1939–45', *Irish Historical Studies*, 39(155), 2015, pp. 417–38.
51 Yvonne McEwen, 'Deaths in Irish regiments 1939–1945 and the extent of Irish volunteering for the British Army', *The Irish Sword*, Vol. 24, 2004–5, pp. 81–98.
52 Patterson, *Ireland Since 1939*, p. 36.
53 Brian Barton, *Northern Ireland in the Second World War* (Belfast: Ulster Historical Foundation, 1995), pp. 25–6.
54 Ibid., p. 78.
55 'Ulster and the war', *Belfast News Letter*, 29 May 1940.
56 Barton, *Northern Ireland in the Second World War*, p. 21. See also p. 43.

4. WHIPPING UP THE NEW RECRUITS

1. Ultach, *Orange Terror: The Case Against Partition* (pamphlet, 1943), p. 3. Archived at: http://bibliotheque.idbe-bzh.org/data/cle_11_fevrier_2016/cle_14_18_fevrier_2016/cle17/cle_17/Orange_Terror_The_partition_of_Ireland_.pdf (accessed 1 May 2021).
2. *Belfast News Letter*, 17 April 1941.
3. Ibid.
4. Ibid.
5. Northern Ireland House of Commons Hansard, 22 April 1941, Vol. 24, Col. 640.
6. *Belfast News Letter*, 17 April 1941.
7. Northern Ireland House of Commons Hansard, 22 April 1941, Vol. 24, Col. 631–2.
8. *Belfast News Letter*, 19 April 1941.
9. Philip Ollerenshaw, 'War, industrial mobilisation and society in Northern Ireland, 1939–1945', *Contemporary European History*, 16(2), 2007, p. 188.
10. Walker, *A History of the Ulster Unionist Party*, p. 90.
11. PRONI, MIC155, Spender Diaries, entry for 15 May 1941.
12. Ibid.
13. Walker, *A History of the Ulster Unionist Party*, p. 90.
14. Barton, *Northern Ireland and the Second World War*, p. 44; Ollerenshaw, 'War, industrial mobilisation and society in Northern Ireland', p. 179.
15. Ollerenshaw, 'War, industrial mobilisation and society', p. 173. As Walker points out, this was 'due mainly to Brooke's moderately successful efforts to acquire contracts for war work', though it was 'insufficiently dramatic to earn the government any popular gratitude'. Walker, *A History of the Ulster Unionist Party*, p. 90.
16. Ollerenshaw, 'War, industrial mobilisation and society', p. 174.
17. Ibid.
18. PRONI, COM 28/7, Sir Walter Smiles to Harold Macmillan, 15 April 1941. Cited in ibid., p. 179.
19. Walker, *A History of the Ulster Unionist Party*, p. 91. See also Walker, *The Politics of Frustration*.
20. PRONI, MIC155, Spender Diaries, entry for 26 November 1941.
21. Northern Ireland House of Commons Hansard, 13 May 1941, Vol. 24, Col. 834.
22. Richard Froggatt, 'Herbert Dixon (1880–1950)', *Dictionary of Ulster Biography*. Archived at: www.newulsterbiography.co.uk/index.php/home/printPerson/1813 (accessed 28 October 2021).
23. PRONI, D1327/12/1, Reverend W. Martin to Lord Glentoran, 28 January 1942.
24. Ibid., Lord Glentoran to Reverend W. Martin, 29 January 1942.
25. Ibid.
26. Ibid., Fullerton to Glentoran, 3 February 1942.
27. Northern Ireland House of Commons Hansard, 20 May 1941, Vol. 24, Col. 865.
28. Ibid.

29 Northern Ireland (Imperial Contributions), House of Commons Debates (Hansard), 15 April 1943, Vol. 388, Col. 1406–7W.
30 Ollerenshaw, 'War, industrial mobilisation and society', p. 187.
31 Ibid., p. 197.
32 Walker, *A History of the Ulster Unionist Party*, p. 93.
33 Ibid., p. 90.
34 Northern Ireland House of Commons Hansard, 31 August 1943, Vol. 26, Col. 1528.
35 Ibid. Throughout the first half of the 1940s, the labour movement was represented in the Northern Ireland House of Commons by Jack Beattie, Paddy Agnew and Harry Midgley – Midgley was expelled from the NILP and formed his own Commonwealth Labour Party. Despite their full-time presence in the House of Commons, the NILP made 'no real advance' in this period according to E. Rumpf and A.C. Hepburn, *Nationalism and Socialism in Twentieth Century Ireland* (Liverpool: Liverpool University Press, 1977), p. 200.
36 Aaron Edwards, *A History of the Northern Ireland Labour Party: Democratic Socialism and Sectarianism* (Manchester: Manchester University Press, 2009), p. 23.
37 Russell Rees, *Labour and the Northern Ireland Problem, 1945–1951: The Missed Opportunity* (Dublin: Irish Academic Press, 2009), p. 28.
38 Author interview with David Bleakley, 21 March 2006.
39 Ibid.
40 Walker, *A History of the Ulster Unionist Party*, p. 97.
41 John Privilege and Greta Jones, 'Crisis and scandal: Government, local government and health reform in Northern Ireland, 1939–44', *Irish Economic and Social History*, 42, 2015, p. 50.
42 Ibid.
43 Ibid.
44 Northern Ireland House of Commons Hansard, 20 February 1945, Vol. 28, Col. 27.
45 Ibid., Col. 33.
46 Ibid., Col. 34.
47 Ibid., Col. 37.
48 Ibid.

5. RESPONSIBLE MEMBERS OF THE COMMUNITY

1 Bertrand Russell, *Authority and the Individual: The Reith Lectures for 1948–9* (London: George Allen and Unwin Limited, 1949), p. 111.
2 *Belfast News Letter*, 18 July 1945.
3 *Belfast News Letter*, 21 July 1945.
4 Ibid.
5 Ibid.
6 Ibid.

7   Northern Ireland House of Commons Debates (Hansard), 31 August 1945, Vol. 29, Col. 55.
8   Ibid.
9   For more on the NILP see Edwards, *A History of the Northern Ireland Labour Party*.
10 *Belfast News Letter*, 4 July 1945.
11 Stopford Green, *Ourselves Alone in Ulster*, pp. 28–9.
12 Ibid.
13 Walker, *A History of the Ulster Unionist Party*, p. 100.
14 Oliver, *Working at Stormont*, p. 75.
15 Ibid.
16 Ibid.
17 Ibid., pp. 75–6.
18 Sayers, 'The political parties and the social background', p. 59.
19 Ibid.
20 Barton, 'Relations between Westminster and Stormont during the Attlee premiership', *Irish Political Studies*, 7, 1992, p. 19.
21 TNA, CAB 21/1842, Note of a conversation between Attlee and Brooke at Chequers, 20 November 1948.
22 Ibid.
23 *Belfast News Letter*, 23 November 1948.
24 Ibid.
25 Paul Bew, Henry Patterson and Paul Teague, *Between War and Peace: The Political Future of Northern Ireland* (London: Serif, 1997), p. 19.
26 Aaron Edwards, 'Social democracy and partition: The British Labour Party and Northern Ireland, 1951–64', *Journal of Contemporary History*, 42(4), 2007, p. 596.
27 Hugh Shearman, *Ulster* (London: Robert Hale Limited, 1949), p. 221.
28 Museum of Orange Heritage, Belfast, Grand Orange Lodge of Ireland, Central Committee Meeting, Sandy Row Orange Hall, 10 October 1951.
29 Museum of Orange Heritage, Belfast, Grand Orange Lodge of Ireland, Special Central Committee meeting, 7 November 1951.
30 Alvin Jackson suggests that the Unionist Party at Westminster 'and Ulster Unionism as a whole benefited from the generally favourable image of Northern Ireland that the war had helped to furnish'. Brooke was astute enough to resist the urge to rock the boat. Alvin Jackson, 'Tame Tory hacks? The Ulster Party at Westminster, 1922–1972', *The Historical Journal*, 54(2), June 2011, p. 466.
31 Paul Ward, *Unionism in the United Kingdom, 1918–1974* (Basingstoke: Palgrave Macmillan, 2005), p. 163.
32 PRONI, D1083/9, Viscount Charlemont, to [Sir] Basil [Brooke]. A copy of a letter relating to the appointment of Dame Dehra Parker to the office of Minister of Health, 28 August 1948.
33 Ward, *Unionism in the United Kingdom*, p. 170.

34 Northern Ireland House of Commons Debates (Hansard), 29 November 1955, Vol. 39, Col. 2898.
35 PRONI, D1327/18/360, Dehra Parker to Lord Glentoran, 2 November 1955.
36 PRONI, D1327/18/360, W.J. Alexander to Dehra Parker, 8 February 1956.
37 Walker, *A History of the Ulster Unionist Party*, p. 140.
38 PRONI, D/3702/C/9, Sam Napier Papers, *Where Ulster Labour Stands* (1953).
39 Clement Attlee was Labour leader 1935–55 and Hugh Gaitskell 1955–63.
40 Gaitskell had even travelled to Belfast prior to the 1958 Stormont election to offer his personal encouragement to the party.
41 Edwards, *A History of the Northern Ireland Labour Party*, p. 47.
42 Rumpf and Hepburn, *Nationalism and Socialism in Twentieth Century Ireland*, p. 195.
43 PRONI, D3233/7/2, Oldpark Divisional Labour Party, letter from Vivian Simpson, 1 April 1958.
44 *Belfast News Letter*, 2 April 1958.
45 Ibid.
46 Ibid.
47 1957 saw the publication of a report by two academic economists from Queen's University Belfast who were critical of the unionist government's economic policies. The report was ordered by the Stormont government in 1947 and delivered in 1955 but withheld for two years to prevent haemorrhaging of votes to the NILP. See K.S. Isles and Norman Cuthbert, *An Economic Survey of Northern Ireland* (Belfast: HMSO, 1957). See also, Patterson, *Ireland Since 1939*, pp. 136–43.
48 Roy Wallace, *The Road to Ballyhightown: A History of Rathcoole and the Rathcoole Self Help Group – New Edition* (Belfast: Rathcoole Self Help Group, 2020), p. 39. My thanks to Roy Wallace for providing me with a copy of his book.
49 McIntosh, *The Force of Culture*, p. 220.
50 Ibid.
51 Ibid., pp. 220–1.
52 BBC Archive, On This Day 1957: Ulster Mirror Reported from the Latest Jewel in the Northern Ireland Housing Trust Crown, the Rathcoole Estate. Accessible at: https://archive.org/details/twitter-1097446727680962560.
53 *Belfast News Letter*, 1 April 1958.
54 Ibid.
55 Ibid.
56 Much later, during the Troubles, loyalist paramilitary groups in local areas would be known as 'the boys'. Although this colloquialism runs back to the Peep o' Day Boys and other martial groups of the late eighteenth century, it would take on a local significance in places like Rathcoole where these groups became organised around sports clubs. They were also known as 'teams'.
57 *Belfast News Letter*, 1 April 1958.

58 'Teaching girls to become responsible citizens: Aims of Rathcoole Club', *Belfast News Letter*, 1 April 1958.
59 Ibid.
60 Ibid.
61 Ibid.
62 Ibid.
63 Ward, *Unionism in the United Kingdom*, p. 176.
64 Ibid. Parker served as the Council for the Support of Music and the Arts (CEMA) chairman in Northern Ireland from 1949 until 1960.
65 High culture is a term traditionally used to denote the aesthetic tastes of the upper classes who tend to find intellectual nourishment in art originating from classical antiquity, as opposed to the 'low culture' or 'popular culture' of the masses.
66 Northern Ireland House of Commons Debates (Hansard), 2 April 1958, Vol. 42, Col. 65.
67 Ibid., Col. 71.
68 Author interview with Beatrice Boyd, 21 February 2005.
69 Ibid.
70 Author interview with David Bleakley, 21 March 2006.
71 Northern Ireland House of Commons Debates (Hansard), 2 April 1958, Vol. 42, Col. 34.
72 Author interview with David Bleakley, 21 March 2006.
73 David Bleakley, *Peace in Ulster* (Oxford: Mowbrays, 1972), p. 19.
74 Harbinson, *Ulster Unionist Party*, pp. 109–13.
75 Brian Faulkner, *Memoirs of a Statesman*, edited by John Houston (London: Weidenfeld and Nicolson, 1978), pp. 22–3.
76 PRONI, D2022/1/44, John Kerr Papers, Letter from Edmund Warnock to John Kerr, dated 12 October 1962. Apart from the four NILP MPs, Frank Hanna (Ind Lab), Gerry Fitt (IrLP) and Harry Diamond (RLP) held seats in Belfast Central, Dock and Falls respectively.
77 Aaron Edwards and Maria Hadjiathanasiou, 'Brothers in arms? How the IRA and EOKA insurgencies transcended the local and became transnational', *Small Wars & Insurgencies*, 32(4–5), 2021, pp. 642–64.

6. AN ULSTER DIVIDED AGAINST ITSELF

1 Hutcheson, *A Short Introduction to Moral Philosophy in Three Books*, p. 226.
2 PRONI, HA/20/A/1/24A, Seized IRA Documents.
3 Brian Hanley and Scott Millar, *The Lost Revolution: The Story of the Official IRA and the Workers' Party* (Dublin: Penguin, 2016), p. 7.
4 IRA, *A Handbook for Volunteers of the Irish Republican Army on Guerrilla Warfare* (Issued by General Headquarters, 1956). Copy in author's possession.
5 Mick Ryan, *My Life in the IRA: The Border Campaign* (Cork: Mercier Press, 2018), pp. 70–2.

6   Ed Moloney, *The Secret History of the IRA: Second Edition* (London: Penguin Books, 2007), p. 50.
7   Mícheál MacDonncha, 'Border campaign — '50s republicans deserve recognition and gratitude', *An Phoblacht,* 14 December 2006.
8   Ryan, *My Life in the IRA*, pp. 51–2.
9   Ibid., pp. 52–3.
10 Ibid., pp. 58–9.
11 TNA, WO 32/17577, Óglaigh na hÉireann General Army Convention 1956.
12 Ibid.
13 Ibid.
14 TNA, WO 32/17577, RUC Special Branch report on the IRA, dated April 1957.
15 Ibid.
16 TNA, CAB 128/30/101, Cabinet Conclusions, 17 December 1956.
17 House of Commons Debates (Hansard), 19 December 1956, Vol. 562, Col. 1265.
18 Ibid., Col. 1267.
19 Moloney, *The Secret History of the IRA*, p. 50.
20 PRONI, HA/32/1/1317, Activities of the IRA, dated August 1957.
21 Ibid.
22 Imperial War Museum, interview, 28 April 1992, Reel 6. Accessible at: www.iwm.org.uk/collections/item/object/80012283.
23 Ibid.
24 TNA, WO32/17577, JIC, The Security and Intelligence Situation in Northern Ireland, 1958.
25 Ibid., Bill Magan to Brigadier C.H. Tarver, Dated 22 November 1957.
26 Ibid., War Office Report on the IRA, dated 16 June 1958.
27 Ibid.
28 *Over the Bridge* dramatised 'the historical impotence of socialist ideals in the face of sectarian violence', cultural critic Edna Longley once wrote. It marked 'one juncture where culture and politics effectively reunited and won a famous victory over the Unionist establishment which attempted to suppress the play'. Edna Longley, 'Progressive bookmen: Politics and Northern Protestant writers since the 1930s', *The Irish Review*, 1, 1986, pp. 50–7. Sam Thompson died of a heart attack on 15 February 1965 while campaigning for the NILP.
29 Connal Parr, 'Sam Thompson (1916–1965)', *Oxford Dictionary of National Biography*, 11 April 2019. Archived at: https://doi.org/10.1093/ref:odnb/96485 (accessed 28 October 2021).
30 House of Commons (Debates), 30 March 1960, Vol. 620, Col. 1404.
31 Ibid., Col. 1434.
32 TNA, WO32/17577, IRA Threat as at October 1960, 19 October 1960.
33 Ibid.
34 Seán Mac Stíofáin, *Memoirs of a Revolutionary* (London: G. Cremonesi, 1975), p. 89.

35 'Former head of IRA who saw himself as successor to Wolfe Tone – Obituary: Ruairí Ó Brádaigh', *The Irish Times*, 8 June 2013.
36 Mac Stíofáin, *Memoirs of a Revolutionary*, p. 90.
37 Moloney, *The Secret History of the IRA*, p. 51; Barry Flynn, *Soldiers of Folly: The IRA Border Campaign, 1956–1962* (Cork: The Collins Press, 2009), p. 200.
38 Seán Cronin, *Irish Nationalism: A History of Its Roots and Ideology* (New York: Continuum, 1980), p. 174.
39 Mac Stíofáin, *Memoirs of a Revolutionary*, pp. 91–4; see also Flynn, *Soldiers of Folly*, p. 204.
40 'Marxist IRA gunman who became leader of Official Sinn Féin — Obituary of Seán Garland', *The Irish Times*, 22 December 2018.
41 Moloney, *The Secret History of the IRA*, p. 278.
42 Oliver, *Working at Stormont*, p. 78.
43 Museum of Orange Heritage, Belfast, Grand Orange Lodge of Ireland, Central Committee Minutes, dated 2 October 1964. The letter from Craig was dated 6 July 1964.
44 Ibid.
45 *Belfast News Letter*, 28 August 1964,
46 *Belfast News Letter*, 2 October 1964.
47 Ibid.
48 Ibid.
49 *Belfast News Letter*, 3 October 1964.
50 Ibid.
51 Roy Garland, *Gusty Spence* (Belfast: Blackstaff Press, 2001), pp. 35–6.
52 TNA, CJ 4/5853, Life Sentence Prisoner Augustus (Gusty) Spence, 'Augustus (Gusty) Andrew Spence – NIO Briefing Note', documents dated December 1984.
53 Garland, *Gusty Spence*, p. 39.
54 Ibid., pp. 37–42.
55 Ibid., p. 48.
56 *Belfast News Letter*, 6 April 1963.
57 Cited in Ben Pimlott, *Harold Wilson* (London: HarperCollins, 1993), p. 304.
58 *Belfast News Letter*, 6 April 1963.
59 Terence O'Neill, *The Autobiography of Terence O'Neill: Prime Minister of Northern Ireland, 1963–1969* (London: Rupert Hart Davis, 1972), p. 47.
60 Garland, *Gusty Spence*, pp. 48–9.
61 PRONI, HA/32/2/8, Documents on the Fiftieth Anniversary of the Easter Rising and Loyalist Response. See also Edwards, *UVF*, pp. 9–22.
62 For more on the UVF, see Edwards, *UVF*.
63 O'Neill, *Autobiography*, p. 81.
64 Clifford Smyth, *Ian Paisley: Voice of Protestant* Ulster (Edinburgh: Scottish Academic Press, 1987), p. 8.

65. Protestant Unionists, *The Way These Orangemen Celebrate the 'Glorious Twelfth'* (n.d. likely 1966). Copy in author's possession.
66. Ibid.
67. Museum of Orange Heritage, Belfast, Grand Orange Lodge of Ireland: Report of the Half-Yearly Meeting held at Castlerock Orange Hall, 14 June 1967.
68. Ibid.
69. *Belfast News Letter*, 13 July 1967.
70. Ibid.
71. Paddy Devlin, *Straight Left: An Autobiography* (Belfast: Blackstaff Press, 1993), p. 80.
72. Bob Purdie, *Politics in the Streets: Origins of the Civil Rights Movement in Northern Ireland* (Belfast: Blackstaff Press, 1990); Marc Mulholland, *Northern Ireland at the Crossroads: Ulster Unionism in the O'Neill Years, 1960–9* (Basingstoke: Palgrave Macmillan, 2000); Thomas Hennessey, *The Origins of the Troubles* (Dublin: Gill & Macmillan, 2005).
73. Purdie, *Politics in the Streets*, p. 123.
74. Simon Prince, *Northern Ireland's '68: Civil Rights, Global Revolt and the Origins of the Troubles* (Dublin: Irish Academic Press, 2007).
75. Ibid., p. 124.
76. PRONI, D2991/B/95/3, Healy to Warnock, 17 November 1967.
77. PRONI, D2991/B/95/2, Warnock to Healey, November 1967 [day not given].
78. Elliott, *Heartlands*, p. 161.
79. Chris Reynolds and Connal Parr, 'Northern Ireland's 1968 at 50: Agonism and Protestant perspectives on civil rights', *Contemporary British History*, 35(1), 2021, pp. 1–25.
80. Stewart, *The Narrow Ground*, p. 183.
81. Ibid.
82. Author interview with Eamonn McCann, 21 December 2007. For a more detailed analysis of the NILP and civil rights see Aaron Edwards, 'Unionist Derry is Ulster's Panama': The Northern Ireland Labour Party and the civil rights issue', *Irish Political Studies*, 23(3), 2008, pp. 363–85.
83. PRONI, D/3026, CDU Papers, Statement from the Northern Ireland Labour Party.
84. Paul Bew and Gordon Gillespie, *A Chronology of the Troubles, 1968–1999* (Dublin: Gill & Macmillan, 1999), p. 3.
85. *Belfast News Letter*, 7 October 1968.
86. *Belfast News Letter*, 4 January 1969.
87. PRONI CAB/9B/205/8, Television Broadcast by Captain Terence O'Neill, Prime Minister of Northern Ireland, on 9 December 1968. This document is available at the wonderful CAIN repository at Ulster University: https://cain.ulster.ac.uk/proni/1968/proni_CAB-9-B-205-8_1968-12-09.pdf.
88. UUP, *Ulster at the Crossroads: The Ulster Unionist Party's Declaration of Principle and Statement of Policy for the General Election, 1969* (UUP: Belfast, 1969), p. 2.
89. Ibid., p. 3.
90. Richard English, *Armed Struggle: A History of the IRA* (London: Macmillan, 2003), p. 120.

7. A REGIME UNDER FIRE

1. Richard Rose, *Governing Without Consensus: An Irish Perspective* (London: Faber and Faber, 1971), p. 218.
2. PRONI, PM/5/81/5A, Freeland to Chichester-Clark, 8 January 1970.
3. Cited in Andrew Sanders and Ian S. Wood, *Times of Troubles: Britain's War in Northern Ireland* (Edinburgh: Edinburgh University Press, 2012), p. 32.
4. Tommy McKearney, *The Provisional IRA: From Insurrection to Parliament* (London: Pluto, 2011), pp. 68–70.
5. For an incisive analysis of minimum force see Andrew Sanders, 'Principles of minimum force and the Parachute Regiment in Northern Ireland, 1969–1972', *Journal of Strategic Studies*, 41(5), 2018, pp. 659–83.
6. David Benest, 'Aden to Northern Ireland, 1966–76' in Hew Stachan (ed.), *Big Wars and Small Wars: The British Army and the Lessons of War in the Twentieth Century* (London: Routledge, 2006), p. 128.
7. Imperial War Museum Sound Archive, Christopher Lawton Oral History, Reel 8. Accessible at: www.iwm.org.uk/collections/item/object/80026382. Lawton was a soldier in the Durham Light Infantry, serving in Cyprus and then Northern Ireland.
8. Benest, 'Aden to Northern Ireland', p. 128.
9. House of Commons Debates (Hansard), 21 January 1970, Vol. 794, Col. 139W.
10. Michael Dewar, *The British Army in Northern Ireland* (London: Arms and Armour Press, 1985), p. 49; House of Commons Debates (Hansard), 12 March 1970, Vol. 797, Col. 1585.
11. James Cowan Obituary. Archived at: https://royalleicestershireregiment.org.uk/entity/133314-cowan-james-alan-comrie-cbe (accessed 8 December 2020).
12. David Charters, *Whose Mission, Whose Orders?: British Civil-Military Command and Control in Northern Ireland, 1968–1974* (Montreal: McGill-Queen's University Press, 2017), p. 59.
13. PRONI, CAB/9/G/91/2, Prime Minister's Meeting with the Home Secretary, 4 February 1970. Archived at: https://cain.ulster.ac.uk/proni/1970/proni_CAB-9-G-91-2_1970-02-04.pdf.
14. PRONI, CAB/9/G/89/2, Notes on points to be discussed with the GOC on Wednesday, 22 April 1970 at Stormont Castle.
15. O'Doherty, *The Trouble With Guns*, pp. 62–4.
16. Thomas R. Mockaitis, *British Counterinsurgency in the Post-Imperial Era* (Manchester: Manchester University Press, 1995), p. 100.
17. House of Commons Debates, 7 April 1970, Vol. 799, Col. 269–270.
18. Ciarán de Baróid, *Ballymurphy and the Irish War*, New Edition (London: Pluto Press, 2000), p. 5.
19. Ibid.
20. Rod Thornton, 'Getting it wrong: The crucial mistakes made in the early stages of the British Army's deployment to Northern Ireland (August 1969 to March 1972)', *Journal of Strategic Studies*, 30(1), 2007, p. 83.

21 Devlin, *Straight Left*, p. 126.
22 British Army, *Operation Banner: An Analysis of Military Operations in Northern Ireland* (London: Ministry of Defence, 2006), paragraph 215.
23 Ibid.
24 Ibid.
25 Simon Winchester, *In Holy Terror: Reporting the Ulster Troubles* (London: Faber and Faber, 1974), p. 59.
26 Ibid., p. 58.
27 Ken Wharton, *A Long Long War: Voices From the British Army in Northern Ireland 1969–98* (Solihull: Helion and Company, 2009), p. 79.
28 Ibid., p. 59.
29 Devlin, *Straight Left*, p. 126.
30 Ibid., p. 127.
31 Gearóid Ó Faoleán, 'The Ulster Defence Regiment and the question of Catholic recruitment, 1970–1972', *Terrorism and Political Violence*, 27(5), 2015, p. 844.
32 Frank Kitson, *The Northern Ireland Insurgency – Talk to U.S. Army War College*, dated 29 January 1973. Copy in author's possession.
33 Ibid.
34 Walker, *A History of the Ulster Unionist Party*, p. 189.
35 Northern Ireland House of Commons Debates (Hansard), 27 January 1971, Vol. 78, Col. 1070.
36 Ibid., Col. 1073.
37 Ibid., Col. 1096.
38 Walker, *A History of the Ulster Unionist Party*, p. 190.
39 Gerry Fitt, '50 years of sectarianism', *Fortnight*, 21, 9 July 1971, p. 6.
40 Ibid.
41 Ibid.
42 Ibid.
43 Author interview with David Bleakley, 21 March 2006.
44 Ibid.
45 Ibid.
46 *Belfast News Letter*, 26 March 1971.
47 *Strabane Chronicle*, 17 April 1971.
48 Ibid.
49 *Belfast Telegraph*, 20 March 1958.
50 Aaron Edwards, 'Labour politics and sectarianism: Interpreting the political fortunes of the Northern Ireland Labour Party, 1945–75' (QUB: PhD Thesis, 2006), pp. 176–7.
51 *The Irish Press*, 1 May 1971.
52 *Belfast News Letter*, 3 May 1971.
53 Edwards, *A History of the Northern Ireland Labour Party*, pp. 180–2.
54 Martin J. McCleery, 'Debunking the myths of Operation Demetrius: The introduction

of internment in Northern Ireland in 1971', *Irish Political Studies*, 27(3), 2012, p. 428. See also McCleery's groundbreaking *Operation Demetrius and Its Aftermath: A New History of the Use of Internment Without Trial in Northern Ireland 1971–75* (Manchester: Manchester University Press, 2015).

55 Paul Dixon and Eamonn O'Kane, *Northern Ireland Since 1969* (Harlow: Pearson, 2011), p. 29.
56 Kay Kennedy, 'When the Shankill gave way to fear', *Belfast Telegraph*, 18 August 1971.
57 Ibid.
58 Ibid.
59 *Evening Herald*, 20 August 1971.
60 The first recorded meeting of the Ulster Vanguard and its linked Loyalist Association of Workers was held in Belfast on 24 January 1972. *Belfast News Letter*, 25 January 1972.
61 John Darby and Geoffrey Morris, *Intimidation in Housing: Northern Ireland Community Relations Commission Research Paper* (Belfast: Northern Ireland Community Relations Commission, February 1974), p. 35.
62 Ibid., p. 36.
63 Ibid., p. 28.
64 Ibid. p. 29.
65 Ibid., p. 30.
66 House of Commons Debates (Hansard), 24 March 1972, Vol. 833, Col. 1859. The measures were designed to be temporary but, in the absence of political progress, would remain.

8. A VERY LOYALIST COUP

1   Michel Foucault, *Society Must Be Defended: Lectures at the Collège de France, 1975–1976* (London: Penguin Books, [1997], 2020), p. 96.
2   Chris Ryder, 'Paddy Devlin', *The Guardian*, 16 August 1999.
3   Paddy Devlin speaking at Stormont, Northern Ireland House of Commons Debates, Vol. 76, Col. 2165, 2 July 1970.
4   Northern Ireland House of Commons Debates, Vol. 72, Col. 1619, 17 June 1969.
5   Northern Ireland House of Commons Debates, Vol. 76, Col. 2166, 2 July 1970.
6   NILP, *Ulster British or British Ulster?* (1969).
7   Northern Ireland House of Commons Debates, Vol. 76, Col. 2166, 2 July 1970.
8   Moloney, *The Secret History of the IRA*, p. 91.
9   Ibid., p. 95.
10 Ibid., p. 97.
11 Faulkner, *Memoirs of a Statesmen*, p. 138.
12 Desmond Hamill, *Pig in the Middle: The Army in Northern Ireland, 1969–1984* (London: Methuen, 1985), p. 77.

13   Thomas Hennessey, *A History of Northern Ireland, 1920–1996* (Basingstoke: Macmillan, 1997), p. 201.
14   Ibid., p. 202.
15   CAIN, *Security and Defence* (2019). Accessible at: https://cain.ulster.ac.uk/ni/security.htm.
16   Simon Winchester, '13 killed as paratroopers break riot', *The Guardian*, 31 January 1972.
17   Faulkner, *Memoirs of a Statesman*, p. 141.
18   Author interview with a former parliamentary researcher for James Molyneaux, August 2022.
19   Ibid.
20   Faulkner, *Memoirs of a Statesman*, p. 149.
21   House of Commons Debates (Hansard), 24 March 1972, Vol. 833, Col. 1860.
22   Hennessey, *A History of Northern Ireland*, p. 208.
23   House of Commons Debates (Hansard), 24 March 1972, Vol. 833, Col. 1871–2.
24   Patterson, *Ireland Since 1939*, p. 226.
25   *The Guardian*, 25 September 1972.
26   Gordon Gillespie, 'The Ulster Workers' Council strike: The perfect storm' in David McCann and Cillian McGrattan (eds), *Sunningdale, the Ulster Workers' Council Strike and the Struggle for Democracy in Northern Ireland* (Manchester: Manchester University Press, 2017), p. 22.
27   The National Archives (TNA), CJ 4/146, Note of a meeting between the PUS [Permanent Under Secretary of State for Northern Ireland], Mr Roy Bradford, and representatives of the UDA held at 7.30 p.m. on 17 October 1972.
28   Ibid.
29   TNA, CJ 4/266, Draft paper by General Officer Commanding Northern Ireland [GOC NI], 'Military operations in the event of a renewed IRA campaign of violence', 9 July 1972. Cited in Huw Bennett, 'From direct rule to Motorman: Adjusting British military strategy for Northern Ireland in 1972', *Studies in Conflict & Terrorism*, 33(6), 2010, p. 516. Further research is required to determine the extent of the contacts between the British Army and UDA, which must be viewed in light of British attempts to manage the security situation, a strategic decision-making process that included covert contacts and talks with IRA leaders in 1971–2.
30   Renagh Holohan, 'UDA men agree to Army barricades', *The Irish Times*, 4 July 1972.
31   'Devlin warning on law and loyalists', *The Irish Times*, 13 June 1972.
32   CAIN, *An Index of Deaths From the Conflict in Ireland – Statistical Summary* (revised in 2002). Accessible at: https://cain.ulster.ac.uk/sutton/book/index.html#append.
33   Peter Taylor, *Loyalists* (London: Bloomsbury, 1999), p. 116.
34   Sarah Nelson, *Ulster's Uncertain Defenders: Protestant Political, Paramilitary and Community Groups and the Northern Ireland Conflict* (Belfast: Appletree Press, 1984), p. 126.

35 The Official IRA called an indefinite ceasefire in the wake of the hostility generated by their killing of Ranger Willie Best in Derry on 21 May 1972. In practical terms this meant that there was effectively only one IRA now – the Provisionals – which continued to operate at the forefront of violent nationalism. See Peter Taylor, *Provos: The IRA and Sinn Féin* (London: Bloomsbury, 1997), p. 136.
36 M.L.R. Smith, *Fighting for Ireland? The Military Strategy of the Irish Republican Movement* (London: Routledge, 1995), p. 119.
37 Henry Patterson, '"1974 – Year of Liberty"? The Provisional IRA and Sunningdale' in McCann and McGrattan (eds), *Sunningdale, the Ulster Workers' Council Strike and the Struggle for Democracy in Northern Ireland*, p. 148.
38 Smith, *Fighting for Ireland?*, p. 119.
39 English, *Armed Struggle*, p. 160.
40 CAIN, *Text of the Sunningdale Agreement, 1973* (2019). Accessible at: https://cain.ulster.ac.uk/events/sunningdale/agreement.htm.
41 House of Commons Debates (Hansard), 13 December 1973, Vol. 866, Col. 675.
42 Paddy Devlin, *The Fall of the N.I. Executive* (Belfast: self-published, 1975), p. 88.
43 *The Irish News*, 15 May 1974.
44 TNA, Director of Operations Brief, 14/15 May 1974.
45 *The Irish News*, 15 May 1974.
46 *Belfast News Letter*, 16 May 1974.
47 Robert Fisk, 'Loyalists' general strike coupled with threat of barricades could bring Ulster to a standstill', *The Times*, 16 May 1974.
48 *The Irish News*, 15 May 1974.
49 Ibid.
50 *The Irish News*, 16 & 17 May 1974.
51 Ibid.
52 'The bomb run', *Belfast Telegraph*, 2 May 1974.
53 *The Irish News*, 18 May 1974.
54 Ibid.
55 Ibid.
56 Ibid.
57 'The loyalist offensive', *The Times*, 20 May 1974.
58 Robert Fisk, 'Mr Rees recognizes new Ulster nationalism as a major force', *The Times*, 1 June 1974.
59 House of Commons Debates (Hansard), 3 June 1974, Vol. 874, Col. 880.
60 Ibid., Col. 880–1.
61 Devlin, *The Fall of the N.I. Executive*, p. 88.
62 Devlin, *Straight Left*, p. 237.
63 My thanks to Dr Connal Parr for reminding of the origins of this critique, which can be found in the chapter on Joe Law in Marilyn Hyndman (ed.), *Further Afield: Journeys from a Protestant Past* (Belfast: Beyond the Pale Publications, 1996); Connal Parr and

ENDNOTES

Aaron Edwards, 'Breaking from the herd: The 'Rotten Prod' tradition in Ulster Labour history', *Social Justice Review – Essays in Honour of Joe Law* (Belfast: Trademark, 2017), pp. 7–10.
64 Clifford Smyth, *Rome – Our Enemy* (Belfast: Puritan Printing, 1974), Preface.
65 Ibid., p. 64.
66 Ibid., p. 63.
67 Smyth, *Ian Paisley*, p. 93.
68 Ibid.
69 Ibid.
70 Eamon Sweeney, 'Tributes paid to leader of '74 loyalist strike', *Belfast Telegraph*, 25 October 2017.
71 Tony Craig, 'From backdoors and back lanes to backchannels: Reappraising British talks with the Provisional IRA, 1970–1974', *Contemporary British History*, 26(1), 2012, pp. 97–117; Tony Craig, 'Laneside, then left a bit? Britain's secret political talks with loyalist paramilitaries in Northern Ireland, 1973–1976', *Irish Political Studies*, 29(2), 2014, pp. 298–317.
72 Craig, 'Laneside, then left a bit?', p. 302.
73 TNA, CJ 4/3963, Note of a Meeting at Laneside with Mr Andy Tyrie, 28 October 1976.
74 Ibid.
75 David McKittrick, 'UDA backs call to end direct rule', *The Irish Times*, 1 December 1976.
76 Ibid.
77 Craig, 'Laneside, then left a bit?', p. 312.
78 TNA, CJ 4/3208, John McMichael to Jim Prior, 29 October 1981.
79 Ibid.
80 Arthur Aughey, 'Between exclusion and recognition: The politics of the Ulster Defence Association', *Conflict Quarterly*, 5(1), 1985, p. 44.
81 Richard Reed, *Paramilitary Loyalism: Identity and Change* (Manchester: Manchester University Press, 2015), p. 58.
82 TNA, CJ 4/4225, Blatherwick to Wyatt, 'Meeting with Ulster Loyalist Democratic Party', 19 November 1981.
83 Ibid.
84 Ibid.

9. PRISONERS OF THE IRA'S STRATEGY

1 Dáil Éireann Debates, 17 November 1981, Vol. 330, No. 12.
2 House of Commons Debates (Hansard), 2 July 1981, Vol. 7, Col. 1057.
3 Richard O'Rawe, *Blanketmen: An Untold Story of the H-Block Hunger Strike* (Dublin: New Island, 2005).
4 Author interview with Tommy Gorman, 23 June 2010.
5 *Belfast News Letter*, 15 November 1981.

6 Ibid.
7 Interview with Witness A for the ULET Legacy Archive, 25 October 2017. Cited with permission.
8 House of Commons Debates, 16 November 1981, Vol. 13, Col. 19.
9 Ibid., Col. 19.
10 Ibid., Col. 21.
11 'Riddle of gun attack on Paisley', *Belfast Telegraph*, 4 July 1981.
12 Ibid.
13 *Belfast Telegraph*, 29 January 1982.
14 TNA, CJ 4/3334, Note of Secretary of State's Meeting with Representatives of the Ulster Unionist Party on 17 September 1981, dated 18 September 1981.
15 Ibid.
16 TNA, CJ 4/3334, Note by S.J. Leach for the Record: Frank Millar, 1 October 1981.
17 Author interview with a former member of the UUP, 1 December 2021.
18 TNA, CJ 4/3334, Note by Mike Bohill, Billy Bleakes UUP, 7 October 1981.
19 Ibid.
20 TNA, CJ 4/3334, Shifts in Unionist Opinion, note by D.E.S. Blatherwick, 16 October 1981.
21 TNA, CJ 4/3334, Mr Scott's Meeting with a Unionist Deputation – 14 November 1981.
22 Ibid.
23 Ibid.
24 Padraig O'Malley, *The Uncivil Wars: Ireland Today* (Belfast: Blackstaff Press, 1983), pp. 140–1.
25 TNA, CJ 4/3334, Speech by James H. Molyneaux to the AGM of the UUC, Holywood, County Down, 11 June 1982.
26 Ibid.
27 Author interview with a former UUP parliamentary researcher, 1 August 2022.
28 D.E.S. Blatherwick to Wyatt, 'David Trimble', 9 April 1981.
29 D.E.S. Blatherwick, 'Note for the record: Conversation with David Trimble', 10 November 1981.
30 Dean Godson, *Himself Alone: David Trimble and the Ordeal of Unionism* (London: HarperCollins, 2004), p. 72–4.
31 TNA, PREM19/815 f6, Northern Ireland: Whitmore note for Boys-Smith (Sloan-Abbott conversations) [UUC claims against official; reference also to David Trimble], dated 30 June 1982.
32 Ibid. See also Godson, *Himself Alone*, pp. 72–3.
33 Ibid
34 TNA, PREM19/816 f177, S.W. Boys-Smith letter to Clive Whitmore, 1 July 1982.
35 TNA, PREM19/816 f150, Michael Hopkins to Clive Whitmore, 12 July 1982. Payne was allegedly a senior MI5 officer who had previously served as Director and Controller of Intelligence in Northern Ireland in the mid-1970s.

36   Private information, August 2022.
37   *Belfast Telegraph*, 30 September 1982.
38   Charles Townshend, 'Northern Irish Initiatives', *London Review of Books*, 4(14), 5 August 1982.
39   TNA, CJ 4/3334, Note by S.J. Leach on a meeting with Ken Maginnis, 16 July 1982.
40   Newton Emerson, 'Licensing next war is Adams's real legacy', *The Irish Times*, 23 November 2017.
41   Ibid.
42   *Belfast Telegraph*, 15 November 1983.
43   Ibid.
44   David Watson and Robin Morton, 'Assembly gives its backing to segregation of prisoners', *Belfast Telegraph*, 17 November 1983.
45   Ibid.
46   Robin Morton, 'Separation call unlikely to change Govt. policy', *Belfast Telegraph*, 18 November 1983.
47   Robin Morton and Ken Devlin, 'Unionists push for devolution', *Belfast Telegraph*, 21 November 1983.
48   Dáil Éireann Debates, 19 November 1985, Vol. 361, Col. 11.
49   Ibid.
50   Ibid. My emphasis. I met former Taoiseach Fitzgerald at a conference in UCD in 2005 and found him an unassuming, down-to-earth individual who was generous with his time and, above all, a great political thinker with an intellect unmatched by many other politicians I have met over the years.
51   Garret FitzGerald, *Towards a New Ireland* (London: Charles Knight and Co. Limited, 1972), p. 91.
52   House of Commons Debates (Hansard), 18 November 1985, Vol. 87, Col. 22.
53   Ibid., Col. 23.
54   *Belfast Telegraph*, 9 November 1985.
55   House of Commons Debates (Hansard), 18 November 1985, Vol. 87, Col. 23.
56   *Belfast Telegraph*, 18 November 1985.

10. THE DUISBURG FORMULA

1   William Magan, *Umma-More: The Story of an Irish Family* (Dorset: Element Books, 1983), p. 427.
2   *Belfast Telegraph*, 25 November 1985.
3   Ibid.
4   Ibid.
5   Smyth, *Ian Paisley*, p. 126.
6   Steve Bruce, *Paisley: Religion and Politics in Northern Ireland* (Oxford: Oxford University Press, 2007), p. 210.

7   Ibid., p. 211.
8   Ibid.
9   Jackson, *The Two Unions*, p. 331.
10 Author interview with Matthew, 24 December 2021.
11 Cited in Edwards, *UVF*, p. 184.
12 Police Ombudsman for Northern Ireland (PONI), *Statutory Report on the Murders at the Heights Bar, Loughinisland, 18 June 1994 – Revised* (Belfast: PONI, August 2020), p. 30.
13 Ibid., p. 36, Desmond de Silva, *The Report of the Pat Finucane Review. The Rt Hon Sir Desmond de Silva QC – Volume I* (London: The Stationery Office, 12 December 2012), p. 106.
14 PONI, *Statutory Report on the Murders at the Heights Bar, Loughinisland*, pp. 34–5.
15 Ibid., p. 35.
16 'Johnny Adair: Ulster Resistance weapons were "godsend" to loyalists', *Belfast Telegraph*, 6 October 2019.
17 House of Commons Debates (Hansard), 18 November 1985, Vol. 87, Col. 28.
18 Ibid., Col. 22.
19 *The Guardian*, 16 November 1986.
20 Brendan O'Leary, 'The Anglo-Irish Agreement: Folly or statecraft?', *West European Politics*, 10(1), 1987, p. 10.
21 Colm Tóibín, *Bad Blood: A Walk Along the Irish Border* (London: Picador, 1987), p. 28
22 Freya McClements, 'Veterans return to Ballygawley to mark 30th anniversary of bus bombing', *The Irish Times*, 19 August 1988.
23 Noel McAdam, 'Carnage on a country road', *Belfast Telegraph*, 20 August 1988.
24 Bimpe Archer, 'Ballygawley bus bombing – 30 years after "walking into hell", survivors still bear scars', *The Irish News*, 18 August 2018.
25 Noel McAdam, 'Carnage on a country road', *Belfast Telegraph*, 20 August 1988.
26 Ibid.
27 'Northern Ireland after the Tyrone bombing: Former officer with the experience for tackling terrorism', *Financial Times*, 22 August 1988.
28 House of Lords Conduct Committee, *The Conduct of Lord Maginnis of Drumglass* (London: House of Lords, 2 December 2020), p. 101. Archived at: https://publications.parliament.uk/pa/ld5801/ldselect/ldcond/185/185.pdf.
29 Richard Ford, Michael Evans, Ronald Faux and David Sapsted, 'Tough moves to counter IRA violence – Crackdown agreed as eight held over bomb', *The Times*, 25 August 1988.
30 Ibid.
31 Paul Vallely and Richard Ford, 'IRA suspects shot dead in SAS ambush', *The Times*, 31 August 1988.
32 House of Lords Conduct Committee, *The Conduct of Lord Maginnis of Drumglass*, p. 101.
33 Martin J. McCleery, 'Sectarianism and the Provisional Irish Republican Army', *Small Wars & Insurgencies*, 32(4–5), 2021, p. 682.

34 Ibid., p. 681.
35 Chris Ryder, 'No peace for Ulster at the inn', *Daily Telegraph*, 4 February 1989.
36 TNA, CJ 4/8071, Quentin Thomas, 'Political developments and the Anglo-Irish Agreement: The Duisburg Riddle', dated 4 April 1989.
37 TNA, CJ 4/8071, I.M. Burns to Private Secretary to the Secretary of State, 31 October 1988.
38 TNA, CJ 4/8071, Dr Eberhard Spiecker to Tom King, 30 January 1989. The letter was delivered by the Moderator of the Presbyterian Church a week after it was sent.
39 Ibid.
40 Chris Ryder and George Jones, 'Secret talks leak damages hopes of Ulster deal', *Daily Telegraph*, 3 February 1989.
41 Ibid.
42 Ryder, 'No peace for Ulster at the inn'.
43 Chris Ryder, 'Unionist leads knew of secret talks over Ulster', *Daily Telegraph*, 4 February 1989.
44 TNA, CJ 4/8071, Private Secretary to Tom King reply to Dr Eberhard Spiecker (n.d.).
45 Ibid.
46 Judt, *Postwar*, p. 627.
47 David Watson and Oliver McGuckin, 'Hands stretched in protest', *Belfast Telegraph*, 15 November 1989.
48 Ibid.

11. AN IMAGE PROBLEM

1 Frank Wright, 'Northern Ireland and the British–Irish Relationship', *Studies: An Irish Quarterly Review*, 78(310), Summer 1989, p. 154.
2 *Belfast Telegraph*, 4 April 1990.
3 *Belfast Telegraph*, 15 March 1990; *The Irish Press*, 5 April 1990.
4 Edwards, *UVF*, p. 199.
5 Mary Kelly, 'Rathcoole victim was jailed for bid to kill UDR man', *Belfast Telegraph*, 5 April 1990.
6 Ibid.
7 Ibid.
8 PRONI, ENV/21/3/15, Liaison with Rathcoole Community Group, Rathcoole Self Help Group (RSHG), *Rathcoole: What Is To Be Done* (1991), p. 33. Meeting held on 12 March 1991.
9 *The Belfast Gazette*, 30 November 1973, p. 907.
10 PRONI, ENV/21/3/15, J.A. Steele to Theo Gallagher, 31 January 1991.
11 Ibid.; see also PRONI, ENV/21/3/15, RSHG, *Rathcoole: What Is To Be Done*, p. 2. There was a disparity between NIHE statistics and those produced by RSHG – the latter underestimated the number of people in receipt of state benefits, in many ways

reinforcing the sober analysis they had provided for the NIHE and other statutory bodies. Interestingly, the British government was keen to boast of its successes in tackling unemployment. In a question on employment trends, Richard Needham told Roy Beggs that the total number of people employed in the six counties stood at 605,400, an increase of 7,000 since its previous peak in 1979. Employment had increased year on year since 1983, growing by almost 51,000 or 9.2 per cent, with the private sector and self-employment accounting for most of the increases. House of Commons Debates (Hansard), 2 May 1991, Vol. 190, Col. 328W.
12 Ibid.
13 PRONI, ENV/21/3/15, J.A. Steele to Theo Gallagher, 31 January 1991.
14 Richard Needham, *Battling for Peace: Northern Ireland's Longest-Serving British Minister* (Belfast: Blackstaff, 1998), p. 295.
15 Ibid., pp. 296–7.
16 House of Commons Debates (Hansard), 11 July 1991, Vol. 194, Col. 1074.
17 PRONI, ENV/21/3/15, Liaison with Rathcoole Community Group, RSHG, *Rathcoole: What Needs To Be Done!* (Rathcoole: Self Help Group, December 1990).
18 Ibid., p. 32.
19 Private information, 1990s.
20 Gary Grattan, 'Man charged with murder of Bawnmore youth worker', *Belfast Telegraph*, 24 September 1991.
21 'Bomb smuggled in condoms', *Belfast Telegraph*, 15 September 1993.
22 Development proposal placed in *Belfast Telegraph* classified ads on 1 April 1993.
23 David Watson, 'Video plan to foil the wreckers', *Belfast Telegraph*, 10 January 1994. Adjusted for inflation, that figure would be half a million pounds.
24 Ibid.
25 RSHG, *Rathcoole: What Needs To Be Done!*, p. 33.
26 Langhammer would top the poll in 1997 and come second in 2001, a sign of his personal standing within the Rathcoole community. He was recognised and respected as a local representative who got things done for his constituents.
27 For more on the Opsahl Commission see Marianne Elliott, 'The role of civil society in conflict resolution: The Opsahl Commission in Northern Ireland, 1992–93', *New Hibernia Review*, 17(2), 2013, pp. 86–102.
28 *Belfast Telegraph*, 19 June 1993.
29 'Support for Labour', *Belfast Telegraph*, 16 July 1993.
30 I recounted this episode in an article for the *Belfast Telegraph*. See Aaron Edwards, 'For as long as we fail to challenge the perverse logic behind republican and loyalist thuggery, we risk a return to widespread violence', *Belfast Telegraph*, 31 December 2018.
31 Rachel Monaghan, '"An imperfect peace": Paramilitary "punishments" in Northern Ireland', *Terrorism and Political Violence*, 16(3), 2004, p. 456.
32 Ibid., p. 449.

33 Steve Bruce, 'The problems of "pro-state" terrorism: Loyalist paramilitaries in Northern Ireland', *Terrorism and Political Violence*, 4(1), 1992, p. 74.
34 Ibid.
35 Rob Wiener, *The Rape and Plunder of the Shankill: Community Action – The Belfast Experience: Second Edition* (Belfast: Farset Co-operative Press, 1980), p. 74.

12. LIFTING THE SIEGE

1 Editorial, 'Making peace: Loyalist declaration', *Belfast Telegraph*, 13 October 1994.
2 Jo Corcoran, 'Gusty is heading south again', *Irish Evening Press*, 2 December 1989.
3 Ibid.
4 Ibid.
5 In his biography of Spence (p. 269), Roy Garland dates this as October 1992, though newspaper reports confirm it was earlier in December 1989.
6 Ibid.
7 Garland, *Gusty Spence*, p. 172; Tony Novosel, *Northern Ireland's Missed Opportunity: The Frustrated Promise of Political Loyalism* (London: Pluto Press, 2013), p. 87.
8 Novosel, *Northern Ireland's Missed Opportunity*, p. 87.
9 Garland, *Gusty Spence*, pp. 203–5.
10 Author interview with Billy Mitchell, 4 May 2001.
11 Edwards, *UVF*, p. 148.
12 Aaron Edwards, 'Democratic socialism and sectarianism: The Northern Ireland Labour Party and Progressive Unionist Party compared', *Politics*, 27(1), 2007, pp. 24–31; Aaron Edwards, 'The Progressive Unionist Party of Northern Ireland: A left-wing voice in an ethnically divided society', *British Journal of Politics and International Relations*, 12(4), 2010, pp. 590–614.
13 Edwards, *UVF*, p. 147.
14 Garland, *Gusty Spence*, pp. 225–6.
15 Ibid., p. 227.
16 Ibid., p. 248.
17 TNA, CJ 4/5853, Michael McAtamney to S.C. Jackson, 18 March 1981.
18 TNA, CJ 4/5853, Assistant Governor Bradley interview with Gusty Spence, 26 February 1982.
19 TNA, CJ 4/5853, Secret Assessment of Gusty Spence, 16 March 1982.
20 Ibid.
21 Ibid.
22 TNA, CJ4/5853, Philip Woodfield to Lord Lowry, Lord Chief Justice, 14 February 1983.
23 TNA, CJ4/5853, Robert J. Andrew, Permanent Under Secretary at the NIO to Secretary of State for Northern Ireland, Gusty Spence – Release, dated 5 December 1984.
24 Garland, *Gusty Spence*, p. 256.
25 Henry Sinnerton, *David Ervine: Unchartered Waters* (London: Brandon, 2003), p. 126;

Graham Spencer, *The State of Loyalism in Northern Ireland* (Basingstoke: Palgrave, 2008), p. 77.
26 Garland, *Gusty Spence*, p. 278
27 Edwards, *UVF*, p. 204.
28 Progressive Unionist Group (later rebranded the Progressive Unionist Party), *Proposed Democratic Devolved Administration for Northern Ireland* (Belfast: PUP, 1979). Copy in author's possession.
29 PUP, *Sharing Responsibility* (Belfast: PUP, 1985). Copy in author's possession.
30 Garland, *Gusty Spence*, p. 286.
31 Author interview with Chris Hudson, 6 February 2007.
32 *Joint Declaration on Peace: The Downing Street Declaration*, Wednesday 15 December 1993. Accessible at: https://cain.ulster.ac.uk/events/peace/docs/dsd151293.htm.
33 Joint Declaration on peace in Northern Ireland: Motion, Dáil Éireann Debates, Vol. 437, No. 5, 17 December 1993.
34 Ibid.
35 Two members of the UUP, Michael and Chris McGimpsey, took a case to the Supreme Court in Dublin that the Anglo-Irish Agreement was incompatible with Articles 2 and 3 of the Irish Constitution. The court ruled that the Agreement did not weaken the constitutional imperative to reunite the island. The outcome merely heightened unionist fears about Irish irredentism. For more on the case see Feargal Cochrane, *Unionist Politics and the Politics of Unionism Since the Anglo-Irish Agreement* (Cork: Cork University Press, 2001), p. 24.
36 Author interview with Chris Hudson, 6 February 2007.
37 Ibid.
38 Rory Godson, 'UVF: We want to stop', *Sunday Tribune*, 11 September 1994.
39 Ibid.
40 Combined Loyalist Military Command Ceasefire Statement, 13 October 1994. Accessible at: https://cain.ulster.ac.uk/events/peace/docs/clmc131094.htm.
41 Lindy McDowell, 'Shankill poised to meet the challenge of peace', *Belfast Telegraph*, 14 October 1994.
42 Billy Hutchinson, *My Life in Loyalism* (Dublin: Merrion Press, 2020), pp. 196–7.
43 Ibid., p. 198.
44 Ibid., p. 199.
45 Northern Ireland Information Service, Opening Statement by HM Government, Exploratory Dialogue with Progressive Unionist Party (PUP) and Ulster Democratic Party (UDP), 15 December 1994. Copy in author's possession.
46 Ibid.
47 Joseph P. O'Grady, 'Forcing the question of Northern Ireland: The Brooke-Mayhew talks, 1990–1992', *New Hibernia Review*, 5(4), 2001, pp. 73–92.
48 John Major, *John Major: The Autobiography* (London: HarperCollins, 2000), p. 435.
49 Ibid.

ENDNOTES

50 Vincent Kearney, 'Molyneaux warns on joint authority', *Belfast Telegraph*, 25 June 1994.
51 NIO, Opening Statement by HM Government, Exploratory Dialogue with PUP and UDP, 15 December 1994. Copy in author's possession.
52 Ibid.
53 Ibid.
54 Needham, *Battling for Peace*, p. 190; see also Kevin Bean, *The New Politics of Sinn Féin* (Liverpool: Liverpool University Press, 2007), p. 28.
55 Ibid., p. 320.
56 Miller, *Queen's Rebels*, p. 150.
57 Ibid.
58 Hutchinson, *My Life in Loyalism*, p. 199.
59 HMG, *Northern Ireland Constitution Act 1973 Chapter 36* (London: HMSO, 1973).
60 HMG, *The Ireland Act 1949 Chapter 41* (London: HMSO, 1949).
61 HMG, *Joint Declaration on Peace: The Downing Street Declaration, Wednesday 15 December 1993*. Accessible at: https://cain.ulster.ac.uk/events/peace/docs/dsd151293.htm.
62 NIO, Opening Statement by HM Government, Exploratory Dialogue with PUP and UDP, 15 December 1994.
63 Ibid.
64 Ibid.
65 Ibid.
66 Eamonn O'Kane, *The Northern Ireland Peace Process: From Armed Conflict to Brexit* (Manchester: Manchester University Press, 2021), p. 54.
67 *Belfast Telegraph*, 15 December 1994.
68 Author interview with Clifford Peeples, 18 January 2022.
69 According to a well-placed MI5 agent inside the UVF leadership, Wright threatened to break from the Shankill-based strategy in January 1996, but he was not formally expelled by the group – under threat of death – until August 1996. Billy Wright Inquiry, SS01 0004-0007, Intelligence Document dated 31/01/1996 (Other Intelligence Documents). Archived at: https://webarchive.nationalarchives.gov.uk/ukgwa/20101210143042/http://www.billywrightinquiry.org/evidence/52/ (accessed 17 January 2022).
70 Desmond McCartan, 'Framework plan revealed', *Belfast Telegraph*, 22 February 1995.
71 HMG, *The Framework Documents, 22 February 1995: A New Framework for Agreement*. Accessible at: https://cain.ulster.ac.uk/events/peace/docs/fd22295.htm.
72 Ibid.
73 Ibid.
74 Ibid.
75 For more on the deterioration of the relationship between Molyneaux and Paisley, see Cochrane, *Unionist Politics and the Politics of Unionism since the Anglo-Irish Agreement*, pp. 318–23.

76 Desmond McCartan, Vincent Kearney, Mark Simpson and Michael Devine, 'Unionists sick: It could not be worse claims Trimble', *Belfast Telegraph*, 22 February 1995.
77 Ibid.
78 Vincent Kearney, 'Dublin "breaking peace promises"', *Belfast Telegraph*, 15 August 1995.
79 Ibid.
80 Ibid.
81 Billy Wright Inquiry, SS01 0004-0007, Intelligence Document dated 31/01/1996 (Other Intelligence Documents). Archived at: https://webarchive.nationalarchives.gov.uk/ukgwa/20101210143042/http://www.billywrightinquiry.org/evidence/52/ (accessed 17 January 2022).
82 Walker, *A History of the Ulster Unionist Party*, p. 248.
83 Cochrane, *Unionist Politics*, p. 336.
84 Author interview with a former UUP parliamentary researcher, 1 August 2022.
85 Ibid.

13. ULSTER'S ANSWER TO LEADERLESS RESISTANCE

1 David Trimble, Nobel Lecture, 10 December 1998. Archived at: www.nobelprize.org/prizes/peace/1998/trimble/lecture/ (accessed 24 January 2022).
2 Darwin Templeton, 'Events that led to stand-off at Orange march', *Belfast Telegraph*, 10 July 1995.
3 Correspondence with Kenny McClinton, 3 July 2017.
4 Ibid.
5 Darwin Templeton, David Walmsley and Nigel Gould, 'March deadlock over', *Belfast Telegraph*, 11 July 1995.
6 Correspondence with Kenny McClinton, 3 July 2017.
7 For more on the confrontations at Drumcree see Edwards, *UVF*, pp. 239–54.
8 Private information, October 2021.
9 O'Kane, *The Northern Ireland Peace Process*, pp. 54–5.
10 For more on Louis Beam's 'iconic status' see: www.splcenter.org/fighting-hate/extremist-files/individual/louis-beam (accessed 26 March 2022).
11 Louis Beam, 'Leaderless resistance', *Inter-Klan Newsletter & Survival Alert* (Hayden Lake, Idaho, 1983). Archived at: https://simson.net/ref/leaderless/1983.inter-klan_newsletter.pdf (accessed 7 March 2022).
12 Ibid.
13 Reed, *Paramilitary Loyalism*, pp. 197–8.
14 Ibid. Dr Reed's comparison of the Covenant-based loyalism of Billy Mitchell and the American Patriot and Militia movements is apposite, though neither Mitchell nor Reed connected these concepts to the work of Francis Hutcheson, who had significant influence on intellectual ideas prevalent in the revolutionary 'golden age' of the American Founding Fathers.

15 Paul Connolly, 'A staunch defender of Ulster's heritage', *Belfast Telegraph*, 18 July 1996.
16 Ibid.
17 Ibid.
18 Norman Porter, *Rethinking Unionism: An Alternative Vision for Northern Ireland* (Belfast: Blackstaff, 1996), p. 8.
19 'No reason to kill me, says Wright', *Belfast Telegraph*, 30 August 1996.
20 *Belfast Telegraph*, 12 September 1996.
21 Author interview with Clifford Peeples, 26 January 2022.
22 Ibid.
23 The so-called 'Triple Lock' meant that that the parties to the talks process must agree, then the two supervising governments must agree, followed by the people via a referendum.
24 Author interview with Clifford Peeples, 26 January 2022.
25 Henry Patterson and Eric Kaufmann, *Unionism and Orangeism in Ireland Since 1945: The Decline of the Loyal Family* (Manchester: Manchester University Press, 2007), p. 223.
26 Author interview with Stephen Cooper, 3 August 2022.
27 ARK, Northern Ireland Assembly Elections. Accessible at: www.ark.ac.uk/elections/fa98.htm.
28 Billy Mitchell, 'Democratic socialism and Progressive Unionism', *New Irelander*, 9 (1998), p. 2.
29 Ibid.
30 Edwards, 'Democratic socialism and sectarianism', pp. 24–31; Edwards, 'The Progressive Unionist Party of Northern Ireland', pp. 590–614.
31 Ibid.
32 Mitchell, 'Democratic socialism and Progressive Unionism'.
33 David Trimble, Nobel Lecture, 10 December 1998. Archived at: www.nobelprize.org/prizes/peace/1998/trimble/lecture/ (accessed 24 January 2022).
34 Christopher Farrington, *Ulster Unionism and the Peace Process in Northern Ireland* (Basingstoke: Palgrave Macmillan, 2006), p. 127.
35 Northern Ireland Assembly Debates (Hansard), 15 December 1998.
36 Ibid.
37 Ibid.
38 Author interview with Lee Reynolds, 25 January 2022.
39 Farrington, *Ulster Unionism and the Peace Process*, p. 123.
40 Esmond Birnie, 'The future of unionism', *Studies: An Irish Quarterly Review*, 89(355), 2000, p. 271.
41 O'Kane, *The Northern Ireland Peace Process*, p. 106.

14. THE CHANGING OF THE GUARD

1. Northern Ireland Assembly Debates (Hansard), 13 September 2001.
2. Ashleigh Wallace, 'Lady Hermon leads the way for the women', *Belfast Telegraph*, 9 June 2001.
3. Ward, *Women, Unionism and Loyalism in Northern Ireland*, p. 159.
4. Author interview with Lee Reynolds, 25 January 2022.
5. Smyth Harper, 'Dishing the dirt in the battle of Upper Bann', *Belfast Telegraph*, 9 June 2001.
6. Kathryn Torney, 'Paisley romps to record win', *Belfast Telegraph*, 9 June 2001.
7. DUP, 'Leadership to put things right! Parliamentary and district council election manifesto 2001'. Archived at: https://cain.ulster.ac.uk/issues/politics/docs/dup/dup01.pdf (accessed 21 October 2021).
8. Ibid.
9. Ibid.
10. Colin Irwin, 'Devolution and the state of the Northern Ireland Peace Process', *The Global Review of Ethnopolitics*, 2(3–4), 2003, p. 72.
11. James W. McAuley, 'Whither new Loyalism? Changing loyalist politics after the Belfast Agreement', *Irish Political Studies*, 20(3), 2005, p. 334.
12. O'Kane, *The Northern Ireland Peace Process*, p. 139.
13. Edwards, 'Democratic socialism and sectarianism', pp. 24–31; Edwards, 'The Progressive Unionist Party of Northern Ireland', pp. 590–614.
14. David Ervine, *Redefining Loyalism – A Political Perspective*, IBIS Working Papers, 4 (Dublin: UCD, 2001), p. 5.
15. Author interview with Billy Mitchell, 4 May 2001.
16. Ibid.
17. Ibid.
18. O'Kane, *The Northern Ireland Peace Process*, p. 138.
19. 'A night to remember', *Belfast Telegraph*, 8 September 2005.
20. Lindy McDowell, 'Keep them at arm's length, for our sakes', *Belfast Telegraph*, 10 September 2005.
21. *Belfast Telegraph*, 12 September 2005.
22. Max Hastings, 'The last writhings of a society left beached by history', *The Guardian*, 15 September 2005.
23. Noel McAdam, 'Plans set to build up unionists' confidence', *Belfast Telegraph*, 26 September 2005.
24. 'Behind the flames', *Belfast Telegraph*, 26 September 2005.
25. Ed Curran, 'Stormont is going to be a work-in and not a love-in', *Belfast Telegraph*, 8 June 2007.
26. Ed Curran, 'The ordinary man in the street has come out and backed me', *Belfast Telegraph*, 11 June 2007.

15. A PEOPLE UNDER SIEGE (AGAIN)

1. Eric Hobsbawm, 'Identity politics and the Left', *New Left Review*, 1(217), 1996, p. 40.
2. I visited Billy Hutchinson on the Shankill in September 2012 where he prophetically pointed to the growing frustration of loyalists. We did not know how this would be channelled, but it was obvious that street protest could well be one option, which would come to pass within a few weeks.
3. Mitchell died in July 2006.
4. Billy Mitchell, 'Nationalist euphoria – unionist despondency', *The Blanket: A Journal of Protest and Dissent*, 11 August 2002. Archived at http://indiamond6.ulib.iupui.edu:81/nateuphoria.html (accessed 21 October 2021).
5. The UDP changed its name back to the Ulster Political Research Group after failing to register with the Northern Ireland Electoral Commission.
6. Author interview with Jamie Bryson, 8 July 2021.
7. Ibid.
8. I coined the phrase 'de-Britification' to describe the radicalisation of the republican base in lieu of a real strategic win after the Provisional IRA's long war. It was in homage to the process of de-Baathification which had taken place in Iraq since 2003, a process which was designed to demolish an old state-based identity without any attempt to build a new consensus based on support from different communities.
9. Alan Meban, 'Billy Hutchinson: Talking at rallies and protests doesn't necessarily make you a leader', Slugger O'Toole, 17 May 2013. Archived at: https://sluggerotoole.com/2013/05/17/billy-hutchinson-talking-at-rallies-and-protests-doesnt-necessarily-make-you-a-leader/ (accessed 24 February 2022).
10. Ibid.
11. Richard Reed and Aaron Edwards, 'Loyalist paramilitaries and the peace process', *Fortnight*, 477, 2011, p. 6.
12. Ibid.
13. Ibid.
14. Ibid. See also Northern Ireland Statistics and Research Agency, Northern Ireland Multiple Deprivation Measure 2010: Summary Measures (administrative geographies). Archived at: www.ninis2.nisra.gov.uk/public/PivotGrid.aspx?ds=6350&lh=73&yn=2010&sk=137&sn=Deprivation&yearfilter=2010 (accessed 24 February 2022).
15. Henry McDonald, 'Northern Ireland unionist parties blamed for fuelling flag protests', *The Guardian*, 2 March 2013.
16. John MacVicar, 'So where to now?', *Shankill Mirror*, 191, January 2013.
17. Claire Graham, 'DUP does U-turn by voting for designated flag days at Down District Council', *Belfast Telegraph*, 27 November 2013.
18. Paul Nolan, Dominic Bryan, Clare Dwyer, Katy Hayward, Katy Radford and Peter Shirlow, *The Flag Dispute: Anatomy of a Protest* (Belfast: Queen's University Belfast, December 2014), p. 26.
19. Author interview with a former senior PSNI officer, 30 November 2020.

20   Meban, 'Billy Hutchinson: Talking at rallies and protests doesn't necessarily make you a leader'.
21   Author interview with Julie-Anne Corr-Johnston, 31 January 2022.
22   Ibid.

16. TOPPLING THE NEW TOWER OF BABBEL

1   C.S. Lewis, *All My Road Before Me: The Diary of C.S. Lewis, 1922–1927*, edited by Walter Hooper (Orlando, FL: Harcourt Brace Jovanovich Publishers, 1991), p. 105.
2   See the Prologue for a definition of 'Imagined Community'. I explore this concept in more scholarly detail in the following: Aaron Edwards, 'Collective memory, Ethno-national forgetting, and the limits of history in Northern Ireland: Misremembering the past?' in James W. McAuley and Graham Spencer (eds), *Troubled Past: Identity and Collective Memory in Northern Ireland* (Manchester: Manchester University Press, 2023).
3   Donald Horowitz, *Ethnic Groups in Conflict* (London: University of California Press, 2000), p. 52. As Hutchinson and Smith observe, these ethnic communities – what they call *ethnies* – tend to exhibit the following characteristics: 'a named human population with myths of common ancestry, shared historical memories, one or more elements of common culture, a link with a homeland and a sense of solidarity among at least some of its members'. John Hutchinson and Anthony D. Smith (eds), *Ethnicity* (Oxford: Oxford University Press, 1996), p. 6.
4   The principal weapon for perpetuating and accentuating division comes in the form of historical narratives – stories retold that perpetuate fear and distrust and are, ultimately, designed for advantage in a conflict, according to renowned Sociologist Professor John Nagle, which is 'inextricably bound up with contests over political legitimacy and state sovereignty'. See John Nagle, 'From the politics of antagonistic recognition to agonistic peace building: An exploration of symbols and rituals in divided societies', *Peace and Change*, 39(4), October 2014, p. 475. This struggle for recognition by competing groups, Nagle argues, is 'highly resistant to peaceful transformation since both groups' desire for national self-determination cannot be realized'.
5   Nicholas Sambanis and Moses Shayo, 'Social identification and ethnic conflict', *The American Political Science Review*, 107(2), 2013, pp. 294–325.
6   Rogers Brubaker, 'Ethnicity without groups', *European Journal of Sociology*, 43(2), 2002, p. 164.
7   For more on this point see the excellent survey-based research undertaken by John Garry and Kevin McNicholl, *Understanding 'Northern Irish' Identity*, Knowledge Exchange Seminar Series (Belfast: QUB, 2015). Archived at: www.niassembly.gov.uk/globalassets/documents/raise/knowledge_exchange/briefing_papers/series4/northern_ireland_identity_garry_mcnicholl_policy_document.pdf (accessed: 27 March 2022).

8   As Professor Jennifer Todd has written, 'To call this package of beliefs, values and expectations "identity" is to point to the fact that it is at once historically embedded, deeply personalised and politically organised. There is thus a dynamic of identity change – underlying changes in experienced content, meaning and oppositionality occur as social practice changes and more sudden changes in identity categories happen as new group alliances are forged in response at once to political events and to changing everyday meanings.' Jennifer Todd, 'Unionism, identity and Irish unity: Paradigms, problems and paradoxes', *Irish Studies in International Affairs*, 32(2), 2021, p. 57. In Northern Ireland, however, the 'sibling' identities of unionism and nationalism have remained mostly fixed, with the former perceived to have 'hardened' in recent years.

9   Census 2011: Key Statistics for Northern Ireland, December 2012. Archived at: www.nisra.gov.uk/sites/nisra.gov.uk/files/publications/2011-census-results-key-statistics-statistics-bulletin-11-december-2012.pdf (accessed 10 March 2022).

10 Census 2011: Detailed Characteristics for Northern Ireland on Health, Religion and National Identity, 16 May 2013. Archived at: www.nisra.gov.uk/sites/nisra.gov.uk/files/publications/2011-census-results-detailed-characteristics-statistics-bulletin-16-may-2013.pdf (accessed 21 July 2021). Of all those surveyed in the census, 89 per cent were born in Northern Ireland. This number had fallen from 98 per cent in the 2001 Census, suggesting Northern Ireland was becoming more diverse in terms of drawing in people from outside, even if the political identities remained somewhat static.

11 Census 2011: Detailed Characteristics for Northern Ireland on Health, Religion and National Identity.

12 The 2021 Census is likely to show consistency in the dominant categories of British and Irish.

13 Matthew J. Goodwin and Oliver Heath, 'The 2016 referendum, Brexit and the left behind: An aggregate-level analysis of the result', *Political Quarterly*, 87(3), 2016, p. 331.

14 Ibid.

15 John Garry, *The EU Referendum Vote in Northern Ireland: Implications for Our Understanding of Citizens' Political Views and Behaviour* (Belfast: QUB, 2016). Archived at: www.qub.ac.uk/brexit/Brexitfilestore/Filetoupload,728121,en.pdf (accessed 10 March 2022).

16 Yvette Shapiro, 'EU Referendum: Growing support in Northern Ireland for Brexit but balance of power lies with the undecided', *Belfast Telegraph*, 20 June 2016.

17 Yvette Shapiro, 'NI Says No to Brexit', *Belfast Telegraph*, 26 May 2022.

18 Ibid.

19 Author interview with Lee Reynolds, 25 January 2022.

20 Donna Deeney, 'Brexit risks peace process and the UK itself, former rivals Blair and Major say', *Belfast Telegraph*, 10 June 2016.

21 Ibid.

22 Ibid.

23   Ben Lowry, 'Major and Blair warn of threat to NI settlement posed by Brexit vote', *Belfast News Letter*, 10 June 2016.
24   Ibid.
25   'Peace in province is safe, say Brexit supporters – Foster, Dodds and Hoey all fiercely dismiss the ex-PMs', *Belfast News Letter*, 10 June 2016.
26   House of Commons Debates (Hansard), 9 June 2016, Vol. 611, Col. 1349.
27   Kate Hoey, 'Yesterday's men: Major and Blair', *Belfast News Letter*, 10 June 2016.
28   Ibid.
29   There was also eager anticipation at the time that the inquiry into the Iraq War, chaired by former Northern Ireland Permanent Under-Secretary Sir John Chilcot, would be publishing its findings. For political reasons, the Chilcot Report was delayed and later issued some weeks after the EU referendum, on 6 July 2016.
30   Jonathan Tonge, Máire Braniff, Thomas Hennessey, James W. McAuley and Sophie A. Whiting, 'Same but different? The Democratic Unionist Party and Ulster Unionist Party Compared', *Irish Political Studies*, 35(3), 2020, p. 409.
31   Ibid., p. 411.
32   Ibid., pp. 413, 419. Tonge *et al.* argue that the Free Presbyterian sect is pre-eminent amongst its membership, but 'whilst still notable, is rapidly being reduced'.
33   Ian R.K. Paisley in a debate on Freedom and Security for Union Citizens, 4 May 2004. Archived at: Debates – Tuesday, 4 May 2004 – Freedom and security for Union citizens (europa.eu) (accessed 18 February 2021).
34   Mary C. Murphy and Jonathan Evershed, 'The DUP and the European Union: From contestation to conformance and back again ...', *Irish Political Studies*, 35(3), 2020, p. 381.
35   Ibid.
36   House of Commons Debates (Hansard), 27 October 1971, Vol. 823, Col. 1760.
37   Author interview with Clifford Peeples, 30 July 2019.
38   Jamie Bryson, 'Editorial: Academics like Professor Pete Shirlow are out of touch with current loyalist thinking', *Unionist Voice*, 4 November 2019. Archived at: https://unionistvoice.com/news/outoftouchacademics/ (accessed 24 March 2022).
39   Ben Lowry, 'Loyalist protest meeting in Portadown against Boris Johnson's "Betrayal Act" was packed and angry', *Belfast News Letter*, 25 November 2019.
40   Author interview with John Kyle, 29 July 2019.
41   Ibid.
42   Ibid.

17. CIRCLING THE WAGONS

1   Peter Robinson, 'The prime cause of the trouble is the Northern Ireland Protocol', *Belfast News Letter*, 9 April 2021.
2   House of Commons, Northern Ireland Affairs Committee, Oral Evidence: Brexit and the

Northern Ireland Protocol, HC 157, Meeting with the Loyalist Communities Council, 19 May 2021.
3   Susan McKay, 'What is smart, young Joel Keys doing with loyalist paramilitaries?', *The Irish Times*, 21 May 2021.
4   Ben Lowry, 'If Joel Keys, aged 19, wants to help unionism, he should get a law degree', *Belfast News Letter*, 22 May 2021.
5   'Multitude of factors behind street disorder', *Belfast News Letter*, 9 April 2021.
6   Brendan Hughes, 'Northern Ireland riots: Why is there rioting and disorder in loyalist areas of Northern Ireland?', *Belfast Live*, 6 April 2021.
7   Twitter, 7 April 2021. Archived at: https://twitter.com/borisjohnson/status/1379895030077394950 (accessed 11 March 2022).
8   Toby Helm, Lisa O'Carroll and Michael Savage, 'Boris Johnson refuses calls for summit on violence in Northern Ireland', *The Observer*, 11 April 2021.
9   Sam McBride, 'On the streets and in Stormont, the next few months look bleak for Northern Ireland', *Belfast News Letter*, 10 April 2021.
10 PSNI, *Chief Constable's Accountability Report to the Northern Ireland Policing Board Financial Year 2020–2021* (Belfast: PSNI, 1 April 2021), p. 5. Archived at: www.psni.police.uk/globalassets/news-and-appeals/latest-news/news-stories/2021/march-2021/april-2021-chief-constable-accountability-report-to-nipb-final.pdf.
11 House of Commons, Northern Ireland Affairs Committee, Meeting with the Loyalist Communities Council, 19 May 2021.
12 House of Commons, Northern Ireland Affairs Committee, Oral Evidence: Brexit and the Northern Ireland Protocol, HC 157, Meeting with Councillor Billy Hutchinson, PUP Leader, 9 June 2021.
13 Author interview with Trevor Greer, 8 July 2021.
14 Ibid.
15 See my remarks in 'Anger and division among loyalists over the Northern Ireland protocol: The guns are still packed away, but the threat is there', *The Economist*, 13 March 2021; and McBride, 'On the streets and in Stormont, the next few months look bleak for Northern Ireland'; Philip Bradfield, 'UVF "may now be persuaded of the need to act" rather than permit "spontaneous" street violence, after Simon Coveney security alert', *Belfast News Letter*, 2022.
16 Jamie Bryson, 'The next DUP leader must tune into the beat of the loyalist drums', *Belfast Live*, 21 June 2021. Accessible at: www.belfastlive.co.uk/news/belfast-news/jamie-bryson-next-dup-leader-20863973.
17 Connla Young, 'Struggle for the soul of Ulster loyalism as concerns grow over escalation in anti-protocol tension', *The Irish News*, 21 June 2021.
18 Aaron Edwards, 'The battle for the soul of unionism', *Fortnight Magazine*, 485, 2022, pp. 2–4.
19 High Court of Justice in Northern Ireland Judicial Review by Clifford Peeples and the Prime Minister, the Secretary of State for Northern Ireland and Chancellor for the

Duchy of Lancaster: Applicant's Skeleton Argument, 7 May 2021. Copy in author's possession.

20 Author interview with Clifford Peeples, October 2021.

21 Both attempts at legal redress were resubmitted to the Court of Appeal in early 2022. Again, they were dismissed. In concluding his remarks, the judge acknowledged how the 'issues raised by these appeals are of incontestable constitutional importance', and had 'generated much public debate and reaction, including public disorder'. Significantly, it appeared that the judge was making his decision in the context of 'potentially profound consequences in Northern Ireland and throughout the 27 Member States of the EU. Instability, uncertainty and confusion would inevitably ensue'. Her Majesty's Court of Appeal in Northern Ireland, Jim Allister *et al.* and Secretary of State for Northern Ireland and Clifford Peeples and the Prime Minister, Secretary of State for Northern Ireland and Duchy of Lancaster, 14 March 2022. Copy in author's possession.

22 Author interview with Jamie Bryson, 7 July 2021.

23 Esmond Birnie, 'The Protocol steers Northern Ireland towards being a less productive economy', *Belfast News Letter*, 22 July 2022.

24 Author interview with Stephen Cooper, 3 August 2022.

25 Stephen Cooper, 'Belfast Agreement formally rewarded IRA violence', *Unionist Voice*, 11 April 2021. Archived at: https://unionistvoice.com/opinions/belfast-agreement-formally-rewarded-ira-violence-by-cllr-stephen-cooper/ (accessed 29 December 2021).

26 Author interview with Nigel Gardiner, 8 July 2021.

27 Seamus McKinney, 'Appeals for calm after fourth night of loyalist riots in Derry', *The Irish News*, 2 April 2021.

28 David Young, '"No basis" for unionists to continue to back peace accord, says PUP leader', *Belfast Telegraph*, 8 November 2021.

29 Author interview with Julie-Anne Corr-Johnston, 31 January 2022.

18. POLITICAL UNIONISM AND THE GREATER GOOD

1 Francis Hutcheson, *Philosophical Writings: Essays on Ethics, Taste, Laughter, Politics, Economics*, edited by Robin Downie (Edinburgh: Birlinn, 2019), p. 353. The quote is taken from *A System of Moral Philosophy*, which was written in 1733–7 while Hutcheson was Professor of Moral Philosophy at Glasgow University and published posthumously in 1755.

2 Francis Hutcheson, *An Inquiry into the Original of Our Ideas of Beauty and Virtue; In Two Treatises – Second Edition* (London: J. Darby, 1726), p. 177.

3 Utilitarianism is the theory that an action is right if it leads to the greatest happiness of the greatest number. Its provenance lies in classical Greek philosophy but originated in its modern guise in the work and teachings of the Earl of Shaftesbury and Francis Hutcheson, though its most famous adherents were Jeremy Bentham (1748–1832) and John Stuart Mill (1806–1873).

4   Hutcheson, *An Inquiry into the Original of Our Ideas of Beauty and Virtue*, pp. 177–8.
5   Francis Hutcheson, *An Inquiry Concerning the Original of Our Ideas of Virtue or Moral Good* (1725; Treatise II of *An Inquiry into the Original of Our Ideas of Beauty and Virtue*); Francis Hutcheson, *An Essay on the Nature and Conduct of the Passions and Affections, With Illustrations Upon the Moral Sense* (1728).
6   Steven Pinker, *Enlightenment Now: The Case for Reason, Science, Humanism and Progress* (London: Penguin Books, 2018), p. 8.
7   Hutcheson, *A Short Introduction to Moral Philosophy in Three Books*, pp. 300–1.
8   Fukuyama, *Identity*, p. 164.
9   McKay, *Northern Protestants*, p. 53.
10 Author interview with Julie-Anne Corr-Johnston, 31 January 2022.
11 Ibid.
12 For a copy of the *Principles of Loyalism* see: www.pup-ni.org.uk/loyalism/principlesdocument.aspx (accessed 28 March 2022).
13 Graham Walker, 'The Scottish dimension of the Union' in John Wilson Foster and William Beattie Smith (eds), *The Idea of the Union: Great Britain and Northern Ireland – Realities and Challenges* (Belfast: Belcouver Press, 2021), pp. 65–77.
14 Edna Longley, 'Opening up: A new pluralism', *Fortnight*, 256, 1987, pp. 24–5.
15 Ibid., p. 25.
16 Ibid.
17 Geoffrey Sloan, 'Ireland and the geopolitics of Anglo-Irish relations', *Irish Studies Review*, 15(2), 2007, p. 172.
18 Ibid., p. 173.
19 Her Majesty's Government, The Integrated Review (March 2021). Archived at: https://assets.publishing.service.gov.uk/government/uploads/system/uploads/attachment_data/file/975077/Global_Britain_in_a_Competitive_Age-_the_Integrated_Review_of_Security__Defence__Development_and_Foreign_Policy.pdf (accessed 21 March 2022).
20 House of Commons (Hansard), Vol. 691, Col. 52W, 24 March 2021.
21 Francis Hutcheson, *A System of Moral Philosophy in Three Books: Volume II* (London: R. and A. Foulis, 1755), p. 223. This volume is housed in the John Adams Library housed in the Boston Public Library.
22 Ibid., p. 215.
23 Ibid., p. 221.
24 Porter, *Rethinking Unionism*, pp. 169–70.
25 Ibid., p. 170.
26 The so-called Barnett Formula is used by the Treasury to allocate block funding to the devolved administrations. In 2019–20 it saw the allocation of £32 billion in Scotland, £16 billion in Wales and £12 billion in Northern Ireland. For more on this see: www.instituteforgovernment.org.uk/explainers/barnett-formula (accessed 28 March 2022).

27 John Denham, 'Nationhood and belonging: The purpose of patriotism', *Renewal*, 29(4), 2022, pp. 62–74.
28 Ibid., p. 63.

EPILOGUE

1 Author interview with Julie-Anne Corr-Johnston, 31 January 2022.
2 George Orwell, *The Lion and the Unicorn: Socialism and the English Genius* (London: Secker and Warburg, [1941], 1962), p. 16.
3 Ibid.
4 Ibid., pp. 87–8.
5 Christopher Hitchens, 'What is patriotism?', *The Nation*, 15–22 July 1991. Cited in Christopher Hitchens, *And Yet … Essays* (London: Atlantic Books, 2015), p. 321.
6 Marianne Elliott, 'Northern Ireland's uneasy centenary', *Financial Times*, 7 May 2021.
7 For the full recorded video interview, see The Brendan Mac Lua Commemorative Lecture 2021 – Understanding Northern Ireland Loyalism: An Interview with Dr John Kyle, 23 September 2021. Archived at: www.youtube.com/watch?v=ldcA2osadJo (accessed 23 March 2022).
8 Ibid.

BIBLIOGRAPHY

Newspapers, Journals and Online Sources

An Phoblacht
Belfast Live
Belfast News Letter
Belfast Telegraph
The Blanket
Cork Examiner, The/Irish Examiner
Daily Mirror
Daily Telegraph
Dictionary of Ulster Biography
Dublin Review of Books
Evening Herald
Financial Times
Fortnight
Guardian, The
History Ireland
Irish Evening Press
Irish Independent and Sunday Independent
Irish News, The
Irish Times, The
London Review of Books
New Irelander
North American Review
Oxford Dictionary of National Biography
Shankill Mirror
Slugger O'Toole
Strabane Chronicle
Sunday Tribune
Times and Sunday Times, The
Unionist Voice

Archives

CAIN, Ulster University, Derry/Londonderry

Irish Defence Forces Military Archives, Dublin
Liddell Hart Centre for Military Archives, London
Museum of Orange Heritage, Belfast
Public Records of Northern Ireland, Belfast
The National Archives, Bishop Street, Dublin
The National Archives, Kew, London

Official Reports

Dáil Éireann Debates
Northern Ireland House of Commons Debates
Northern Ireland Senate Debates
Seanad Éireann Debates
UK House of Commons Debates
UK House of Lords Debates

Memoirs

Beattie, Geoffrey, *We Are the People: Journeys Through the Heart of Protestant Ulster* (London: Mandarin, 1993).
—, *Corner Boys* (London: Orion, 1998).
—, *Protestant Boy* (London: Granta Books, 2004).
—, *Selfless: A Psychologist's Journey Through Identity and Social Class* (London: Routledge, 2020).
Blair, Tony, *A Journey* (London: Arrow Books, 2011).
Campbell, T.J., *Fifty Years of Ulster, 1890–1940* (Belfast: Irish News, 1941).
Devlin, Paddy, *The Fall of the Northern Ireland Executive* (Belfast: self-published, 1975).
—, *Straight Left: An Autobiography* (Belfast: Blackstaff Press, 1993).
Elliott, Marianne, *Heartlands: A Memoir of the White City Housing Estate in Belfast* (Belfast: Blackstaff, 2017).
Faulkner, Brian, *Memoirs of a Statesman* (London: Weidenfeld and Nicolson, 1978).
Fitzgerald, Garret, *Towards a New Ireland* (London: Charles Knight and Co. Limited, 1972).
—, *All in a Life: An Autobiography* (London: Macmillan, 1991).
Hutchinson, Billy, *My Life in Loyalism* (Dublin: Merrion Press, 2020).
Major, John, *John Major: The Autobiography* (London: HarperCollins, 2000).
O'Neill, Terence, *The Autobiography of Terence O'Neill: Prime Minister of Northern Ireland, 1963–1969* (London: Rupert Hart Davis, 1972).
Oliver, John Andrew, *Working at Stormont* (Dublin: Institute of Public Administration, 1978).
Ryan, Mick, *My Life in the IRA: The Border Campaign* (Cork: Mercier Press, 2018).
Trimble, David, *To Raise up a New Northern Ireland: Speeches and Articles by the Rt. Hon. David Trimble MP MLA, 1998–2001* (Belfast: The Belfast Press, 2001).

Winchester, Simon, *In Holy Terror: Reporting the Ulster Troubles* (London: Faber and Faber, 1974).

Books and Articles

Anderson, Benedict, *Imagined Communities: Reflections on the Origins and Spread of Nationalism* (London: Verso, [1983], 2006).

Arrington, Lauren, 'St John Ervine and the Fabian Society: Capital, empire and Irish Home Rule', *History Workshop Journal*, 72(2), 2011, pp. 52–73.

Ash, Timothy Garton, *We the People: The Revolution of '89 Witnessed in Warsaw, Budapest, Berlin and Prague* (London: Penguin Books, 1999).

Aughey, Arthur, 'Between exclusion and recognition: The politics of the Ulster Defence Association', *Conflict Quarterly*, 5(1), 1985, pp. 40–52.

—, *Under Siege: Ulster Unionism and the Anglo-Irish Agreement* (Belfast: Blackstaff, 1989).

Barritt, Denis P. and Charles F. Carter, *The Northern Ireland Problem: A Study in Group Relations – Second Edition* (Oxford: Oxford University Press, 1972).

Bartlett, Thomas and Keith Jeffery (eds), *A Military History of Ireland* (Cambridge: Cambridge University Press, 1996).

Barton, Brian, *Brookeborough: The Making of a Prime Minister* (Belfast: Blackstaff, 1988).

—, *Northern Ireland in the Second World War* (Belfast: Ulster Historical Foundation, 1995).

Bell, Desmond, *The Protestants of Ulster* (London: Pluto Press, [1976], 1987).

—, *The Twilight of Unionism: Ulster and the Future of Northern Ireland* (London: Verso, 2022).

Bew, Paul, *Ideology and the Irish Question: Ulster Unionism and Irish Nationalism, 1912–1916* (Oxford: Oxford University Press, 1998).

—, Peter Gibbon and Henry Patterson, *Northern Ireland, 1921–2001: Political Forces and Social Classes* (London: Serif, 2002).

Birnie, Esmond, 'The future of unionism', *Studies: An Irish Quarterly Review*, 89(355), 2000, pp. 267–73.

Bleakley, David, *Peace in Ulster* (Oxford: Mowbrays, 1972).

Bourke, Richard, *Peace in Ireland: The War of Ideas* (London: Pimlico, 2003).

Bourke, Richard and Ian McBride (eds), *The Princeton History of Modern Ireland* (Princeton, NJ: Princeton University Press, 2016).

Bowman, Tim, *Carson's Army: The Ulster Volunteer Force, 1910–22* (Manchester: Manchester University Press, 2007).

Brown, Kris, '"Our father organization": The cult of the Somme and the unionist "golden age" in Modern Ulster Loyalist Commemoration', *The Round Table – The Commonwealth Journal of International Affairs*, 96(393), 2007, pp. 707–23.

Brubaker, Rogers, 'Ethnicity without groups', *European Journal of Sociology*, 43(2), 2002, pp. 163–89.

Bruce, Steve 'The problems of "pro-state" terrorism: Loyalist paramilitaries in Northern Ireland', *Terrorism and Political Violence*, 4(1), 1992, pp. 67–88.

—, *The Edge of The Union: The Ulster Loyalist Political Vision* (Oxford: Oxford University Press, 1995).

—, *The Red Hand: Protestant Paramilitaries in Northern Ireland* (Oxford: Oxford University Press, 1995).

—, *Paisley: Religion and Politics in Northern Ireland* (Oxford: Oxford University Press, 2007).

Bryson, Jamie, *Brexit Betrayed: Writings from the Referendum to the Betrayal Act* (Donaghadee: Unionist Voice Publications, 2021).

Buckland, Patrick, *Ulster Unionism and the Origins of Northern Ireland, 1886-1922* (Dublin: Gill & Macmillan, 1973).

Coakley, John and Michael Gallagher (eds), *Politics in the Republic of Ireland*, Fourth Edition (London: Routledge, 2005).

Cochrane, Feargal, *Unionist Politics and the Politics of Unionism Since the Anglo-Irish Agreement – Second Edition* (Cork: Cork University Press, 2001).

Colley, Linda, *Acts of Union and Disunion: What Held the UK Together – and What Is Dividing It?* (London: Profile Books, 2014).

Coogan, Tim Pat, *The IRA: New Edition* (London: HarperCollins, 1995).

Craig, Tony, 'From backdoors and back lanes to backchannels: Reappraising British talks with the Provisional IRA, 1970-1974', *Contemporary British History*, 26(1), 2012, pp. 97-117.

—, 'Laneside, then left a bit? Britain's secret political talks with loyalist paramilitaries in Northern Ireland, 1973-1976', *Irish Political Studies*, 29(2), 2014, pp. 298-317.

Dawe, Gerald, *The Sound of the Shuttle: Essays on Cultural Belonging & Protestantism in Northern Ireland* (Dublin: Irish Academic Press, 2020).

de Baróid, Ciarán, *Ballymurphy and the Irish War*, New Edition (London: Pluto Press, 2000).

Denham, John, 'Nationhood and belonging: The purpose of patriotism', *Renewal*, 29(4), 2022, pp. 62-74.

DePaor, Liam, *Divided Ulster* (London: Penguin Books, 1970).

Devlin, Paddy, *Yes We Have No Bananas: Outdoor Relief in Belfast, 1920-39* (Belfast: Blackstaff Press, 1981).

Dewar, Michael, *The British Army in Northern Ireland* (London: Arms and Armour Press, 1985).

Drennan, William, *Fugitive Pieces in Verse and Prose* (Belfast: F.D. Finlay, 1815).

Dudgeon, Jeffrey, *H. Montgomery Hyde: Ulster Unionist MP, Gay Law Reform Campaigner and Prodigious Author* (Belfast: Belfast Press, 2018).

Dudley Edwards, Ruth, *The Faithful Tribe: An Intimate Portrait of the Loyal Institutions* (London: HarperCollins, 2000).

Edwards, Aaron, 'Democratic socialism and sectarianism: The Northern Ireland Labour Party and Progressive Unionist Party compared', *Politics*, 27(1), 2007, pp. 24-31.

—, '"Unionist Derry is Ulster's Panama": The Northern Ireland Labour Party and the civil rights issue', *Irish Political Studies*, 23(3), 2008, pp. 363-85.

—, *A History of the Northern Ireland Labour Party: Democratic Socialism and Sectarianism* (Manchester: Manchester University Press, 2009).

—, 'The Progressive Unionist Party of Northern Ireland: A left-wing voice in an ethnically divided society', *British Journal of Politics and International Relations*, 12(4), 2010, pp. 590–614.

—, *Defending the Realm? The Politics of Britain's Small Wars Since 1945* (Manchester: Manchester University Press, 2012).

—, *UVF: Behind the Mask* (Dublin: Merrion Press, 2017).

Edwards, Aaron, and Maria Hadjiathanasiou, 'Brothers in arms? How the IRA and EOKA insurgencies transcended the local and became transnational', *Small Wars & Insurgencies*, 32(4–5), 2021, pp. 642–64.

Elliott, Marianne, *Wolfe Tone: Prophet of Irish Independence* (New Haven, CT: Yale University Press, 1989).

English, Richard, *Armed Struggle: A History of the IRA* (London: Macmillan, 2003).

—, *Irish Freedom: The History of Nationalism in Ireland* (London: Macmillan, 2006).

English, Richard and Graham Walker (eds), *Unionism in Modern Ireland: New Perspectives on Politics and Culture* (Dublin: Gill & Macmillan, 1996).

Ervine, David, *Redefining Loyalism – A Political Perspective*, IBIS Working Papers No. 4 (Dublin: University College Dublin, 2001).

Ervine, St John, *Craigavon: Ulsterman* (London: Allen and Unwin, 1949).

Estyn Evans, Emyr, 'The personality of Ulster', *Transactions of the Institute of British Geographers*, 51 (1970), pp. 1–20.

Farrell, Michael, *Northern Ireland: The Orange State* (London: Pluto Press, 1976).

—, *Arming the Protestants: The Formation of the Ulster Special Constabulary* (London: Pluto, 1983).

Farrington, Christopher, 'Ulster unionist political divisions in the late twentieth century', *Irish Political Studies*, 16(1), 2001, pp. 49–71.

—, 'Ulster unionism and the Irish historiography debate', *Irish Studies Review*, 11(3), 2003, pp. 251–61.

—, *Ulster Unionism and the Peace Process in Northern Ireland* (Basingstoke: Palgrave Macmillan, 2006).

Fitzgerald, Garret, *Towards a New Ireland* (London: Charles Knight and Co. Limited, 1972).

Follis, Bryan A., *A State Under Siege: The Establishment of Northern Ireland, 1920–1925* (Oxford: Oxford University Press, 1995).

Foster, John Wilson and William Beattie Smith (eds), *The Idea of the Union: Great Britain and Northern Ireland* (Belfast: Belcouver Press, 2021).

Foster, R.F., *Modern Ireland, 1600–1972* (London: Penguin Books, 1988).

Foucault, Michel, *Society Must Be Defended: Lectures at the Collège de France, 1975–1976* (London: Penguin Books, [1997], 2020).

Fukuyama, Francis, *Identity: The Demand for Dignity and the Politics of Resentment* (New York: Farrar, Straus and Giroux, 2018).

Garland, Roy, *Gusty Spence* (Belfast: Blackstaff Press, 2001).

George Boyce, D. and Alan O'Day (eds), *Defenders of the Union: A Survey of British and Irish Unionism Since 1801* (Abingdon: Routledge, 2001).

Gibbon, Peter, *The Origins of Ulster Unionism* (Manchester: Manchester University Press, 1975).

Gibbons, Ivan, *Partition: How and Why Ireland Was Divided* (London: Haus Publishing, 2020).

Godson, Dean, *Himself Alone: David Trimble and the Ordeal of Unionism* (London: HarperCollins, 2004).

Goodwin, Matthew J. and Oliver Heath, 'The 2016 referendum, Brexit and the left behind: An aggregate-level analysis of the result', *Political Quarterly*, 87(3), 2016, pp. 323–32.

Graham, Brian, 'The past in the present: The shaping of identity in loyalist Ulster', *Terrorism and Political Violence*, 16(3), 2004, pp. 483–500.

Greacen, Robert, *The Sash My Father Wore: An Autobiography* (Edinburgh: Mainstream Publishing, 1997).

Greer, James and Graham Walker, 'Awkward Prods: Biographical studies of progressive Protestants and political allegiance in Northern Ireland', *Irish Political Studies*, 33(2), 2018, pp. 167–83.

Hamilton, Lord Ernest, *The Irish Rebellion of 1641: With a History of the Events Which Led Up To and Succeeded It* (London: John Murray, 1920).

Hanley, Brian and Scott Millar, *The Lost Revolution: The Story of the Official IRA and the Workers' Party* (Dublin: Penguin, 2016).

Harbinson, John F., *The Ulster Unionist Party, 1882–1973: Its Development and Organisation* (Belfast: Blackstaff Press, 1973).

Hennessey, Thomas, *A History of Northern Ireland, 1920–1996* (Basingstoke: Palgrave Macmillan, 1997).

—, *The Northern Ireland Peace Process: Ending the Troubles?* (Dublin: Gill & Macmillan, 1999).

—, *Northern Ireland: The Origins of the Troubles* (Dublin: Gill & Macmillan, 2005).

—, *The Evolution of the Troubles, 1970–72* (Dublin: Irish Academic Press 2007).

Hepburn, A.C., 'The Belfast Riots of 1935', *Social History*, 15(1), 1990, pp. 75–96.

Hewitt, John, *The Collected Poems of John Hewitt*, edited by Frank Ormsby (Belfast: Blackstaff, 1992).

Hill, Jacqueline, 'The meaning and significance of "Protestant ascendancy", 1787–1840' in *Ireland After the Union*, Proceedings of the Second Joint Meeting of the Royal Irish Academy and the British Academy, London, 1986 (Oxford: Oxford University Press, 1989), pp. 1–22.

Hitchens, Christopher, *And Yet … Essays* (London: Atlantic Books, 2015).

Hobbes, Thomas, *Leviathan* (London: Penguin Books, [1651], 1987).

Hobsbawm, Eric, 'Identity politics and the left', *New Left Review*, 1(217), 1996, pp. 38–47.

Horowitz, Donald, *Ethnic Groups in Conflict* (London: University of California Press, 2000).

Howe, Stephen, *Ireland and Empire: Colonial Legacies in Irish History and Culture* (Oxford: Oxford University Press, 2000).

Hughes, Brian, *Defying the IRA? Intimidation, Coercion, and Communities During the Irish Revolution* (Liverpool: Liverpool University Press, 2016).

Hume, David, *The Ulster Unionist Party, 1972–1992: A Political Movement in an Era of Conflict and Change* (Lurgan: The Ulster Society, 1995).

Hutcheson, Francis, *An Inquiry into the Original of Ideas of Beauty and Virtue in Two Treatises I. Concerning Beauty, Order, Harmony, Design & II. Concerning Moral Good and Evil*, Second Edition (London: J. Darby et al., 1726).

—, *A Short Introduction to Moral Philosophy in Three Books Containing the Elements of Ethics and the Law of Nature – Translated from the Latin – Second Edition* (Glasgow: Robert & Andrew Foulis, 1753).

—, *A System of Moral Philosophy in Three Books: Volumes I–III* (London: R. and A. Foulis, 1755).

—, *An Essay on the Nature and Conduct of the Passions and Affections, With Illustrations on the Moral Sense*, Third Edition (Glasgow, 1769).

—, *Philosophical Writings: Essays on Ethics, Taste, Laughter, Politics, Economics*, edited by Robin Downie (Edinburgh: Birlinn, 2019).

Hutchinson, John and Anthony D. Smith (eds), *Ethnicity* (Oxford: Oxford University Press, 1996).

Hyndman, Marilyn (ed.), *Further Afield: Journeys from a Protestant Past* (Belfast: Beyond the Pale Publications, 1996).

Isles, K.S. and Norman Cuthbert, *An Economic Survey of Northern Ireland* (Belfast: HMSO, 1957).

Jackson, Alvin, *Home Rule: An Irish History, 1800–2000* (Oxford: Oxford University Press, 2003).

—, 'Tame Tory hacks? The Ulster Party at Westminster, 1922–1972', *The Historical Journal*, 54(2), 2011, pp. 453–75.

—, *The Two Unions: Ireland, Scotland, and the Survival of the United Kingdom, 1707–2007* (Oxford: Oxford University Press, 2012).

Judt, Tony, *Postwar: A History of Europe Since 1945* (London: Vintage Books, 2005).

Kaufmann, Eric P., *The Orange Order: A Contemporary Northern Irish History* (Oxford: Oxford University Press, 2007).

Kenna, G.B., *Facts and Figures of the Belfast Pogrom, 1920–1922* (Dublin: The O'Connell Publishing Company, 1922).

Kennedy, Liam, 'One island, two peoples: Ethical Perspective on Ireland's constitutional future', *Irish Studies in International Affairs*, 32(2), 2021, pp. 448–76.

Kissinger, Henry, *World Order* (New York: Penguin Books, 2014).

Le Bon, Gustav, *The Crowd: A Study of the Popular Mind* (New York: Macmillan, 1896).

Lewis, C.S., *Till We Have Faces: A Myth Retold* (New York: Harcourt Brace and Company, 1956).

Longley, Edna, 'Progressive bookmen: Politics and Northern Protestant writers since the 1930s', *The Irish Review*, 1, 1986, pp. 50–7.

Lynch, Robert, 'The people's protectors? The Irish Republican Army and the "Belfast Pogrom", 1920–1922', *Journal of British Studies*, 47(2), 2008, pp. 375–91.

McAuley, James W., *The Politics of Identity: Protestant Working Class Politics and Culture in Belfast* (Aldershot: Avebury, 1994).

—, '"Just fighting to survive": Loyalist paramilitary politics and the Progressive Unionist Party', *Terrorism and Political Violence*, 16(3), 2004, pp. 522–43.

—, 'Whither new loyalism? Changing loyalist politics after the Belfast Agreement', *Irish Political Studies*, 20(3), 2005, pp. 323–40.

—, *Ulster's Last Stand? Reconstructing Unionism After the Peace Process* (Dublin: Irish Academic Press, 2010).

—, *Very British Rebels? The Culture and Politics of Ulster Loyalism* (London: Bloomsbury Academic, 2015).

—, 'Memory and belonging in Ulster loyalist identity', *Irish Political Studies*, 31(1), 2016, pp. 122–38.

McAuley, James W. and Graham Spencer, *Ulster Loyalism After the Good Friday Agreement: History, Identity and Change* (Basingstoke: Palgrave Macmillan, 2011).

— (eds), *Troubled Past: Identity and Collective Memory in Northern Ireland* (Manchester: Manchester University Press, 2023).

McBride, Ian, *The Siege of Derry in Ulster Protestant Mythology* (Dublin: Four Courts Press, 1997).

—, *Scripture Politics: Ulster Presbyterians and Irish Radicalism in the Late Eighteenth Century* (Oxford: Oxford University Press, 1998).

—, *Eighteenth-Century Ireland: The Isle of Slaves – The Protestant Ascendancy in Ireland* (Oxford: Oxford University Press, 2009).

—, 'The edge of Enlightenment: Ireland and Scotland in the eighteenth century', *Modern Intellectual History*, 10(1), 2013, pp. 135–51.

McCann, David and Cillian McGrattan (eds), *Sunningdale, the Ulster Workers' Council Strike and the Struggle for Democracy in Northern Ireland* (Manchester: Manchester University Press, 2017).

McCartney, Robert, *Reflections on Liberty, Democracy, and the Union* (Washington, DC: Academica Press, 2001).

McCleery, Martin J., 'Sectarianism and the Provisional Irish Republican Army', *Small Wars & Insurgencies*, 32(4–5), 2021, pp. 665–86.

McDonald, Henry, *Trimble* (London: Bloomsbury, 2000).

McEwen, Yvonne, 'Deaths in Irish regiments 1939–1945 and the extent of irish volunteering for the British Army', *The Irish Sword*, 24, 2004–5, pp. 81–98.

McGarry, Fearghal, *The Rising: Ireland: Easter 1916* (Oxford: Oxford University Press, 2016).

McKay, Susan, *Northern Protestants: An Unsettled People* (Belfast: Blackstaff, 2000).

—, *Northern Protestants: On Shifting Ground* (Belfast: Blackstaff, 2021).

McKearney, Tommy, *The Provisional IRA: From Insurrection to Parliament* (London: Pluto, 2011).

McKittrick, David, Seamus Kelters, Brian Feeney and Chris Thornton, *Lost Lives: The Stories of the Men, Women and Children Who Died as a Result of the Northern Ireland Troubles – Revised and Updated* (Edinburgh: Mainstream, 2001).

McNeill, Ronald, *Ulster's Stand for the Union* (London: John Murray, 1922).

Miller, David, *Queen's Rebels: Ulster Loyalism in Historical Perspective* (Dublin: University College Dublin Press, [1978], 2007).

Mitchell, Arthur, *Labour in Irish Politics: The Irish Labour Movement in an Age of Revolution* (New York: Barnes and Noble Books, 1974).

Mockaitis, Thomas R., *British Counterinsurgency in the Post-Imperial Era* (Manchester: Manchester University Press, 1995).

Moloney, Ed, *A Secret History of the IRA: Revised and Updated Edition* (London: Penguin, 2007).

—, *Ian Paisley: From Demagogue to Democrat* (Dublin: Poolbeg, 2008).

Monaghan, Rachel, 'The return of "Captain Moonlight": Informal justice in Northern Ireland', *Studies in Conflict and Terrorism*, 25(1), 2002, pp. 41–56.

—, '"An imperfect peace": Paramilitary "punishments" in Northern Ireland', *Terrorism and Political Violence*, 16(3), 2004, pp. 439–61.

Mulholland, Marc, *Northern Ireland at the Crossroads: Ulster Unionism in the O'Neill Years, 1960-9* (Basingstoke: Palgrave Macmillan, 2000).

Munck, Ronnie and Bill Rolston, 'Oral history and social conflict: Belfast in the 1930s', *The Oral History Review*, 13, 1985, pp. 1–21.

—, *Belfast in the Thirties: An Oral History* (Belfast: Blackstaff Press, 1987).

Murphy, Dervla, *A Place Apart* (London: John Murray, 1978).

Murphy, Mary C. and Jonathan Evershed, 'The DUP and the European Union: From contestation to conformance and back again ...', *Irish Political Studies*, 35(3), 2020, pp. 378–98.

Nelson, Sarah, *Ulster's Uncertain Defenders: Protestant Political, Paramilitary and Community Groups and the Northern Ireland Conflict* (Belfast: Appletree Press, 1984).

Novosel, Tony, *Northern Ireland's Missed Opportunity: The Frustrated Promise of Political Loyalism* (London: Pluto Press, 2013).

O'Callaghan, Margaret and Catherine O'Donnell, 'The Northern Ireland government, the "Paisleyite Movement" and Ulster Unionism in 1966', *Irish Political Studies*, 21(2), 2006, pp. 203–22.

O'Connor, Steven, 'Irish identity and integration within the British Army forces, 1939–45', *Irish Historical Studies*, 39(155), 2015, pp. 417–38.

O'Doherty, Malachi, *The Trouble With Guns: Republican Strategy and the Provisional IRA* (Belfast: Blackstaff Press, 1998).

Ó Faoleán, Gearóid, 'The Ulster Defence Regiment and the question of Catholic recruitment, 1970–1972', *Terrorism and Political Violence*, 27(5), 2015, pp. 838–56.

O'Grady, Joseph P., 'Forcing the question of Northern Ireland: The Brooke-Mayhew talks, 1990–1992', *New Hibernia Review*, 5(4), 2001, pp. 73–92.

O'Kane, Eamonn, *The Northern Ireland Peace Process: From Armed Conflict to Brexit* (Manchester: Manchester University Press, 2021).

O'Leary, Brendan, 'The Anglo-Irish Agreement: Folly or statecraft?', *West European Politics*, 10(1), 1987, pp. 5–32.

—, *A Treatise on Northern Ireland: Volume 1 – Colonialism* (Oxford: Oxford University Press, 2019).

—, *A Treatise on Northern Ireland: Volume 2 – Control* (Oxford: Oxford University Press, 2019).

—, *A Treatise on Northern Ireland: Volume 3 – Consociation and Confederation* (Oxford: Oxford University Press, 2019).

Ollerenshaw, Phillip, 'War, industrial mobilisation and society in Northern Ireland, 1939–1945', *Contemporary European History*, 16(2), 2007, pp. 169–97.

Orwell, George, *The Road to Wigan Pier* (London: Penguin Books, [1937], 1966).

—, *The Lion and the Unicorn: Socialism and the English Genius* (London: Secker and Warburg, [1941], 1962).

Parr, Connal, *Inventing the Myth: Political Passions and the Ulster Protestant Imagination* (Oxford: Oxford University Press, 2017).

—, 'Expelled from yard and tribe: The "Rotten Prods" of 1920 and their political legacies', *Sijis*, 11, 2021, pp. 299–321.

Patterson, Henry, *Class Conflict and Sectarianism: The Protestant Working Class and the Belfast Labour Movement, 1868–1920* (Belfast: Blackstaff, 1980).

—, 'The limits of "New Unionism": David Trimble and the Ulster Unionist Party', *Éire-Ireland*, 39(1&2), 2004, pp. 163–188.

—, *Ireland Since 1939: The Persistence of Conflict* (Dublin: Penguin Books, 2006).

Patterson, Henry and Eric Kaufmann, *Unionism and Orangeism in Northern Ireland Since 1945: The Decline of the Loyal Family* (Manchester: Manchester University Press, 2007).

Pinker, Steven, *Enlightenment Now: The Case for Reason, Science, Humanism and Progress* (London: Penguin Books, 2018).

Porter, Norman, *Rethinking Unionism: An Alternative Vision for Northern Ireland* (Belfast: Blackstaff, 1996).

Prince, Simon, *Northern Ireland's '68: Civil Rights, Global Revolt and the Origins of the Troubles* (Dublin: Irish Academic Press, 2007).

Pringle, D.G., 'Electoral systems and political manipulation: A case study of Northern Ireland in the 1920s', *The Economic and Social Review*, 11(3), 1980, pp. 187–205.

Privilege, John and Greta Jones, 'Crisis and scandal: Government, local government and health reform in Northern Ireland, 1939–44', *Irish Economic and Social History*, 42, 2015, pp. 33–52.

Purdie, Bob, *Politics in the Streets: Origins of the Civil Rights Movement in Northern Ireland* (Belfast: Blackstaff Press, 1990).

Reed, Richard, *Paramilitary Loyalism: Identity and Change* (Manchester: Manchester University Press, 2015).

Rees, Russell, *Labour and the Northern Ireland Problem, 1945–1951: The Missed Opportunity* (Dublin: Irish Academic Press, 2009).

Rowthorn, Bob and Naomi Wayne, *Northern Ireland: The Political Economy of Conflict* (Cambridge: Polity Press, 1988).

Reid, Colin, 'Protestant challenges to the "Protestant State": Ulster Unionism and Independent Unionism in Northern Ireland, 1921–1939', *Twentieth Century British History*, 19(4), 2008, pp. 419–45.

Roche, Patrick and Brian Barton, *The Northern Ireland Question: Perspectives on Nationalism and Unionism* (Tunbridge Wells: Wordzworth Publishing, 2020).

Robbins, Caroline, '"When it is that colonies may turn independent": An analysis of the environment and politics of Francis Hutcheson (1694–1746)', *The William and Mary Quarterly*, 11(2), 1954, pp. 214–51.

Rose, Richard, *Governing Without Consensus: An Irish Perspective* (London: Faber and Faber, 1971).

Rumpf, E. and A.C. Hepburn, *Nationalism and Socialism in Twentieth Century Ireland* (Liverpool: Liverpool University Press, 1977).

Russell, Bertrand, *Authority and the Individual: The Reith Lectures for 1948–9* (London: George Allen and Unwin Limited, 1949).

Sambanis, Nicholas and Moses Shayo, 'Social identification and ethnic conflict', *The American Political Science Review*, 107(2), 2013, pp. 294–325.

Scott, William Robert, *Francis Hutcheson: His Life, Teaching and Position in the History of Philosophy* (Cambridge: Cambridge University Press, 1900).

Shearman, Hugh, *Ulster* (London: Robert Hale Limited, 1949).

Shirlow, Peter, *The End of Ulster Loyalism?* (Manchester: Manchester University Press, 2012).

Shirlow, Peter and Mark McGovern, *Who Are the People? Unionism, Protestantism and Loyalism in Northern Ireland* (London: Pluto Press, 1997).

Sinnerton, Henry, *David Ervine: Unchartered Waters* (London: Brandon, 2003).

Sloan, Geoffrey, 'Ireland and the geopolitics of Anglo-Irish relations', *Irish Studies Review*, 15(2), 2007, pp. 163–79.

Smyth, Clifford, *Ian Paisley: Voice of Protestant Ulster* (Edinburgh: Scottish Academic Press, 1987).

Southern, Neil, 'Ian Paisley: A Critical Comment', *Studies: An Irish Quarterly Review*, 99(394), 2010, pp. 139–52.

Spencer, Graham, *The State of Loyalism in Northern Ireland* (Basingstoke: Palgrave, 2008).

Stewart, A.T.Q., *The Narrow Ground: The Roots of Conflict in Ulster*, New Edition (London: Faber and Faber, 1989).

Stopford Green, Alice, *Ourselves Alone in Ulster: New Edition With Notes* (Dublin and London: Maunsel and Company, 1918).

Todd, Jennifer, 'Two traditions in unionist political culture', *Irish Political Studies*, 2, 1987, pp. 1–26.

—, 'Unionisms and the challenges of change', *Irish Political Studies*, 35(3), 2020, pp. 335–55.

—, 'Unionism, identity and Irish unity: Paradigms, problems and paradoxes', *Irish Studies in International Affairs*, 32(2), 2021, pp. 53–77.

Todd, Selina, *The People: The Rise and Fall of the Working Class* (London: John Murray, 2014).

Tonge, Jonathan, *Northern Ireland: Conflict and Change: Second Edition* (Essex: Person Education Limited, 2002).

Tonge, Jonathan, Máire Braniff, Thomas Hennessey, James W. McAuley and Sophie A. Whiting, 'Same but different? The Democratic Unionist Party and Ulster Unionist Party compared', *Irish Political Studies*, 35(3), 2020, pp. 399–421.

Urquhart, Diane (ed.), *The Minutes of the Ulster Women's Unionist Council and Executive Committee, 1911–40* (Dublin: Irish Manuscripts Commission, 2001).

Walker, Brian, '1641, 1689, 1690 and all that: The unionist sense of history', *The Irish Review*, 12, 1992, pp. 56–64.

Walker, Graham, 'Protestantism before party!' The Ulster Protestant League in the 1930s', *Historical Journal*, 28(4), 1985, pp. 961–7.

—, *The Politics of Frustration: Harry Midgley and the Failure of Labour in Northern Ireland* (Manchester: Manchester University Press, 1985).

—, *A History of the Ulster Unionist Party: Protest, Pragmatism and Pessimism* (Manchester: Manchester University Press, 2004).

Ward, Paul, *Unionism in the United Kingdom, 1918–1974* (Basingstoke: Palgrave Macmillan, 2005).

Ward, Rachel, *Women, Unionism and Loyalism in Northern Ireland* (Dublin: Irish Academic Press, 2006).

Wells, H.G., *The Fate of Homo Sapiens* (1939).

Wiener, Rob, *The Rape and Plunder of the Shankill: Community Action – The Belfast Experience, Second Edition* (Belfast: Farset Co-operative Press, 1980).

Willis, Gary, *Inventing America: Jefferson's Declaration of Independence* (Boston, MA: Mariner Books, [1978], 2002).

Wichert, Sabine (ed.), *From the United Irishmen to Twentieth-Century Unionism: A Festschrift for A.T.Q. Stewart* (Dublin: Four Courts Press, 2004).

Wilson, Thomas, *Ulster Under Home Rule: A Study of the Political and Economic Problems of Northern Ireland* (London: Oxford University Press, 1955).

Wright, Frank, 'Ideology and politics in Ulster', *European Journal of Sociology*, 14(2), 1973, pp. 213–80.

—, 'Northern Ireland and the British-Irish relationship', *Studies: An Irish Quarterly Review*, 78(310), 1989, pp. 151–62.

—, *Northern Ireland: A Comparative Analysis* (Dublin: Gill & Macmillan, 1992).

—, *Two Lands on One Soil: Ulster Politics Before Home Rule* (Dublin: Gill & Macmillan, 1996).

ACKNOWLEDGEMENTS

IT IS CUSTOMARY TO THANK those who have had a significant impact on helping me to shape the ideas that resulted in producing the book you now hold in your hands. First and foremost, I would like to thank my friend Harry Donaghy and the other members of the Fellowship of the Messines Association Project in Belfast for inviting me to prepare several research papers upon which three chapters are based. I was fortunate to deliver a presentation at the Somme Heritage Centre on the forty-fifth anniversary of the UWC strike in May 2019 and to share a platform with several of those who were involved in events at one level or another at the time. My thanks to Dr Seán Farren and the other panellists who gave me feedback on my talk, as well as those in the audience who offered their own perspectives from the period. Another friend of the Messines Project, Dr Brian Hanley, was generous with his remarks on a paper I gave at Edinburgh University in February 2018. I would like to thank Dr Roseanna Doughty and Dr Tommy Dolan for their comments on that occasion too, and for subsequently inviting me to contribute my thoughts on unionism and loyalism to the excellent 'Writing the Troubles' blog. Thanks also to Jim McDermott, Dr Connal Parr, Dr Seán Brennan, Anne Devlin, Deirdre McBride and Harry Donaghy for feedback on what formed the basis of my chapter on the formation of Northern Ireland.

Thanks also to Malachi O'Doherty, Rudie Goldsmith and, latterly, Tom Hadden at *Fortnight* magazine for publishing my work over the years, as well as the PSA and PSAI for the opportunity to present my work at annual conferences and other events. Professor Jim McAuley, Professor Jon Tonge, Dr Eamonn O'Kane and Dr Alan Greer – not forgetting the remainder of 'the usual suspects' – have been generous with their feedback over the years.

The origins of the ideas for this book lie in my time as a graduate student at Queen's University Belfast in the early to mid-2000s. While there I encountered a range of inspirational academics, such as Dr Christopher

Farrington, Professor Margaret O'Callaghan and Professor Richard English, who helped forge my engagement with unionism and loyalism at an intellectual level. However, it was Professor Lord Bew, who supervised my MA thesis, and Professor Graham Walker, who supervised my PhD, who both helped shape my ideas in the most rewarding of ways. Along with Professor Arthur Aughey, Professor James W. McAuley, Professor Henry Patterson, Professor Jennifer Todd and Ian S. Wood, I owe them all an intellectual debt in terms of my understanding of unionism and loyalism. Any merits in *A People Under Siege* are thanks to my engagement with these scholars and their work. Arthur and Graham were particularly helpful as I moved the book towards completion. Having said that, I am fully responsible for the analysis presented here.

My friends Dr Seán Brennan, Dr Stephen Bloomer, Dr Paddy Hoey, Dr Marty McCleery and Dr Connal Parr were on hand at various points to assist me with test-driving some thoughts. Thanks also to the late Henry McDonald, Clifford Peeples, Dr Marisa McGlinchey and Richard O'Rawe for engaging with me and my research, and for their comradeship, over the years.

The team at Merrion Press have helped enormously as I prepared the manuscript amidst other personal and academic commitments. Thanks to Conor Graham for commissioning the book, to Wendy Logue for steering the project towards completion, and to my copy editor, Heidi Houlihan, for ensuring consistency across the manuscript.

Finally, I would like to thank Jim, Barbara, Ryan, Stephanie for their support in various ways over the years. And, of course, I owe an unpayable debt of gratitude to Charlotte for being there when it mattered most, especially during the final stages of revisions of the manuscript when we were preparing for the imminent arrival of our daughter, Bethany.

INDEX

Abbott, Clive, 146–7
Act of Union (1801), the, 4, 241, 242
Action for Community Employment (ACE) programme, the, 166–7, 168
Acton, Maj. Gen. Thomas, 110
Adams, David, 183
Adams, Gerry, 156, 213, 214
Agnew, Paddy, 56, 68
Allen, Jack, 159
Allen, Samuel, 80
Alliance Party, the, 125, 160, 201, 211, 216
Allister, Jim, 217, 241
Alpha Boys Club, Newtownabbey, the, 80
American evangelical community, the, 195
Andrews, John L.O., 78, 167
Andrews, John Miller, 41–2, 43–4, 47–9, 51, 60, 65, 74, 75
Andrews, Thomas, 41
Anglo-Irish Agreement (1985), the, 12, 149–50, 151–4, 156, 160, 161, 168, 178, 185, 187, 191
Anglo-Irish Defence Agreement (1938), the, 48
Anglo-Irish Treaty (1921), the, 27–8
Apprentice Boys of Derry, the, 105, 153
Arbuckle, Const. Victor, 108
arms decommissioning, 186, 203, 204, 214, 220
arms importations, 18, 155–6
Armstrong, Charles, 148
Armstrong, Robert, 147
Articles 2 and 3 of Bunreacht na hÉireann, 45–6, 181, 208
Ashley-Cooper, Anthony, 248
Atlee, Clement, 71, 73, 74
Aughey, Arthur, 258
authoritarian laws to curb civil unrest (*see* Special Powers Act (1922), the)

B Specials, the, 109
Babington, Anthony Brutus, 33
Baillie, Harry, 107
Baillie, Thomas, 65
Baird, James, 24
Baldwin, Stanley, 31
Ballygawley coach atrocity (August 1988), the, 157–8
Barr, Andy, 129
Barr, Glenn, 131, 134–5, 137
Bates, Sir Richard Dawson, 34, 35
Battle of the Diamond, Loughgall (1795), the, 4, 49

Beam, Louis, 195–6
Beattie, Geoffrey, 170–1
Beattie, Jack, 30, 31, 65, 78
Beggs, Roy, 169
Belfast Agreement (Good Friday Agreement) (1998), the, xv, xvi, 13, 200, 204–5, 208, 229, 232, 236, 241–3, 245; and referendum on, 200, 205 (*see also* Framework Documents, the; peace process, the)
Belfast Corporation, 29–30, 37
Belfast Shops Stewards' movement, the, 60
Benn, Tony, 231–2
Beyond the Religious Divide (policy document), 136
Bill of Rights proposal, 210, 211
Bingham, John, 155
Birnie, Esmond, 205, 242
Black, Sir Harold, 126
Blair, Tony, 204, 205, 229, 230
'blanket' protests, the, 139
Blatherwick, David, 137
Bleakes, Billy, 143, 144
Bleakley, David, 66, 78, 82, 83–4, 103, 116–17, 118, 216 (*see also* Northern Ireland Labour Party, the)
Blelloch, John, 144
Bloody Sunday (30 January 1972), 123
border areas and Unionist siege mentality, 156–7, 159, 163
Border campaign (1956–62), the, 9
border issues and Brexit, 229–30
border poll proposals for a united Ireland, 260–1
Boundary Commission, the, 8, 31, 32
Boyd, Beatrice, 82–3
Boyd, Billy, 78, 82, 103, 116
Boyd, Tom, 78, 84, 103, 216
Boyle, Kevin, 10, 12
Bradford, Robert, 138–9, 140–1, 144, 149, 162, 175
Bradley, Roger, 165
breakaway loyalist elements after the ceasefire, 193–8
Brexit referendum (2016), the, 14, 224, 227–31, 232–3, 240, 258–9; and the Northern Ireland Protocol, 236, 237, 239–43, 244, 246, 255, 257, 260
British Army, the, 20, 56, 88, 90–1, 106, 107–8, 109–11, 112–14, 120, 122, 123, 126–7, 132, 174, 256; 36th Ulster Div, xii; Battalions: 1st Bn Light Infantry, 112, 157–8; 2nd Bn Queen's

Regiment, 112; Royal Green Jackets, 126; and Catholic/nationalist perceptions of, 108, 109; Military Intelligence, 91–2, 135; Regiments: KRH (King's Royal Hussars), 90, 91; Royal Irish Rangers, 200; Royal Irish Regiment, xvii; and the Territorial Army, 87
British general elections: (1923), 30; (1924), 30–1; (1945), 71; (1964), 98, 103; (1970), 113
British government policy, 10, 18–19, 89–90, 113, 148, 166, 196, 252–3; and the Anglo-Irish Agreement, 149–50, 156, 160, 163; and devolution and power-sharing, 128–9, 143, 160; and direct rule, 10, 12, 119, 120, 123–5, 135–6; and the Downing Street Declaration, 179, 184–7; and guarantees of the constitutional position of Northern Ireland, 74, 179, 184–5, 186; and initial deployment of the British Army, 108, 110; and the principle of consent, 184, 186–7, 188–90; and the UWC general strike, 131, 132 (*see also* NIO (Northern Ireland Office), the)
Brooke, Peter, 184, 190
Brooke, Sir Alan, 68, 74
Brooke, Sir Basil (Lord Brookeborough), 26, 40, 64, 65–6, 67–8, 71, 72, 73–5, 76, 79, 82, 90, 92, 97, 167
Brooks, Sydney, 6
Bruce, Steve, 154
Bruton, John, 188
Bryson, Jamie, 217–18, 233, 240, 241, 245
Bunreacht na hÉireann (Constitution of Ireland), 45–6, 181, 208
Bunting, Maj. Roland, 104
Burke, Edmund, 13, 14, 203, 253
Butler, 'Rab', 9, 89
Byrne, Chief Const. Simon, 236

Caldwell, Colin, 168
Cameron, David, 224, 227
Campaign for Labour Representation (CLR), the, 224
Campbell, Ken, 140, 141
Campbell, Thomas J., 39
Camplisson, Joe, xiv
capacities for change and identity politics, 226
Carroll, Gerry, 223
Carson, Sir Edward, 7, 16, 18, 21, 22, 27–8, 31, 32, 41–2, 48
Catholic Church, the, 10, 46, 50, 134
cell-based systems, 195–6
Chichester, Col Robert P.D. Spencer, 76
Chichester-Clark, Maj. James, 107, 110, 114, 214
Churchill, Lord Randolph, 5
Churchill, Sir Winston, 71, 204

civil unrest and violence in Northern Ireland: (1919–22), 21–2, 26–7; due to unemployment, 34–5, 36
Clark, Sir Ernest, 22–3
Clark, Sir George, 94–5, 99, 100
Clarke, Edward J., 35–6
class distinctions within unionism, 9, 31, 32, 37–8, 47–8, 59, 71–2, 85, 143, 211, 219 (*see also* NILP (Northern Ireland Labour Party), the; working-class interests in Northern Ireland)
class issues and Brexit, 227–8
Combined Loyalist Military Command (CLMC), the, 183–4, 197
Commonwealth Labour Party, the, 67
Communist Party of Northern Ireland, the, 67
Community Relations Commission, the, 120
confederal Ireland scenario, 146–7
Conservative and Unionist Party, the, 71, 74, 113, 143, 168, 255, 257 (*see also* Cameron, David; Heath, Edward (Ted); Major, John; Thatcher, Margaret)
Conservative–Liberal Unionist alliance, the, 5
Constitutional Convention, the, 134
Coole Social Club, the, 165
Cooper, Robert, 130
Cooper, Stephen, 200–1, 242–3
Corbyn, Jeremy, 224, 255
coronavirus restrictions, 236, 244, 256
Corr-Johnston, Julie-Anne, 221–2, 245–6, 249–51, 254, 256
Cosgrave, W.T., 31
Costello, John A., 73–4
Council of Ireland, the, 128, 129
Countess of Kilmorey, the, 6
Covenant Unionism, 211, 251
covenanting, 2–3
Cowan, James, 110
Craig, Bill, 94, 119, 124–5, 128, 130, 134
Craig, Sir James (Lord Craigavon), 22–3, 27, 28, 51, 52, 56–7, 60, 62, 76; and the Boundary Commission, 31, 32; on the nature of the Northern Ireland state, 8–9, 40–1, 51, 54; and the Protestant working-class, 30, 31, 32, 35; and relations with Irish nationalists, 39, 45, 48, 53–4, 55–6
Craven, Joe, xiv
criminal activity among loyalist paramilitaries, 220–1
Cronin, Seán, 87, 93, 94
Crumlin Road gaol, Belfast, 168
Currie, Austin, 103, 160
Curtis, Gunner Robert, 114

Darlington talks (September 1972), the, 125

INDEX

Davison, Sir Joseph, 47, 51
de Valera, Éamon, 23, 27, 46, 48, 51, 53, 54–5
deaths, xiii, 44, 49, 58, 59–60, 61, 94, 106, 108, 114, 123, 133, 149, 199; during the 1916–22 revolutionary period, 18, 21, 22, 26; of British Army, 114, 157–8; from German Luftwaffe raids, 58, 59–60, 61; by the PIRA, xvii–xviii, 112, 127, 140–1, 142, 148, 157–8, 168; by the UDA/UFF, xiv, 127; by the UVF, xiv, 98, 108, 164–5, 168, 173
Defenders, the, 4, 49
demilitarisation after the Belfast Agreement, 200
democratic socialism in Northern Ireland, 29–30, 202, 255; and the NILP and PUP, 66–7, 201–2, 221, 222, 223, 224; as a perceived threat, 42–3
Democratic Unionist Party (DUP), the, 134, 136–7, 156, 199, 209, 217, 245, 258; and Brexit and Euroscepticism, 230–1, 232, 234, 255, 257; on devolution and power-sharing, 125, 128, 143; and electoral performance, 13–14, 201, 207, 223, 243; and the Joint Declaration and the Belfast Agreement, 189, 199–200, 201, 205, 207–8; and protests on flag restrictions, 199–200, 205, 220; and the UUP, 162, 189, 207, 211, 230
demographics, xv, 9, 166, 216, 226–7
Denham, Prof John, 254–5
Derry civil rights march (October 1968), 103–4
designated days policy on flag-flying, the, 220
Devlin, Anne, 103
Devlin, Bernadette, 206
Devlin, Paddy, 34, 36–7, 100–1, 104, 112, 113, 114, 121–2, 129, 133
devolution of political power, the, 12, 17; and devolved government proposals, 142–3, 146–7, 160, 177–8 (see also power-sharing)
Dickie, George, 108
discrimination, 9, 39–41, 42, 43–5, 55, 100, 115
Dissenters and Ulster Presbyterianism, 3
Divis Street riots (September 1964), 95–6, 174
Dixon, Herbert (see Glentoran, Lord (Herbert Dixon))
Dixon, Thomas, 62
Dodds, Nigel, 230
Donaldson, Jeffrey, 211
Downey, Hugh, 71, 74
Downing Street Declaration (Joint Declaration on Peace) (1993), the, 12, 179, 180, 184, 186–7, 188, 191
Drennan, William, 4
Drumcree parade stand-off (July 1995), the, 192–5
Dublin and Monaghan car bombings (May 1974), the, 131, 174

Duisburg talks (October 1988), the, 159–62, 163
Duncairn Women's Unionist Association, the, 32–3

Easter 1916 Rising, the, 18, 89, 98
economic prospects for Protestant working-class youth, 218–19
economic war, the, 48
Eden, Anthony, 89–90
electricity supply during the general strike, 131–2
Elizabeth, Princess, 69–70
Elliott, Billy, 137
Elliott, Marianne, 17, 259
Ellis, James, 92
English, Joe, 182, 183
English, Richard, 5
enlistment from Northern Ireland in the British war effort, 56, 57, 62
Ervine, Brian, 222
Ervine, David, 174–5, 177, 178, 181–2, 183, 188, 203, 207, 209, 210, 222, 261
Ervine, St John, 16–17, 23
Established Episcopalian Church, the, 3
ethnic diversity due to immigration, 227
European Economic Community (EEC), the, 122, 232 (see also EU (European Union), the)
European Union (EU), the, 231, 232–3, 246
Euroscepticism, 231–2
Evans, Emyr Estyn, 22
Evans, Gerry, xvii
Executive Authority (External Relations) Act (Éire, 1936), the, 73
expulsions of Catholic workers, 20–1

fall of Stormont and impact on Unionism, the, 10–12, 119, 120, 121, 124–5, 126, 142, 148, 186
Farrar-Hockley, Maj. Gen. Anthony, 110
Farrington, Christopher, 205
Faulkner, Brian, 85, 100, 114–15, 117, 118, 120, 122, 123–4, 128, 129, 132, 133, 189, 214
Fermanagh Vigilance, 26
Fernhill House, Glencairn, 182–3
Fianna Fáil, 180 (see also de Valera, Éamon; Lemass, Seán)
Fitt, Gerry, 103, 111, 115–16, 117, 141
FitzGerald, Garret, 138, 149, 150–1
flag protests against restrictions on council-owned buildings, 14, 215–17, 218, 219, 237
Foreign Office, the, 90
Forsythe, Ellen, 118
Foster, Arlene, 211, 229–30
Framework Documents, the, 188–9, 190, 200, 201
Free Presbyterians, the, 230
Freeland, Lt Gen. Sir Ian, 107, 109, 110, 111

Fulton, Capt. Norman, 37–8
Future of Northern Ireland: A Paper for Discussion, The, 12

Gardiner, Nigel, 243–4
Garland, Roy, 175
Garland, Seán, 94
Garvaghy Residents Group, 193
general strike (May 1974), the, 129–33
geopolitics of Anglo-Irish relations, the, 252
Getgood, Bob, 70–1, 74
Gibson, John, xvii
Gildernew, Michelle, 206–7
Girls Club, Rathcoole, Newtownabbey, 80–1
Glentoran, Lord (Herbert Dixon), 62, 63–4
Gorman, Tommy, 139
Gossip, Alex, 36
Gould, Matilda, 98
Goulding, Cathal, 94
Government of Ireland Act (UK, 1920), the, 8, 32, 39; as a Bill, 19, 20
government perceptions of loyalty and disloyalty, 39–40
Gracey, Harold, 193
Graham, Edgar, 149
Grant, William, 42, 47
Green Party, the, 223
Greencastle, Belfast, xii–xiv; and LOL 658, xii, xiv, xv, xvi, 47
Greenwood, Sir Hamar, 23, 24–5
Greer, Trevor, 238–9
Griffiths, Thomas, 24
gunrunning at Larne and Donaghadee, 18

Hain, Peter, 212, 213
Hanna, John A., 24
happiness and the extension of goodwill, 247–8, 249
Hardie, Keir, 66
Harland & Wolff, Belfast, 20, 47, 66, 86, 129–30
Harris, Eoghan, 202
Hastings, Max, xviii, 212–13
Hawe, Herbert, 108
Hazard, Herbert, xiii
Healey, Denis, 110
Healy, Cahir, 39, 101
Healy, David, 211
Heath, Edward (Ted), 120, 123–4, 125, 189
Henderson, Tommy, 29–30, 37–8, 45, 51, 65
Hendron, Máire, 216
Hennessey, Thomas, 123
Henry, Sir Denis, 40
Herbert, Christopher, 107
Hermon, Chief Const. John, 144

Hermon, Lady Sylvia, 206
Herron, Tommy, 126
Hewitt, Jackie, 183
Hewitt, John, 44–5
Hitchens, Christopher, 258
Hobbes, Thomas, 1–2, 3, 11, 120, 253
Hobsbawm, Eric, 21
Hoey, Kate, 230
Holmes, Erskine, 103
Home Rule, 5–8, 10, 17, 19, 31–2
homelessness due to violence, 118
housing, 65, 67, 76, 78–80, 82, 166, 167, 169
Hudson, Brig. Peter, 107, 110, 112
Hudson, Chris, 178–9, 180, 181, 190
human rights and the constitution, 210
Hume, David, 3, 248
Hume, John, 151, 160, 161, 190
hunger strikes, the, 139, 142
Hungerford, Sir Wilson, 41
Hutcheson, Francis, 1, 3–4, 5, 14, 87, 202, 247–9, 253
Hutcheson, John, 3
Hutchinson, Billy, 174–5, 183, 186, 203, 211, 216, 218, 220, 221, 222, 223, 238, 245

identity politics and the nation state, 1–2, 215, 225–6, 230, 249
Imperial Contributions from Northern Ireland, 64
Independent Labour, 19, 24, 169
Independent Unionists, 31, 32, 37, 45, 51, 62, 65, 121
industrial unrest, 60, 64, 70, 85–6; and the UWC general strike, 129–33
information campaign by breakaway loyalists, 197–8, 199–200
intelligence, 91–2, 93 (*see also* MI5)
inter-state party dialogue, 10, 23, 31, 46, 99, 178–9, 180, 181–2, 183, 185
intergovernmental approach to Northern Ireland governance, 187 (*see also* Anglo-Irish Agreement (1985), the; Belfast Agreement (Good Friday Agreement) (1998), the; Downing Street Declaration (Joint Declaration on Peace) (1993), the)
international tensions before World War II, 51–2
internment, 90, 117–18, 122, 124
intimidation: of election candidates, 24–5, 31; of workers, 129–30, 131
intra-Unionist divides, 31, 33, 34, 37, 38–9, 62–3, 98–100, 101
Ireland Act (UK, 1949), the, 74, 77, 186
Irish Association, the, 174
Irish government, the, 151, 156, 179, 180, 185, 187, 190; and irredentism, 9–10, 48, 51, 53, 54–5, 73–4, 181, 246

INDEX

Irish National Liberation Army (INLA), the, xiv, 148
Irish nationalism, 4, 14–15, 27, 150–1; criticisms of, 16–17
Irish People's Liberation Organisation (IPLO), the, 164
Irish Republican Army (IRA), the, 8, 9, 52–3, 55, 101, 246; and the 1919–22 guerrilla campaign, 21–2, 26–7, 28; and the 1956–62 Border Campaign, 86, 87–9, 90, 91, 92, 93–4 (*see also* PIRA (Provisional IRA), the)
Irvine, Sgt Robert, xvii
Irwin, Colin, 208

Jamison, Dougie, 258
Jenkins, William, 99
Joint Intelligence Committee (JIC), the, 91, 92
Johnson, Boris, 236, 238, 241
joint republican/loyalist assassination plot allegation, 149
Jones, Mervyn, 216

Kant, Immanuel, 4, 248
Kennedy, Kay, 118
Keppel, Captain the Hon. Derek, 59
Keppel, Lady Mairi, 59
Keys, Joel, 235, 237
Kidd, R.J. 'Bob,' 169–70
Kilfedder, James, 97, 175, 191
King, Tom, 162
Kinner, Eddie, 175
Kirkham, Tommy, 183
Kitson, Brig Frank, 113–14
Kyle, Dr John, 216, 223, 233–4, 254, 259–61
Kyle, Sam, 30

Labour Party (Britain), the, 71, 73, 97, 98, 113, 130, 132, 169, 224, 255
Laneside talks (April 1974), the, 135–6
Langhammer, Mark, 167, 169, 170, 258
Lavery, Fred, 62
'leaderless resistance' and infiltration, 195–6
legal action against the British government over the Northern Ireland Protocol, 241
legal case on the Irish Constitution, 181
'legitimate targets,' xvii, 142, 148
Lemass, Seán, 99
Lend-Lease Agreement, the, 71
Liddle, David, 96
Lloyd George, David, 18–19
lobbying for an Ulster state, 8
Local Government Bill (Northern Ireland, 1922), the, 32
Locke, John, 4, 248

London bombings (February 1939), 52–3
Londonderry Loyalists, 243
Long Kesh Detention Centre, 174–5
'Long March' (January 1969), the, 104
Longley, Edna, 252
Loughrey, Geordie, 35
Lowry, Lord Chief Justice, 177
Loyalist Association of Workers, the, 129
Loyalist Communities Council (LCC), the, 235
loyalist delegation to meet British government (December 1994), 183–4, 185–8, 189
Loyalist Labour, 64–5
loyalist paramilitaries, 143–4, 155, 235, 237, 239, 244, 257, 258; ceasefire of, 182–3, 186, 187–8, 196; in Rathcoole, 165–6, 170–1
Loyalty League, the, 35–6
Loyalist Volunteer Force (LVF), the, 197, 212
Luftwaffe bombings of Belfast, the, 58–60, 61, 62, 65
Lyttle, Tommy 'Tucker,' 137

Mac Stíofáin, Seán, 94
MacDermott, John, 61
Macmillan, Harold, 62
MacSwiney, Terence, 139
MacVicar, John, 219
Magan, Brig. Bill, 91, 92, 93, 153
Maginnis, Ken, 144, 158–9, 163, 207
Mahood, Jackie, 183
Major, John, 179, 184–5, 188, 189, 229, 230
Mallon, Seamus, 261
Marquess and Marchioness of Londonderry, the, 59
Martin, Rev. W., 63
Mary Anne, 2nd Duchess of Abercorn, 6
Mason, Roy, 136
mass protests in the 1960s, 102, 104
Mawhinney, Gordon, 160
May, Theresa, 234
McAleese, Mary, 212
McAtamney, Deputy Chief Const. Michael, 17
McAteer, Eddie, 103, 116–17
McBride, Thomas, xiii
McCann, Eamonn, 102, 103, 116, 223–4
McCartney, Robert, 149, 191, 200, 203, 204
McCleery, Martin, 118
McClinton, Bill, 167, 258
McClinton, Kenny, 192–3
McClinton, Wendy, 192
McConnell, John, xvii
McConnell, Thomas, 29–30
McCullough, Myna, 167
McCurrie, Mary, 137
McCusker, Harold, 144, 145–6, 175
McDonald, Jackie, 212

McDonald, Jim, 175, 182
McDonald, Mervyn, xiv
McDowell, Lindy, 183, 212
McEwen, Yvonne, 56
McFarland, Alan, 191
McGimpsey, Chris, 181
McGimpsey, Michael, 181
McIntyre, Anthony, 216
McKay, Mary, 80
McKay, Susan, xviii, 235, 249
McKearney, Tommy, 108
McLaughlin, Patricia, 83
McMichael, Gary, 182, 183
McMichael, John, 136
McMillen, William 'Billy', 95
McMullen, William, 30
McNally, Hugh, xiii
McNally, Thomas, 26–7
McNeill, Ronald, 7–8
McQuade, Johnny, 116
McQuaid, Fr John Charles, 46
McRoberts, Brian, 95
McTasney, Peter, 168
Meehan, Martin, 113
Menzies, Sadie, 67
MI5, 91, 107, 147, 176, 190–1
Middleton, David, 135
Midgley, Harry, 24, 30, 31, 41, 62, 66, 67, 117 (*see also* NILP (Northern Ireland Labour Party), the)
Military Aid to the Civil Power (MACP), 90, 106
Millar, Frank, 143
millenarian loyalism, 95, 259
Milne-Barbour, Sir John, 61
Minford, Nat, 75–6
Mitchell, Billy, 174–5, 201–2, 209–11, 216–17, 251
Molyneaux, James, 124, 142–3, 144, 145–6, 149, 153, 154, 159, 161, 162, 185, 189, 191, 204 (*see also* UUP (Ulster Unionist Party), the)
Montgomery, Maj. Gen. Hugh Maude de Fellenberg, 43–4
Murray, Harry, 129

Napier, Oliver, 175
Napier, Sam, 78
nation state and identity politics, the, 1–2, 215, 225–6, 230, 249
National Amalgamated Furnishing Trades' Association, the, 36
National Health Service (NHS), the, 71
nationalist and Catholic community in Northern Ireland, the, 39–41, 44, 55, 101, 187, 225
Nationalist Party, the, 5, 19, 32, 39, 40, 45, 55, 82
nationalists in Greencastle, Belfast, xii–xiii
Neave, Airey, 148

Needham, Richard, 166, 185–6
Nelson, Brian, 155
New Ulster Political Research Group, the, 178 (*see also* ULDP (Ulster Loyalist Democratic Party), the)
Newell, Geordie, 214
Newtownabbey Council, 169
Newtownabbey Urban District Act (Northern Ireland, 1957), the, 78
Nixon, Insp John, 45, 65
Nobel Peace Prize Committee, the, 202
Nocher, David, xiv
non-aligned population of Northern Ireland, the, 9
North Belfast and the Union, 249–51
Northern Bank robbery (July 1987), the, 155
Northern Ireland Affair Committee, the, 237
Northern Ireland Assembly, the, 152, 188
Northern Ireland Assembly elections: (1973), 128; (1974), 134; (1998), 201; (2005), 211; (2016), 223, 224
Northern Ireland Civil Rights Association (NICRA), the, 101, 102, 103–4, 122
Northern Ireland Civil Service, the, 55, 58, 61, 72
Northern Ireland Constitution Act (UK, 1973), the, 186
Northern Ireland Constitutional Proposals (paper), 128
Northern Ireland economy during World War II, the, 61–2, 64, 68
Northern Ireland Executive, the, 129, 134
Northern Ireland general and local council elections (2001), 206–7
Northern Ireland general elections: (1921), 23–4; (1925), 31; (1933), 37–8; (1941), 62; (1949), 74–5; (1958), 78; (1969), 105, 121
Northern Ireland Government Agent's office, London, 51
Northern Ireland Housing Executive (NIHE), the, 166
Northern Ireland Housing Trust, the, 76, 78–9, 80–1, 119
Northern Ireland Labour Party (NILP), the, 24, 32, 102–3, 116–17, 121–2, 125, 130, 170, 216, 223–4; and crossing the religious divide, 41, 82; and democratic socialism, 66–7, 201; and electoral performance, 19, 20, 30, 62, 78, 103, 121; as opposition to the UUP, 34, 45, 56, 57, 64, 65, 68, 72, 77–8, 82, 83–5, 86, 97, 105; and the PUP, 175, 201, 208; and working-class unionists, 30, 55, 70–1, 78, 133
Northern Ireland local government elections: (1920), 19–20; (1924), 32; (1993), 169; (2014), 222, 243

INDEX

Northern Ireland Neighbourhood Information Service, the, 219
Northern Ireland Office (NIO), the, 120, 147, 160, 161, 166, 177, 185, 187, 198, 214, 221; and devolution talks, 143, 145–6; and militant loyalism, 135–6, 175–6, 177, 183–4
Northern Ireland Policing Board, the, 236
Northern Ireland Protocol, the, 236, 237, 239–43, 244, 246, 255, 257, 260
Northern Ireland Public Prosecutions Service, the, 236
Northern Ireland state, the, 8–9, 17, 22–3, 27, 28, 31

Ó Brádaigh, Ruairí, 94, 127, 131
O'Doherty, Shane Paul, 174
Offences Against the State Act (Éire, 1939), the, 53
Official IRA, the, 109, 112, 131
Oliver, John, 55, 72–3, 94
O'Neill, Terence, 10, 84, 97–100, 103, 104–5, 116, 119, 214
opposition politics in Stormont, 45, 56, 65–6, 68, 83–4, 85, 121 (see also NILP (Northern Ireland Labour Party), the)
Opsahl, Prof. Torkel, 169
Opsahl Commission, the, 169
oral traditions, xi, xvi
Orange Order, the, 29, 48, 54, 94–5, 115–16, 153; and civil and religious liberty, 75–6, 99–100; and influence of, 31–2, 40, 42, 76, 95, 111; LOL (Loyal Orange Lodge) 658 Greencastle, xii, xiv, xv, xvi, 47; and parades, xi–xii, xvi, 111–12, 192–3, 212, 256; purpose and aims of, 4, 49–51
Orde, Chief Const. Hugh, 212
O'Reilly, Emily, 155
Orr, Capt. Lawrence, 93
Orwell, George, 29, 257–8
Official Unionist Party (OUP), the (see Ulster Unionist Party, the)
outdoor relief riots, the, 35, 36
Overend, David, 175

Paine, Thomas, 4
Paisley, Eileen, 142
Paisley, Ian, Jr 193
Paisley, Rev. Ian, 9, 98, 125, 144, 161, 175, 189, 193, 206, 207, 213, 214, 231; and the Anglo-Irish Agreement, 151, 153–4, 156, 162; on murders of Unionist politicians, 141–2, 148–9; as a rabble-rouser, 95, 99, 100, 104, 174; and the UWC general strike, 134, 135 (see also Democratic Unionist Party, the)
Parker, Adm. H.W., 76

Parker, Dehra, 76–7, 79, 81–2, 167
parliamentary democracy and control of destiny, 232
partition, 17, 18–19, 53, 86, 115, 156; and the Boundary Commission, 8, 31, 32
patriotism and conservatism, 257–8
Payne, Denis, 147
peace process, the, 188–9, 197, 202, 203, 205, 208, 209, 214, 217–18, 229, 240, 244
Peake, John, 80
Peep o'Day Boys, the, 4, 49
Peeples, Clifford, 188, 197–8, 199–200, 232, 241
Penal Laws, the, 49
People Before Profit Alliance (PBPA), the, 223, 224
People's Democracy (PD), the, 104
Phillips, Morgan, 78
physical force nationalism, 16–17, 18 (see also Irish Republican Army, the; Provisional IRA, the)
Police Service of Northern Ireland (PSNI), the, 212, 220–1, 236–7, 244 (see also Royal Ulster Constabulary, the)
political unions and stability, 253, 261
Porter, Norman, 196–7, 254
Porter, Robert, 107
Pounder, Rafton, 10, 12
Powell, Enoch, 141, 146
power-sharing, 13–14, 125–6, 128, 129, 134, 145, 187, 214, 232
principle of consent, the, 12, 179, 184, 186–7, 189–90, 199, 245, 249
Prior, Jim, 136, 142, 143, 144, 147
prison seminars for UVF detainees, 174–5
'progressive patriotism' and the future of Unionism, 255
Progressive Unionist Party (PUP), the, xv, 175, 186, 197, 224; as alternative Unionist thought, 160, 177–8, 208–11, 222–3; and the Belfast Agreement, 200, 201; and Brexit and the Northern Ireland Protocol, 233–4, 238, 240, 243–4; and democratic socialism, 201–2, 222, 223, 224; and engaging with Sinn Féin and republicans, 216–17, 218; and impact of new members, 221–2; and the loyalist ceasefire, 182, 183; and the peace process, 187–8, 240, 244–5
proportional representation single transferable vote method, the, 20, 23, 32, 124, 134, 161
Proposed Democratic Devolved Administration for Northern Ireland (policy document), 177–8
Protective Patrol, 26
Protestant Unionist Party, the, 99
Provisional IRA (PIRA), the, xvi, 109, 113–14, 119, 122, 131, 137, 139, 163, 173, 186, 196, 229, 236, 242–3; and arms decommissioning,

200, 205; and the Ballygawley coach atrocity, 157, 158; and ceasefire, 182, 213; as defenders of the Catholic/nationalist community, 106, 109, 110–11; and dialogue leading to the peace process, 177, 182; murders by, xvii–xviii, 112, 127, 140–1, 142, 148, 157–8, 159, 168; and the Tactical Use of Armed Struggle, 198, 199; and targeting of Unionist politicians, 140–1, 142, 148, 149, 156; and use of the Republic as a 'safe haven,' 150, 151 (*see also* IRA (Irish Republican Army), the; Sinn Féin)
public discontent after *Luftwaffe* bombings, 60–1
'punishment beatings,' 170
Purvis, Dawn, 222
Pym, Francis, 128–9, 131

Rankin, William, xiv
Rathcoole Defence Association (RDA), the, 119–20
Rathcoole estate, Newtownabbey, xii–xiv, xv–xvi, 79–81, 119–20, 164, 165–6, 167–9, 170–2
Rathcoole Self Help Group (RSHG), the, 167, 169, 258
Rea, Jim, 138
Red Hand Commando (RHC), the, 203, 235
Rees, Merlyn, 131, 132–3
referendum on the Belfast Agreement, 200, 232
Reid, Fr Alec, 160, 177, 182
Rent Restriction Bill (Northern Ireland, 1943), the, 65
Representation of the People Act (Northern Ireland 1928), the, 6
representatives with links to paramilitary violence, 203, 204 (*see also* PUP (Progressive Unionist Party), the)
Republican Clubs, the, 131
Republican Labour party, the, 103
revolutionary ideals in late eighteenth-century Ireland, 4, 5
Reynolds, Albert, 179, 180
Reynolds, Lee, 191, 204, 211, 228–9
rioting, xii, xiv, xv, 20, 35, 43, 44, 95–6, 105–6, 108, 112, 113–14, 174, 235–6, 237, 239–40, 244, 257
Robb, Lindsay, 183
Robinson, Henry, 79
Robinson, Iris, 206
Robinson, Mary, 188
Robinson, Peter, 142, 159–60, 162, 175, 206, 235
Rosalind, 3rd Duchess of Abercorn, 23
Rose, Richard, 107
Rousseau, Jean Jacques, 248
Royal Black Preceptory, the, 95
Royal Irish Constabulary (RIC), the, 22, 25

Royal Ulster Constabulary (RUC), the, 36, 39, 94, 99, 114, 131, 144, 170, 198; and intelligence on the IRA, 87, 90, 91; and loyalist paramilitaries, 165, 168, 176; and management of riots and marches, xi, 33–4, 35, 44, 95–6, 101, 102, 104, 193; and replacement of, 200; and request for MACP (Military Aid to the Civil Power), 90, 106, 108; and Special Branch, 89, 98 (*see also* Police Service of Northern Ireland, the)
Royal visit (July 1945), the, 69–70
Russell, Sean, 52
Russell, T.W., 31
Ryan, Liam, 173
Ryan, Mick, 88
Ryder, Chris, 161–2

Sands, Bobby, 139–40
Saville Inquiry, the, xviii
Sayers, Jack, 73
Scott, Kenneth, 144
Scottish Enlightenment, the, 3–4
Scullion, John, 98
sectarianism, xii–xiii, 12, 26–7, 57, 66, 77, 87, 95–6, 104, 117, 118, 122, 159, 169, 173, 185, 224, 236; of militant loyalism, 98–9, 164–5, 168, 170; of the Orange Order, 75–6, 100, 111–12; through discrimination, 8–9, 34, 39–41, 42, 43, 44–5, 55, 100, 115; against the working-classes, 20–1, 25, 37
Shankill riots (October 1969), the, 108
Sharing Responsibility (policy document), 160, 178
Shorts Aircraft, 70
Simpson, Vivian, 78, 103
Sinn Féin, xii, 6, 17, 21, 25, 26, 31, 92, 142, 148, 203, 214, 229, 232, 260; and the Belfast Agreement, 13, 242–3; and electoral performance, 19, 20, 24, 206–7, 211, 223; and flags and emblems, 216–17, 218; and Unionist perceptions of British concessions to, 204, 205, 206, 207 (*see also* PIRA (Provisional IRA), the)
Skey, Robert, 168
Sloan, Thomas, 31
Smiles, Lt Col Sir Walter, 54, 62
Smith, Adam, 3, 248
Smith, Plum, 175, 183
Smyth, Clifford, 99, 134, 135
Smyth, Hugh, 175, 182
Smyth, Rev. Martin, 162
social cohesion in loyalist areas, 171–2 (*see also* Rathcoole estate, Newtownabbey)
Social Democratic and Labour Party (SDLP), the, xiv, 13, 125, 128, 129, 133, 134, 141, 142, 146, 151, 160, 211

INDEX

social engineering in housing, 79–81
social teachings of the Catholic Church, 46
Solemn League and Covenant, 2, 7, 211, 251, 254
South Down Unionist Association, the, 63
Special Powers Act (1922), the, 34, 102, 117
Spence, Augustus Andrew 'Gusty', 96–7, 98, 99, 173–5; and the PUP, 175, 178, 182, 183, 222; and release from prison, 175–7
Spence, Billy, 97
Spender, Wilfred, 61, 62–3
Spiecker, Dr Eberhard, 159, 160–1, 162
Spring, Dick, 179, 180
Springfield Road, Belfast, as a flashpoint, the, 111, 112, 212
SS *Titanic*, 41
Steele, Frank, 126
Steele, J.A., 166
Stewart, Sir Robert, 2
Stewart, Sir William, 2
Stopford Green, Alice, 18, 72
Storey, Bobby, 236
Stormont Parliament suspension (March 1972), the, 10–12, 119, 120, 121, 124–5, 126, 142, 148, 186
Strain, Mrs. M.E., 81
Stronge, James, 142
Stronge, Sir Norman, 142
Sullivan, Jim, 112
Sunningdale Agreement (November 1973), the, 128–9, 132, 134, 154, 178, 205, 208

Tartan gangs, the, 120, 126
Tawney, R.H., 202
Taylor, John, 135, 148
Teebane atrocity (January 1992), the, xvii
Thatcher, Margaret, 141, 149, 153, 156, 158
theory of perpetual conflict, the, 1–2, 3
Thirty Years' War (1618–48), the, 1, 2
Thompson, Sam, 92
threat of civil war, the, 156
Toal, Malachy, 131
Tóibín, Colm, 93, 157
Toler, Maj. Gen. David, 110
Tone, Theobald Wolfe, 4
trade union movement, the, 45, 60, 66, 67, 117; and socialism, 19, 36
Traditional Unionist Voice (TUV), the, 217, 221, 223, 241, 242
Trainor, Malachy, 164–5
Treaty of Rome, the, 232
Trimble, David, 13, 146, 147, 149, 189, 191–2, 193, 200, 202–3, 204–5, 207, 213
Troubles, the, xiv–xv, xvii, 10, 103–4, 105–9; causes of, 115–16; and governance during, 111, 112, 113–14, 117–18, 122, 144; and possibility of reform, 115, 117
Tuzo, Sir Harry, 126
Twelfth of July, the, xi–xii, xv–xvi, 21, 50, 54, 99, 100, 256–7
Tyrie, Andy, 135–6, 137

UK Unionist Party, the, 200, 201, 203
Ulster Defence Association (UDA), the, 128, 130, 131, 149, 155–6, 170, 171, 182, 186, 193, 194, 212, 235, 238; as a mass vigilante group, 109, 123, 126–7; and UDI, 132, 135–7, 178; and the UPRG, 217, 244; and Vanguard, 119, 134
Ulster Defence Regiment (UDR), the, 110, 113, 148, 158, 165, 198, 200
Ulster Democratic Party (UDP), the, 182, 183, 186, 187–8, 200
Ulster Ex-Servicemen's Association (UESA), the, 20, 25
Ulster Freedom Fighters (UFF), the, xiv, 127, 182, 194
Ulster Loyalist Democratic Party (ULDP), the, 136, 137, 178
Ulster Army Council, the, 128
Ulster Group Theatre company, the, 92
Ulster Imperial Guards, the, 26
Ulster Political Research Group (UPRG), the, 217, 244
Ulster Presbyterians, 3, 4, 9, 65, 230
Ulster Protestant Association (UPA), the, 25
Ulster Protestant League (UPL), the, 43
Ulster Resistance, 155
Ulster Special Constabulary (USC), the, 22, 26
Ulster Unionism, xvi–xvii, xviii–xix, 5–6, 41, 49–50, 54, 134–5, 196–7, 212–13, 225–6, 230–1; and the Anglo-Irish Agreement, 151–4, 155, 160, 161, 162, 163, 168, 191; and attitudes to British rule, 12–13, 137, 143, 148–9, 168, 175, 189, 234, 246; and the Belfast Agreement, 200–1, 211, 217–18, 222, 229, 241–3, 245; and breakaway groups and suspicions about the peace process, 193–9, 200–1; and class distinctions, 9, 31, 32, 37–8, 47–8, 59, 71–2, 85, 143, 211, 219; and Euroscepticism and Brexit, 231, 232–4; and impact of the fall of Stormont, 10–12, 119, 120, 121, 124–5, 126, 142, 148, 186; and intra-Unionist divides and schools of thought, 10–11, 13, 14, 31, 33, 34, 37, 38–9, 62–3, 98–100, 101, 132, 135–7, 143–4, 160, 177–8, 201, 208–11, 217, 221, 222–3, 251, 259; and the Northern Ireland Protocol and the mood among loyalists, 237, 238, 240–3, 244; opposition to Home Rule and Irish nationalism, 6–8, 10, 17–18, 20, 31–2; and

perceived threats, 9–10, 42–3, 45–6, 48–9, 51, 53–4, 55, 64, 106, 120, 134, 144–5, 150–5, 156–7, 167, 179, 180–1, 185, 188, 190, 197, 198, 205, 208, 241, 242–3, 245–6, 258; perceptions of, 5–6; and power-sharing, 125–6, 128, 134, 145, 187; and pragmatism about the future, 248–52, 253–5, 259–61; and the siege mentality, 156–7, 159, 163, 259

Ulster Unionist Council (UUC), the, 5, 18–19, 22, 24, 31, 62, 97, 129, 145

Ulster Unionist Labour Association (UULA), the, 19, 38–9, 41–2, 47

Ulster Unionist Party (UUP), the, 8, 10, 84–5, 128, 134, 135, 148, 162, 211, 230, 242, 245; and adjusting to the welfare state, 72–3, 84–5; after the fall of Stormont, 10–12, 121, 124; and the Anglo-Irish Treaty, 27–8; attitudes to socialism and trade unionism, 9, 20, 42–3; and the Belfast Agreement, 204–5, 207; and challenge from the NILP, 34, 45, 56, 57, 64, 65, 72, 77–8, 82–6, 97, 105; and the DUP, 162, 189, 207, 211, 230; and electoral performance, 19, 24, 30–1, 62, 64, 74–5, 204, 206, 207, 243; and governance of Northern Ireland, 8–9, 20, 45, 56–7, 62, 97–8, 104–5, 110, 114–15, 253; and housing and community vision, 76–7, 79–82, 120; and internal dissent and tensions, 62–3, 143, 189, 191, 207, 211; and IRA campaign 1919–21, 21–2; and leadership of Molyneaux, 142–3, 144, 145–6, 189, 191, 204; and management of working-class supporters, 68, 81–2, 83, 86, 143; and O'Neill's modernisation agenda, 97, 103, 105; and overtures to nationalists and Catholics, 13, 101, 104, 105, 120; and the Provisional IRA, 88, 89, 92, 93, 94–5, 158–9; and reorganisation of, 63–4, 65, 66

Ulster Volunteer Force (UVF), the, 10, 47, 98–9, 123, 128, 135, 155, 178–9, 180, 211, 235; from 1914–21, 18, 22, 26, 108, 182; and Billy Wright, 190–1, 192, 193, 194, 196, 197, 212; and bombings, 105, 109, 131; and ceasefire and arms decommissioning, 182, 186, 203, 220; and criminal activity, 220–1; and killings, xiv, 98, 108, 164–5, 168, 173; and the peace process, 240, 244; in Rathcoole, Newtownabbey, 165–6, 170 (*see also* PUP (Progressive Unionist Party), the; Spence, Augustus Andrew 'Gusty')

Ulster Workers' Council (UWC), the, 129, 130, 131, 132–3

Ulster Women's Unionist Council (UWUC), the, 6–7, 23, 67

unemployment, 33, 34–5, 61, 68, 70, 82, 166, 167, 218

Unilateral Declaration of Independence (UDI) option, the, 132, 135–7, 178
Unionist Associations, 63–4, 66, 77
United Irishmen, the, 4
United Ulster Unionist Council (UUUC), the, 134

vandalism, 166, 167, 168–9
Vanguard Unionist Party, the, 119, 128, 134
Varadkar, Leo, 239
vigilante-style groups, 26, 118–19, 120; and the UDA, 109, 123, 126–7
violence and the use of force, 17, 53, 93–4, 108, 131, 154, 163, 186, 190, 214, 235
Vote Leave campaign, the, 228–9

Walker, Brian, xvi
Wallace, Andree, 167
Wallace, Roy, 167
War of Independence, the, 21–2, 26–7, 28, 139
Ward, Peter, 98, 173
Warnock, Edmund, 57, 85–6, 101
Webster, John, 26
Weiner, Rob, 172
welfare state, the, 71, 72–3, 84–5, 122, 166
West, Harry, 134
White, John, 127, 182, 183
Whitelaw, Willie, 128
Wilson, Harold, 97, 98, 132
Winchester, Simon, 113, 123
Withdrawal Agreement, the, 233, 234, 241
women and equality of representation, 207
Woodfield, Philip, 176–7
Wooldridge, Capt. Alan, 90–1
Workers' Party, the, xiv
working-class interests in Northern Ireland, 64–5, 117, 165, 239; and economic prospects, 218–19, 233–4; and the NILP, 30, 55, 56, 66, 68, 70–1, 77, 78, 117, 133; for Protestants and loyalists, 115–16, 143, 168, 172, 218–19, 243; and socialist politics, 32–3, 70–1, 72, 169, 175, 177–8, 223; and Unionist detachment from, 60–1, 68, 77, 81–2, 83, 86, 143, 219
Workman and Clark, Belfast, 20
World War II, 51–2, 58–9, 60
Wright, Billy, 188, 189, 190, 192–3, 194, 196, 197, 198–9

youth instruction in the Unionist community spirit, 80–1
Youth Welfare Act (Northern Ireland, 1944), the, 82